ARCHITECTURE IN THE AGE OF REASON

Baroque and Post-Baroque in England, Italy, and France

By

EMIL KAUFMANN

DOVER PUBLICATIONS, INC., NEW YORK

Published in Canada by General Publishing Company, Ltd., 30 Lesmill Road, Don Mills, Toronto, Ontario.

Published in the United Kingdom by Constable and Company, Ltd., 10 Orange Street, London WC 2.

This Dover edition, first published in 1968, is an unabridged and unaltered republication of the work originally published in 1955. It is reprinted by special arrangment with Harvard University Press, publisher of the original edition.

International Standard Book Number: 0-486-21928-3
Library of Congress Catalog Card Number: 68-17252

Manufactured in the United States of America
Dover Publications, Inc.
180 Varick Street
New York, N. Y. 10014

IN MEMORY

OF MY PARENTS

MAX AND FRIEDERIKE KAUFMANN

FOREWORD

THIS is a timely and rewarding book: timely because it brings into focus, at a moment when our architecture is submerged under an excess of dogma, the humane and searching thought of the eighteenth century, and rewarding because it clarifies with new insight the engaging art of humanism. The author has made the period lying between the Renaissance and our own day his special field. He writes with distinction and vitality.

I do not know of any work in which one could find a more complete and illuminating account of that idea—harmonious integration—which for three hundred years haunted the minds of European architects. Mr. Kaufmann follows this idea—the idea which most perfectly expresses the aspirations of the Renaissance—from the time when, with "astounding clarity," it was first expressed by the friar Francesco Colonna, through its many restatements in the academic pages of Alberti, Serlio, and Scamozzi, through Palladio's theories of beauty and the adaptations made by Guarini to suit the sensual mood of the Baroque, to its summary in the ordered and logical works of Jacques-François Blondel.

This by way of prelude to the author's central theme, which is concerned with the dissolution of the Italian idea in the colder light of eighteenth-century France. Blondel saw clearly the rationalist's challenge to the traditions of classicism: he was the first to propose a conciliation between form and practical necessity. He saw also the approaching wave of romance: "Character is more important than visual beauty." Mr. Kaufmann would send us back to Blondel that we may learn what has happened to architecture.

Mr. Kaufmann also takes us to England, where architects, finding integration an impossible ideal—and anticipating cubism—attempted to salvage the Renaissance idea by substituting a "clarity of appearances" for the interplay of the parts. He shows us the beginnings, in Italy, of the functionalist doctrine—for example, in the astonishing teachings of the Venetian Dodoli, who, as early as 1780, would "show in architecture only that which derives from the strictest necessity"—and we follow the growth of this doctrine in the unrest generated by the approach of the French Revolution.

The reader will be delighted by the author's original and penetrating characterizations of buildings and architects—for example, his exposition of the Baroque elements in Palladio and in François Mansart, his enlightening account of the confused mind of Soane, and, especially, his interpretations of Ledoux's exciting fantasies. Mr. Kaufmann is an authority on the work of Ledoux.

"Looking back to our ancestors," writes Emil Kaufmann, "is a deeply human trait, a prerogative of the human species." It is a practice which ought to be congenial and invigorating to architects.

Dover, Massachusetts   Joseph Hudnut
December 3, 1954

PREFACE

SINCE THE history of art established itself as an independent field of research, the exploration of the different periods of the past has proceeded in chronological order, and at almost equal intervals. In the middle of the eighteenth century the study of the works of antiquity was started with scientific thoroughness rather than with the enthusiastic dilettantism of the Renaissance. About 1800 the artistic production of the Middle Ages was considered to be worthy of careful investigation. Half a century later, the Swiss scholar Jakob Burckhardt laid the foundation of a new appreciation of the Renaissance. About 1900 his compatriot Heinrich Wölfflin and the Austrian Alois Riegl opened the eyes of mankind to the intrinsic qualities of the Baroque. So in the middle of the twentieth century it might be timely to scrutinize the post-Baroque development. Anyone devoting himself to this task faces a situation similar to that which confronted the rediscoverers of the earlier periods. He, too, has to deal with a period that has been badly underrated and misunderstood. Again, the revaluation of the era will of necessity bring about its rehabilitation.

I did not at first intend to continue the work of those pathfinders by attempting to describe the transition from the Baroque to the nineteenth century. After having published the first monographs on Ledoux and Boullée, in 1933 and 1939, I merely planned to investigate French architecture of their period on a large scale. Soon it seemed imperative to me to go beyond the French border. Thus widening the field of my research, I found out that the great change of the late eighteenth century was ushered in by extraordinary efforts to get rid of the heritage of the past, in England and Italy, while at a somewhat later date the French worked out certain basic formulas of an entirely new architecture. A better understanding of nineteenth-century architecture will become possible through the new knowledge of its origins.

The different parts which the three nations played, in the overthrow of the older architectural ideal by a younger one, each required a different treatment. The Italian development demanded, categorically, the discussion of the ultimate fate of the Baroque in the country where it had originated and unfolded in amazing grandeur. In displaying the English and the French development I had to reëxamine the performances of the well-known protagonists, and restore to their right places the achievements of many architects who had fallen into undeserved oblivion. I felt I should not begin by setting forth my historical concept, using the works merely as illustrations, as some commentators do in other fields; so I decided to present the material in approximately chronological sequence, proceeding from architect to architect, from work to work, interested in the interrelationship between the whole and the constituent parts rather than in the forms and formal qualities, and developing the guiding ideas from the analysis of the individual creation. I do not believe that I have solved the momentous problem of how the architectural transformation of about 1800 came to pass. However, I trust this new approach will prompt further research, systematic studies as well as monographic ones. Omissions and errors may be excused in an investigation covering so wide a field, with such large stretches previously unexplored. Yet my endeavor has been not to omit any English or French eighteenth-century architect of significance. In the illustrations the emphasis is on unknown works rather than such as can be easily found in other publications. Comments on architectural theories from the Renaissance down to 1800 and frequent quotations from the old treatises will complement the criticism of the buildings and projects. The bibliographical references in the notes will be useful to those who seek more factual data or more illustrations.

Note of Acknowledgment

In the years devoted to the preparation of this book it meant very much to me that several distinguished art historians and architects followed its progress with the kindest interest. My sincere gratitude goes to M. Jean Adhémar, Bibliothèque Nationale, Paris; Professor Turpin C. Bannister, University of Illinois, Urbana, Ill.; Dr. Rudolf Berliner, Rhode Island School of Design, Providence, R. I.; Professor Kenneth J. Conant, Harvard University; Professor John Coolidge, Harvard University; Professor Donald Drew Egbert, Princeton University; Professor Paul Frankl, Institute for Advanced Study, Princeton, N. J.; Professor Talbot F. Hamlin, Columbia University; Professor Julius Held, Columbia University; Professor Henry-Russell Hitchcock, Smith College, Northampton, Mass.; Architect Philip Johnson, Museum of Modern Art, New York, N. Y; Professor Wilhelm Koehler, Harvard University; Professor Paul Kristeller, Columbia University; Professor George A. Kubler, Yale University; Professor Charles L. Kuhn, Harvard University; Professor Carroll L. V. Meeks, Yale University; Professor Erwin Panofsky, Institute for Advanced Study, Princeton, N. J.; Professor Meyer Schapiro, Columbia University; Professor John Shapley, Catholic University, Washington, D. C.; Professor James Grote Van Derpool, Columbia University; Professor Paul Zucker, Cooper Union Museum, New York, N. Y. I am also deeply indebted to my brother, Dr. Maurice E. Kaufmann, for his understanding helpfulness.

My chief indebtedness in this work is to the American Philosophical Society, Philadelphia, for having made to me an award from the Penrose Fund which enabled me to carry out my project.

It is my pleasant duty to offer my best thanks to the staffs of the libraries which extended to me many privileges, above all the Avery Library of Columbia University, New York, N. Y.; the Library of Congress, Washington, D. C.; the libraries of Harvard, Princeton, and Yale Universities, the University of California and the University of Southern California and the William Andrews Clark Memorial Library, Los Angeles, Calif.; the libraries of the Cooper Union Museum and the Metropolitan Museum of Art, New York; the Art Institute of Chicago, Ill.; the Philadelphia Museum of Art, Philadelphia, Pa.; the Huntington Library, San Marino, Calif. I owe, of course, very much to the hospitality of many European institutes, especially to the libraries of the British Museum, the Royal Institute of British Architects, the John Soane Museum, the Victoria and Albert Museum, London, the Bibliothèque Nationale and its Cabinet des Estampes, Bibliothèque de l'Ecole des Beaux-Arts, Bibliothèque Historique de la Ville de Paris, Musée Carnavalet, Bibliothèque d'Art et d'Archéologie, Bibliothèque Mazarine, Bibliothèque Sainte-Geneviève, Paris; Biblioteca Apostolica Vaticana, Biblioteca di Archeologica e Storia dell'Arte, Biblioteca Romana Sarti, Rome; Biblioteca Nazionale, Biblioteca Marucelliana, Florence; Biblioteca di Brera, Milan; Biblioteca Marciana, Venice; Biblioteca Universitaria, Genoa; the libraries of the universities of Brussels, Oslo, Uppsala, Valencia, Zurich; the Rijksmuseum, Amsterdam; the Royal Library and the Kunstakademiets Bibliotek, Copenhagen; the Municipal Library of Göteborg; the National Museum, Stockholm; the Biblioteca Nacional, Madrid.

The following institutions graciously gave me permission to illustrate original drawings from their collections: the Bibliothèque Nationale, Cabinet des Estampes, Paris (figs. 102, 142, 145–150, 162, 169–171, 174, 209, 210); the Bibliothèque de la Ville de Besançon, Besançon (figs. 180–183); the Cooper Union Museum for the Arts of Decoration, New York (figs. 76–92, 103, 212). Professor Nils G. Wollin, Stockholm, obliged me by allowing illustrations from his monograph on Desprez (figs. 175–178). I wish also to thank the following for permission to reproduce photographs: Campbell's Press Studio, Ltd., London (fig. 62), the National Buildings Record, London (figs. 25, 32), and the Warburg Institute of London University, London (figs. 4, 5, 8, 9, 10).

Paris, May 1951   E. K.

Publisher's note: Dr. Emil Kaufmann died in 1953, before the editorial work on this book was finished.

CONTENTS

ILLUSTRATIONS

(following page 118)

PART I

ENGLAND

1

ENGLISH BAROQUE AND ENGLISH PALLADIANISM

THE ARCHITECTURE of the eighteenth century in England reveals several opposing currents which can be distinguished without difficulty. It has become customary to subsume them under various headings, as English Baroque, English Palladianism, Neoclassicism, and Romanticism. However, apart from these major trends there were powerful undercurrents which remained unnoticed, but which were to foretell the direction architecture was to take in the future. The question of ancestry is largely settled. It is now time to attempt to identify the germs of further development, which in the end was to replace all traditional principles. One cannot summarize the significance of these undercurrents in a few introductory words. Presenting them and commenting upon them is one of the major aims of this investigation. It may be asked why these currents were ignored by practically all historians. Several factors contributed to this oversight. In the first place, the foremost exponents of the new trends, the French architects of the revolutionary era, were almost completely forgotten. There was, or, to be fair, there could be no understanding for their achievements, at least not in the nineteenth century. Many symptoms of the deep-going renewal of architecture appearing in the extraordinary designs of the eighteenth-century reformers and experimenters could be comprehended only in a new period of abstract art. Moreover, most architectural historians were guided by aesthetics handed down from the Renaissance which they considered not as the expression of a particular period, but as eternally valid. Basing their judgment on an obsolete and nearly petrified doctrine, they could not but charge all deviations to the imperfection of the artists.

To obtain a better insight into the eighteenth-century development, or, for the sake of a fuller comprehension of the transformation of the Baroque, we have to turn to the latter's earlier stages. This will be done in Part II, which is devoted to the role of Italy in the process of architectural reorientation. One may question why, then, this investigation does not begin with Italy. The reason is that its topic is the eighteenth century, and especially its reform tendencies, in which we shall see that England was earliest, whereas Italy merely reached the critical stage of traditional building, but contributed little in the way of fresh solutions. Here as in Germany only a rather feeble resonance of the daring efforts of the French innovators accompanied the downfall of the Baroque. In conclusion, before entering into details, it may be said that we shall not have to do with some new "style," but with a great movement of reorientation and reorganization, slowly rising and slowly expanding, yet full of promise for the future.

Five years after St. Paul's in London was "happily finished" by Sir Christopher Wren, Colen Campbell brought out the first volume of the *Vitruvius Britannicus*.[1] At its very beginning he illustrates Wren's cathedral and St. Peter's in Rome. His intention is not to present the two churches as models, but rather to prove he knows how to provide a better scheme. At first glance one can recognize that his church, designed "at the Desire of some Persons of Quality and Distinction" for Lincoln's Inn Fields* in 1712, is obviously a modification of the two, but not an invention of his own.[2] Whether it really shows some improvement over its predecessors need not be discussed here. Yet it is interesting to note what these modifications aimed at. He comments:

The Plan is reduced to a Square and Circle in the Middle, which, in my weak Opinion, are the most perfect Figures. In the Front I have removed the Angular Towers at such a distance, that the great *Cupola* is without any Embarrass . . . the whole is dress'd very plain, as most proper for the sulphurous Air of this City, and, indeed, most conformable to the Simplicity of the Ancients.[3]

"The Simplicity of the Ancients"!—this sounds rather like an utterance from the end of the eighteenth century than from its beginning, when the vivid, luxuriant, agitated art of the Baroque still had its sway over Europe. It does not matter that these views were expressed by an architect whom we today consider an artist of minor importance. His words were written and his scheme was set forth in England, at a time when no one on the continent held similar views. We shall have to come back to Campbell's viewpoint later. First, let us look at the architectural situation in England in the days immediately before and after the *Vitruvius Britannicus* appeared.

One of the earliest of Christopher Wren's works, the Sheldonian Theatre at Oxford (1663–1669), is still Renaissance in the character of its decoration, in the clarity of its design, and in its reticent relief.[4] Yet the façade also shows symptoms of the Baroque: the semipediments on the sides, leading up to the central pediment; the upper pilasters which combine with the engaged columns of the basement to tie together the stories; the rather heavy entablature which unifies it horizontally; and, above all, the emphasis on the center itself. Quite a few of these features call to mind typical Baroque façades. The motifs of unification and centralization appear in many later designs by Wren, as exemplified in those for Whitehall Palace (1669–1683),[5] and in another one for the same building (1698).[6]

---

* All buildings, streets, etc., for which no location is given are in London.

At Marlborough House, on St. James' Park (1709),[7] the unifying elements are the long-stretched balustrades, and the pilasters in the "French manner," that is, with rustication of stones "of the same Extent."[8] The wall itself does not play any important role in the composition; high apertures prevail. Two typically Baroque tendencies were common in the works of Wren's contemporaries: that toward the "concatenation" of the parts, as Robert Morris termed it;[9] and that toward the negation of the wall. One instance may be cited, that of the "Pilastrade" of Buckingham House, "conducted by the learned and ingenious Capt. Wynne, Anno 1705."[10]

Progressing from multiplicity to unity in his façades, Wren also went over from the single, vast, crowning feature developed in the great wood model for St. Paul's (1673)[11] to the pictorial grouping of the cathedral as it was ultimately carried out. The anecdotal report that Wren wept "in bitter disappointment" because of the rejection of the wood model may be true, yet despite his personal disillusionment he seems to have sensed that the model was not in harmony with the times. The Warrant Design of 1675 indicates how he struggled after exalting the dome over the required Latin cross by enhancing it with a superimposed steeple.[12] The cathedral, as it was executed, offers a solution in the Baroque sense. The towers on either side, with the pediment of the front and the dome, form a group of several subordinates and a dominant. Thus Wren, imbued with the principles of contemporary French architecture, and deeply impressed by Bernini whom he had met in Paris in 1665,[13] reached the level his rival John Vanbrugh was attaining in the great houses of his early period. Very soon after the climax of English Baroque composition a sudden and profound change was to occur in Vanbrugh's later structures, foreshadowed, perhaps, in several capricious steeples of Wren's City churches and the Orangery at Kensington Palace.[14]

Perfect grouping through concatenation and gradation is the characteristic feature of the first manner of Vanbrugh. Nevertheless, in many works of his the trend toward variety is even stronger than in Wren's designs. It may be that Vanbrugh's predilection for richness was inherited from his Flemish ancestors. The combination of lavish decoration and conventional composition in some of his early work makes him England's most Baroque architect, his ardor to overcome the inherited concepts, her most personal one. Joshua Reynolds, in the frequently quoted passage in his *Thirteenth Discourse*,[15] has very well characterized Vanbrugh's first manner: the receding and advancing masses, the scenic arrangement on different planes; in short, the pictorial as well as the picturesque character of Castle Howard, Yorkshire (1701–1714),[16] and Blenheim Palace, Oxfordshire (1705–1724).[17] From the Baroque viewpoint, the plan of Blenheim being the more mature, the core formed by its great hall and salon is hardly inferior in unifying power to the most advanced achievements of the continental Baroque. The façades of Castle Howard bear rich sculptural adornment. The balustrade, the main cornice, the giant orders, the pilasters of the lantern, and the ribs of the dome convey the idea of coherence.

The conventional means used in binding the parts together on Castle Howard are replaced by more vigorous ones at Blenheim Palace with its heavy segmental colonnades tying the main pile to the wings and its new, extremely significant manner of interlocking masses. The decorative variety of Castle Howard is given up in favor of strong contrasts. Blocklike masses seem to protrude from, or intrude into, each other. Fantastically shaped superstructures antagonize the massive angle turrets, round and square apertures, vases and statues add to the impression of unrest.[18] Stressed contrasts play a still more important role in Vanbrugh's later works, particularly at Seaton Delaval.

Thomas Archer, inspired more by Italy than by Vanbrugh,[19] wanted to give to architectural work the plastic quality which distinguished Italian and German Baroque building but was rather rare in England. In St. Philip's at Birmingham (1709–1715) the apsis was curved, sharp edges were avoided by chamfering the steeple, and the dome was combined with the bell stage by scrolls.[20] The same tendency toward unification appears on the church of St. John Evangelist, erected on Smith Square, London (1713–1728).[21] His integration of the parts into a whole finds its most outspoken expression in the garden pavilion of the Duke of Kent at Wrest, Bedfordshire, which Archer built on a triangular plan in 1709.[22] Here we find concatenation of the parts in space. The dome and the protruding curved walls suggest the unity of a single body. Archer's Baroque feeling also strongly manifests itself in many single features on St. Paul's, Deptford (finished 1730),[23] especially in the way the structure is tied to the ground by the curved stairs in front and the stairs on the sides. There is, moreover, a definite, throughgoing movement leading from the pedestals on the front stairs through the columns up to the tower.

An English architect-sculptor of the type that played such an important part in the artistic development of Italy all through the Renaissance and the Baroque was Thomas White of Worcester, to whom a few buildings are attributed.[24] But his rich sculptural embellishments on the Guildhall at Worcester (1718–1723),[25] lack the function which the decorations of Castle Howard provide, that is, of forming a coherent pattern of lights and shadows. White would rather achieve the integration of the parts by the use of curves. Segmental pediments unify the central parts of the Guildhall, the Deanery,[26] and St. Nicholas at Worcester,[27] just as Wren emphasized the central bays on Christ's Hospital in London (1682).[28]

The plastic character of both the single features and the architectural body in the works of James Gibbs show he belonged to the group of Wren and Archer. St. Mary-le-Strand in London (1714–1717),[29] reveals how this pupil of Carlo Fontana[30] proceeded, with much taste, along the traditional line. Yet one should not understand "tradition" as simply to mean the use of classic features. What it means, above all, is a certain preconceived idea of the relationship of the parts to the whole. In his *Book of Architecture* (1728), Gibbs makes the following statement:

It is not the Bulk of a Fabrick, the Richness and Quantity of the Materials, the Multiplicity of Lines, nor the Gaudiness of the Finishing, that give the Grace or Beauty and Grandeur to a Building; but the Proportion of the Parts to one another and to the Whole, whether entirely plain, or enriched with a few Ornaments properly disposed.[31]

When we compare St. Mary-le-Strand with the Banqueting House by Inigo Jones,[32] we find that the latter has only straight-headed windows on the upper floor, while the side elevation of St. Mary's presents a rhythm of alternating triangular and segmental pediments above the main cornice and strong rhythmical accents all over the surface. The vertical and horizontal ligaments and the attempt to group the single features are the chief characteristics of Gibbs's church. In quite a different manner did he obtain the concatenation of the parts in his design for the "Publick Building" at Cambridge (fig. 1) one wing of which, the Senate House, was built between 1722 and 1730.[33] Here the balustrade and the cornice play the foremost role in horizontal binding, while the colossal half-columns and pilasters achieve unity between the two stories.

Akin to Gibbs's Senate House, and to the much earlier Buckingham House by Wynne,[34] are some structures by Francis Smith of Warwick. On Stoneleigh Abbey, Warwickshire (about 1720),[35] three stories are tied together by colossal Ionic pilasters. Sutton Scarsdale, Derbyshire (1724),[36] with only two stories, is still more like the Senate House at Cambridge.[37]

In his publication on the orders, Gibbs decided to follow Palladio's proportions;[38] as he followed him also in the plans of many country houses. The type most common among Palladio's villas, a dominating pile with lower pavilions "join'd to the House by circular Arcades,"[39] reappears in a great number of Gibbs's designs.[40] The more exceptional plan of the Villa Rotonda—a square with a circular main hall in the center—inspired Gibbs in two instances.[41]

However, besides these designs of little originality, Gibbs produced others with a curious, unwonted emphasis on elementary geometrical forms. The Radcliffe Camera at Oxford (1737–1749)[42] is a massive cylindrical structure rising on a "regular polygon of sixteen sides."[43] Several earlier pavilions and summer houses are composed in plain circular or octagonal shapes.[44] The Octagon at Orleans House, Twickenham (1720), is regarded as a masterwork of Gibbs.[45] We do not know whether aesthetic or merely practical considerations were responsible for the form of the Radcliffe Library; but the variations of the pavilions indicate a definite predilection for the elementary forms. The most striking instances of this predilection are two "round draughts" (1721) among the projects for St. Martin-in-the-Fields (fig. 2).[46] These were rejected because they were too costly,[47] but the architect must have rated them highly, for he inserted them in his book. The cylindrical shape of the main body in these projects is not the only remarkable thing about them. Still more characteristic is the way in which the body is squeezed between the prisms of the west and east ends (fig. 3). The feeling for concatenation, typical of other edifices of Gibbs, is gone. Instead of an organic whole, there is an aggregate of geometrical elements. On the exterior of the actual church, the antagonism of the "disparate elements of temple and tower" (fig. 4)[48] is equally significant as a symptom of the tendency toward a new order of the constituents.

Now we become aware that Colen Campbell's praise of the "Square and the Circle" as "the most perfect Figures" was in no way fortuitous. Nor was the tendency toward the independence of the parts shown in the "round draughts" merely an occasional aberration. Soon we shall see how elementary geometrical forms found an ardent advocate in Robert Morris, and shall learn that Vanbrugh, in the same manner as Gibbs, progressed from Baroque concatenation and gradation to a more individualized treatment of the parts. Also various other designs on unusual plans were published, for example the circular and octagonal houses ascribed to Inigo Jones.[49] The trend toward the geometric gained momentum in the eighteenth century when the far more significant attempts at a new order of the components became the main concern of the architects.

We have been able to distinguish two different manners in the work of Gibbs who was a traditionalist in the double meaning of adhering to Baroque principles and of following Palladio. Yet he also exhibited strange and novel traits in his work. John Soane, in an opinion similar to mine, noted the mingled concepts in St. Mary-le-Strand and in the execution of St. Martin's. St. Mary-le-Strand looked to him like the work of Borromini, Vanvitelli, and Fuga. Soane characterized it as "divided and subdivided into so many parts, and . . . crowded with Decorations of every kind" and, above all, objected that "there is no principal feature . . . to which every other must be subservient . . ." The great merit of St. Martin's, however, consisted, for him, in that "there is sufficient Variety to keep the mind employed with an Uniformity and Simplicity that reminds us of the Temples of the Ancients," although it has deficiencies, too, for it "partakes of the fashion of the day, to which Gibbs himself contributed greatly by his rustics, consoles, and other incongruities," and is to be censured for "the interruption caused by the discordant, unmeaning, and clumsy rustication of the Doors and Windows."[50]

From this criticism we may gain insight into two important factors which will be corroborated by many instances in the course of this investigation. First, we learn that this neoclassicist of the late eighteenth century was opposed only to the overdecoration of the Baroque, but not to its compositional principles.[51] Second, we may infer that those "incongruities" of the "fashion of the day," which, in later stages, were to play an increasing role, were akin to the symptoms of disintegration in late Baroque composition. Later we shall become aware that there was no sudden break in the eighteenth-century development, but a consistent evolution. From the dissociation of the old, a new order was to rise. Only for the short period between about 1760 and 1790, when the transformation reached its highest peak, particularly in France, may one speak of a revolutionary movement. Then the rising and subsiding currents were so intermingled that to the retrospective view the continuity disappears in the uproar.

If, now, we turn to Isaac Ware, it is chiefly to consider his publication, *A Complete Body of Architecture*. Published perhaps in 1735, it contains the quintessence of the architectural doctrines embodied in all eighteenth-century work of the conventional type. Although Ware thoroughly treats "the Ornamental Parts of Buildings,"[52] as well as the practical details, he emphatically warns the student not to lose sight of the whole:

> . . . the orders of architecture, which give the greatest beauty that can be communicated to a building, . . . are not essential parts, because very good, nay very elegant, edifices . . . may be erected wholly without them. . . .[53] The student may be assured that he will never execute that design well which he contrives by piece-meal. All must be planned together, and every part regulated upon a just idea of the whole.[54]

Ware condemns everything which might impair the integral nature of the structure:

> In houses which have been some time built, and which have not an out of proportion room, the common practice is to build one to them: this always hangs from one end, or sticks to one side, of the house, and shows to the most careless eye, that, though fastened to the walls, it does not belong to the building.[55]

These passages were written still in the spirit of Leone Battista Alberti who had seen in "Beauty . . . a harmony of all the parts . . . fitted together with such proportion and connection that nothing could be added, diminished or altered, but for the worse."[56] The parts should be integrated in the structure, and the building itself integrated into the environment. "The first thing he [the architect] is to consider is the outline of the edifice; he is to study what figure will best lie upon the spot, will best fill it, or best become it."[57]

This admonition may seem in no way remarkable. Yet let us state here that when these words were written, architecture had already reached the threshold of a new era, with definitely different views on composition; an era in which the building was no longer expected to merge into its surroundings, but abruptly to part company with them and to rise in splendid isolation.

Ware still recommends supple curves which lack "harshness in the angles,"[58] and thus are apt to combine one feature with the other, the main pile with the outbuildings, the "fabrick" with nature. Like the Baroque architects of the early century, Ware is fond of harmonious variety:

> It is certain that variety is the source of great pleasure to the eye, yet there is to be an uniformity preserved in buildings.[59]

. . . there ought to be, in this apparent external division, what we recommended to him [the young builder] before so strongly for that within, a conformity of all the parts, first to the whole building, and next to one another.[60]

This great precept is brought out repeatedly in Ware's book,[61] in varying contexts. We cannot doubt that this was his own belief and not merely a doctrine taken over from some revered authority. In addition to his general remarks on "the disposition of parts in an edifice,"[62] he puts forth precepts concerning particular problems which likewise are in concordance with the practice of the early eighteenth century. Ware wants the traditional *enfilade* to be observed regardless of its practical disadvantages:

. . . it may be laid down as an unanswerable rule, that the entrance, or principal door, of a house ought always to be in the centre; and that we must content ourselves with this string of unbroken or uninterrupted apartments in the upper floor, and even there it is often attended with great inconveniencies.[63]

From the belief in the importance of unified composition, Ware ascends to the ultimate dogma of the Baroque creed. He advocates gradation: "Variety . . . may be given in a building of some extent, by the *various elevation of different parts*"[64] (my italics). The differentiation of the constituents is the best help against monotony:

Though it be incumbent upon the architect to give a proportion and harmony to the whole building, and to make every part of it as suitable to that whole as its nature will admit, yet he must not endevour to make all equally elegant.[65]

The symbolism of the rusticated basement appealed to Ware as to any Baroque architect: "It looks as a rock upon which all the rest is raised."[66]

Such was the thought of Isaac Ware. The plans and elevations he illustrates are conceived in the spirit of Baroque composition (fig. 5).[67] Whether his façades are rich or plain, they present gradation and reciprocity of the parts. Besides *A Complete Body of Architecture*, Ware brought out a translation of the *Four Books* of Palladio with the assistance of the Earl of Burlington (1738).[68] We must give credit to the scrupulousness of both men who coöperated in this endeavor to provide an "exact copy" in "a strict and literal translation, that the sense of our author might be delivered from his own words."[69] Thus, they declare themselves to be adherents of Palladio, as, indeed, they were recognized to be by almost all commentators. Is there a contradiction between this view and the one which holds that Ware was a Baroque architect? The label "Palladianist" has been used in architectural history again and again in a rather vague manner. It may therefore be good to review, at least briefly, the teachings and the practice of Palladio himself. The elucidation of Palladio's intentions is a necessary preparatory step before we attempt to comprehend the ways of eighteenth-century architecture.

There were times in which Palladianism meant restraint, simplicity, and clarity. There were other times in which it was identical with academic correctness and cool aloofness. Only too often a few features, or a few buildings, were singled out in Palladio's work and set forth as representative of his style. Some authors of textbooks content themselves with the simple equation: pediment plus portico equals Palladian.[70] These features were obviously not characteristic of him alone. What he made out of them is important. In order to grasp the essence of his artistic will, we have first to find out his attitude towards that most basic problem of all architecture, "composition."[71]

Each architect is guided in his work by a leading compositional ideal, an architectural *Gestalt-Ideal,* which he shares with his contemporaries. We may speak of any period of time as being of one and the same artistic epoch as long as the very same ideal of configuration dominates. The arrangement of the parts of every single work, and quite particularly their relationship to the whole, derives from the compositional ideal of the era. The "architectural system" is the visualization of the particular *Gestalt-Ideal.* (For the moment, the historically extremely important overlapping of different trends may be disregarded. Part II of this book will discuss more extensively my understanding of the architectural system.)

Only a few passages in Palladio's *Four Books on Architecture* reveal his ultimate goal in composition, yet these passages speak a clear language. In the first chapter of his First Book he gives a definition of beauty:

Beauty will result from the form and correspondence of the whole, with respect to the several parts, of the parts with regard to each other, and of these again to the whole; that the structure may appear an entire and compleat body, wherein each member agrees with the other, and all necessary to compose what you intend to form.[72]

Thus he advocates the concatenation of the parts, and their integration into the whole; to which precept he adds another, demanding that there shall be one ruling part:

I have made the frontispiece in the fore-front in all the fabricks for villas, and also in some for the city, in which are the principal gates; because such frontispieces shew the entrance of the house, and add very much to the grandeur and magnificence of the work . . . the fore-part being thus made more eminent than the rest.[73]

Because of the significance of the matter, another quotation may be cited:

The loggia's have frontispieces, which . . . give no small grandeur to the fabrick; making it more elevated in the middle, than it is in the flanks, and serve to place the ensigns.[74]

His third chief goal, therefore, is the differentiation of the parts by distinguishing between dominant and subordinate. None of these three goals of concatenation, integration, and gradation, has anything to do with the imitation of the ancients, but each was a contributing factor building up the theory of proportions which was to fill so many pages of Renaissance and Baroque treatises. Concatenation, integration, and gradation were the fundamental principles which made the Renaissance and the Baroque one system in spite of all differences between the two stages.[75]*

In Ware's time the doctrine of Palladio was still alive. Many a doctrinaire was just able to pick from it the utterances of reverence toward antiquity. However, Palladio was revered by the true architects so long as they held the same views on composition, whether they were more conservative or went on to the utmost possibilities of the Baroque system.

Finally, a word must be said about Palladio's attitude toward the material. The above-quoted passage on "beauty" throws some light on this point. The building is to him a "body" and the parts are its "members." It is extremely important to recognize this concept of organic architecture. Concerning this point, two more quotations may find a place here: "I say therefore, that architecture, as well as all other arts, being an imitatrix of nature, can suffer nothing that either alienates or deviates from that which is agreeable to nature."[76] And, in dealing with his Villa Mocenigo, he speaks of the "Four loggia's which, like arms tend to the circumference, seem to receive those that come near the house."[77]

Palladio's buildings conform to his theory. Yet one should not illustrate the Rotonda (or Villa Capra, Vicenza), as the archetype of Palladianism, as it has become customary to do. Its form is exceptional in his work. He himself felt he had to justify it: "It is upon a small hill . . . and therefore, as it enjoys from every part most beautiful views . . . there are loggia's made in all the four fronts."[78] All the other villas, however, most certainly follow the Baroque system. Especially characteristic are those with side pavilions connected by aisles to the central pile, for example, the Villas Badoer[79] or Barbari,[80] or the beautiful group of Villa Trissini.[81] The frequent use of colossal orders is likewise in conformity with the Baroque system. Nor can one overlook the Baroque climax in the cupolas of the Redentore and San Giorgio, in Venice.

Giacomo Leoni was one of the early eighteenth-century "Palladianists" to whom the spirit of Palladio's architecture meant more than the pedantic obedience to immediate details. Isaac Ware blamed Leoni for having dealt too freely with Palladio's text when bringing out the *Four Books*.[82] In Leoni's works, such as Lyme Hall,[83] and the house at Moor Park, Hertfordshire,[84] both of the 1720's, there is "Palladian" concatenation by the use of colossal columns or pilasters, and gradation by the emphasis on the center and the opposition of the "Rustick" basement to

---

* In my comments on the changes in the eighteenth century I shall use, for the sake of brevity, the term "Baroque system" instead of "system of the Renaissance and the Baroque." Concatenation, integration, and gradation were disregarded by the Mannerists, in that stage between Renaissance and Baroque formerly known as the Late Renaissance. On Mannerism see Part II.

the smooth upper walls. Leoni connected the main building at Moor Park with the outbuildings by curved colonnades,[85] which were removed in 1785.[86]

Lord Burlington is commonly regarded as the most prominent figure of English Palladianism. It is interesting to see how Burlington, with all his admiration for the great Italian master, moved away from him. Like many of his countrymen, Burlington possessed far more originality than art history has so far recognized in eighteenth-century English architecture. Rudolf Wittkower rightly notes in Burlington's Tottenham Park, Wiltshire, of 1721 a certain "staccato" quality and remarks, "every one of [its] parts forms a distinct unit of its own."[87] Yet I believe one should not consider this as Palladian. The somewhat similar plan of Villa Mocenigo shows how dear to Palladio were the tying curves. Still farther away from Baroque compositional principles is Chiswick House, Middlesex (about 1727). In support of this view I should like to refer to the excellent observations made by Fiske Kimball and Wittkower. Both authorities point out the pattern of the garden front of Chiswick, on which little is left of the traditional centralization.[88] Wittkower, moreover, remarks about the relation of the villa to a wing connecting it to an older building, that "the break between them was made quite definite."[89] Also in the details, Burlington was far from copying Palladio's Villa Rotonda. He appended to both main fronts imposing open stairs and thus made a concession to the pictorial tendency of the scenic Baroque. These lively flights of steps link the architectural body to the ground with greater intensity than the straight stairs of the Rotonda. Likewise un-Palladian,[90] though in quite a different way, are the overarched Venetian windows of the north front.[91] These deserve particular attention because they were to become very popular in the course of the century. They represent a definitely un-Baroque variation of the Palladian motif, for the outer arch deprives the central light of its predominance. In spite of his academic conviction, Burlington, the artist, deviated from Palladio's models, both when he was more Baroque—as in the exceptional feature of the stairs and the lofty dome of Chiswick—and when he was less Baroque—as in the total composition and the garden-front windows.

The Assembly Rooms at York (1730–1736) may have been inspired by Palladio's drawings of Roman halls. More noteworthy, here, however, seems to be the appearance of a new compositional principle. The goal now is no longer unifying the parts, but contrasting them. The curved vestibule is opposed to the straight front wall above; the arcades to the oblong windows; the balustrades to the pediments.[92] How Burlington ultimately aimed at modern plainness can be seen in his project for Kirby Hall, Ouseburn (about 1750), which was carried out by Roger Morris.[93]

It happened of course eventually that so-called Palladian devotees misunderstood the architect of Vicenza. Thus it came about, for example, that the Palladian Bridge at Wilton House, Wiltshire, by Roger Morris, as well as that at Prior Park near Bath,[94] misses the basic idea of Palladio's bridge[95] with its three loggias climaxing in the high middle one, although they show the noble proportions and the purity of design so often exalted as truly Palladian.

We have seen that Colen Campbell believed himself to be able to improve on St. Paul's of London. Another ambitious aim of his was to surpass the Villa Rotonda.[96] His improved, or, as he modestly asserts, altered version of Mereworth Castle near Maidstone, Kent,[97] completed in 1723, is just as exceptional in his work as the Rotonda is in that of Palladio. In general Campbell follows the regular patterns of the Palladian Baroque. He emphasizes the center, either by a porch (Wanstead House, for Richard Child, Essex),[98] or by a loggia (design of a house inscribed to the Earl of Halifax in 1715)[99] or by two superimposed orders (design for Lord Percival, 1715).[100] Often he presents a change in texture by setting the rusticated basement against the smooth upper walls, as, for instance, in the design of a house inscribed to the Earl of Islay (1715)[101] and Burlington House in Piccadilly (1717).[102] He adopts the Baroque system in the interior, also, making the great hall and the salon the core of the whole, and linking the rooms together by the *enfilade* (Wanstead,[103] houses for Lords Halifax[104] and Percival[105]). Campbell makes a significant remark about the Halifax design, which reveals that he no longer liked the Baroque ways of treating the walls: "Here the Windows are placed at due distance, and free from that bad Effect we so frequently see when they are crowded, which destroys that Repose and Appearance of Strength, so necessary in Architecture."

In several cases it is easy to trace the Palladian models. The square forecourt of the Percival house shows a certain dependency on the Villa Marco Zeno[106] or the Villa Ragona.[107] The plan of Goodwood, Sussex (1724),[108] with its curved colonnades is apparently inspired by the Villa Badoer[109] or the Villa Trissini.[110] Nevertheless, significant deviations from Palladio are not rare in Campbell's *oeuvre*. His houses are more restrained than even Palladio's plainer structures, and much more so than the Basilica of Vicenza or the Loggia del Capitano. In the first project inscribed to Robert Walpole, Campbell "endeavored to introduce the *Temple* Beauties in a private building,"[111] but usually he prefers rather plain fronts, as in the Hotham house at Beverley, Yorkshire,[112] Hedworth House in County Durham (1716),[113] Walpole's Houghton Hall, Norfolk,[114] and Goodwood. Goodwood has two mezzanines which disturb the equilibrium of the stories. Here, as on Hedworth, the center is only slightly stressed. Remarkable originality appears in the layout of Houghton Hall (carried out for Walpole, 1722–1735). Its pavilions are connected with the main house by colonnades, and yet seem to be self-contained units.

Two of the earlier projects follow the layout of the Villa Francesco Pisani, which is unique in Palladio's work, for the main house and the outbuildings are equal in depth and almost equal in height.[115] Similarly, in the first design for Walpole[116] and the house of Charles Hotham, the office buildings run parallel to the main building and are only loosely connected to it by a gallery or by a "Rustick Arch."[117] The project for Walpole must have been particularly dear to Campbell. He presents it for a second time with certain modifications at the end of the third volume of the *Vitruvius Britannicus,* dating the design 1724.[118]

The loose connection of main house and pavilions characterizes also the house which was built about 1710 for Lord Bingley, Bramham Park near Leeds.[119] Two wings projecting from the central structure were connected by Tuscan colonnades to outer pavilions. The wings belong, bodily, to the center, but in appearance, to the pavilions. This inconsistency of the whole, as well as the stressed cubism of the masses, is new, and very characteristic of the changed concepts of composition. "The Front is of an elegant, though plain Manner."[120]

In his text, Campbell attacks the "excessive ornaments"[121] of Bernini, Fontana, and Borromini, but does not blame Wren, Vanbrugh, Hawksmoor, and Archer for their tamer performances.[122] It may be that out of personal regard he spared the English architects. Yet his praise of simplicity again and again occurs in his book. In speaking of a church design of his, he boasts of having "abstained from any unnecessary Ornaments."[123] Just as he commends the "plain Manner" of Bramham Park, so does he praise the "Majestick Simplicity" of Inigo Jones's St. Paul's, Covent Garden (1638).[124] He seems to have been recommending himself by taking the part of reticence. Now we understand better his criticism of St. Paul's Cathedral and of St. Peter's of Rome. Clarity of appearance meant more to him than the Baroque interplay of the parts.

To sum up: As early as the beginning of the eighteenth century, Colen Campbell's work manifests deviations from the Baroque, in an inconspicuous yet unmistakable way. We can sense the coming of a definite anti-Baroque feeling in both his works and his words. The first, however, who truly shattered the Baroque system was Vanbrugh in his second manner.

II

THE FIRST OPPONENTS OF TRADITION

WE MAY measure the "greatness" of an artist according to an aesthetic canon we ourselves have chosen as a yardstick, or we may find larger significance in his versatility and independent thinking. If we prefer the latter qualities, then Vanbrugh, so often disparaged and even ridiculed, will come out as the most prominent personality of England's eighteenth-century builders. When I speak of his first and second manners this should not be understood as denoting early and late works. "First manner" rather refers to those designs in which he followed Baroque principles more or less closely; "second manner," to those in which, primarily, he struggled to get rid of inherited modes. The two manners ran parallel through all his work. Yet the second seems always to have been the stronger and more in accord with his proper will. It showed already in the Goose-Pie House in Whitehall,[125] of about 1700: in its composition this house went ahead of the most progressive achievements of the eighteenth century. Because of its odd shape Jonathan Swift called it "a monstrous pile." It was a revolting sight to contemporary eyes; it seems revolutionary to posterity. In the opinion of Geoffrey Webb it might "be ignored as evidence of style." I cannot share this view, either with regard to Vanbrugh's personal style, or to that of the period. The house with its vigorous and somewhat bizarre handling of both masses and details was truly Vanbrughian. And it appears to be highly expressive of the rising century, as soon as we desist from thinking merely in terms of the commonly accepted styles and, eventually, their revivals. Having become aware that there was not, perhaps, just one more "style" in the Age of Reason, but a momentous movement of artistic reorientation, I recognized the little house as one of its first manifestations, and Vanbrugh, though certainly not its creator—for such movements originate on a wide front—as one of its greatest exponents.

Goose-Pie House was distinguished by dissonances both on the surface and in the masses, by emphasis on cubes, and by the "disproportionate height, and the scale of the rustication." Unhampered by the usual regard for a patron, Vanbrugh here tried out what could be done for the redemption of architecture from traditional tenets.

In 1710 Vanbrugh started to work on King's Weston in Gloucestershire.[126] Its calmness and sobriety are exceedingly striking beside the richness of Castle Howard.

We have seen how the far less original Campbell hastened to show his understanding of the newly arising trend toward simple, elementary forms. Apart from the row of chimneys, there is nothing on King's Weston to be compared with the fantastic skyline of Blenheim Palace. Nor is there any reminiscence of the play of light and shadow of Castle Howard on the flat walls of the Gloucestershire structure with its prevailing horizontals.[127] Richly decorated walls suggest the continuity of inner and outer space; undecorated walls stress the mutual independence of these areas. Sculpture was not an incidental but an integral part of the architectural system of the Baroque. It had a definite and very important part in the realization of the great concept of integration; it was supposed to be the mediator between the limitations of the interior and the infinity of nature. King's Weston, however, looks almost hostile in its surroundings. Here the architect has passed from the all-embracing Baroque composition to the new principle of isolation, about which we shall soon learn more. The transition from effusiveness to reserve is a historical fact of great significance. It should be so considered, no matter whether our individual taste agrees with the older attitude, or with the modern one.

The unwonted aspect of the exterior is not the only curious thing at King's Weston. Avray Tipping has published a series of projects made for it about 1718 which display Gothicizing features.[128] It is not known whether Vanbrugh himself, or a certain "Mr. Price of Wandsworth," is responsible for these. Yet it is interesting to see that in one and the same moment the discontent with the Baroque found a twofold expression: in the progressive attempt to evolve a new principle of composition, and in the reintroduction of features of a remote past. "The time was not yet ripe for the picturesque and romantic," Tipping rightly remarks.[129] It was still less ripe for a new concept of the general arrangement. Vanbrugh's own "castle"[130] and Maze Hill House[131] next to Greenwich Park (1717) are further instances of that "false dawn of the Gothic revival"[132] appearing on some minor structures of Castle Howard.[133]

More significant than the appearance of Gothicizing features is Vanbrugh's treatment of the details. We find in it, beyond his personal style, the reflection of the general unrest that was to increase steadily in the course of the century. In the center of the east front of King's Weston, under the heavily projecting cornice, a straight window heading carried by brackets protrudes boldly.[134] The entrance door is subdued by all the heavy motifs above. Near the castle, hidden behind shrubbery, the brewhouse stands, with a machicolated frieze. Most noteworthy is the vigorous treatment of the arched door. Its oversized keystone and the heavy blocks flanking it seem to struggle against the projecting window sill above.[135] On the house in St. Michael's Street, Oxford, commonly ascribed to Vanbrugh, and named after him,[136] the short cornice in the center below the top story recalls the similar motif on King's Weston. It is, once more, a feature rebelling against being integrated into the whole.

The curious belvederes on top of the angle towers of Eastbury Park in Dorset (1718) were truly Vanbrughian features. The plan differs markedly from the architect's earlier works, the Baroque scheme of wings spreading from the central body being replaced by the loose appendage of the outbuildings.[137] Campbell reached only the stage of a hardly perceivable weakening of the traditional pattern; Vanbrugh made an important step ahead. At Seaton Delaval, Northumberland (1721) (fig. 6),[138] the struggle between the elements breaks loose. There is nothing more of the Baroque harmonizing and blending of the parts. The crowning pediment, the chimneys, and the roof balustrades of the lateral towers rival for dominance; octagonal angle turrets are contrasted to ringed column shafts. The change of the wall texture adds to the uproar. The center of the entrance front is rusticated, but flanked by smooth sides and topped by a smooth attic wall. A bold intruder, it tears the front apart. The tripartite door, the group of three windows high up (both remote descendants of the Palladian motif), and the lunette oddly inserted between them have nothing in common with the oblong windows of the sides. Discord reigns between the elements. Still greater incongruities become apparent in the protruding square towers on the sides which contain the staircases.[139] On these the rustication runs high up and is contrasted to the flat top story with big Palladian windows. No trace is left of the old proportionality and the old equilibrium. Almost any part of the structure is a menace to the others.

Grimsthorpe Castle, Lincolnshire,[140] partly rebuilt by Vanbrugh in 1723, is far more composed. It was in Seaton Delaval, that grandiose protest against convention and the apogee of his second manner, that Vanbrugh said the last he had to say as an architect.

We have distinguished between the first manner of Vanbrugh, showing him close to the Baroque, and his second manner, revealing him as an opponent of its principles. But we should not pass over yet another possible interpretation, for it is the task of the historian to pave new approaches rather than to set forth a dogmatic view. The second interpretation would place Vanbrugh's whole production on a common denominator. The multiplicity of features and the consequent unrest, both recognizable in his work, or the unmistakably oppositional character of all his designs, could be regarded as a return to the English concept of building prior to Inigo Jones, and thus as a protest of the vernacular against Italian formalism. But the subsequent development did not lead in this direction, excepting, perhaps, only certain side currents of romanticism. Both architects and patrons usually preferred to accept the Italian fashion, rather than to go back to an Elizabethan Revival. It will, of course, remain an open question whether Vanbrugh was guided by the idea of reviving the older style, or was aiming at a new order. The latter alternative seems to be more in accord with the general trends, as the following investigation will show by a great many works of a great many architects.

Another architect who in his structures opposed the Baroque system in the strongest way was Nicholas Hawksmoor. He discarded the Baroque plan, disrupted unity by bizarre forms, and at the same time liked to emphasize solid walls. Antithesis of the elements is the basic idea of all of his designs. Lord Leimpster's house, Easton Neston, mainly completed in 1702,[141] is still a Baroque group in the general layout as well as in its elevations with their continuous lines and the climaxing central part. Yet the Baroque scheme is abandoned in the plan of the main building. The single rooms do not tend toward a dominant center, but are freely arranged. Hawksmoor's proper style can be found on the east front of the Queen Anne Block of Greenwich Hospital (1705–1715).[142] The windows in the center are set in deep recesses forming a striking contrast to the massiveness of the piers and the side walls. The antagonism of the elements is also the main characteristic of the architect's churches. St. Mary Woolnoth (1716–1727)[143] shows a definite predilection toward cubes. Yet while the façade of Wren's St. Lawrence Jewry,[144] likewise cubic, is adorned with engaged columns and alleviated by high windows and niches, that of St. Mary's is conspicuous by the massiveness of its walls. On the latter, the boldly projecting cornices of the tower, the unorthodox design of the main front, and, still more, the three gigantic niches with inserted small windows, on Lombard Street, tell of the unrest that had taken hold on architecture. The lanterns of St. Anne's, Limehouse (1712–1724),[145] and St. George-in-the-East (1715–1723)[146] are "set diagonally upon the square towers." The opposition of the straight cornices and the broken contour of the steeples is particularly impressive.

On these churches the tendency appears to go beyond, and, possibly, to surpass, classical building. James Peller Malcolm understood the architect's intentions perfectly, yet in the heyday of Revivalism he could not but blame them: "Mr. Hawksmoor appears to have erred principally in his designs by attempting more than Grecian architecture will permit."[147] Still, with the help of classical features Hawksmoor strove to revolutionize building. Whether he had the Mausoleum of Halicarnassus in mind when he erected St. George's, Bloomsbury (1720–1731) (figs. 7, 8), or not, is of secondary importance. Yet his boldness in piling a pyramid on top of a tower proves that he could do better than simply reproduce Wren's diversified inventions.[148] The oversized keystones on the undercroft openings of this church recall Vanbrugh. The time was not yet ripe for entirely new solutions. But in the exaltation of single features the revolutionary spirit speaks out loudly.

Christ Church, Spitalfields (1723–1729) (fig. 9), is also full of antagonisms showing particularly in the two gigantic, fantastically transformed Palladian motifs, the upper one on the tower challenging the mightier lower one of the porch.[149] On the east end Hawksmoor placed a huge Venetian window between upper circular and lower arched windows, whereas Gibbs, on the east end of St. Martin-in-the-Fields (fig. 10), still had tried to bring unity into his composition by identically framing the windows as well as the blind windows, and by tying them with semicolumns. Hawksmoor hardly cared about unity, but presented a pattern of unconnected motifs, which became frequent in French revolutionary architecture. At Queen's College, Oxford (1733), the airy canopy is markedly set off against the supporting massive wall.[150] In this city, if you stand in the gateway of the north quadrangle of All Souls, you can make an interesting comparison by looking from Hawksmoor's agitated gothicizing twin towers (about 1721) to the firm plastic forms of Gibbs's Radcliffe Camera. It may be that the different characteristics combined in Hawksmoor's works resulted from his having been a colleague of both Wren and Vanbrugh. The problem of the "cross-fertilization" of the three has been interestingly discussed by Sitwell.[151] Yet there is no doubt that Hawksmoor, quite independently, was searching for new ways. In no instance should he be considered as a typical representative of the Baroque.[152] His strongly personal manner was often pointed out, for example in 1742 by John Gwynn, who saw in Hawksmoor's and Vanbrugh's designs a "wild Heap of inconsistent Things";[153] in 1803 by Malcolm ("Mr. Hawksmoor proceeded according to a set exclusively his own")[154] and in this century by Avray Tipping who speaks of his "eccentric attempts."[155] And John Summerson is right in his remark: "The more detailed aesthetic character of Hawksmoor's architecture is extraordinarily hard to analyze."[156] One may try to come nearer to the source of the phenomenon of his style by taking it strictly as the expression of his personality. Yet more promising than the psychological approach would be an endeavor to place his achievements historically as important links in the chain of attempts to overcome the Baroque. Thus his eccentricities become more easily comprehensible. Vanbrugh's and Hawksmoor's "failure to found a school"[157] most certainly resulted from their being too bold for their time.

The work of William Kent also manifests the tendency to depart from the Baroque.[158] The projects for the Houses of Parliament (1732–1739),[159] reveal the decay of the old, rather than any traits of the architecture to come. However, the strong accentuation of the sides already points toward the future. Kent was not as great a reformer in building as he was in landscape architecture.[160] In the plan of Holkham Hall, Norfolk (begun 1734), reminiscences of the Baroque wing scheme live on, though markedly modified.[161] The hall and the salon are no longer lined up on the main axis, but are on different floors, separated by stairs.[162] Thus the main artery of the Baroque organism is disrupted. The symptomatic value of this arrangement should not be underrated. Moreover, the four corner pavilions have not the intimate correlation to the main structure which Baroque pavilions had. The center of the northern front is hardly accentuated.[163] The entrance doors are inconspicuous apertures in the basement. Great emphasis is laid on the solid walls on which we meet, again, overarched Palladian windows. On the west front of the Horse Guards, Whitehall,[164] the changes of texture call to mind the dramatization of the front of Seaton Delaval. It is not merely a feeling of our own that the parts forming the Horse Guards antagonize each other. William Chambers explained the "general dislike" of it by the very fact that the conventional unity is missing in . . . "a building of so complicated a figure, both in its Plan and Elevation, that it is impossible to form a distinct idea of the whole at once."[165]

In this dramatized composition something new appears, the predominance of cubes. Others had gone ahead in this direction, to name only John Price in St. George's, Southwark (1734),[166] and Isaac Ware (or else Edward Shepherd) at 71 South Audley Street (1736).[167] Yet the Horse Guards is remarkable, first, because of its vigor, and second, because Kent, with all the intransigence of a man who at last has found a new way—a way not leading back to Palladio but forward to our own time—strove to realize the new concept of antagonistic cubes within the old pattern of a ruling central pavilion and subordinated sides.

Soon we shall see that cubism was to play an ever increasing role in eighteenth-century architecture. If it has been said that neoclassic architects did not think in terms of cubic masses, this is true perhaps only of the upper crust of weak traditionalists or revivalists. The progressive architects in England and, even more violently though much later, in France, struggled after mastery of space with the means of cubism. The Horse Guards is not a failure, but a promise.

Two designs of "garden seats" by Kent are compositionally remarkable for the accumulation of incongruous features. The one for Charles Hotham is a plain house with a prostyle, a high attic, and a saucer dome.[168] The other, for Lord Cobham at Stowe, presents a pedimented front opening in a huge niche and connected by arcades to massive rusticated pavilions.[169] The parts are connected materially, but not related aesthetically.

The characteristics shown in these works appear with greater intensity on Worcester Lodge at Badminton Park, Gloucestershire.[170] The lodge consists of strongly contrasted upper and lower portions. The walls of the upper portion are smooth, those of the lower, framing the huge archway, show heavy rustication. Yet the textural differentiation is not all. There are additional contrasts in shape and size. The cupola and the polygonal drum are set against the comparative flatness of the upper story, while the squareness of the entire structure is opposed to the pyramidal finishings of the loosely appended pavilions. Minor features contribute to the strange appearance of the lodge, above all the square sunken panels under the main cornice, and the semicircular niches. Compositionally, the building has almost nothing in common with previous architecture.[171] It is hard to understand how it could be styled "a triumph of Palladian architecture in England."[172] The group of the large central window and the two niches is derived from the Palladian motif, but in shape and proportions thoroughly altered. Apart from this feature which we know was not exclusively Palladio's, everything on the lodge is as anti-Palladian as it can be. There is no harmonization and no integration of the parts, and still less than on the Horse Guards and the "garden seats" can we find here what was most dear to Palladio: "the entire and complete body, wherein each member agrees with the other." If you go through the whole *oeuvre* of the Vicentine master, you cannot find any design like Worcester Lodge. Finally, almost complete lack of decoration characterizes the façades of Kew Palace, "executed from Designs of Kent."[173]

Roger Morris is sometimes confused with his relative, Robert Morris, the writer. In speaking of Roger's buildings, Blomfield finds that "his originality is excessively dull."[174] Yet Morris' work seems to be interesting in many respects. No doubt many of his designs are on an average level, distinguished perhaps only by a definite predilection for plainness (His Majesty's Lodge in Richmond Park, by Morris and Stephen Wright,[175] and the house of Thomas Wyndham at Hammersmith[176]). However, Combe Bank,[177] house of the Duke of Argyle, is almost entirely independent of models of the past, different from the common run of buildings of his day, and in no way "weak." The whole structure and its single features are vigorously handled, especially the sturdy towers attached to the four corners. Morris deserves full recognition for this dignified piece of architecture. It has been compared with Kent's Holkham,[178] Inigo Jones's Wilton (about 1649),[179] and Campbell's Houghton Hall.[180] But on all these the towers are rather slight projections from the main façade and belong to the body of the house. Morris' corner towers are nearly independent units, loosely attached to the central block. This makes quite a difference from the viewpoint of the architectural system.

We have already mentioned the "Palladian" Bridge at Wilton, and found that it was not Palladian at all, with only two coördinated loggias, while Palladio's prototype has three, with a dominant one in the center.[181] Mere juxtaposition of classic features without gradation should not be termed "Palladian."

Robert Morris' writings have been either almost completely disregarded, or heavy blame has been put upon them. His main publications, *Essay in Defence of Ancient Architecture, Lectures on Architecture, Rural Architecture,* and *Architecture Improved,*[182] are only little known.[183] Blomfield is disgusted by the *Lectures,* branding them "most tedious and rhetorical," and the designs contained in them "as weak and pretentious as his letterpress."[184]

In the plates of *Rural Architecture* (1750), Robert Morris deviated but little from the Baroque system. Yet one should not minimize his efforts in making some first steps toward a new arrangement. *Rural Architecture* must have met with interest, for in 1755 a new edition came out under the title *Select Architecture.* However, aside from the title, the new edition was otherwise unchanged. We gain the impression from it, as well as from the little *Architecture Improved,* that Morris was gifted with an inventive mind and anticipated the playfulness of John Soane in some regards. This can be said, for instance, of his experiments with the plan. He tries to combine rooms of diversified shapes (figs. 11, 12, 13),[185] or plays with the variations of a one-room garden house.[186] He enjoys drawing uncommon though not very significant façades,[187] and among his designs in Halfpenny's *Modern Builder's Assistant,* House No. 13 shows cylindrical corner turrets set against a plain cube.[188] Altogether, his designs show that some symptoms of unrest have crept into architecture.

Morris' dissatisfaction with the architecture of his day made him oppose the overdecorated Baroque, and by censuring Palladio, he criticized Palladianism as well. "I shall endeavour to shew you his Blemishes as well as Perfections," he wrote.[189] His criticism is contained in the fourteen lectures given by him from October 22, 1730, to January 13, 1735, and printed in two parts in 1734 and 1736. He reproaches Palladio for the superimposed orders—"two *Orders* erected one over the other in the same Range of Building, is contrary to all the stated Rules of *Architecture.*"[190]—and he blames the architects "who have made Ornament or Dress the principal Part of their Performance."[191] In later years he placed still greater emphasis on this particular point: "Redundancy of Members, Ornament, and Dress, are the Productions of unthinking Geniuses. Undecorated Plainness . . . in a well proportioned Building will ever please." And he adds to this admonition the following:

. . . the great End of Appropriation terminates in Convenience: Your Structure must answer the End for which it was erected, and the Ornament be suited to the Dignity of the Inhabitant; but all such additional Embellishments should be rather the Intent of internal than external Gaiety.[192]

Besides this criticism he voices positive views of still greater interest. These views do not point in one direction exclusively. You can find as many contradictions in his words as in the writings of most architects, and particularly in writings that originated in a time of marked transition. The pioneer who struggles to free himself from what he was taught will always carry along with him remnants of the past.

In Morris' *Lectures* the well-established Baroque doctrine appears side by side with some basically new ideas. It is still a typical Baroque thought, derived from the concept of the building as a picture, when he demands that it should be carried out so "as to invite the Beholder to consider the taking in of the whole Scene at one View . . . and which should be at such an Angle that the whole may be seen without moving the Eye."[193] Quite Baroque also are the following passages:

The Entrances should be Grand, the Rooms Noble and Spacious, and should be contiguous to each other, without the Interruption of Passages or Staircases.[194]

Each Room may bear an Analogy and Connexion to each other.[195]

The Joint Union and Concordance of the Parts, in an exact Symmetry, forms the whole, a compleat Harmony, which admits of no Medium; it is agreeably blended through the whole.[196]

As to a Knowledge of the Five Orders of *Architecture,* indeed they are commendable, but it is only the Entrance, the first Branches of the Art; the great and valuable Parts of it consist in designing well, to appropriate the several Parts to Use, and make them have an Affinity with the whole.[197]

. . . a proper Design compos'd to blend Art and Nature together, must . . . give an unspeakable Pleasure to the Eye of every Beholder.[198]

. . . a Vista through the Middle of the Building should be always had . . . and the Doors of one Room, in a Range of Rooms should be dispos'd to answer each other in a Line [the *enfilade!*], to preserve a Grandeur proportion'd to the Magnitude of the Building.[199]

If the Offices are continued long in a Range with the Front, they should fall gradually away, by Breakings, and terminate, as it were in a Point.[200]

Morris repeatedly asks for "utmost Symmetry and Exactness."[201] In the Introduction to the *Rural Architecture,* he still speaks of the "concatenation" and "gradation" of the parts as vital principles of the composition:

The Parts should be so disposed, that, from the highest Station, in those little Communities, all the subservient Apartments should be join'd by an easy Gradation, that every Link in the Concatenation should be justly regulated; and in this Light I would be understood, that they could no where else be so well placed.[202]

No one could better have expressed the basic idea of the Baroque system than Robert Morris has done here; and the same can be said of the comparison immediately following, which calls to mind the famous passage in Joshua Reynolds' *Thirteenth Discourse:*

As in History Painting, one principal Figure possesseth the superior Light, the fore Ground and Eminence of the Piece, and the subordinate Figures are placed, Part in Sight, Part in Groups and Shade, for Contrast, and keeping in the Design; so in Building, all the subservient Offices should terminate by gradual Progression in *Utility* and *Situation*.[203] [His italics]

In a passage like this the concept of the Baroque hierarchy seems to be fully alive, and yet the feeling for the well-rounded-off unity was already somewhat weakened. We may learn about this change by turning back from the written testimony of the theorist Morris, to the examples set by the architect Morris. The latter—we already know this from Combe Bank—was the more progressive of the two relatives. The former, in his lecture of December 16, 1734, illustrates a façade with an emphasized central pile, wings, and pavilions. But he remarks that some more pavilions might be added: "This Range might be still continued."[204] Instead of the finite scheme—Palladio's *uno intiero, e ben finito corpo*[205]—he allows a composition *ad infinitum,* that is, juxtaposition and disregard of the almost sacrosanct Baroque hierarchy. We who today know what was to happen in architecture in the later eighteenth century recognize in this incidental remark a first sign of an underlying trend that we are bound to follow down to its ultimate supremacy.

Another suggestion by Morris, also diametrically opposed to the principles of the Baroque, takes up a good deal of space in the *Lectures*. Morris proposes to use as the element of composition one of the simplest geometrical forms, the cube.[206] He adds a plate showing various ways of combining cubes simply by adding one to the other vertically or horizontally (fig. 14) In support of his idea he illustrates several projects, all starting from the cube (fig. 15)[207]

The BUILDING which I would erect on that *Spot,* is the Plan and Profile before us, compos'd of three cubes.[208] In delineating the Plan or Elevation of a Building, the Outline is to be first form'd, as in the Plan and Profile before us, which are composed of 3 Cubes, as represented by the circumscribing Circles. It is from thence the internal Parts, as well as the *ornamenting* and *disposing* the proper Voids, and Decoration of the Front, are to be regulated.[209] [His italics]

Thus the architect recommends the cube not merely as a single feature, but as the formative element of the whole.

To make his intention perfectly clear, he adds in his illustrations the "circumscribing" circles,[210] to underline the concept of cubic compartments which are to compose the building. Had he omitted the circles, or not referred to them in the text, we could hardly grasp the compositional idea behind the conventional façades. The concept of the cube as the cell-unit of the whole must have been particularly dear to him. When, many years later, he adorned the title pages of *Rural Architecture* and *Select Architecture,* he again used one of these model façades with their meaningful circles.[211] These designs and ideas indicate that Morris was far more than another classicist "pyrating one Member of this order, another of that,"[212] and toying with the rules of proportionality.[213]

The Ninth and Eleventh to Fourteenth Lectures present examples of the new way in composition. In the Fifth Lecture, containing the table with the combinations of cubes, he also attacks the Baroque fancy of giving shrubs the shapes of men or animals, and praises the new landscape garden: "Our Modern way of planning Gardens is far preferable to what was us'd 20 Years ago, where, in large Parterres, you might see Men, Birds, and Dogs, cut in Trees."[214]

Robert Morris was fully aware of the novelty of his "singular way of Thinking."[215] After the passage about how "the internal Parts, as well as . . . the decoration of the Front, are to be regulated,"[216] he remarks:

It may perhaps appear an Innovation, as well as Novelty, to introduce in Architecture a Method so different from the common Ideas people have conceived of Building, and which has been an established Rule so long practised; but if Men would impartially divest themselves of such mistaken Principles, which may have misled their Genius, I cannot see what Objection can be made to this Method.[217]

In order to appreciate rightly his position as a forerunner, two personal confessions of his may be cited:

I love to strike out of a beaten Path sometimes, only to walk the more easy, or at least to prevent Disturbance from the busy Multitude; and then I have more Room for the Imagination to work upon.[218]

The second passage also demonstrates that he sensed the significance of the new doctrine:

The Task I have undertaken, may have underwent severe Criticisms . . . I have purposely started out of the *common Road,* not only as an *Amusement* to myself, but to exercise the Pens of abler Artists.[219] [His italics]

In 1728 when Morris wrote the *Essay in Defence of Ancient Architecture* he had not yet formed the concept of a cubist architecture laid down later in the *Lectures.* In that earliest publication he pointed at the works of the Ancients as models, as did Colen Campbell and many others all through the eighteenth century.[220] Yet he recommended them not for that reverence which every erudite scholar since the Renaissance believed was due to antiquity, but because he saw in them "those unerring Rules, those perfect Standards of the Law of Reason and Nature, founded upon Beauty and Necessity."[221] Although he did not draw the far-reaching conclusions which the Italian friar Carlo Lodoli was soon to reach, the ideal of architectural consistency meant much to him.[222] What is more, in the very years when the pageant of the late Baroque reached its climax in Germany and Italy, Morris warned against the sensuous beauties in architecture.[223] Afraid that Puritan crudeness might be offending, he pointed out the direction which later Romanticism was to take. He advocates impressing the *mind* rather than the eye. This seems to him "a Task more particularly adapted for those who move in a higher Sphere, superiour to that where bodily Exercise has the greatest share, and whose Support is sustain'd by a Labour far less pleasing than that of the Mind."[224] In the *Essay,* Morris foresees the next development; in the *Lectures,* he attempts to find a more advanced way, the way of cubism. Yet the *Essay* reveals something more. It depicts the unsatisfactory conditions which made Morris search for a remedy. One of his illustrations, a building designed by an anonymous author in 1724, serves as a warning example (fig. 16). One might suppose that this design presents the exaggerations of the late Baroque; yet not the slightest trace of the latter can be found in it. The "Irregular" House of 1724, to adopt Morris' disapproving term, was, he says, not exceptional, but typical.[225] Therefore it is worthwhile to look closer at it. What he dislikes most on such houses is "the disagreeable Affinity the Windows have to each other" and, in general, "the disproportionate Unity of their Magnitudes."[226] To complement his comment we may list a few of the features appearing in the design: the tiny keystones of the lower windows, the oversized segmental gables of the attic, the insignificant door which seems to be subdued by the gigantic window above, and the way in which the latter intrudes into the pediment. A remarkably negative characteristic is the lack of tying elements. The house is a perfect illustration of Morris' words, "there is a daily Application of combined Force to destroy that Beauty, Sweetness, and Harmony united in the Composition of ancient Architecture."[227] We have seen the drama of Seaton Delaval; here on a much smaller scale we face similar disharmony and harshness. Besides the constructive trend toward cubism there was already in the early eighteenth century a destructive undercurrent, violent and bold, hostile both to the graces of the Rococo and to classic regularity and serenity. And here was the man who stood up against the "un-ruly," against those who aimed, as he wrote, at the "overthrow" of architecture.[228] But he could not change the way of destiny. Architecture was bound to go through a revolutionary crisis before it could reach new consolidation.

Other instances of "irregular" houses with "Varieties of incoherent Parts"[229] were Archer's Roehampton House (Wandsworth, Surrey) of 1712 for Thomas Cary (fig. 17),[230] Vanbrugh's derided Goose-Pie House (1702) and his "New Design for a Person of Quality in Dorsetshire" (1716) as well as Burlington's design of the school of Sevenoaks, Kent.[231] And if further demonstration were needed of what Morris may have understood under "the decaying Principles of Novelty and Singleness"[232] we could simply list almost all the works of Hawksmoor.

Morris' views on landscape architecture are rather unimportant if compared with the idea of an entirely new concept of architectural composition. Yet these, too, show him far ahead of his continental contemporaries. To him, the natural surroundings are already the fitting spot for a "pleasing REVERIE"[233] where "in the *cooler Hours* of Reflection, a Man might retire, to contemplate the Important *Themes* of *Human Life;* recluse from gay Fancies, he might secrete himself" (his italics).[234] House and park are no longer to be for ostentation, but to satisfy "a speculative Mind."[235] As early as 1734, Morris advocated the sentimental, romantic landscape garden. Out of the many passages[236] reflecting an attitude towards nature which was to be predominant during the following hundred years I should like to quote just one:

Care should be taken so to lay out and dispose of the several Parts, that the neighbouring Hills, the *Rivulets,* the *Woods* and little *Buildings* interspers'd in various Avenues, . . . should render the Spot a kind of *agreeable Disorder,* or *artful Confusion;* so that by shifting from Scene to Scene, and by serpentine or winding Paths, one should, as it were, accidentally fall upon some remarkable beautiful Prospect, or other pleasing Object. [His italics][237]

While in architecture Morris' ideas were to bear fruit only later, in garden planning before very long the world was ready to follow him and earlier English landscape architects.

Like Vanbrugh and Hawksmoor, Morris personifies the tragedy of English architecture in the early eighteenth century. Each felt that architecture was to be reformed, not only superficially, as perhaps by the introduction of more correct classic features, or Gothic, or exotic ones, but basically. Yet neither the great builder Vanbrugh, nor the fanciful searcher Hawksmoor, nor the solitary thinker Morris, was able to carry out the new ideas to their conclusion. But we should not censure them as art history of the nineteenth century would have done. The main thing for the retrospective view is to learn when new ideas sprang up for the first time, and to see what became of them; whether they were fertile or barren, whether the man who voiced them first was able to translate them into reality, or whether others were chosen to bring the new message to the world. Vanbrugh, Hawksmoor, and the anonymous builder of the Irregular House of 1724, each started to disrupt the Baroque integer, but found no satisfactory substitute. Morris wanted the cube to be the controlling feature in building. Yet he did not attempt to bring it into being, undisguised. We must look behind his "tedious" designs to understand him and to do him justice.

The position assigned to an artist by history does not so much depend on "absolute" merit, as on how his manner appears to the era looking at him. After having witnessed the architectural development of the twentieth century it is comparatively easy to grasp the meaning of Morris' cubism; easier, of course, than it would have been some forty years ago. Goya found the right appreciation only in the era of Impressionism, El Greco in that of Expressionism. People who grew up in the aesthetics of the nineteenth century could never appreciate the Baroque, far less the goals of this early "cubist," had he been known to them at all. After an artist's rediscovery—not so much by an individual, as by a congenial era—his work will arouse bewilderment and suspicion and its significance will be ridiculed, or at least minimized, especially by those who feel guilty for having themselves overlooked it. But before long its merits will be extolled, perhaps even exaggerated. Its meaning will then be understood by everyone, and now he will fare better than his scholarly rediscoverer.

Pattern-book designs by William and John Halfpenny and T. Lightoler look quite modern from the viewpoint of our time, because they almost completely lack decoration. Yet, in composition, the designs of country houses by John Halfpenny follow the Baroque pattern.[238] Lightoler's publication *The Gentleman and Farmer's Architect* also shows how the Baroque system lived on in the elevations of his plain Parsonages and Farmhouses (fig. 18).[239] We see it also in a lodge, or keeper's house (fig. 19), with gothicizing features, and in a lodge house "in the Chinese Taste" (fig. 20). In the *Builder's Assistant* he presents fascinating plain façades on Baroque plans.[240]

William Halfpenny's work presents an interesting development. In his later publications, in which John Halfpenny participated, the exoticism and eclecticism of the ending century appears in a sort of Rococo version.[241] But his earlier production is full of stimulating experiments. His design for Holy Trinity, Leeds, in some details, especially its steeple, reminds one of Hawksmoor's St. George's, Bloomsbury.[242] The plain walls with unframed openings in most designs of the *New and Compleat System of Architecture*[243] recall Robert Morris' aversion to "Redundancy of Ornament, and Dress." But in this volume there are also designs marked by a definite unrest. The "Fore Front" of House No. 21 presents an unusual arrangement of differently sized rectangular windows,[244] while on House No. 29 (fig. 21) engaged columns, sculptural pilasters, and statues in great number disrupt the unity of the façade. In addition, William Halfpenny attempts to impart life to his structures by building them up on variegated, unorthodox plans and by composing the fronts with contrasting masses. In these regards William Halfpenny went beyond Morris, who, according to the preface of the *New and Compleat System,* was his friend and counselor. The highly original "summer-lodge" (House No. 30) is designed on a Greek cross,[245] the still more interesting House No. 31 (fig. 22) on an equilateral triangle.[246] The plans of the summerhouses, Nos. 11, 13, and 15, are polygonal or circular.[247] In the more common inventions the free arrangement of the rooms and Baroque reminiscences appear side by side. William Halfpenny likes bold contrasts and achieves them by opposing elementary solids (cubes and cylinders on Nos. 25,[248] 26,[249] and 27, fig. 23) or by the interpenetration of cubic masses (House No. 10).[250] His desire for innovation also shows in *The Modern Builder's Assistant,* in the elevations and in the plans (House No. 10, etc.) (fig. 24). Looking over his entire development we see that William Halfpenny went the way of all architecture of the eighteenth century, from the rise against tradition—born of reasoning—to the search for a new order, and finally to revivalism. Vanbrugh's and Hawksmoor's works were passionate outbursts of minds at variance with the reigning taste. The Morris-Halfpenny group shows the patient, assiduous endeavor to bring the revolutionary thinking in line with everyday exigencies. The highflying ideas of the forerunners soon were to reach the stage of popularity.

Another who departed from the Baroque was Henry Flitcroft. Two main works of his may show how far he went on the new way. St. Giles-in-the-Fields, London (1731–1734),[251] has been compared with Gibbs's St. Martin-in-the-Fields[252] because of the similarity of the steeples.[253] However, by singling out just one feature we are likely to miss the mark. Gibbs's church has a hexastyle portico and colossal pilasters on the sides. The steeple, although markedly set off from the "temple" below, nevertheless continues the upward movement of the columns and pilasters. The wood model for the church presents, moreover, a roof balustrade with vases. Flitcroft's church is a clumsy block with almost no emphasis on the verticals, and terminated by a heavy cornice. Thus the tower is independent of the substructure. Yet there is still some stress laid on the central part, by the pediment and the big openings. One may say St. Giles combines Baroque remnants with symptoms of disintegration. The same is true of Flitcroft's alteration of Wentworth Woodhouse, Yorkshire (1740). Its long stretched-out front lacks the coherency of Baroque composition. The central block is accompanied by wings and low structures attached to them. At the far end of each side a towerlike pavilion rises. Reginald Blomfield characterizes this house very well; "Flitcroft seems to have designed this building piece-meal, or rather to have pieced it together from other designs. . . . The lower blocks of buildings, at the sides, are reasonable enough as isolated designs."[254] The parts of a truly Baroque building are never so self-contained.

Many churches all over England were similar in composition to St. Giles, with its tower superposed on the main mass; to name only a few: St. Mary's, Ingestre (Staffordshire, 1673), ascribed to Wren, All Saints' at Oxford, rebuilt by Henry Aldrich (1707), Blandford church by John and William Bastard (1731–1739), Daventry church by William and David Hiorn (1752), and St. George's, Hanover Square, London, by John James (1712–1724).[255] Apparently such individualizing treatment of the components must have been agreeable to many English builders.

Calmness and sobriety distinguish Thomas Ripley's Admiralty, Whitehall, of about 1726,[256] from Baroque structures.[257] It belongs to the U-shaped type—a square court with an open side—and has a pedimented portico on the central front. Ripley's Wolterton Hall, Norfolk,[258] of 1724,[259] is closely related, in its general character, to the Admiralty; the horizontals prevail, the center is rather inconspicuous.

From the standpoint of stylistic development, the Mansion House in London, built between 1739 and 1753 by George Dance the elder, is very noteworthy. We have, of course, to consider its original state, with the twin stories atop the roof.[260] Dance piled the two oblong blocks astride the main block and thus defied the idea of unity. The high windows on the side fronts break through the main cornice and thus disrupt its continuity. They have not the dynamics of the central motif of the northern front of Seaton Delaval,[261] yet they say essentially the same thing. The elements are no longer in harmonious unison, but oppose each other. It is no wonder that such a break from traditional composition encountered "hostile criticism," and that the offending twin stories were removed later, "very much to the advantage of the design," as Reginald Blomfield finds. A more recent critic, A. E. Richardson, has a better understanding of Dance: "Although the design and proportion of these features were exaggerated, their removal leaves something lacking in the aspect of the building."[262] Blomfield illustrates the building without the superimposed stories; Richardson, however, brings out an old engraving showing the building with them, just as Dance would have it. Similarly, it is not, as Blomfield has it, a shortcoming of Dance's St. Leonard's, Shoreditch (1736–1740) that "there is no cohesion between the tower and the steeple over it;" it is rather a symptom of the changed attitude toward composition.[263]

The antagonism of the main pile and the superstructures, or, to put it in a more general way, the incongruity of shapes, is the chief characteristic of the Mansion House. Incongruity in sizes makes an earlier work commonly ascribed to Dance, St. Luke's, Old Street (1727–1733) (fig. 25), interesting.[264] We should take this church building seriously, not in spite of but because of its strange shape. It stands in line with Hawksmoor's achievements. First, there are outer similarities. The fluted obelisk forming the spire reminds one, by its boldness, of the steeple of St. George's, Bloomsbury;[265] the emphasis on the solid walls recalls the deeply recessed windows of Greenwich Hospital and St. Anne's, Limehouse.[266] Second, and more important, is the identity of the motivating forces behind the strange features. The overheavy keystones so frequent in Hawksmoor's work and the overtall spire of St. Luke's manifest the builder's desire to express something which could never be expressed by the conventionally balanced composition. They protested against the old order and tended toward a new one.

In the early eighteenth century no European country had architects as progressive as the British. Many of them were searchers, gifted with great inventiveness and daring minds. Contemporaries of David Hume, they, too, were forerunners of a deep-going reorientation of thinking, a revolution that would trace its lineage from the original, and definitely un-Palladian, builders Vanbrugh, Hawksmoor, Kent, Dance the elder, and their followers, Dance the younger, Soane, and Nash.

III

BELATED BAROQUE

WHILE CERTAIN new ideas began to germinate in the centers of building activities, the Baroque was to triumph once more in the little city of Bath. Quite a few of the houses erected there in the first half of the eighteenth century present the customary patterns of Baroque façades as well as the plasticity of single features. Nassau House[267] shows how well softly modeled, supple forms agree with the Baroque system. Here are reversed brackets applied to the parapet of the roof, leading down to engaged columns; gently sloping curves on either side of the parapet; little scrolls connecting the framing of the top windows with the wider framing of the openings beneath. The various nuances of the relief, from the flat scrolls to the round columns, make the wall vibrate. Likewise, the interplay of light and shade plays the foremost role on Marshal Wade's house.[268] Its boldly projecting cornice, the fluted pilasters, the garlands below the window sills reveal the same sense of plasticity that permeates the best continental works, only with a little more reticence. Describing his Belcomb Brook house (1734), John Wood the elder remarks:

The Windows of the principal Story are dressed so as to become compleat Tabernacles . . . and the Mouldings in the whole Front, proper to be carved, are all enriched in the best Manner the Workmen were then Masters of.[269]

Various features on the houses of Bath show the Baroque predilection for high relief, for example: the segmental pediment of Weymouth House,[270] the consoles shaped like griffins on a house in St. James Street,[271] the door heads of Nos. 3 and 4 Abbey Gate Street,[272] the eagles perching on pedestals and the mask above the door of Beau Nash's last dwelling.[273] Lastly, I should like to point out a small yet significant feature of Widcombe House (1727),[274] which has been described as follows: "The architecture is happily connected with the garden by the treatment of the plinth moulding under the pilasters, which ramps down as it leaves the building and becomes the coping of the balustrade."[275] The charming building is full of Baroque vitality.

Such was the atmosphere in which John Wood the elder started on the great scheme of the further embellishment of Bath. The town house of Ralph Allen which he erected in 1727[276] is a good specimen of Baroque florid decoration and negation of the wall.[277] The same can be said of Titan Barrow Loggia, erected in

1748.[278] Thomas Jelly's Grammar School, Broad Street (1752),[279] still shows the fondness for high relief, yet no attempt has been made to unify the openings by horizontal or vertical members.[280]

In city building John Wood's chief aim was to weld the single houses into, at least exteriorly, a homogeneous whole. He did so when designing the buildings of Queen Square in 1728.[281] The twentieth century objects to a façade concealing inner arrangement instead of revealing it. But about 1730 architectural practice favored monumental sham façades like those on the north side of Queen Square, effacing the independence of the units behind them.[282] Sheer practical considerations—the wishes of the prospective tenants—forced Wood to abandon his scheme for the west side of the square and to erect instead three separate units.[283] The center of Queen Square was marked by an obelisk.

The intimate connection of a house with its park was not an exclusive characteristic of sumptuous structures. At Belcomb Brook, built by Wood in 1734,[284] flights of stairs with baluster rails lead from the small villa down to the garden.[285] These flights continue the diagonals of the house plan. One might very well compare them with roots parting from the trunk of a tree. This motif is not conditioned by the sloping ground; it serves a distinctly artistic purpose: the architect wanted to tie the building to the environment. The concept of the most intimate connection of the parts also inspired Wood's plan for Prior Park near Bath (1735–1743).[286] Its single features are insignificant. If one pointed out that a portico with a pediment was attached to the house, he would merely mention a trait common to a great many buildings of various periods. Only by seeing the general arrangement as a whole can one observe the stylistic position of the structure. The mansion is connected by colonnades to the pavilions and the stables. (This was the original plan; the execution differed slightly.) Even the location of the basin in front of the edifice was as carefully calculated as that of the obelisk on Queen Square, that is, with regard to the whole "picture."

Here I should like to point out an architectural curio of Bath, the corner house at 41 Gay Street. This house was designed by John Wood the elder in 1740.[287] The strange thing is that it presents several rare features which were to appear somewhat later in French architecture. It shows a corner "splayed off to receive an elaborately decorated bow," very similar in shape to Michel Chevotet's Pavillon de Hanovre, on the Boulevard des Italiens, of 1760,[288] and even more similar to the still extant Maison Deshayes on the Boulevard de la Madeleine, by André Aubert.[289] Moreover, the plan with the "principal room placed diagonally to command a view across Queen Square" foreshadows the plan of Ledoux's Hôtel Montmorency, while the Palladian window of the second floor presents twin columns coupled by rustic blocks not so much in the manner of Serlio as in the manner of some of Ledoux's barrières.[290] I must leave the question open whether the Frenchmen knew about the small house at Bath. Yet it is noteworthy that this strange design turned up on both sides of the Channel about mid-century. At Bath a similar corner treatment can be seen on the house at 103 New Sydney Place, erected shortly after 1800.[291] Instead of searching for interdependence, which hardly existed, we would do better to follow the thought of one of the great inaugurators of the Age of Reason, Gianbattista Vico, who combatted the concept of "the scholastic succession of nations," the error which "consists in thinking that when two nations have a similar idea . . . one must have learned it from the other."[292] Fortunately, today, history has passed beyond the narrow positivism which had already been branded by Ledoux in the words: *La plupart des hommes instruits ne jugent que lorsqu'ils comparent: compilateurs exacts, ils s'appuient sur tous les exemples qui servent de boussole.*[293]

In 1753 Wood planned the layout of the Circus at Bath.[294] His son carried out the scheme after the father's death. The circus is composed of three segments. A maximum of unity has been attained. Here Wood still presents the plasticity of the walls so much cherished by the builders of Bath. The engaged columns are not a merely superficial decoration. Their relief is to reconcile the inner with the outer space. By effacing the rigidity of the bordering walls the enclosed area is brought to life.

With the semi-elliptic Royal Crescent, begun in 1767,[295] John Wood the younger inaugurated a series of similar groups of buildings to be erected in Bath in the following decades (Camden Crescent by John Eveleigh, 1788,[296] Lansdown Crescent by John Palmer, about 1794[297]). Thus a typically Baroque feature was to survive by many years the era in which it had originated. The huge columns and pilasters running up through two stories enliven the far-sweeping fronts of the Royal Crescent, and in a more subdued way those of the other crescents. Thomas Baldwin's Somersetshire Buildings (1782), on Milsom Street, were also made up of two-storied orders above the rusticated basement, a strongly protruding cornice, and a roof balustrade.[298] The central parts form a segmental projection giving a swelling effect to the whole front.

Meanwhile, a new trend of architecture had come to Bath, bringing with it calm, undisturbed walls instead of the late modeled façades. Representative of this trend are the flanks of Baldwin's Guildhall, of about 1775.[299] Similarly modern were the Assembly Rooms (1769) by the younger Wood. In church design, Wood went even beyond Flitcroft's piecemeal composition by making the tower of Hardenhuish church (1779) penetrate the main mass.[300] Old and new overlapped for a length of time. Before the old style died away, it manifested itself, once more, on the Old Grosvenor Hotel erected by John Eveleigh in 1790.[301] Its façade is rich in carvings and the main cornice is broken round the engaged columns which run up through the two main stories.

Better than in any other building at Bath the ultimate fate of the Baroque is revealed in Pulteney Bridge, the only structure erected there by Robert Adam (about 1770).[302] Obviously, this bridge is derived from the one which Palladio shows in the thirteenth chapter of his Third Book.[303] Adam's bridge is also tripartite, with an accentuated central part. Originally, the entrances were marked by porticoes. Two rows of shops run from one end to the other. Here is still something left of the Palladian rhythm, which is missing on other English "Palladian" bridges. And yet, Adam's work is already far removed from its model. Both concatenation and gradation have become exceedingly weak. Palladio stressed the latter by the contrast of the open loggias and the massive walls of the connecting low aisles, as well as by the sudden rise of the entablature in the center. On Pulteney Bridge, the main cornice runs through, almost unbroken. The wall, too, is continuous. All the parts are welded into an undifferentiated mass. The rise and fall of the entablature on Palladio's bridge and the array of columns along its walls produce the impression of movement in the horizontal. On Pulteney Bridge, only a few pilasters flank the center. Between them is the bare mute wall. The horizontal movement in Palladio's design is counteracted by a vertical movement, this antagonism of the two directions bringing additional life to the whole. The bearers of the upward movement are not only the tall columns of the central loggia and the pediments, but also the tabernacles on the spandrels above the piers. There is throughgoing continuity, starting with the statues in the tabernacles and their pediments, passing through the statuary of the loggia, and finally ending in the statues on the roof. Adam's central pediment is low-pitched. The contrast between it and the cornice is subdued. Adam, too, felt the aesthetic necessity of filling the spandrels with some decoration. Yet, instead of the tabernacles with statues, he applied roundels, that is, instead of an upward leading feature, he added an ornament that does not point in any particular direction but is the true representative of static indifference. In the center of Pulteney Bridge, we find the Palladian window motif breaking into the low-pitched pediment. But even the application of this arch-Baroque feature should not make us believe that the Baroque is still alive in Adam's work. For the main characteristic of the Palladian motif, apart from its rhythm, is the dominance of the center over the sides. Adam deprives the motif of its very meaning by drawing a parallel outer circle around the archivolt. The dynamics of the motif are gone. We have seen Burlington, Kent, and others reintroducing the overarched Palladian motif. Adam developed a particular predilection for it.

Whatever Baroque features there are on the Pulteney Bridge, all life has been taken out of them. They are no longer expected to exhibit the living forces which permeate Baroque structures. They are embedded in the rigid wall like petrifactions. The last agony of the Baroque system has begun, though there is no trace of anything new on Pulteney Bridge which might replace it.

Adam saw in himself a modernist. "We have not trod in the path of others, nor derived aid from their labours," he wrote, and even boasted "to have brought about, in this country, a kind of revolution in the whole system of this useful and elegant art."[304] There is a good deal of self-deception in this statement. For Adam was imbued with the concepts of the ancients which he ardently studied, and "trod," though lamely, in the path of Palladio. He was rather a decadent heir, than an innovator, let alone a revolutionary. He did nothing to change the old "system" radically, but we shall see that he, too, participated in the new efforts.

If we look at some of his designs made at Rome about 1757,[305] we observe that he caught only superficially the ideas of variety and gradation, and amassed in his compositions the most diverse elements taken from here and there. He was not able to amalgamate the parts. He lacked the quality which made the Roman Baroque great; the power to weld the parts into a higher unity, binding and differentiating them at the same time. This deficiency is characteristic not only of his youthful Roman essays, but also of his later projects, such as the design for a house for General Hervey,[306] or the proposed elevation of the Findlater house of the early seventies.[307] Each is a gay mixture of incongruous features. Hervey's house virtually mimics Baroque gradation. But the combination of the domed central rotunda and the gables of the wings, and the contrast of the plasticity of the colonnade with the flatness of the sides, reveal that the traditional harmonization of the parts was aimed at no longer.

When, in 1784, Adam made a design for the south side of the quadrangle of King's College, Cambridge, he did not care much about unity.[308] The building seems to fall apart into two halves, separated by the central loggia. Thus the dome does not find any support from forces tending toward the center, but looks as if it were floating above the house like a balloon. Various elements of the Baroque system are present: the entablature and the balustrades finishing the entire front, the enhancement of the center, and the attempt to achieve rhythmical composition. But whatever Baroque motifs are recognizable, all have lost their former vigor. The façades of Fitzroy Square (1790), show monotonous rows of openings.[309] You can trace the vestiges of Baroque concatenation and gradation in these façades, but you will look in vain for the liveliness of the mature Baroque. Some of the new feeling for massiveness mingles rather oddly with the overabundant piercing of the walls.

It may be taken for a symbol that Adam was to erect the screen of the Admiralty at the outset of his career, in 1760.[310] For it was his destiny to reproduce the compositional patterns of the Baroque and at the same time to deprive them of their vitality. Adam was, of course, not the only one who closed a U-shaped forecourt with a colonnaded screen. Yet there is a marked difference between his screen and, for example, that of the castle of Compiègne by Jacques-Ange Gabriel.[311] The latter's colonnade abuts the lateral faces of the projecting wings, thus tying them together and continuing their rusticated basements. Adam, however, set the screen in front of the wings, making it look like an appendage, not a tie. Its cornice running from end to end virtually strikes out the house behind it. Again, it is not the single feature which counts, but the use which has been made of it. Adam lacked the verve of the great architects of the Baroque, although he held in high esteem the "movement" of Baroque structures, and flattered himself that he had outdone his predecessors in this regard. However, we do not find in his works the "movement" which, in his own words,

is meant to express, the rise and fall, the advance and recess, with other diversity of form, in the different parts of a building, so as to add greatly to the picturesque of the composition . . . the convexity and concavity [which] serve to produce an agreeable and diversified contour, that groups and contrasts like a picture, and creates a variety of light and shade.[312]

All the features in his works look frozen. The very life of the Baroque has come to a standstill in them. If we compare his drawing for Harewood House, Yorkshire (1760),[313] with the engravings in the *Vitruvius Britannicus* after the plans of John Carr of York,[314] we must note the superiority of Carr's work—that is, the superiority from the Baroque point of view. (The question of which solution we like better is a matter of taste and must not enter into this discussion. However, the question of which better conforms to the Baroque system can be answered positively, if we have formed a definite concept of the Baroque system.) A chief characteristic of any Baroque architectural work is the interrelationship of its parts. In Carr's drawing there is such interrelationship between the central pediments and the pitched roofs of the end pavilions. Moreover, the window heads of the passages of the south elevation are similar to those of the central part. On the north side Carr applied a balustrade with rhythmically arranged vases on top of it. The up and down of the pediments and the vases produces the impression of an undulatory movement emanating from the center. Adam's wings and end pavilions, however, have little in common with the main pile. He presents a group with a dominant part and subordinate ones, but there is no longer the flux and reflux which pulses through truly Baroque structures. Particularly the straight balustrades of the pavilions have no relation to the central pediment. The same can be said of Adam's design for the south front of Stowe, Buckinghamshire (1771).[315] As a further instance of the "Frozen Baroque" may be cited his design for the "Board-Room for the Paymaster General and the Office for Invalids" at Whitehall, illustrated in the *Works*.[316] The upward movement of the twin pilasters is counteracted by the heavy pedestals over them and the lion and the unicorn peacefully resting on top of all.

The tendency to neutralize Baroque "movement" reveals itself also in the frequent use of horizontal bands dividing the wall and counteracting the upward aiming force of the colossal order. Thus the effective antithesis of the basement and the upper stories is destroyed and the equilibrium resulting from the opposition of two lighter stories to a heavier one is lost. Examples of this are the south front of Kenwood, Hampstead (1768);[317] the Society for the Encouragement of Arts in the Adelphi;[318] the house of Watkin Williams Wynn, 20 St. James Square;[319] Drury Lane Theatre;[320] the Office for Invalids, Whitehall;[321] and the houses in Portland Place.[322] The Palladian motif had to undergo noteworthy changes, too. Adam liked to deprive it of its meaning, as we have already seen, either by drawing a parallel outer semicircle around the central arch (Society for the Encouragement of Arts; back-court offices of 20 St. James Square),[323] or by thinning the inner arch and separating it from the window below by an entablature (Office for Invalids); or by replacing the inner arch by a pediment (entrance front of Newliston House).[324]

The term "Frozen Baroque" is to designate the last stage of the Baroque development. This is not to intimate that all its productions are "weak." The Frozen Baroque was not confined to England alone. Instances of it may be found all over Europe, commonly subsumed under the vague notions of Louis Seize, the Directoire, the Empire; or under the still vaguer category of "Classicism."[325] The new term may be helpful in disentangling the various trends of the period, which availed themselves, in the main, of the same traditional features, but which derived from basically different architectural concepts.

Adam was an adroit interior decorator. Indoors, the weakness of his design did hardly impair the general effect. But on the exterior his decorations are mere inexpressive trimmings, calling to mind the confectioner's "art." This is particularly true of the bridge designed for Syon,[326] the gateway designed for Carlton House (1767),[327] and the south wall in the back court of the Williams Wynn house.[328] In a few works Adam departed from the ways of the Baroque, as for instance in the design for David Hume's tomb, 1778,[329] and in several others of greater significance to be dealt with later, which proves his ability to adapt himself to models quite different from those he once followed. Because of some gothicizing features appearing here and there in Adam's work, and because he tried his hand at the "Castle Style,"[330] we are told he "is to be regarded as a forerunner of that stirring of the romantic spirit which was to dominate the succeeding century."[331] If so, then he would simply have been the forerunner of the most infertile and infantile trend in nineteenth-century architecture. But there were "romantics" long before him. Nor is it correct to assert that "Robert Adam was destined to revolutionize the older traditional school."[332]

Even the most comprehensive monograph on Adam, crammed with laboriously gathered eighteenth-century society news and anecdotes, is not in a position to devote more than a few pages to "Robert Adam's Ideas," half of which are quotations from his meager text.[333] And yet, of the prevalent opinions, either that he was a "past-master of the taste of his time,"[334] or that his work was distinguished only by its "elegant mannerism,"[335] neither gives the whole picture. For Adam shared in the new architectural endeavors and grappled with the new problems.

This receptiveness does him more credit than all the patterns which Arthur Bolton believes to have recognized in his *oeuvre,* the "mood of Fragonard" as well as "the spirit of revived antiquity," the "spirit of the age of Bernini," the "romantic spirit," and the belief in Palladio.[336]

A first indication that Adam attempted to change the conventional façades can be found in the project of Findlater House[337] and the design for the British Coffee House,[338] both in the 1770's. Still more interesting are some of his cubistic experiments. A Deputy Ranger's Lodge (1768) presents a pattern which, at about the same time, became rather popular in France, namely the insertion of a cylinder into a cubic mass.[339] The end pavilions of Luton Park House, Bedfordshire (1767–1771), are shaped as semicylinders.[340] Its southern side front has almost no decoration and is made effective by the contrast of the huge entrance niche and the flanking prismatic projections.[341]

The desire for a new arrangement of the masses, which already shows on Luton Park House, manifested itself with greater strength on the church at Mistley. Here Adam added, to a preëxisting oblong structure, porticoes on each front and towers on the sides (1776).[342] His occasional modernism also allows us to understand the semicircular plan of Great Saxham (1779).[343] It is one of Adam's attempts to keep pace with the newly rising trend toward the geometric. If we do not limit ourselves to comparing single features with models of the past we shall also grasp the form of the addition made to Culzean Castle in 1787, that "excursion in the Castle Style."[344] It is worthwhile to analyze this, for practically all revivalistic work was similarly based on promiscuous formal concepts. On the sea front of Culzean Castle Adam emphasized the geometric forms cherished by eighteenth-century rationalism, the cylinder and the prism. But the plan with the circular salon in the center is an offspring of the Baroque. The concept of the boldly projecting cylinder had been in Adam's mind long before, as can be seen in Mersham-le-Hatch, Kent, a work of the 1760's without any medieval aspects.[345] Gossford House in East Lothian, Scotland, completed after the architect's death, is an agglomeration of blocks with a slight predominance of the central mass.[346] Recesses separate the latter from the sides, in a way similar to Culzean Castle. In all these designs a new attitude toward composition becomes apparent, which is far more interesting than the question whether the architect preferred classic or Gothic forms. In some late works Adam seems to have joined those who aimed at a complete reorientation of architecture. The design of the north side of Charlotte Square, Edinburgh (1791), is still a Baroque scheme without Baroque liveliness, still Frozen Baroque, whereas the entrance to the University of Edinburgh (about 1790) gives the impression of a composition of heavy blocks.[347] Nobody would deny that there is a certain grandeur in this work. Yet at the time when it originated such stern monumentality was no longer new.

It is somewhat astonishing that, on the whole, Robert Adam was rather conservative. For already in the work of his father, William Adam, certain modern traits can be detected. We should point out here that the latter, beside much conventional work, produced also several advanced designs in Scotland.[348] Forceful and original is his circular church at Hamilton. Plain cubic masses show in Haddo House, Dun House, and Lonmay House. The front of Niddrie House is distinguished by a niche running up to the roof. The composition *ad infinitum*, of which we have learned in dealing with Morris' theory, is recognizable in Cumbernauld House, Dumbarton County, where twin houses are appended to the main block, and in the dog kennels at Hamilton, consisting of two juxtaposed twin structures.

John Carr, on the north front of Tabley House, Cheshire (1761),[349] finished the central Palladian window with a parallel outer semicircle. Like Adam, he neutralized the rhythmical gradation of the motif. But he framed it with heavy rustication, and thus made it stand out as an independent element. He obviously preferred such masculine decoration to Adam's daintiness. On Carr's Court House of York (1765),[350] the horizontal band across the wall opposes the columns and contradicts the very concept of the building. It is an intruder into the well-balanced arrangement of the whole. Carr's Stable Court at Castle Howard (1782) is a group of aesthetically independent blocks.[351]

A certain negative attitude toward the Baroque marks several works of Sir Robert Taylor. The center of Stone Buildings, Lincoln's Inn (1756),[352] is not emphasized at all, and its walls are bare. The differentiation between the rusticated basement and the plain upper stories is almost the only Baroque residue. The villa of Sir Charles Asgill, at Richmond, is an interesting experiment with the plan.[353] Polygonal bays give the structure an air of self-contained compactness diametrically opposed to the wings of the Baroque which "like arms," seem to embrace the surroundings. This villa looks as if shunning contact with nature. Many later examples will show that such reticence was to become quite common before long. Parenthetically, whenever a novel trait is pointed out in this book for the first time, it will not simply be deduced from the instance just dealt with, but from a large number of cases to be amplified later.

Taylor's Ely House, in Dover Street (1772), presents the severe pattern of juxtaposition of equivalent elements.[354] In the works of Adam, Carr, and Taylor the moment had come when architecture began to turn away from the Baroque system, which gathered the forces of all the parts and associated them with a leader. The decline of the old system was accompanied by experiments with new forms and new arrangement.

IV

THE SECOND CRISIS OF TRADITIONAL COMPOSITION

IN THE LAST third of the eighteenth century, Sir William Chambers so carried out several buildings as to prove that there can be merit enough in the performances of the Frozen Baroque. On Peper Harow House, Surrey (about 1765), the center is still enhanced, and all the parts bear some relationship to each other.[355] But there is no trace of the Baroque dynamics. Calmness reigns throughout. In Chambers' greatest work, Somerset House, London (1776),[356] the horizontals dominate and there is scarcely any perceptible movement although there still are reminiscences of Baroque unity and Baroque rhythm. Chambers' skill is manifested in his manner of bringing out the chosen rhythm on the far-stretched river front clearly and yet unobtrusively. You may mark the Baroque heritage in the building, or you may note its classicizing motifs and pass by, unaware of its veritable character. For Somerset House reveals more of the problems of the era than most of the monumental classicistic piles, with their annoying monotony. Its front toward the river contains some strange features, such as the inconspicuous, dwarfed dome, and the three colonnades inserted in the façade. One cannot believe that the architect, matured in the classic tradition, did not comprehend that the dome of an edifice is the recipient of all its force, and the herald of its might. Yet Chambers must have had the feeling that a dome lording over the whole structure was no longer timely. He added it for reasons of convenience perhaps, or because he was expected to add it; more probably, because his inherited sense for Baroque rhythm still demanded an apex. Thus he compromised and made the dome almost ridiculously small. As is true of most compromises, this one, too, is unsatisfying. But it tells of the doubts of the period as distinctly as Adam's uncertainty does, or perhaps even more clearly. Chambers still wanted the traditional crowning feature, and simultaneously tried to stress the blocklike body. The three colonnades looking like temple fronts are intruders undermining the unity of the structure. Thus Somerset House offers an amazing spectacle with its crowning feature degraded to a superfluous accessory and the three colonnades in revolt against the whole, but still in bondage.

Chambers' *Treatise on Civil Architecture* is a conservative textbook, but in some passages his sense for dramatization manifests itself just as strongly as in the assembly of classical features of Somerset House. He wants the architects to turn

41

away from the conventional features to the greater effects of the masses "for it is sufficient if the General Form be distinct, and the principal masses strongly marked" and he suggests that they be content with "a few rough strokes."[357]

In a little polemic against the French Jesuit Laugier, who defended columns and expressed his dislike for pilasters, Chambers decides in favor of the latter. The problem in question is of secondary importance. What matters is that Chambers' viewpoint reflects the rising new trend toward expressiveness:

The transition from light to shade in the Column is gradual and easy, but in the Pilaster it is abrupt, and strongly contrasted. The variations in the surface of the Column are flowing, and insensible; those in the surface of the Pilaster are rapid, and in directions very opposite; and consequently more apt to produce sudden and violent impressions on the imagination.[358]

While the time for arguing about trifling differences in the proportions of the orders was nearing its end, the dawn of an era of masses struggling against each other and the whole had come. Chambers' words reveal that, to the "imagination" of the eighteenth century, the suavity of harmonious and rhythmical display already meant less than the grandiosity of vigorous contrasts.

Chambers' gateways at Blenheim[359] and at Wilton[360] do show gradation of the components and plasticity of the members. But these Baroque qualities are counteracted by the blocklike character and the rigidity of the masses. Particularly the Wilton gate, with its wings, justifies the classification of Frozen Baroque. There may be, of course, in some cases a difference of opinion, whether a design is mature Baroque, or "frozen," or perhaps already a representative of the new consolidated architecture which will be dealt with more fully later. For there are, of course, no definite borderlines in historical development. The new factor which plays such an important role in the gates at Blenheim and Wilton is self-contentedness—the unwillingness of the parts to communicate with each other and with the environment. This factor became decisive also for the shape of Chambers' Casino at Marino, Clontarf (near Dublin),[361] despite its richer appearance. The Casino is planned on the Greek cross. Tuscan columns support the boldly projecting entablature that runs around the building in many breaks. There is much plasticity and even movement in the Casino. But the movement is counteracted by the heavy superimposed block extending from the entrance side back to the west elevation. This configuration reminds one of Dance's Mansion House.[362] In all these works the basic concept is that of the obstruction of the living forces which the Baroque was anxious to visualize.

Regarding Chambers' Casino, or Robert Taylor's Heveningham Hall, Suffolk, of about 1778,[363] one hesitates to use the term, Frozen Baroque, afraid that some depreciative connotation may result from it. The intent is not to intimate any qualitative inferiority, but only to designate the stage of development when the Baroque quieted down. The truly grand Heveningham Hall has something of the calmness and reserve of Ely House.[364] The parapet crowning the central block, adorned with rather inconspicuous sculptural decoration, is to counteract the upward movement of the colossal central order. Little is left of the expanding forces of the earlier Baroque, though the composition as a whole is still unchanged.

In Heveningham Hall, the cubic character of the body is disguised by the apparatus of columns and statues; in the church of All Saints, Nuneham Courtenay, Oxfordshire, by the "Athenian" James Stuart (1764), it is strongly emphasized.[365] Stuart's, the archaeologist's, church is rather modern in its contrast between the cubic mass and the cylindrical drum, and in the inorganic additions of the porches.

James Paine belonged to the generation of Robert Taylor, though his work is markedly advanced. It looks still more progressive when compared with the achievements of the much younger Robert Adam. Yet we had to deal first with the latter in order to show better the evolution of architectural thought. A strictly chronological presentation would have furnished a distorted picture. Paine inveighed against the "blind veneration for inconsistent antiquated modes,"[366] and presented in his Middlesex Hospital (1755-1775) a composition of revolutionary boldness.[367] Only some of his early work has *rocaille* character. (The Mansion House at Doncaster (1745-1748) has cartouches in the pediments and luxuriant interior decoration, especially in the banquet room.)[368] His later production shows increasing restraint in decorative accessories. The bridges over the Derwent and the Trent[369] are distinguished by their noble, quiet outline. Most remarkable are his attempts to free himself from traditional composition in many façades and, occasionally, in the organization of the body itself. His work shows how slowly the English development advanced, step by step. There was no such sudden, spectacular, and radical change as in France when the time had come for the old system to give way.

Paine dispensed with vertical ties on three sides of Gosforth Hall, Northumberland (fig. 26);[370] the court front of Sir Matthew Featherstonhaugh's house in Whitehall (later York House), 1754;[371] the fronts of Serlby, Nottinghamshire;[372] Axwell Park, Durham (1758) (fig. 27);[373] and the interesting park front of Shrubland Hall, Suffolk.[374] The framing of the windows, on all these buildings, is very Featherstonhaugh's house[375] is not emphasized. Instead, there is juxtaposition poor, or there is no framing at all. The center of the richly decorated park front of of equivalent motifs reminiscent of the row of overarched Palladian windows on Burlington's Chiswick House. At Axwell Park the central window of the east front is framed, and finished by a segmental pediment. Yet there is no response from the neighboring unframed windows, so that the central one stands isolated in the wall. The lateral overarched Venetian windows excel in size and decoration. At last Paine proceeded to sacrifice the continuity of the rooflines (Stockeld Park, Yorkshire, of 1758, fig. 28, and Bywell, Northumberland).[376] Each of these fronts is broken up into three almost unrelated compartments and is full of incoherent features. There is no doubt—a certain unrest had come into architecture which was to lead, ultimately, to the independence of the parts. Those were the years in which Hogarth, in his *Analysis of Beauty,* hinting at the diversified interests and the novel goals of the period, wrote, "there is at present such a thirst after variety." Though an admirer of the graces of the Rococo with its "serpentine lines," he nonetheless understood the signs of the times: "The moderns have carried simplicity, convenience and neatness of workmanship to a very high degree of perfection, particularly in England."[377] In the plans of Paine the centralized arrangement is still the rule. Only exceptionally, as at Shrubland Hall, the traditional formality is given up.

Many of Paine's façades would have been regarded as "irregular" by Robert Morris. Soon architecture proceeded toward establishing some new order of the components, or, to trying out new patterns. Interestingly enough, such patterns can be found on many small houses.[378] However, the most consistent attempts in this direction were made only later, in France.

A new treatment of the masses characterizes George Dance the younger's Newgate Prison, begun in 1770.[379] The whole was composed of incongruous, unrelated blocks. In the accentuation of the horizontals, in the stress on the rusticated walls and in the cubic character of the parts appears the tendency to build on lines diametrically opposed to the principles of the Baroque. Newgate Prison has rightly been regarded as an outstanding performance, impressive and thoroughly sound. Only the prominence of the Governor's House in the center is a last remnant of Baroque gradation. One might be tempted to explain the forbidding form of the prison from its purpose. Yet several single features reveal the formal intention with great distinctness. The entrance lodges and the niches enshrining aedicules visualize the new individualistic tendencies. The parts struggle against the whole. Certain antagonisms have already been marked by other authors. "The unpleasant conflict between the arched window-heads and the massive squareness of the rest of the building . . . is the one fault of the design," declares Sir Reginald Blomfield who, otherwise, is full of admiration for the "huge bare walls."[380] A. E. Richardson is enthusiastic about the building "unprecedented in its forcefulness," and adds: "that Dance risked such a contrast in placing a building of domestic character in the midst of a fortress structure, is sufficient proof of his confidence in his own powers: that he succeeded is unquestionable."[381] Newgate Prison is symptomatic of the era. The great problem confronting architects since has been to find the way out of the conflict between the whole and the rebelling parts. There were different possibilities of contrasting blocklike masses in a rather composed way, without the dramatic accents of Newgate Prison. One solution became very popular both in England and in France: the virtual interpenetration of the blocks, of which a villa in Hertfordshire (1778), by James Lewis was an early instance.[382]

In designing the elongated front of the Customs House, Dublin (1781), James Gandon was obviously dependent on the principal work of his teacher Chambers, but went beyond him in emphasizing the cubic volume of the wings.[383] He similarly stressed the blocklike character of the County Hall of Nottingham.[384] The saucer dome of the Four Courts at Dublin (begun by Thomas Cooley, 1776) is a crowning feature lacking the upward movement of Baroque domes. King's Inns, Dublin, erected between 1795 and 1800, calls to mind Paine's last attempts.[385] Its front is subdivided into five aesthetically independent parts. Above the center a small circular colonnade rises as an independent element. The whole has blocklike character. Gandon's pupil Richard Morrison continued in the cubistic manner.[386]

The emphasized contrast of massive enclosure and domed rotunda appears in the addition by Henry Holland to York House (after 1787).[387] A noteworthy instance of the beginning redemption of the parts is the façade of Carlton House as it was restored by Holland about 1784.[388] At Newgate Prison the elements revolted; on King's Inns, they began to exhibit their individuality; on Carlton House, they showed no interrelation, although materially coherent. The central part resembled a temple entrance, the sides were massive blocks. Behind the discrepancy of the parts, the concept of an ostentatious center accompanied by subservient wings was still present. Holland's Royal Pavilion at Brighton (1787)[389] had some characteristic particularities. The rooms on the east front came forward in segmental bays. That was another and soon very common way of breaking up the consistency of the Baroque front, and at the same time, a glorification of the elementary forms. The two projecting half-cylinders on each side echoed the mighty cylinder rising in the center. This very reverberation proves that a formal ideal was at work. The walls were undecorated, the openings unframed.

Some designs by the almost completely disregarded architect William Thomas are of a very advanced character. There are no vertical ties and no window framings on Mr. Mirehouse's house in Pembrokeshire (1783) (fig. 29). The plan presents a compromise between the Baroque layout and greater practicality. The project of the Mausoleum (1781) (fig. 30) is an outstanding specimen of the predilection for elementary geometry. A heavy cylindrical superstructure rises over the plain pedimented entrance, while the sides are topped by pyramids. An interesting experiment was Surrey Chapel in St. George's Road, Southwark (1783) (fig. 31), the plan of which is a sixteen-sided polygon. Again the walls are bare, the windows unframed. These designs show that the modern ideas had already to some extent become popular about 1780. The few remaining classical features appear to be just a hindrance to their full development.

Interesting also were the experiments which Thomas Rawlins made: the "Building for a Gentleman of opulent Fortune," and the "Banquetting-Room," with original patterns on their fronts; the Triangular Building and the Octangular Church (he submitted designs for the Octagon Chapel, Norwich).[390]

Between 1786 and 1789 David Stephenson built the large elliptical church of All Saints at Newcastle-on-Tyne with its originally shaped spire and blocklike wings flanking the entrance hall.[391]

The desire for innovation never died during the last decades of the century. In Charles Middleton's *Picturesque Architecture* (1793), we find a circular cottage and several villas with unusual façades,[392] in Richard Elsam's *Essay on Rural Architecture* (1803), triangular and polygonal plans, and a highly elucidating comment on the triangular Pettyward House, Suffolk (1794), which reads like the program of the moderns around 1800:

This idea for a Villa . . . will be considered rather *outré* by those who are not in the habits of venturing out of the ordinary style in the formation of their plans; but to the admirers of Messrs. Nash, Soane, Dance . . . it will prove a subject not unworthy of attention, interesting from its novelty of form, as well as from the agreeable and picturesque effects it will produce . . .[393]

This was what the pioneers of the late eighteenth century wanted: venturing out of the old forms and patterns and searching for new ones. And to Elsam the chief merit of this house appears that it was "divided into distinct masses by bold projectures" and "valuable in itself from its sudden, defined, and marked contrast."

Art history has paid little attention to George Steuart although he was the author of one of the most original churches in the British Isles. Among his country residences Stoke Park House, Wiltshire, carried out between 1786 and 1791, is a composition of cubic masses.[394] The house of Lord Berwick at Attingham, Shropshire (1789), presents a square main pile with loosely attached pavilions.[395] Of greater interest is St. Chad's, in Shrewsbury (1791) (fig. 32).[396] It consists of four distinctly set-off portions, namely, the entrance hall preceded by a portico, the two-storied tower, the staircase containing two flights of stairs leading to the galleries of the main room, and the church hall proper. Seen from the outside, the group of the tower and entrance hall is opposed to the cylindrical staircase and the big cylinder of the church hall. Correspondingly, the interior presents an array of rooms of different shapes. Each room is self-centered, and just as independent from the others as are the different masses outside. It is a far cry from the intersecting curves of the Baroque to these self-contained shapes of St. Chad's. Many people who consider it the worst architectural failure of Shrewsbury are certainly not aware that it represents a noteworthy phase of architectural development. For though the architect still used traditional features, he nonetheless passed to a new compositional principle, with the help of geometrical masses. In the many Pantheon imitations of about 1800 the builders, perhaps, just wanted to show their familiarity with antiquity. On St. Chad's the new compositional ideal is prominent.

A definite continuity emerged from these new attempts. The revolution against the Baroque was to establish a new tradition. Many buildings, which will be discussed later, will corroborate this thesis. Here I should like to point out, only as a first instance, Bayfordbury House in Hertfordshire, which was begun in 1759, but was entirely remodeled (1809-1812) by an unknown architect.[397] It is composed of plain blocks which are neatly set apart from each other. It differs from the rebellious Newgate Prison by its composure. The goal for which the architects around 1770 began to strive was reached about 1800. Bayfordbury House was already a common type, then. Once more I wish to draw the attention to the many, mostly disregarded, smaller buildings in which the modern traits showed, such as the King's Weigh House Chapel in Eastcheap, with its plain walls, originally disposed windows, and cubic masses.[398] Such buildings often allow a deeper insight into the artistic aims of the period than conventionally monumental ones do.

V

ROMANTICISM AND REVIVALISM

THE ESSENCE of the architectural development of the nineteenth century was to be the parallelism of two main currents, a conservative and a revolutionary one. The first was more conspicuous because it affected chiefly the surface and provided the forms. The second, however, became increasingly decisive for the shape of the architectural body, and for the interrelationship of the elements. It reveals the new system. The Janus-faced nineteenth century was anticipated in the work of James Wyatt.

The discussion of three of his performances—Heaton House, in Lancashire, of 1772,[399] Castle Coole, at Fermanagh, Ireland, of about 1790, and Ashridge Castle, Hertfordshire, erected between 1808 and 1813[400]—will suffice to determine his historical position. The first, with its south front by Wyatt, belongs to the category of buildings which do not depart radically from Baroque centralization, but show the rising interest in novel shapes. At Heaton House there is, again, a striking discrepancy between the main pile with its semicylindrical projecting bay and the octagonal end pavilions. The chimneys above the connecting colonnades introduce an element of the picturesque. The main body and the sides contain overarched Palladian windows. There is a variety of features that give the house a personal touch and express at the same time the desire for innovation characteristic of the period.[401]

On Castle Coole, too, the Baroque ancestry is patent. But its end pavilions have considerably gained in independence, whereas on Heaton House the ideal of the pictorial ensemble still played a major role. The fronts of the end pavilions of Castle Coole are not in line with the main front, but stand at right angles to it. Here we see architecture on the way from the unilateral display of one, or two, exalted façades to the equivalence of all fronts.[402] Once again the composition tells more about the aspirations of the era than do the forms.

The much later Ashridge Castle was thought to evoke the impression of a medieval building with the help of gothicizing features.[403] The Baroque arrangement still lingers in the plan,[404] but the body is an agglomerate of cubic and polygonal masses. The architect Wyatt indulged in looking backward to a remote past while striving, simultaneously, for a basically new configuration. Toward a structure of this kind, different critical attitudes are possible. The easiest reaction

48

is to ridicule the futile attempt at reviving bygone times. I believe one would do better not to take this standpoint. For looking back to our ancestors is a deeply human trait, a prerogative of the human species. The opposite attitude of questioning whether every possible "correctness" was obtained was rather too common during the nineteenth century. Certainly, the critics were right who condemned Wyatt for having produced a Gothic construction that was "not pure enough."[405] But the criterion of authenticity is, at best, of secondary importance, for we are not to decree how a work of the past should have been done, but take it as it is. Wyatt's castle is a structure of the earliest nineteenth century. It tells of its romantic aspirations and it reflects its will to create a new, particular, and distinctive general form. These three houses reveal how Wyatt set out from attempts to reform traditional composition and ended with disguising the modern shapes with decoration of the past. Finally, the Radcliffe Observatory at Oxford may be mentioned; begun by another architect, it was "materially altered, and completed by Mr. Wyatt in 1786."[406] Its curious appearance is highly significant of the uncertainty of the period. Wyatt made use of many conventional features, but his main concern seems to have been the original arrangement. He piled the octagonal tower upon the almost Baroque house, contrasted the low wings to the main mass, and repeated the pedimented portico high up in the oversized window of the tower front.

John Carter, Wyatt's adversary, furnishes still better evidence of the architectural unrest in the late Georgian period.[407] Wyatt made resolute attempts to modify the conventional form of the architectural body; Carter came out with some interesting experimental designs. The majority of his designs published in *The Builder's Magazine* between 1774 and 1778 follow the Baroque pattern in the plans and particularly in the façades. Occasionally the sparing decoration and the plainly cut-in windows announce the new trend toward sobriety.[408] Largely he prefers what he calls "the present reigning taste,"[409] recommends rustication for the basement, and wishes that "every part be made to correspond with the whole."[410] In the designs for more luxurious structures, for instance, the Harmonic Pavilion (fig. 33), even the old plasticity is preserved. Balustrades, windows, pediments, and columns still play a prominent role.[411] Only in a few instances is emphasis laid on the rigid wall, as in the designs for a malt house,[412] a "Gentleman's Villa,"[413] and a printing house.[414] In speaking of farmhouses Carter blames the customary "irregular, injudicious manner,"[415] and advocates a "pleasing disposition." When we compare the airy, richly decorated pavilion to the memory of George Frederick Handel (fig. 36) with the memorials the French revolution was to plan, we become aware how far Carter lagged behind.

Beside these more or less traditional schemes stand a few experiments with the plan: the stables with a curiously arranged portico and three cylindrical *conchae*,[416] the public library on an octagonal plan (fig. 34); the keeper's lodge with two lateral apses,[417] and the county gaol.[418] The plans of the Fennick villa show the Baroque arrangement of a central pile with wings and pavilions transformed into an array of squares, circles, and ellipses.[419] A villa with an unusual arrangement of the windows,[420] a watchhouse in cylindrical form,[421] and a tollhouse with a barrel roof,[422] may be pointed out as the boldest of Carter's designs. A charming, playful version of the Palladian motif appears in the design of the door of John Truman's house.[423]

Yet no definite attempt toward a deeper-going reform is traceable in Carter's work. He was one of those who first follow the traditional ways, and then without hesitating join the fashions of the day. He was not of the vanguard, but rather a partisan of the trends in vogue. Paying his tribute to the romantic whims of the era, he covered cottages with thatched roofs (fig. 39)[424] and adorned them with "rough bodies of trees to represent columns,"[425] or he applied rustication to the entire structure (fig. 35).[426] He followed Adam's style in the interiors (fig. 37),[427] yet also joined the fashion of exoticism.[428] He conceived an "Egyptian Pyramidical Dairy," found pleasure in putting sphinxes on top of the classic entablature of a temple,[429] and designed a marble table "inlaid with Japan Paintings"[430] which do not look Japanese at all. His halfhearted experiments did not last long. Very soon he skipped from Baroque schemes to the imitation of Gothic, which was to be his main interest for the rest of his life (fig. 38).[431] This interest led him to compose a series of writings on medieval architecture.[432]

Carter, like all his English colleagues, seems to have taken little note of the efforts of his French contemporaries. From the early Georgian days English architecture moved toward new goals at a slow, steady pace of its own. One who may have formed his style on the continental *avant-garde*—perhaps on De Wailly, Neufforge, or the younger Cuvilliés—was William Robertson. Different characteristics of their works show in his designs.[433] He overemphasized the rustication in the "Garden Seat and Bath," presenting on it a niche running up to the main cornice, and he topped a mausoleum with a fantastic finishing which he describes as follows: "The dome has externally the appearance of a truncated cone, ornamented with masks and drapery."

The further the century progressed, the more the architectural unrest increased in England as well as in France. In each country an architect emerged whose work was to the highest degree expressive of the excitement of the period, as well as its uncertainty: Claude-Nicolas Ledoux, in France, born in 1736, and John Soane, in England, born in 1753. It is amazing how they resembled each other in character and in temperament. Arthur Bolton, in his *Portrait of Sir John Soane,* depicts the English architect as "a man of a highly complex character . . . prepossessed with the idea of secret enemies striking at him in the dark," and "possessing to the full the characteristic Hebrew passion for righteousness."[434] Soane was unable to overcome disappointment.[435] He was anxious to compensate the imagined underestimation of his person by underlining his own merits, as we may learn from several passages of his last publication.[436] The following characterization of Soane also very well applies to Ledoux: "A great fighter, he nevertheless felt deeply the opposition he raised, and he never entirely learnt to refrain from making public his personal misfortunes and grievances."[437]

The achievements of these two men were as different as their characters were similar. The Frenchman strove for remote goals lying far beyond the ultimate performances of the Englishman. This fact is particularly striking when we call to mind that Ledoux was educated by a teacher who almost unrestrictedly adhered to tradition; while Soane studied under his "great master," George Dance the younger,[438] who was a kind of revolutionary himself. Soane was superior to Ledoux in artistic refinement, but remained under the influence of models of the past through all his life. He has been called "the principal exponent . . . of the neo-Greek manner,"[439] yet he also followed the fashion of medievalism wholeheartedly. Thus he may be considered as a precursor of nineteenth-century eclecticism. Lacking a definite, original concept of what architecture should be, he always was ready to dress in borrowed garments. Yet, again, we must inquire what lay behind these disguises, and must therefore devote rather considerable space to Soane's work, for by studying it we may reach a fuller understanding of the eighteenth-century development and may recognize what its architectural inheritance was.

Much of the Baroque is still alive in Soane's best-known work, the Bank of England. This is true of the entrance portico in Threadneedle Street,[440] and the entrance from Lothbury Courtyard.[441] It is particularly true of the Threadneedle Street angle[442] and the Tivoli Corner.[443] Whatever his models were, he knew how to use the various features to express growth, movement, and unity. The history of the Tivoli Corner is significant. In 1804, Soane made many designs for it. These may be divided into two main classes: the "angular treatment" and the "circular sweep forward."[444] Finally, he decided on the latter solution, that is, on the shape which conformed to tradition. Few Baroque architects could have better tied together the converging walls. When we look at other performances of his, quite different in type, we must come to the same conclusion. Soane was Baroque in his executed masterpiece, as well as in the designs for humble rustic structures. He was Baroque in what he termed the "wild effusions of a mind glowing with an ardent and enthusiastic desire to attain professional distinction in the gay morning of youth . . ."[445] and he was still Baroque in the late design for a royal palace, made in 1821 (fig. 40).[446] Through all his life he composed in the old way.

Several of Soane's designs for a triumphal bridge (fig. 41)[447] manifest what he understood in his early years to be good architecture. The bridge reveals the taste of competent contemporaries, for it was awarded a Gold Medal by the Royal Academy in 1776.[448] No bridge was ever expected to bear so heavy a load of classical features as this one was. It is approached by semicircular colonnades flanked by richly decorated halls. The colonnades, topped by small cupolas, continue on to the bridge itself. Between them three mighty pavilions rise. Statues rim the skylight of the dome of the central pile, while still larger crowds of statues enjoy the vista of the river and the mountains from the heights of the end pavilions. Despite the tremendous number of architectural and sculptural features, Soane succeeded in visualizing the Baroque crescendo. The extensive use of colonnades serves to bind the parts into the whole. The bridge voices the unrest of the era, yet it does so by conventional means, and was, therefore, acceptable to the Royal Academy.

Three years later while still in Rome, Soane designed a Royal Palace of similar character (fig. 42), again with cupolas in abundance, statues in overabundance, porticoes, and various other features, on a triangular plan. Once more the masses are firmly held together by the colonnades with continuous entablatures; again some features are emphasized. The will to create something new is unmistakeable. But the architect saw no other way to achieve the new than by heaping old motifs one on top of the other. Nonetheless, the composition is well balanced, for Soane disliked Piranesi's "confusion," as a passage in one of his lectures shows.[449] It is worthwhile to quote, from Soane's book on his house, the description of this palace which "was proposed to have been erected in Hyde Park."[450] Even in his later years he was still satisfied with the scheme of 1779. Proudly he lists the sources from which he had drawn:

In composing this design, I laboured to avail myself of the advantages arising from the contemplation of the remains of the great works of the ancients, as well as of the observations and practice of the moderns. With these feelings, I endeavoured to combine magnificence with utility, and intricacy with variety and novelty. Vignola's celebrated palace at Caprarola suggested the general outline of the plan; and the villa of Adrian at Tivoli, the palace of Diocletian at Spalatro, the immense remains of the imperial palace of the Caesars in Rome, the baths of the Romans, and the interior of the Pantheon, with its superb portico by Agrippa—exemplars of magnificence, intricacy, variety, and movement, uniting all the intellectual delights of classical Architecture,— were objects calculated to call forth my best energies. The portico is copied from that of the Pantheon: in the centre of the building is a dome, under which is another, of a smaller diameter, leaving a space for the admission of light, after the manner of the 'lumière mystérieuse,' so successfully practised in the great church of the Invalids, and other buildings in France.

The architect is right. There is almost everything in his project, except John Soane. Much later, in 1821, Soane designed another Royal Palace for London (fig. 40).[451] It gave him much grief when his plan was not accepted. Compared with the former project, little is changed. There is the same lavishness in decoration, and the same Baroque layout is even more conspicuous. A pompous gateway leads into the large courtyard, with buildings on three sides. The center of the main block is enhanced by a portico, and a round temple on top of the roof. The modernistic teachings of Laugier were well known to Soane,[452] and modern French architecture, certainly, too. But in this design, late as it is, no trace of modernity can be found.

Other fruits of Soane's classical studies were the "National Mausoleum," designed at Rome in the year 1779 in memory of the Earl of Chatham (fig. 43),[453] and the "Castello d'acqua"[454]planned at the same time. Both show some originality in the layout. The probably much later "Bellevue Building" and the "Hunting Casino" may be regarded as attempts to compose in contrasted masses (fig. 44).[455] Each consists of a prismatic substructure and a cylindrical tower. While the "Castello d'acqua" at Wimpole, Cambridgeshire (fig. 45), carried out in 1793, differs from Baroque structures in its compactness, yet even here Soane applied dome and pediments.

It seems as if the interior of the architect's own house and museum (now the Soane Museum), on which he worked from 1812 to his death,[456] was to some extent inspired by Piranesi despite the contempt which he expressed for the latter in his Eighth Lecture.[457] It may also be that Soane was influenced by the weird fantasies of Delafosse's *Iconologie Historique,* which he owned.[458] Anyway, the Museum is the place where at long last we find Soane himself. According to his variegated inclinations he devoted a large part of the house to the cult of antiquity, other parts to the display of works of ancient Egypt and the Middle Ages. He mixed the discrepant features in the oddest manner. The masquerade of garments borrowed from the past has here become a travesty.

Soane built in his house the ruins of a monastery,[459] an Egyptian crypt,[460] and a monk's cell,[461] fancying himself to be Padre Giovanni. The cell, apparently, did not entirely satisfy his romantic whim, so he added the *"Parloir* of Padre Giovanni."[462] Here among his collected treasures, he must have felt at home. The crowd of *objets d'art* filling the *Parloir,* were, according to his belief, apt "to impress the spectator with reverence for the Monk."[463] Architecturally, the rooms are odd. Whimsical forms, as the triple arch between the dining room and the library,[464] may be considered by the observer as remarkable inventions. The ceilings are divided up in geometrical patterns,[465] or kinds of coffers,[466] or adorned with plaster roses,[467] or "enriched with Plaster ornaments in compartments, forming arched canopies."[468] One can also find fun in reading the text of the *Description.* Soane was proud of the thought he spent on the arrangement. He had even cared for the hereafter. "The Tomb of the Monk . . . adds to the gloomy scenery of this hallowed place, wherein attention has been given to every minute circumstance" (fig. 46).[469] One can hardly take seriously the man who, beside much other self-praise throughout the text, extols "the unremitting assiduity of the pious monk."[470] Reading on, we learn a lot of things about the "hallowed place." "The

Stone Structure, at the head of the Monk's grave, contains the remains of Fanny, the faithful companion, the delight, the solace, of his leisure hours."[471] According to one of the many insertions in the book, signed B. H.,[472] Fanny was "a good and true little dog." Over her burial place Soane affixed "a skull crowned with the Alexandrian laurel."[473] After having quoted the inscription on the dog's tomb: "Alas, Poor Fanny!", the architect-monk continues in a matter-of-fact tone: "Amongst these ruins is placed the furnace that heats the water by which the Museum and part of the basement story of the House is warmed."[474] I have dwelt upon some of the oddities of the famous Museum, for here is the key to the failure of Soane as an artist. He certainly carried out several truly great buildings. But he did not have the frame of mind necessary to give to architecture a fresh impulse.

In this preliminary survey we have become acquainted with Soane as an adherent of the Baroque, as an eclectic, and as a rather timid follower of some modern trends. He was not a leader to new goals. He just tried out all the possibilities that he came across. Since in his day the most progressive architects already anticipated essential features of the architecture to come, we can also find traces of them in his work; they appear sporadically, as could not otherwise be expected of a man who was just a receptacle for the most diversified currents. To round off the picture of his attainments a selection of his works may be discussed, not in the order in which they were originated, but in the order of the "styles" which they represent. First, I wish to point out instances of the survival of the Baroque, of the revolutionary unrest, and of the "consolidated" architecture of about 1800. Then examples of nineteenth-century eclecticism will be shown, and patterns foreshadowing Art Nouveau, as well as a few structures with traits resembling the compositional experiments of the French revolutionary architects.

Again and again, in various ways, the Baroque heritage shows in Soane's work. The project for Parliament (1795)[475] manifests dependence on Baroque models in composition and decoration. It lacks the Baroque flexibility but the concept of ruling and subordinate parts is still alive. Also, in his late design for a National Monument, exhibited in the Royal Academy in 1817, Soane could not do without a dominating center, though the individuality of the single cubes composing the whole is notably stressed.[476] The elevations planned for numbers 12, 13, and 14, including his own house (1812), on the north side of Lincoln's Inn Fields[477] show a multitude of openings, which is as typical of the Baroque negation of the wall as it is contrary to the new predilection for massiveness. The same can be said of the design of 1808 for buildings in Princes Street, Lothbury,[478] and of the design for a church—probably Holy Trinity in Marylebone Road (1821)[479]— with its huge nichelike entrance and the high arched windows flanking it.

The Baroque plan, too, lived on in Soane's work. The square plan for an Academy of Arts (about 1776),[480] shows the traditional sequence of vestibule and main hall (the latter serving as a lecture room). The plans for the villa of Wm. Praed and that of Thomas Swinnerton are equally dependent on the Baroque scheme.[481] The rivalry between practical exigencies and the concept of Baroque formality becomes apparent in the Swinnerton house. Soane was so strongly imbued with Baroque principles that even in his late *Lectures* he took the side of sculptural architecture, and inveighed against the modern predilection for plain geometrical forms and the modern incoherency:

An edifice must form an entire whole from whatever point it is viewed, like a group of Sculpture[482] . . . The Ichnography of many of our Buildings consists of a series of squares and parallelograms, and the exterior is formed of discordant parts without that due connection, so necessary to constitute an entire and perfect whole.[483]

He clung to the Baroque tenets, but he could not help letting modern features creep into his designs, in plans as well as in elevations.

Soane was an admirer of Vanbrugh, of whom he said: "Boldness of Fancy, unlimited Variety and Discrimination of Character mark all his productions."[484] All those who not only know Vanbrugh as a dramatist, but who also have a feeling for the dramatic quality of his architecture, especially of his ultimate manner, will agree with Soane's statement: "In his bold flights of irregular fancy, his powerful mind rises superior to common conceptions, and entitles him to the high distinctive appellation of the Shakespeare of Architects."[485] Being fond of Vanbrugh's grand manner Soane could not but dislike the weakness of Adam's exterior architecture, although he appreciated his interior decorations.

It is to the activity of the Messrs. Adam that we are more particularly indebted . . . for the introduction from Ancient Works of a light and fanciful style of Decoration. . . . However well adapted this style might be to internal embellishment, it was ill-suited to external grandeur.[486]

The *Plans, Elevations, and Sections, of Buildings,* which Soane published in 1788, is accompanied by a rather insignificant introduction. Soane had little to say about his own aims. He merely felt obliged to add a text of a few pages to his designs, "since custom has so fully established the propriety of an introductory address from all who present their labours to the public."[487] A good deal of this consists of quotations taken in the main from Vitruvius. There is some praise of the ancients and there are other commonplace remarks, but close to nothing which might reveal the young architect's own goals. A passage of a different tone is the following: "Ornaments are to be cautiously introduced; those ought only to be used that are simple, applicable and characteristic of their situations."[488] Somehow the modern tendencies had come to his attention and he felt no scruple about giving some space to them. For, in the end, he was an adherent of the Baroque by habit, rather than a steadfast defender of the old by personal conviction.

The designs of the *Plans* are utterly exhausted Baroque. On the first project for the parsonage of Saxlingham, Norfolk (fig. 47), the Palladian motif appears in a degenerated version. Broad piers separate the central arched window from the lower side openings. On Malvern Hall, Warwickshire (fig. 48), thin stringcourses run across the entire front; the center is barely emphasized. Here we have the old scheme before us, but now deprived of its former vivacity. The front of the house for Nathaniel Rix, Oulton, Suffolk, looks like a specter of a Baroque façade (fig. 49).

Beyond such timid deviations from the Baroque, Soane paid a tribute to his time by accepting various novel features. The second design for Saxlingham[489] and the projected front of Letton Hall, Norfolk (fig. 51),[490] present semicyclindrical central bays. Yet far from underlining this modern feature, Soane disguises it by trifling ornamental additions. A project for Shottisham, Norfolk, and another for Mottram, Cheshire,[491] present nichelike vaulted entrance halls. This feature was rare with Soane, but very common with Ledoux.

The *Sketches in Architecture* of 1793 tell the same story. Even in the simplest rustic structures the architect appears to be haunted by the ghosts of the defunct Baroque. A glance at plates III, IV, VI, and VII supports this statement. Reminiscences of Baroque gradation and Baroque rhythm survive under thatched roofs. A design like that of plate IX with porticoes on either side of the projecting center shows lack of originality. It is touching in its naïve mixture of classical features and pseudo-rusticity. Also in the *Sketches,* side by side with the sheds, appear more sumptuous villas. Several of these prove that plain surfaces alone do not make a new style, so long as the composition has not changed.[492] Plate xxx presents a cylindrical centerpiece atop the roof. Soane took over this modern feature without having grasped the modern spirit.

Revolutionary unrest manifested itself in England as well as in France in various experiments with form. While the French architects set out to reform architecture basically and boldly attempted to apply their new ideas to any type of building, Soane did not go beyond playing with the novel forms and combinations of forms. In a collection of *Designs* of 1778 presenting little structures for the decoration of gardens and parks, we find an "Obelisk" consisting of conical and cylindrical parts, a "Tea Room" on the plan of a trefoil inscribed in a triangle, a stepped "Pavilion," a "Circular Temple" (fig. 50), and a pyramidal "Garden Building."[493] There are, furthermore, structures composed of heterogeneous features, as a "Rusticated Temple," a "Triangular Temple," and two "Mausolea," one of which is dated 1776.[494] Parallel to the experiments with geometrical shapes runs the interest in the most variegated forms of remote times or faraway countries. This current of exoticism is represented in the *Designs* by a "Gothic Summer House," an "Egyptian Temple," and a "Dairy in the Moresque Stile" (fig. 52).[495]

Late instances of restlessness that had come into architecture are the design for a "Sepulchral Church" at Tyringham (about 1796)[496] and the Cenotaph to William Pitt in the National Debt Redemption Office of 1819.[497] The description of the "Sepulchral Church," by Bolton,[498] reads as follows: "This curious church design is based on a triangular plan with quadrant corners enclosing a spherical dome, which is cut down upon a hexagon. . . . Over the dome is a lantern with Ionic columns. Three porticoes, of four columns each, constitute the main features of the exterior design. . . . It may be only a coincidence that the *Essai sur l'architecture* of P. Laugier, S. J., 1754, a book which Soane appreciated, as is shown by numerous copies in his Library, contains the programme of such a triangular church. . . ." Indeed Soane's dependence seems manifest when we consider not only Laugier's *Essai*,[499] but also his *Observations*.[500] Soane may have taken from the first the triangular plan with the inscribed circle from which the dome rises, the "rotundas" at the three angles, the three entrances on the sides; from the latter, the lantern and the porticoes. Yet it may also be that Soane was inspired by others besides Laugier. We shall learn later that, long before Soane adopted them, experiments with triangular plans were not rare in France; to name but three, there was d'Ixnard's Schoulenbourg House, Neufforge's Temple de la Guerre (about 1760), or the project for a college by Trouard *fils* (1780).[501] We also remember John Carter's triangular Gothic mansion, William Halfpenny's triangular house, and Archer's pavilion for the Duke of Kent,[502] all disregarded by Bolton, but hardly unknown to Soane. There are, of course, considerable differences between Archer's and Soane's performances. The integrality of Archer's pavilion is achieved by the curvature of the walls and the upward movement expressed in the pediments of the porticoes and the ribs of the dome. It is one compact body. However, the exterior of Soane's church, as illustrated in the "Nightview" by Joseph Gandy,[503] is conspicuous for discrepancies in size and shape, especially the contrast between the huge, airy lantern and the massive main structure. The sarcophagi on top of the porticoes and the urns on the dome add to the picturesqueness of the building. In the upper zone of the William Pitt shrine there is "a series of very Soanic, half circular features, spaced with a curious disregard of the columns below."[504] Such inconsistency in the decoration again tells of the perturbation of the era. That at this very moment architecture was already far ahead of Soane does not matter. In the receptacle of Soane's mind things usually came to the surface when they were least expected.

We find also in Soane's work the unrest of the last stages of the revolutionary period, coupled with the new trend toward consolidation. The wood model for a church of 1824 in the Soane Museum is a belated instance of this phase.[505] It offers a striking contrast between open loggia and massive wall, or, we may say, between the Baroque principle of communication between interior and exterior space and the post-Baroque principle of keeping the different realms apart. The curiously shaped steeple indicates the desire for innovation as well as the lack of ability to find something truly new.

Like Letton Hall[506] the project for the Law Courts at Westminster (1820)[507] belongs to that type of "consolidated" architecture which stresses the blocklike character of the masses, while classical features still are loosely applied. Palladian windows appear on the main floor of the Law Courts, not as dominating features, but alternating with square-headed openings. The rounded corner is reminiscent of the new predilection for semicylindrical planes, already known to us from Letton Hall and Holland's Brighton Pavilion.

In the consolidated architecture of about 1800 the raw material began to present itself in a more consistent and rational way, quite different from the organic, mobile character it had assumed in the Baroque. However, one should not lose sight of the major fact that at the very moment when the material solidified the strict formality of the Baroque was given up. Simultaneously, with the redemption of the parts from the whole, matter, too, was redeemed from Baroque rule and was bound to submit to patterns promising greater freedom. The architectural revolution brought about by rationalism was to end in an entirely new concept of art. The Frozen Baroque still involves Baroque composition, with gradation, concatenation, and integration as the main factors, but the components have lost their liveliness and expressiveness. Consolidated architecture, whether it includes worn-out traditional features or not, is, approximately, cubism with all its implications of massiveness, horizontalism, and independence of the parts. A good example of consolidated architecture is Chester Castle by Thomas Harrison (1793–1820).[508] Either "style" is a link in the chain of continuous development. The Frozen Baroque is the earlier stage. It is prerevolutionary, while consolidated architecture, as the first result of the struggle for a new architectural system, is postrevolutionary. ("Revolutionary" refers of course to .the architectural, not to the political, revolution.)

All the different stages from hierarchical formality to free arrangements of the rooms can be traced in Soane's plans. His design for Buckingham House[509] is representative of the earliest stage of the informal plan with slight reminiscences of the past. On the exterior the palace appears in full symmetry with a marked center. So it was to be throughout the nineteenth century: the newly won freedom had to borrow its garb from the *ancien régime*.

The interior of Soane's house is an instance of medieval eclecticism, which played such an important role in the early decades of the nineteenth century. It was followed by the "Renaissanceism" to which Soane turned in the State Paper Office (1829).[510] It is a far cry from Soane's projects in a fantastic Baroque to this dignified but utterly unoriginal edifice. To one modern critic, the main interest in this building is its being "astylar."[511] Columned, or not columned—that is the only question which some have put to the productions of 1800. Yet the historical position of an architectural design can not be recognized by such a simple device.

Among Soane's most noteworthy achievements are to be counted the exterior of the Museum,[512] several rooms of the Bank of England,[513] Pitzhanger Manor at Ealing,[514] Dulwich Gallery,[515] and Tyringham House, Buckinghamshire.[516] They are remarkable not only because of their artistic qualities, but also because they point out, though feebly, still unmistakeably, the direction architecture was to take in the future. It is unfortunate that Soane could not go to the end, and went far astray from the goal, in his confusion over the multitude of possibilities that lay before him. H. J. Birnstingl, whose monograph on Soane contains many fine remarks, very aptly characterizes the front of Pitzhanger Manor, completed in 1802, in these words: "The entrance front is far from satisfactory, the main order seeming to be frankly applied with scarcely an attempt to incorporate it into the design, and this impression is strengthened by the clear demarcation between the two materials of which it is built, for the walls are of brick and the order is of stone."[517] Birnstingl's observation of the incoherence of the parts is excellent, but he should not blame the architect for this deficiency. In the loose application of the columns of Pitzhanger Manor as well as in the detachment of the central portion of the Museum we have to see attempts towards a new order of the constituents. The parts should be delivered from their former captivity within the whole. We know of this tendency from the works of the younger Dance, Holland, and Wyatt. The way in which Soane finished the center of these fronts is also noteworthy. Today we are accustomed to see stepped blocks, yet they were rather new in the days of Soane. Another attempt to break away from the Baroque tradition by dissolving the unity of the whole can be seen in Soane's second design for Brasenose College at Oxford (1807).[518] The entablature of the central portion is discontinued on the annexed aisles, but reappears on the extreme wings. The feature which was one of the strongest ligaments on Baroque structures is disrupted. The parts are materially coherent, but no attempt is made to emphasize their belonging together.

It seems as if the architects of the calm eclectic decades of the nineteenth century forgot the great goals set by the revolution of the eighteenth century, of which we have so far caught only a faint shadow. Thus, another uprising against tradition become inevitable around 1900. It is known as Art Nouveau, or the Secession. We know that this second revolution[519] was, theoretically, very bold, but in practice brought about, at its beginning, merely a change in architectural decoration. Some works of Soane foretell this Revolution of Ornament. There is a somewhat striking resemblance between the playful and capricious inventions of Art Nouveau and Soane's "incised wall surface treatment,"[520] his tendril or stalklike moldings on the outside of the Museum, the walls of several rooms of the Bank, and on the Dulwich Gallery.[521] These decorations of Soane are of a morbid grace— fin de siècle, one would have said fifty years ago. The spirit which created the Dulwich Gallery (1811–1814),[522] was revived in buildings like Josef Hoffmann's Palais Stoclet, at Brussels, about a century later. There is a great similarity between them though each bears the mark of its own era, the former belonging to a period of intensified classical studies, the latter extremely eager to get away from the past. Both are but slightly touched by the new structural aspirations. The exterior of the Dulwich Gallery seemed to a contemporary critic to be a bewildering novelty. In vain he tried to find a name adequate for the perplexing composition:

Now for the Picture Gallery! . . . What a thing! What a creature it is! A Moeso-Gothic, semi-Arabic, Moro-Spanish, Anglico-Norman, a what-you-will production: It hath no compeer, there is nothing like it above the earth, nor under the earth, or about the earth. It has all the merit and emphatic distinction of being unique. Say what you please, and you cannot say anything so delightfully monstrous as is the exterior in question.[523]

People in the 1890's were similarly confused when they faced the fads of the Art Nouveau and equally unaware that they witnessed the birth throes of a new era. They did not grasp the meaning of such odd performances. They expected to be presented with an entirely new architecture at once, not understanding that it could be achieved only through struggle and failure, if at all.

Some very sober designs by Soane form a striking contrast to the fanciful Dulwich Gallery: Malvern Hall,[524] Chillington, Staffordshire,[525] Skelton Castle, Yorkshire,[526] Oulton.[527] The church of Tyringham is an instance of revolutionary unrest, with its mixture of incongruous features and its triangular plan.[528] On the Tyringham mansion, however, a serious attempt has been made to handle the plain cube in an aesthetically satisfying way as the different models and the structure (1793–1798) show.[529] The entrance gateway to Tyringham is a plain, dignified specimen of the new cubism.[530] Perhaps Soane's most advanced design is the project of Butterton House for Thomas Swinnerton (1816).[531] It should have been a terraced building. While the front of the Museum just shows stepped-up blocks as appendages to the front, Butterton House presents the superimposition of blocks of diminishing sizes. But in designing terraced buildings, Ledoux and his pupil Dubut were many years ahead of Soane, as we shall see later.

Soane's *Lectures* cannot be considered a source from which fresh ideas spring. They are just a vehicle for the most diversified currents. As such they are of great interest for anyone who tries to penetrate the mystery of the birth of modern architecture, but they do not afford much credit to their author. The first six lectures were delivered between 1806 and 1809, the last six between 1815 and 1833.[532] They contain numberless contradictions. Soane drew upon any available source. He was able to set forth classical and romantic thought in one breath:

There must be Order and just Proportion, Intricacy with Simplicity in the component Parts, Variety in the mass, and Light and Shadow in the whole, so as to produce the varied sensations of gaiety and melancholy, of wildness, and even of surprise and wonder.[533]

One can infer from his words that in his day the antitraditional doctrines had already taken firm root, for these play a considerable role in the *Lectures*. Yet Soane's designs manifestly show that these utterances are lip service rather than conviction.

Soane, who has copied almost everything, warns against "servile imitation."[534] Soane, who has adorned part of his home with Egyptian motives, inveighs against the "Egyptian mania."[535] Soane the Grecian, apart from condemning such minor features as Caryatides and Persians,[536] attacks the worship of antiquity: "This impropriety of application from the Antique must strike every person, and teach us the necessity of thinking before we blindly adopt what we find in the remains of Antiquity."[537] Soane the maker of fantastic ultra-Baroque projects is against twisted columns,[538] praises simplicity of decoration,[539] and extols the flat roof.[540] Soane the impersonator of any fashion exhorts us to follow nature alone; the burlesque Padre Giovanni preaches rationalism: "All the great principles of Art, whether decorative or constructive, are alike founded on a close imitation of the works of Nature, and on the immutable laws of Reason and of Truth."[541]

We should not conclude this chapter without mentioning some appealing personal traits of the architect. He knew how to appreciate another's merit—his French colleagues, for instance, as we may learn from his *Lectures*[542] as well as from a letter of his pupil, George Basevi,[543] who accompanied him to Paris. He also showed great impartiality in judging contemporary English architects.[544] And if he was not a great reformer, he certainly was one of the most interesting personalities in architectural history.

VI

THE END OF "SCHOLASTIC REGULARITY"

W̲ʜᴇɴ S̲ᴏᴀɴᴇ was confronted with the truly progressive productions of his day, he could not but look at them from the viewpoint of the past. So it was inevitable that he should find fault with Robert Smirke's Covent Garden Theatre of 1809,[545] in his Fourth Lecture disapproving "the Fronts enriched with Columns, Pilasters, and other Architectural Ornaments, while the Flanks are left plain as if belonging to other buildings."[546] He could not bear the lack of relationship between the parts and the whole, and between the parts themselves. Because of this critical remark he was suspended from lecturing at the Royal Academy for a period of time. Not that his colleagues were more modern than he, but there was a regulation issued shortly before he gave that lecture, prohibiting criticism of living artists when lecturing.[547] To us, Smirke's Covent Garden appears to be one of the most advanced English works of its period. On the side elevations we find flat walls with unframed windows, and, still more significant, we find as the basic idea of the whole composition the juxtaposition of individually treated blocks. It was certainly not merely a coincidence that Smirke with his strong feeling for cubism particularly favored concrete.[548]

A few words should now be said about that particular feature of the semi-cylindrical projection which we have already met in different stages: on Adam's Deputy Ranger's Lodge of 1768,[549] on Holland's east front of the Royal Pavilion at Brighton (1787), and on Soane's Letton Hall, prior to 1793.[550] Echoing the cylindrical tower, it shows in the semicircular portico of Smirke's St. Mary's, Wyndham Place (1825),[551] and it occurs again in works by John Nash, on his Casina at Dulwich (1797), and at Rockingham House[552] in Ireland (1810). The "bow with three windows, which projects from the building" appears to have been very popular about 1800, as we may learn from a publication by C. A. Busby and from his houses at Brighton.[553] In the Baroque similar projections were as a rule rather shallow, with a segmental or polygonal circumference. They were like waves gliding over the surface. The semicylindrical projection, however, boldly protrudes and thus reveals the tendency of the central piece to emanicipate itself from the whole. Moreover, the novel shape intimates that there is a close connection between this tendency and the new predilection for elementary geometrical forms. Such forms possess a certain reticence, a self-contained, uncommunicative character, both the shyness and the vigor of the primitive. They seemed to be predestined to become the most appropriate tools of the emancipation. The interdependence of the compositional ideal and its formal media will be dealt with to a greater extent in the following chapters.

From Busby also we may learn a little about the great artistic conflict of his era, the rivalry between "formal architecture," the "classical" and the Baroque, and the "informal" that strove for dominance during revolution and romanticism down to our own individualistic architecture. In his preface Busby briefly points out the two opposing currents. He personally is against informal, "picturesque" architecture and condemns any irregularity in the structure itself.[554]

We remember already having met the opposing trends in earlier publications. John Miller could not part from the basic idea of Baroque composition though he renounced almost any decoration. Yet in several instances he decided for informality in plan[555] just as, eventually, John Crunden, the builder of the original front of Boodle's Club (1765), had done,[556] and, still earlier, T. Lightoler.[557] Various currents of the late eighteenth century show in David Laing's designs of cottages. In some the Baroque patterns still survive, eventually strangely modified. We see for instance in the "Villa intended to be erected in South Devon" the dining room and the library departing diagonally from the central salon and the service rooms loosely appended to the sides. This solution, original as it seems, was in no way new. Later, we will meet similar plans by Juvara, Boffrand, and Cuvilliés *fils*. Laing presents also pentagonal and octagonal plans, plain cubes and houses in which the novel pattern of interpenetrating blocks appears. His best-known work was the Custom House, London (1817), a long-stretched massive structure, later remodeled by Smirke. His Custom House, Plymouth (1810), is distinguished by the quiet juxtaposition and the textural contrast of the two stories.[558]

Since architectural work is the result of practical considerations and formal will, it may be good to caution against certain misconstructions before we deal with a period of increasingly simplified schemes. It is indicative of the stylistic aspirations of a period when an architect applies a complex scheme—like the Baroque plan—to humble buildings. It is equally significant when an architect gives preference to the informal arrangement in the plan of a sumptuous edifice. But it means little if the few rooms of a plain utilitarian building are planned in a free manner. To which I must add that in this context "informal" architecture means lacking in Baroque formality. Later we shall see how the more modern, "free" composition developed a form of its own.

In his *Ferme ornée* (1795), John Plaw refers to a "new method of building Walls for Cottages, etc. as practised in France."[559] This remark, as well as the title of the book indicate that he had learned something from French architects. He illustrates various rustic buildings, among them log cabins with thatched roofs,[560] houses with gothicizing features,[561] and houses of utmost plainness.[562] There are both decentralized[563] and centralized plans.[564] A bathhouse[565] is on a plan very similar to that of Thévenin's "Dairy of the Queen."[566] A "Hunting Box" seems to be influenced by contemporary French experiments.[567] An interesting feature on a "Cow House" is a row of windows running below the roof, separated from each other merely by extremely thin, almost invisible piers.[568]

The designs of the *Ferme ornée* reveal the momentary prevalence of the romantic mood. They are, as the title page states, "calculated for landscape and picturesque effects." Looking over two other publications of Plaw, one a little earlier, the other a little later than the *Ferme ornée,* we become aware how fast the architectural scene changed in those years, or rather, how the different currents run side by side. In the *Rural Architecture,*[569] which first came out in 1785, we see Plaw grappling with the problem of how to combine Baroque grouping with the advantages of a free arrangement of the rooms. His inventiveness makes it worth while to note his varied solutions. The plan for a villa with an arched loggia[570] illustrates how he tried to reconcile Baroque centralization with practicality. Exceptional in this publication is the "Circular House on the great Island, in the Lake of Winandermere in Westmoreland" (fig. 53).[571] It may be that he got his inspiration from French sources.

In 1800 Plaw's *Sketches for Country houses, Villas, and Rural Dwellings* appeared. The preface begins with a profession of the unaltered belief in Baroque principles:

I beg leave to observe, the following Designs are constructed on the principles of symmetry and correspondence of parts; because I am aware some persons think Dwellings on an humble scale, and Cottages, ought rather to be irregular in their forms, and broken in their parts.[572]

Notwithstanding this pronouncement the idea of the free arrangement has crept into the plans.[573] Two curious experiments in the *Sketches* are a circular cottage[574] and another "on a triangular plan." The author says of the latter: "This may be considered . . . a whimsical design, but it affords a pleasing suite of rooms."[575] At the end, a cubic, crenelated house "for a Lady"[576] is illustrated. It has a "free" plan, but a façade with enhanced center. Baroque, romanticism, and cubism are blended in the design. No doubt, here is an architect who adheres to tradition, but at the same time is touched by the new trends. Likewise, in the text, statements of a somewhat "modern" tenor follow the Baroque profession in the beginning. Plaw wishes for "the general appearance snug, low, compact, and dressed in artless and unaffected attire,"[577] and demands consideration for the "natural character of [the] country which must influence the site and disposition of an House."[578] Such a demand is in direct contradiction to the Baroque concept of making the surroundings subject to the building.

"Low, compact, and dressed in artless and unaffected attire" is also Plaw's St

Mary's, Paddington (1788) (fig. 54), "a neat cube with a variety of excrescences not too logically related to it,"[579] and thus a good instance of how the Baroque feeling for unity has gone.

Plaw was eight years older than Soane. Yet we had to deal first with the latter in order to demonstrate how devastating an effect the turmoil of the late eighteenth century had on an architect of greater caliber. Then it becomes easier to recognize the slow but tenacious process of transition in Plaw's humble designs, particularly in his plans. In dealing with the sudden crisis in France we shall gain a more complete picture of what happened in architecture during the eighteenth century. Evolution and revolution headed for the same goals.[580]

"Romantic" cottage architecture was not merely a sentimental aberration. It rather visualizes the struggle for freedom which had begun with Vanbrugh's dramatic protest against traditional formality. Irregularity as the freedom from rule was proclaimed by many authors about 1800. Let us quote as one instance a passage from James Malton's writings:

Though I cannot agree with the author of a late publication [footnote: Smith on Cottages], who, speaking of rural structures in general, observes that, 'so much is irregularity of parts a constituent of beauty, that regularity may almost be said to be deformity;' yet do I most decidedly admit, that a well chosen irregularity is most pleasing.[581]

And Robert Lugar wrote: "In composing Architectural Designs for Dwellings it is not necessary the Artist should be trammelled by the cold rules of the school."[582] For the sake of comparison, a passage from a mid-eighteenth-century treatise by Daniel Garret, also dealing with rural architecture, declares:

The Palace or Cottage require different Forms; and though Decoration and Magnificence are required in the One, and Plainness and Rusticity in the Other, yet Regularity is necessary in Both: Due Proportion in every Object will always attract the Eye and Attention.[583]

Many of Plaw's inventions reappear in the somewhat later publications of another "Little Master," to use the generic name applied to a group of minor Renaissance engravers because of the comparative insignificance as well as the diminutive size of their works. Such a Little Master in architecture was Joseph Gandy. He was in no way an original thinker, rather more of a henchman of the modernists of his day. His *Designs for Cottages*[584] show attractive small buildings, almost all one-storied and consisting of just a couple of rooms, many of only a single room. Therefore one can not reasonably expect any complicated plans, and it does not make sense to see in the simplicity of his plans a stylistic symptom. Neither is the horizontalism of his projects astonishing, nor the lack of upward pointing features and of decoration.[585] Gandy does not seem to have been ambitious, or he may have felt the limitation of his talents. Otherwise he perhaps would have attempted to emulate the great schemes of the architects of the French revolution. The row of broad windows

immediately below the roofline, already applied by Plaw, reappears in many of
Gandy's designs. This resembles the "striped fenestration" of our time.[586] The odd
form of circular rooms was no new experiment when Gandy designed them (fig.
55).[587] These may be impressive in large buildings; they are neither effective nor
practical in small ones. Several projects make it likely that he mimicked the French
avant-garde, for instance in the Cottages of the Winds, each of which is arranged
on a circular plan (fig. 56), the circular village to which they belong,[588] and the
Two Cones as Lodges (fig. 57).

Gandy was not an architect who had a definite formal ideal. Very liberal, he
did not object to anyone changing his designs; he just wished to sell them:

These [cottages] which are regular may be changed into the picturesque, by taking
away one wing; and the picturesque or irregular Designs will become regular by select-
ing a centre, and repeating the parts on each side, if the Builder prefers such dull
monotony.[589]

To suit every taste he designed several "regular," very "dull" houses.[590] The designs in his *Rural Architect* are equally insignificant. Occasionally feeble attempts
at a certain rhythmical arrangement are made.[591]

Whenever novel forms appear it is never long before the toyboxes, too, are filled
with them. However, there is nothing left in Gandy's toys of the grandeur of the
architectural fantasies of the French revolution.[592] Of greater significance than
Gandy's weak designs is a cylindrical structure carried out by Francis Sandys,
though this architect, too, was hardly an independent, creative mind. Frederick
Hervey, fourth Earl of Bristol and Bishop of Derry, wanted two houses made on
circular plans, Ballyscullion, begun in 1787, but never completed,[593] and the "most
remarkable and most eccentric of great Suffolk houses," Ickworth, started by
Sandys about ten years later.[594] In a letter of 1787 Hervey wrote about Ballyscullion:
"The House itself is perfectly circular in imitation of one which I saw upon an
Island in the Westmoreland Lakes."[595] The structure referred to is Plaw's Circular
House[596] whose plan Sandys copied, almost literally, for Ickworth.[597] But while
Plaw's house rose from a square substructure which helped to isolate it from the
environment, curved wings and end pavilions were added at Ickworth. We do not
know whether these additions were asked for by the patron. In any case, the work
is highly indicative of the uncertainty of the period. It attempts to combine the
traditional wing scheme with the elementary form of the central body. But there is
no harmony between the components. The oversized rotunda of Ickworth is markedly set off against the wings and end pavilions, and thus is a further instance of
the emancipation of the central piece, or its extrication from the whole. The
process which at Vanbrugh's Seaton Delaval began with the rebellion of the parts
has developed into the independence of the elements, although they are still materially connected. Only after the idea of independence had become common, chiefly

in "picturesque" building, "great" architecture followed, operating with cubic masses.

The stage of an entirely new organization of the constituents was reached only in the twentieth century. The nineteenth, and particularly its early years, still grappled with the problems which were posed in the Age of Reason. Having dealt already with several works of the latest Georgian period, I would like to point out a few others which may still better visualize the result of eighteenth-century efforts and may serve as an introduction to any investigation into the character of the nineteenth-century development.

Emphasis on cubic masses became increasingly more important than pictorial display or picturesque shapes. The perspective view of a projected villa by William Fuller Pocock, and particularly its plan, show that its chief effect was to be derived from the interpenetration of prismatic blocks.[598] The oversimplified classification "Grecian" or "Greek Revival" is insufficient. First in Pocock's mind was the pattern of elementary forms. Similar patterns can be found in many contemporary works, such as Robert Lugar's "Gentleman's Residence," his Glenlee House at New Galloway in the County of Ayr, though on the latter the "castellated" character strikes the eye,[599] William Wilkins' Grange Park house, Hampshire (about 1810), and James Burton's double villas at St. Leonards, Hastings (about 1830).[600] We also recognize the pattern of interpenetration on Decimus Burton's Greenough Villa (Grove House), in Regent's Park, London (1822), where the corners of the cross are filled in with low blocks (fig. 58).[601] Clear-cut cubes are Jay's Albion Chapel, Moorgate, of about 1816 (fig. 59), and Decimus Burton's Athenaeum Club (1830), in its original shape.[602]

Cubes are self-contained. Thus they could not please people who above all wanted unification of the parts. In post-Baroque times, however, incoherence was no longer considered a defect. On St. George's or Hanover Chapel, Regent Street (1823) (fig. 60), by Charles Robert Cockerell, the towers had no relationship to the main mass. One could have removed them without damaging the whole. The dome, too, was "little connected with the composition of the front arrangement."[603] Similar inconsistencies on other buildings are usually regarded as shortcomings. Yet they seem to indicate a new compositional principle. University College, London, by William Wilkins (1826), has been criticized because "the wings have a painfully abrupt relation to the centre, being married to the portico neither in rhythm nor alignment."[604]

The spirit of experimentation lived on after 1800. An outstanding instance of a highly original façade is that of the United Service Club by Robert Smirke (1816) (fig. 61).[605] The horizontals prevail; there are almost no vertical ties. Groups of straight-headed and arched windows, and oblong panels with reliefs, form a pattern of great refinement. The variegated façades of Regent Street carried out by John Nash about 1820 likewise exemplify the desire for innovation.[606] Particularly note-

worthy is the Suffolk Street elevation of the Haymarket Theatre (fig. 66).[607] Here
we see John Nash striving for a spatial effect with the help of prismatic projections.
The array of projections presents the pattern of juxtaposition in space. On the tower
of St. Anne's, Soho (1803), the classical features are inconspicuous (fig. 62).[608] For
its builder, Samuel Pepys Cockerell, father of Charles Robert and a pupil of Robert
Taylor, cared principally about presenting a sophisticated surface treatment. Instead of plastic decoration in the old sense, pilasters, roundels, flat niches, and curtain motifs above the latter present successive parallel planes. (Another way of intimating depth appears on a work by the same architect, of the 1790's, at Middleton
Hall in Carmarthenshire, Wales, where the receding entrance hall is contrasted to
the bare façade.)[609] The very concept of St. Anne's tower is the antithesis of masses
distinguished either texturally, or by different shapes; white stone is contrasted
against dark stone, the lower cubes to the bell stage and the fantastic finishing.

Returning to Nash, we find that the gothicizing features of St. Mary's, Haggerston (1826) (fig. 67), play a subordinate role if compared with "its extreme od-
dity."[610] The front manifests the eagerness of a man who, though using old forms,
wanted to devise something new. With this view of Nash's intentions we are in a
position to understand the famous church of All Souls (fig. 68) on Langham Place,
London (1822–1824).[611] Commonly, it is looked upon as a whimsical performance.
A recent writer on the Regency style does not even find it worthwhile to comment
on it except by illustrating a contemporary cartoon on the "Nashional" taste, displaying just the spire. Another contemporary ironically found it "something so
sublime as to be beyond comprehension."[612] However, all the incongruities are
expressions of the still continuing architectural unrest, and thus indicative of the
historical position of All Souls. Knowing about the new compositional ideals we
can also recognize its artistic meaning, in the contrast of its circular vestibule and the
tall spire, the unrelatedness of the former to the cubic nave, and the way in which
the vestibule is echoed by the likewise circular tower colonnade. This peculiar shape
distinguishes the church from conventional types. Different solutions might have
been fit for the site, and particularly the changing direction of the street—for instance, a simple domed rotunda. Yet Nash, aiming at a new arrangement, achieved
this highly original design. Compositions in incoherent, antagonistic masses are
also Nash's Cronkhill house, near Shrewsbury, and his first design for Buckingham Palace (1825) with its parts "loosely knit, badly coordinated . . . and hopelessly unrelated."[613] That Nash, later, became self-conscious and denounced his
boldness, does not lessen the significance of his project. Architecture was not
doomed to obey the precepts of the past slavishly, forever.

We remember from Robert Morris's *Essay* that long before the zenith of
romanticism there was a trend in building toward "irregularity" which manifested
itself in what today we would consider cautious deviations from the classical canon.
This formal trend toward the irregular or the free was seconded by that sentimental

trend of the eighteenth century known to everyone from literature. So the "Irregular House" became popular about 1800. Castle Coole by James Wyatt with its independent side façades was just a beginning. More and more, irregularity was sought on artistic grounds rather than because of its sentimental associations. This can be seen in the statement of Samuel H. Brooks: "It is evident that to introduce irregularity of form in buildings is an architectural refinement of the present age . . . The irregular cottage style depends more on its picturesqueness, than on its being an imitation of anything that has previously existed."[614] On Osberton House, Nottinghamshire, by William Wilkins, regularity was given up deliberately.[615] The circular salon protrudes on one of the short sides of the block while the portico is appended to the adjoining long side. It was only a step from here to "picturesque" cottages. James Malton's *Essay on British Cottage Architecture* carries the revealing subtitle, "An Attempt to perpetuate on Principle that peculiar Mode of Building which was originally the effect of Chance."[616] The "free" form did not remain confined to "rustic" huts; it was applied also to houses composed of classical elements. In a design by James Thomson with the significant caption, "Irregular House," the composition speaks for itself. It is characterized by interpenetrating blocks, a predilection for plain solids, and purposeful lack of balance. The accompanying text makes the architect's point still clearer: "Each elevation in this design differs from the rest." The "irregular" structures once criticized by Robert Morris were merely the first negative steps of the architectural reorientation—the revolt against the rules, or, the "regular." Thomson's house reveals the positive goal—the new form of free coëxistence (fig. 63). Painting, after many vicissitudes, reached the same goal in nineteenth-century realism and impressionism.[617]

The comments of Francis Goodwin on a "Villa in the Gothic Style" (fig. 64) reveal similar intentions: "The purpose aimed at" is "to set off" the elements "by the contrast . . . produced." This is also the guiding idea in his "Italian Villa."[618] Goodwin used quite different models to conform to the fashions of the day. But in all disguises he presents his own manner—or rather, the manner of the nineteenth century, which means a new order of the elements in attire taken from the past.

One of the most remarkable visualizations of this new manner is Goodwin's Park Lodge Entrance to Lissadell Court (1830) (fig. 65).[619] Here balance and symmetry are discarded in favor of the vigorous antithesis of the components. The most conspicuous feature is the watch tower, which "offers a striking contrast to the lodge . . . being as much detached from, as united with, the latter by the gate, and the ornamental railing extending between the two buildings." Obviously, "detached" is meant aesthetically, while "united" just indicates the material facts.

Typical products of the nineteenth century are the terraces along Regent's Park in London.[620] Here we find architecture at the crossroads, still dependent on tradition and yet anxious to break away from it. Their builders attempted to reconcile the formal heritage of the Baroque with the new modern practicality of large apartment houses and, simultaneously, to introduce into their designs the patterns developed in the "Age of Reason." Thus there is great historical significance in these terraces. We should not content ourselves with vague phrases in admiration of their singularities, but carefully analyze each of the huge buildings. In doing this we come to distinguish, roughly, three groups of rather different character, though, of course, they have traits in common.

Three structures west of Regent's Park, Hanover Terrace, Cornwall Terrace, and Sussex Place may be termed the "conservative" group. Clarence Terrace on the west side, York Terrace to the south, and Cambridge Terrace on the east side constitute an "oppositional" group. Cumberland and Chester Terrace, east of Regent's Park, and Ulster Terrace adjoining York Terrace, represent the most "progressive" class. All were built in the early 1820's; most of them were damaged in the Second World War.

Hanover Terrace (fig. 69), by Nash,[621] and Cornwall Terrace, by James and Decimus Burton under the direction of Nash,[622] still resemble Baroque compositions. The contemporary writer and architect James Elmes rightly points out the "more grammatical style of architecture" of Hanover Terrace[623] and the "scholastic regularity" of Cornwall Terrace.[624] Sussex Place, after Nash's design, is an offspring of romanticism with its interest in remote times and regions. The "pagoda-like cupolas" form a "whimsical row . . . for the sake of picturesque variety."[625]

On York Terrace (fig. 70) Nash departed from the conventional scheme in two ways.[626] He juxtaposed massive, elongated twin blocks, and by finishing them with heavy attic stories he deprived them of the little movement that was left in their single features. Within each block there is a certain incongruity between the attic story and the main mass. Elmes had already remarked that the former "strays rather too much into the irregular . . . it is in a different key, and is a false concord."[627] Yet, we believe, the builder should not be censured for what appears to be merely the reflection of the rising new trends in composition. Suave harmony was no longer wanted; the natural dissonance between the parts was no longer to be concealed. Cambridge Terrace by Nash (fig. 71)[628] also presents disrupted unity. The whole seems to consist of two houses. This configuration is of greater interest and greater importance than the incised lines on the pilasters, reminding one of Soane, and the coupled rusticated columns, recalling Ledoux. On Clarence Terrace, as shown in Decimus Burton's original drawing,[629] the central pile is still more weakened. The side pavilions, loosely attached by galleries, are not inferior to the center in height and decoration. Instead of the former integration, we witness here dissociation of the elements.

On Ulster Terrace (fig. 72),[630] its façade designed by Nash himself, the main accent has been shifted to the sides with two pairs of cylindrical projections. The compositional ideal intimated only faintly on Clarence Terrace has developed into the new pattern of reduplicated geometrical features on Ulster Terrace. The lavish decoration of Cumberland Terrace (fig. 73), by Nash,[631] might be interpreted as typically Baroque. But we should not forget that the concept of unity has been superseded by a multiplicity of accents well suited to the numerous apartments behind the pompous veil.[632] This, of course, does not mean that each single apartment is expressed in the façade decoration. The development in architecture seems to have been analogous to that of social life. The multitude coming to the fore was in the end to shape the surface itself. With the inner forces menacing the outer pomp, Cumberland Terrace becomes truly representative of the nineteenth century. Chester Terrace (fig. 74), begun a year earlier, brings a new solution.[633] The attenuated front shows five juxtaposed projections. Above the first, third, and fifth the attic is finished by a straight parapet, while the second and fourth projections are crowned with low triangular pediments. Contrary to the Baroque rhythm of subordinate sides and enhanced center (s–C–s or S–s–C–s–S) we see on Chester Terrace the alternating rhythm of straight and pitched finishings. This arrangement could be continued *ad infinitum*, just as Robert Morris had foreseen.[634] To mark the end of the row, Burton appended at right angles triumphal arches terminating in outer pavilions. These appendages are a concession to the old ideal of wholeness. Without them the new pattern of the endless streets of our modern cities could readily be recognized. From sheer juxtaposition of ever repeated identical elements many other terraces derived their artistic effect, for instance John Buonarotti Papworth's Lansdowne Terrace, Cheltenham, and Busby's Brunswick Square, Brighton.[635]

PART II
ITALY

VII

THE ARCHITECTURAL SYSTEM OF THE
RENAISSANCE AND THE BAROQUE

IT IS NOT my intention in this second part of the book to give an exhaustive account of the development of eighteenth-century architecture in Italy, but only to attempt to display her role in the transition from the Baroque to the nineteenth century. To do this I shall first outline the history of the Renaissance-Baroque system in the country of its origin. The momentous symptoms, then, of growing uneasiness about 1750 will not appear as a sudden break with the past, but as the outcome of a century-old process. It may be said in advance that this uneasiness found vent not so much in actual building as in acid criticism of tradition, in the most daring formulation of an entirely new architectural program, and in delineations in the graphic arts which tell of the breakdown of the old outworn system and the desire for a new architectural order.

Before dealing with the vicissitudes of the Renaissance-Baroque system in Italy, it is necessary to discuss the concept of an architectural system in general. I started first with the development in England chiefly because the very first steps leading to the architectural revolution of about 1800 are to be found in that country, and also because this disposition offers a methodical advantage. We obtain a better understanding of the earliest stages of the Renaissance-Baroque system after we have become acquainted with its latest phases.

We are accustomed to conceive of an architectural style as a certain number of structural and decorative features, with some variations, recurring within a given period. Whether we take these features from one outstanding building considered as the purest incarnation of a particular style, or construe the style by features selected from several structures, either way we are apt to view all the performances of the period from a presumed climax. If we thus form our concept from this apex view, before long we shall be in the position of the man who found the solution to the problem of irregular Greek verbs in the formula: one verb is regular, all the others are exceptions. Such fiction is a help in bringing some order to discrepant phenomena—a useful abstraction enabling us to master the confusing variety of different features. But the meaning of the growth and development of architecture will become clearer only as we proceed from the fixation on style to the reality of change. In order to correct the fallacy of a stylistic apex, one must investigate the entire field, out to its very frontiers. From there, and possibly even from neighboring regions beyond, one can gain better insight into one's own territory. On the frontier, where the different currents converge, one becomes aware that there is no dividing line. Today there is hardly a historian who does not share this view. Borderlines are created by and for man for the easier administration of the land. The frontier aspect offers the first corrective of the apex view. There is no reason for the historian who has reached the frontier to give preference to the apex view, to the "purest" Gothic, for instance (if there were such), over the mingling of Gothic and Renaissance features. Such an attitude reveals the weakness of stylistic discrimination based on single features (forms as well as characteristics, the latter including the "categories" of Heinrich Wölfflin). Moreover, the single forms have a certain persistency. Or, to put it the other way round: man does not forget completely the forms his ancestors have devised. They recur time and again. There always have been "revivals," and there always will be. There is, however, a great difference between the Gothic and the Gothic Revival. There is another, deeper-rooted and deeper-going, change besides the periodic appearance and disappearance of forms, namely, the change in the interrelation of the parts—or, in what I propose to term the system. It is the system change that makes the difference between Gothic and Gothic Revival, between Roman and Renaissance architecture, and so forth.

There are profounder reasons for a change of system than for a change in forms, or even in characteristics. Systems depend wholly upon, or, better, derive directly from, the general mental attitude of a particular era. Since attitudes change unceasingly, the architectural systems also are in a state of unceasing flux. The change of a system, moreover, does not concern merely a few elements, but affects the whole. Consequently it is responsible too, for the selection—invention or modification—of the forms at their first appearance in history. It is also responsible for the intensification of the characteristics (pictoriality, plasticity, etc.). Forms and system, however, become antagonistic when forms of an earlier system recur in a later one because of some new scholarly interest in them, or for some other extra-artistic reason. This is why we have the feeling of something unsound in every revival, or even of something insane. Forms recur; systems don't. Through the centuries Greek forms were applied again and again, but never in later times were homes arranged in the Greek manner, just as mankind may eventually copy institutions like the archontate, the consulate, or the senate, but will never again live under Athenian or Roman law.

Wherever changes of the forms occur we may suspect that a change of system is the cause. Borrowed forms can be quickly discovered, as a rule. Usually they are short-lived and sporadic. Generally they undergo a transformation under the new system. Occasionally the sudden emergence of certain new forms gives the impression of a break in the development. But also in such cases a prolonged period of concealed preparation has been taking place. The historic process is a constant and slow evolution. There is no sudden reversal except, perhaps, in the infinitesimal and therefore imperceptible moment of the conception of the new idea.

When novel forms abruptly appear, as for instance the geometrical forms in architecture before 1800, the historian should not yield to the temptation of displaying such an eruption as a sensational event, like a magician anxious to conceal the stages leading up to the startling result. It may well be that some artistic performance looks like an erratic block, grand, imposing, of unknown origin, towering from a stretch of land of quite different character. It has its history. Its ancestry and its progeny will give a good account of it. A simple array of stages, precedent or subsequent, will not be of such help, for history is not chronology. To write history we must distinguish between the different currents, sometimes running parallel, often overtaking each other, occasionally flowing together, but always striving for dominance. Only after such an analysis can we integrate these various aspects into a comprehensive picture.

The concept of system, as used throughout this investigation, does not involve the idea of accomplishment. It merely points to a tendency. No system can ever completely fulfill its specific concepts of interrelation of the parts. From the beginning to the end it has to struggle against opponents. It is the same as in social life: each system proclaims new goals; none reaches them. The unity of an epoch in the visual arts results from the predominance of an immanent idea, but not from the recurrence of single forms. It may be controversial whether configuration (*Gestalt*) comes first in perception. It most certainly comes first in artistic creation. The most irreconcilable opponents of that immanent idea are tradition, practical exigencies, the nature of the materials, and, worst of all, the contradictions in the system itself. All these necessitate unending compromise. Starting from natural self-assertion, there enters into play the tendency toward intensification, toward the strongest exhibition of the underlying principle, leading to overdoing, and still more contradiction. Such exaggeration necessarily precipitates the end. When a system arises, it is expected to overcome its adversaries; it declines when there is no longer hope of getting the better of them. At last it gives way, or is overthrown. This is the inescapable fate of all social systems and is no less true of artistic systems. The inner inconsistencies debilitate the system and diminish its power of resistance against the attacks of the most dreaded of its antagonists. The rising new idea will engender a new system, which in turn will itself in time come to a similar fate.

The concept of the rise and decline of architectural systems has nothing in common with the nineteenth-century concept of blossom, maturity, and decay of the styles, which was at the same time naturalistic and moralizing. I prefer to stress the equal significance of all periods within their epoch, and oppose the assumption of the superiority of any one period. My conception negates the possibility of the ascent to some glorious height of artistic perfection, around which the art writers of the past century liked to display, melodramatically, the picture of a splendid cultural life. May I repeat that, in my opinion, every system struggles hopelessly for fulfill-ment. Every new idea carries death within itself. But before death comes, the new idea has to fight its way against manifold obstacles. This metamorphosis of the system, caused by the counteraction of its opponents, is one of the primary subjects of art history.

Before discussing the transformation of the Baroque to post-Baroque archi-tecture, we must first comment on the inherent weaknesses of the Renaissance-Baroque system, and its outer enemies. The permanent flux in artistic development makes it impossible to fix a point separating the "ascending" from the "descending" system, or the stages of unshaken confidence in its aims to its last frantic efforts for survival, and final resignation. Consequently we will take a general view of the entire postmedieval evolution. This means we must go as far back as any signs of the essential traits of the Renaissance-Baroque system can be traced. These may be detected at the moment which was always regarded as a turning point in art history, the moment of the incipient early Renaissance. This concept of the "Baroque system," as I shall call it briefly, really means the system underlying both the Renaissance and the Baroque proper. My next task, therefore, will be a brief survey of both periods. It is to the credit of the art historians of about 1900 that they elucidated the basic differences between the Renaissance and the Baroque. But from the viewpoint of the architectural system, a common principle underlying both the Baroque and Renaissance becomes manifest in contradistinction to the "medieval system" on the one hand, and to the system of the nineteenth century on the other. The Renaissance was the first stage in an attempt toward a new organization of the constituents; the Baroque represents the last desperate efforts to reach this goal. The Renaissance was the preparatory stage of the Baroque; the Baroque made a harder effort to achieve the common ideal of organization. By this I do not mean to imply any aesthetic superiority of one over the other, but only to clarify the historic position of the two periods. And I might add that this had an analogy in political history. The system of absolute monarchy came closest to its fulfillment in the late seventeenth century.

In the following pages these general remarks will be supported by an outline of the development of the Baroque system in Italy, the country of its origin, but first I should like to be allowed a brief digression which I feel may help toward a better understanding of postmedieval architectural thought. I want to point out what I consider to be the fundamental difference between the ancient theories as summarized by Vitruvius and those of the Renaissance and the Baroque; or, be-tween the compositional ideal of Greco-Roman architecture and that of the cen-turies following the Middle Ages. Vitruvius' aesthetic categories are obscured chiefly because he himself did not reach a clearly defined concept. However, one thing is certain: all his categories had a quantitative significance. Proportionality, or perfect numerical relations between the parts, was of foremost importance to him. The ideal of quantitative beauty appears in *ordinatio* as well as in *symmetria* and *eurythmia*. Today, in the sense of balanced arrangement, these likewise have quantitative significance. Like features placed symmetrically, or at carefully thought-out distances, are of equal value; identical in form or not, there is no differentiation in significance. Each column on an ancient building is of equal rank with the rest; the pediment is higher than, but not superior to, the colonnade. The elements of the Greek temple were coördinated—whereas on the front of the Pazzi Chapel the side compartments were subordinated to the higher and wider central bay. The dome of the Roman Pantheon is inconspicuous, whereas that of St. Peter's rules in size and shape.

The ideal of quantitative perfection lived on in the Renaissance. We know how much thought its theorists gave to the "correct" measurements. But more important, and far more significant than the reintroduction of ancient forms, was the rise of a new compositional principle: the parts now should be presented not only in aesthetically satisfying relationships of size and in mathematical reciprocity, but they should be differentiated as superior and inferior components. Such differentiation would have been strange to antiquity, even to its "Baroque" phases, at any rate within the individual building. The postmedieval composition which emphasized the different values of the parts made of the whole a hierarchy of well-disciplined elements. The means by which this goal was reached are already known to us. They were concatenation, integration, and gradation.

Most historians look upon Filippo Brunelleschi as the first great architect of the Renaissance. Yet they do not deal much with the new elements in his work, preferring to go back to the past to trace the sources from which his manner derives. Ever looking back, Wilhelm Bode denies that the Renaissance architecture of the fifteenth century brought a truly new art.[1] Brunelleschi, "the very creator of Renaissance architecture,"[2] is to Bode just a copyist of antiquity and a follower of the Gothic.[3] William J. Anderson expresses a similar view. Speaking of the Pazzi Chapel, Anderson asserts that "none can contend that in this instance Brunelleschi was merely copying Roman work."[4] Moreover, he refers to "deep marks of the Byzantine tradition,"[5] and "the retention of medieval usage,"[6] in Brunelleschi's work. Hans Willich, too, deals chiefly with the two influences, the classical and the medieval.[7] August Schmarsow points out the survival of the Gothic in Brunelleschi's work. He sees in the even number of bays terminating the transepts and the choir of Santo Spirito, the strongest evidence of Brunelleschi's Gothic feeling.[8] To G. K. Lukomski, Brunelleschi's work is nothing but Gothic with some classical features thrown in.[9] Julius Baum mentions the Gothic character of Brunelleschi's features, but speaks of his composition only in rather vague terms.[10] Charles Herbert Moore[11] and Paul Schubring[12] held similar views to those of Lukomski. Moore's hostile attitude against Brunelleschi culminates in his criticism of the Pazzi Chapel from a functionalistic viewpoint: "it is bad architecture, because the parts have no proper adaptation to their functions."[13] Alone among these, Heinrich Geymüller saw, as we shall see later, more than the mere adoption of classical forms when he wrote that Brunelleschi "invented an architectural style," and Paul Frankl emphasized Brunelleschi's aversion to tradition.[14]

Most of these opinions fit into the concept of permanent flux and do their part in erasing the artificial borderline between the Gothic and the Renaissance. But they give only one partial aspect of Brunelleschi's achievements, certainly not the most significant.

Adolfo Venturi, in speaking of the lantern of the dome of the Florentine Cathedral, finds an opportunity to demonstrate the close relationship of its buttresses with the Gothic and he compares the lantern with Gothic reliquaries.[15] But the scrolls which tie the buttresses to the pillars of the lantern bear greater likeness to Baroque scrolls than to any Gothic form. One single feature may not be of significance were there not several instances of Brunelleschi's work where basic ideas of the Baroque system are already perceivable.[16] The new system is foreshadowed in his first construction, the Foundling Hospital of Florence (founded 1421), which is considered the very first performance of the Renaissance proper.[17] Geymüller sees the principle of concatenation in its arcades framed by tall pilasters,[18] and remarks that the well-differentiated ground plan of the hospital was to have the greatest bearing upon the further development of architecture.[19] Cornel von Fabriczy emphasizes the conscious application of gradation in the rustic work of the Palazzo Pitti.[20]

The Baroque system could hardly have been expressed with greater distinctness than in the Pazzi Chapel (1430). The most remarkable feature here is the five-part portico with the stress on the central portion. The chapel front is the true precursor of the pattern which later became famous as the Palladian motif.[21] The structure is climaxed by the dome, internally as well as externally.[22]

In dealing with an innovator, one should, of course, see him in relation to the future. His importance does not lie in his dependence on the past. It lies in the promise his work holds for further development.

In many structures of the early Renaissance, the classical features play a rather subordinate role.[23] Already the architects were intent upon visualizing the concatenation of the parts,[24] and found an excellent method of marking gradation by working the material in different ways and by carefully thinking out the proportions. Unification and integration become manifest in the simple pattern of vertical pilasters and horizontal bands: for example, on Alberti's Palazzo Rucellai at Florence (1446–1451); Rossellino's Palazzo Piccolomini at Pienza (1462); and the Cancelleria (about 1486) in Rome.[25] Good illustrations of gradation, either by the treatment of the stone, or by the varying height of the stories, are the Palazzi Medici-Riccardi by Michelozzo (1444), Strozzi by Benedetto da Majano (begun

1489), and Gondi by Giuliano da Sangallo (1490).[26] The Palazzo di Venezia in Rome with its crenellation (1455) is commonly regarded as a typical medieval stronghold;[27] only the arcades of its court are recognized as Renaissance on purely formal rather than compositional grounds. But the exterior most certainly belongs to the new era because of its axiality, the emphasis on the central bays, and the gradation of the stories. In northern Italy, too, the new compositional pattern appears, however different the buildings may be from Florentine and Roman work in other respects. It can be found on the Certosa of Pavia with its copious decorations,[28] as well as the colorful church Santa Maria dei Miracoli in Venice, by the Lombardi (1481).[29]

On some of the structures concatenation prevails, on others, gradation. Often an architect imbued with the ideal of Baroque configuration may have pondered how to express it best—should he stress concatenation, or should it be gradation? (Needless to say such pondering was not a conscious process.) If he were to apply both in equal strength, he would risk monotony in his work. The alternatives reveal the first of the difficulties of the system. Assuming that the architect has chosen to stress concatenation, at once the problem arises should he give preference to the horizontals or the verticals? If, on the other hand, he has decided that gradation is to prevail, should he then accentuate one story, or the vertical main axis of the façade? Or, should he compromise and underline both? From such a compromise originated the very common inverted "T" pattern where the ground floor is emphasized and contrasted to the upward surge of the center. With the appearance of the new system, these dilemmas arose and as long as the new ideal of configuration was valid, the architects had to cope with them. Raphael (or Peruzzi) in the Villa Farnesina (1511), and Vignola at Caprarola (1560),[30] were apparently confused by the contradictions the new system presented. Their schemes are full of uncertainty; they dodged the issue. Michelangelo, in the entrance hall of the Laurenziana, faced it.[31] He did not attempt a one-sided solution, nor did he compromise, but bluntly stated the contradictions within the system by exaggerating both gradation and concatenation. The columns, forceful still in the bondage of the walls, are efficiently antagonized by the horizontals. The tragic mood of the interior is a confession of the hopelessness of solving the contradictions. Palladio, in his later years, emphasized vertical unification. By applying colossal orders to the Palazzo Valmarana at Vicenza (1566)[32] and the fronts of San Giorgio (after 1566) and San Francesco at Venice (1562), he disrupted the continuity of the horizontals.

Some of the works which show such contradictions and inconsistencies are looked upon by several historians as specimens of the so-called style of Mannerism. It is not possible to deal with the latter to any extent in this introduction to my topic, the transition from the Baroque to the post-Baroque. I must limit myself to brief remarks only. Those who might be interested in the stimulating problem of the significance of "manneristic" traits may compare my concept of the gradually evolving Baroque system with the elucidating observations on Mannerism made by other historians.[33] For my part, I agree with those who reject the notion of a manneristic style, at least in architecture. What we see in "Mannerism" is uncertainty, dilemma, and bold effort to exhibit, in the strongest terms, contradictory trends. On the one side we see weakness, inconsistency, affectation, and "unnaturalness"; on the other, we find dramatic eruptions. We see changes in balance, distortions of the logical relationship between supported and supporting elements, and attempts to revise the conventional dispositions. All this speaks not so much of a style with positive characteristics, but rather of a phase within the Baroque, tending to negate its own aspirations. Indeed, negative symptoms do not constitute a style. Already in the sixteenth century the Renaissance-Baroque system was seriously menaced by the idea of some new form of coëxistence of the parts, but the danger became acute only in the eighteenth century. In the era of Mannerism the time was not ripe for architectural revolution. For, contrary to the architecture of the late eighteenth century, that of Mannerism never seems to have reached the point of conceiving new compositional principles. Its attitude was strictly negative. Nikolaus Pevsner, a foremost authority in this field, rightly remarks that in Manneristic work there is "no solution anywhere . . . tormenting doubt . . . unconnected bits . . . monotony instead of gradation . . . the total lack of a predominant accent," scorn of pleasing proportions, and even "deliberate attacks on the Renaissance ideal . . . of the balance of all parts." In spite of the challenge of Mannerism the basic Renaissance-Baroque concepts still held their ground firmly. Architects were not yet ready to give up the dream of the possible fulfillment of the Baroque system.

The façade of the Scuola San Rocco,[34] although contemporary with the Laurenziana, has an entirely different appearance, with all the splendor of Venice in it. And yet, there too, are the inner contradictions of the system. The serene optimism of the early Renaissance is gone. Sixteenth-century architects began to realize that there was no solution; that it was impossible to bring the individual parts into a perfect union and at the same time to endow some of them with power. One can strive for the reconciliation of gradation and concatenation, but one can never reach it. Gradation, particularly, is the natural foe of integration.

Yet the architects did not give up. On the contrary, the struggle against the odds became more and more passionate. Architecture was on its way from the serene Renaissance to the excitement of the High Baroque. The climactic point of a system is not when it seems to fulfill itself, but when it makes the utmost effort to reconcile the irreconcilable. We speak of an architectural system as long as one ideal of configuration is valid. Beyond this basic and, perhaps, somewhat nebulous idea there is nothing permanent, there is only change. The relationships of the whole and of the parts, and of the parts to each other, are dictated by the ruling idea of the system, but the variations are infinite. The artist searches for ever new solutions. This is the essence of artistic development. If there were a possibility of fulfillment, or if an accomplishable concept did arise, it would mean the stagnation of artistic development.

And now let us go on to an adversary who seems to foster the goals of the system, but in reality is an enemy. The trend toward intensified self-assertion of the parts strengthened the vertical columns, pilasters, and piers, as well as the horizontal bands and cornices. Even the filling within the framework, and finally the whole surface, and the body itself, began to expand and to move. Everything was increasingly affected by the desire for unification and differentiation simultaneously, until the conflict assumed dramatic proportions. The step from self-assertion to exaggerated self-exhibition looks quite natural, but it is questionable whether this process is automatic or whether such a development would take place, were there not outer spiritual and social forces promoting, or at least, prompting it. Perhaps I had better not dwell on this problem, since the metaphysics of architecture is beyond the scope of this investigation.

The Laurenziana and the Scuola San Rocco reveal not only the clash between the horizontal and the vertical, but also the rival claims of framework and filling. The more the framework is accentuated, the less the wall can demonstrate its quality as a confining element. Only the framework, not the massive wall, is apt to convey the ideas of concatenation and gradation. Therefore the piercing of the façades necessarily increased with the progress of the Baroque. Local Venetian tradition gave preference to the framework at an early moment: Sansovino's Palazzo Corner (1532),[35] and his Library (about 1535).[36] The height of this development can be seen in the façade of Bernini's Palazzo Barberini (1630)[37] in Rome, and in Longhena's Palazzo Pesaro (1679)[38] in Venice. In Baroque church architecture, too, the framework ultimately triumphed over the wall. Framework and wall were still of equal weight on San Luigi dei Francesi by Della Porta (1589)[39] in Rome. The conflict became acute on San Carlo alle Quattro Fontane (1662-1667)[40] by Borromini. The framework dominates in San Giovanni in Laterano (1735)[41] by Alessandro Galilei. Incidentally, while the piercing of the walls is a menace to surface concatenation, it is a help in spatial unification. It tears up the plane but brings the interiors into relationship with the outer world.

Architects did not feel at ease when confronted with the conflict between the vertical and the horizontal. They found a remedy in using those volutes which are some of the most characteristic features of Baroque church architecture. The volutes serve the double purpose of tying the upper story to the lower, and of eliminating or mitigating the conflict between the directions. Such volutes can already be found in their double function on Alberti's front of Santa Maria Novella (1448-1470),[42] and they continue to perform their task deep into the eighteenth century (Cathedral of Syracuse, by Pompeo Picherali, about 1730).[43] One may also consider the introduction of spiral towers as an effort to reconcile the vertical and horizontal (Sant' Ivo by Borromini, 1642–1660;[44] San Gregorio, Messina, by Guarini, 1660[45]). The twisted columns can be interpreted in the same way, although they, too, were favored because they blend more perfectly with space than do straight columns. All the problems of the Baroque are exemplified in the façade of Il Gesù in Rome as completed by Della Porta (1575).[46] Here is the conflict between horizontal and vertical, and here the parts vie for superiority within the whole. The double pediment over the entrance and the scrolls on the sides act as intermediaries between the vertical central axis and the horizontals of the ground floor. Compare this with the impression of composure and balance in the Palazzo Pitti a century before.[47]

The crowning cornice was a problem with which the Renaissance was greatly occupied. Should the main cornice be proportioned to the top floor or to the whole building? Michelangelo resorted to the latter solution on the Palazzo Farnese.[48] It is obvious that an entirely satisfying solution was impossible. Neither the Baroque system, nor any other, can settle the divergent claims of the whole and of the single parts.

To find the way out of all these conflicts, the architects of the Renaissance turned with an almost unshakable faith to the doctrine of the proportions. Many treatises of the later Baroque, as well as frequent reprints of famous Renaissance publications, prove that the architects of the seventeenth and eighteenth centuries, too, clung to this doctrine hopefully. The most renowned early adherent was Leone Battista Alberti, in whose writings we may discover the essence of the theory of the Baroque system. I shall come back to his aesthetics later.[49] At San Andrea of Mantua (1470),[50] Alberti made a remarkable attempt to eliminate the antagonism between the central vertical axis and the horizontal members. Its arcaded porch running through three stories was scarcely imitated. His façade of Santa Maria Novella, however, became the prototype of countless churches, the most influential among them being Il Gesù.[51] The big arch of San Andrea plays down the competition of the verticals and horizontals. Although it helps to unify the façade with the body, unfortunately it tears apart the entire front. Here again is an insoluble problem which occupied the architects through three centuries. Ordinarily, they did not even try to reach unity between the body and the front of the church, and made of the latter an independent piece of decoration. Alberti, however, attempted, though unsuccessfully, to bring the element of depth into harmony with the surface pattern of the façade. Seen side by side, Alberti's two façades show how he struggled against the contradictions latent in the Baroque system.

Further instances of the discrepancy between the façade and the body are Della Porta's San Luigi dei Francesi,[52] Santa Maria della Vittoria in Rome by Carlo Maderna and Giovan Battista Soria (begun 1605),[53] and the Cathedral of Brescia by Gianbattista Lantana (1604).[54] The façade of San Giovanni in Laterano by Alessandro Galilei (1735)[55] is simply a screen, almost independent of the interior, like a stage setting. Nevertheless, the arched openings refer to depth as strongly as any Baroque portal. An exceptional solution of the problem of the façade was tried by Giulio Romano. In the church at San Benedetto Po (1540),[56] he continued the pattern of the main front, on the sides, with an effect of sweeping unity and harmony, but made the dome inconspicuous. The relationship of cupola, nave, and façade was of utmost importance and had many facets. The Baroque architect was expected to harmonize the upward-pointing dome with the rather inert body, and bring both into accord with the two-dimensional front. He was to reconcile the demand for union with the demand for gradation. In the interior his task was made still more difficult by the ritual exigencies. Obviously, the best position for the altar is the end of the main nave. Yet, should the altar be the main feature, or the dome? The Renaissance for a while gave preference to the completely centralized plan. Aesthetically, this was possibly the best compromise between the two main features rivaling for dominance. But it was not the best solution for divine service. Hence the centralized plan had to disappear almost entirely in the seventeenth century. The intricacy of all these problems marks one of the most crucial stages in the struggles of the Baroque system. It would be impossible to discuss all the vicissitudes of this struggle, from Bramante's choir of Santa Maria delle Grazie in Milan,[57] down to the Superga by Juvara near Turin.[58] The history of St. Peter's alone could serve as an illustration. The unification of the parts in every direction and the rule of a crowning feature could most nearly be achieved on circular or polygonal plans. It is significant that the centralized scheme had already appeared in the earliest Renaissance. In studying the plan of Santa Maria degli Angeli (about 1430) by Brunelleschi,[59] to return to him for a moment, we should not hunt for possible distant ancestors like the Cathedral of Aix-la-Chapelle. We must rather look ahead toward Giuliano da Sangallo's Madonna delle Carceri, Prato (about 1485),[60] toward Bramante and Michelangelo. We will then better appreciate the significance of Brunelleschi's work. Let us not overlook the fact that behind the lucidity of the interior of Santo Spirito at Florence there looms already the rivalry between the two opposed principles of church planning. Brunelleschi felt he had to bridge the gulf between the longitudinal nave and the centralized east end, the latter, naturally, being complete only on three sides. To obtain unity, he carried the aisles around the entire room.

Two polar attempts at reconciliation can be seen in San Alessandro at Milan by Lorenzo Binago (about 1602),[61] and in Santa Maria della Consolazione at Todi by Cola da Caprarola (begun 1508).[62] The latter emphasized unification, the cornices tying the parts together with tremendous power. For Lorenzo Binago, hierarchic gradation had the most meaning. His façade climaxes in the central portico; then the upward movement is taken over by the two satellite towers, and finally by the dome. His church as a whole, by its very form, is well tied into its environment, while Santa Maria della Consolazione stands in exalted solitude.

In its youth the Baroque system had attacked all the problems with comparatively little regard for inner contradictions and outer conditions. In the course of time, the compromise of the longitudinal church type won more and more adherents. Peruzzi and Raphael abandoned the centralized scheme when in charge of St. Peter's.[63] The future did not belong to the type of Todi; it belonged rather to that of San Benedetto Po or of San Alessandro, that is, to the differentiated group. This conforms better to practical requirements and fits better into its surroundings. But it is this very differentiation which breeds the coming disintegration. The case of Santa Maria della Salute at Venice by Baldassare Longhena (begun 1631),[64] will help to clarify my point. This church seems to belong to the centralized type, but the octagonal main room and the choir are almost independent of each other. Accordingly, a rivaling lower cupola is seen on the exterior, behind the huge main dome.

In profane architecture there was an analogous development. The Villa Reale at Poggio a Caiano by Giuliano da Sangallo (1483)[65] is a cubic form with a central hall. Later, for example in most of Palladio's villas, elongated houses were preferred to the earlier compact structures. Again, as in church building, there was a turning away from isolation to closer integration with the environment. Thus, we come face to face with another contradiction deriving directly from the general tendency of the system. In striving for the higher unity of house and surroundings, architects were forced to give up the compactness of the building itself. Or, to put it in a more general way, one can not reach "perfect" unity within each part and, at the same time, within the whole.

The exaggeration of details, which is rightly considered particularly characteristic of the Baroque, was of course a consequence of the system's tendency to dramatic self-representation. Thus the minutest feature became heavier and more plastic. Whatever the reasons for the exaggeration of the single feature, the effect was lack of harmony. Ultra-Baroque details which expressed the living forces with particular intensity, ultimately undermining the system, were the twisted columns, the broken or cleft pediments, the pediments consisting of diverging semi-arches, and so on. The desire to underline concatenation was the reason for breaking cornices around the capitals.

Palladianism survived, especially in Western Europe, perhaps because, in its reticence, it better expressed the Baroque system than the ultra-Baroque features which perverted its idea.

The overemphasis on spatial interrelations is already perceivable in the interiors of Palladio's churches of San Giorgio Maggiore and Il Redentore,[66] at Venice (1576–1592), with the airy colonnades screening the main apses. Such overemphasis contributed to the disruption of the system even more than the exaggerated accentuation of single features. It had been expected that the arcades of Renaissance courts would efface the rigid separation of the interiors from the outer world, and that loggias would likewise create spatial unity by blending mass and space. This overwhelming longing for unity finally led from intensified spatial inter-relationship to coalescence of the rooms. The process of discarding all limitations was probably not merely mechanical or self-generating. The physical transforma-tions were effected by metaphysical aspirations; above all, by the desire to melt into the universe. In due course the Baroque system had to pass from the finite to the infinite. This becomes manifest in the increasing dominance of the voids over the walls; the vistas opened through the interiors; the replacing of the panels by mirrors; and the illusionistic paintings on ceilings and walls.

After the compactness of the architectural body was gone, the single parts began to separate. Already, Cornelius Gurlitt has observed,[67] the corner turret of Bor-romini's San Carlo alle Quattro Fontane has no connection with the main mass; the canopy over the central window is also an element apart. The semicircular porches of Santa Maria della Pace by Pietro da Cortona (1655) and Sant' Andrea al Quirinale by Bernini (1678)[68] speak out loudly what Borromini's canopy states rather modestly: the extrication of the parts. The loosely appended portico became common about 1800. Milestones on the way are Bernini's Santa Maria dell'Assunta at Ariccia (1664),[69] and the Superga by Juvara (1718–1731). This last is considered to be the very beginning of neoclassicism.[70]

The disintegration of the interior into single, nearly independent compartments, as foreshadowed already in the Salute, becomes patent in Guarini's church of the Consolata at Turin (1679). The visitor, after having passed the oblong hall, which actually is a second church, is surprised to see several individual, self-centered rooms: the polygonal main hall and the oval altar room on the central axis, and the two circular chapels on each side.[71] Each room has its own cupola. In the earlier San Ambrogio at Genoa (finished by Lantana, 1589) the first, second, and fourth bays of the aisles are finished by cupolas—the third bay coincides with the barrel-vaulted transept—but there the continuity of the aisles was not yet given up. San Ambrogio, the Salute, and the Consolata represent different stages of the dis-integration of the interior, or, the emancipation of its parts. After the concept of all-embracing unity had turned out to be utopian, the parts were restored to their own rights.

The trend toward intensified self-representation also brought the system into conflict with the material. The tendency to express the binding forces at any cost led to more and more disregard for the proprieties of the stone; it was treated as if it were soft, flexible, organic matter. There was only one step from the anthropo-morphic interpretation of the forms—the "male" Doric, the "female" Ionic, the "virginal" Corinthian—to the introduction of the human body or animal forms into the tectonic arts. All those atlantes and caryatids, those furniture legs with joints and paws, those water-spouting lion heads, dolphins, and so on, have a triple origin: the antiquarian interests of the humanists, the contemporaneous animistic concept of the universe, and the particular faculty of organic forms for embodying living forces otherwise strange to inanimate matter but ever present in all things, according to Baroque belief.

The plastic character of the single features, and the anthropomorphic or animistic transformation of the tectonic elements, became main characteristics of the production of the Baroque. One may rightly speak of the era of Brunelleschi-Michelangelo-Sansovino-Bernini as the epoch of the architect-sculptor.

VIII

ITALIAN THEORIES FROM ALBERTI TO LODOLI

ARCHITECTURAL THEORIES, from the early Renaissance to the late Baroque, tell the same story as do the buildings; theory and practice were in perfect accord. The theorists were not the leaders as theorists occasionally pretend to be. They advocated the same compositional ideals that were visualized in buildings.

Quite suddenly, in the midst of the eighteenth century, a new theory arose in Italy which diametrically contradicted all earlier doctrines. These doctrines were entirely formalistic and supported the contemporary aesthetic pattern. The newly arisen doctrine, however, was strictly functionalistic. Its only postulate was rigorous conformity to practicality and to the material. So far as we know, this theory never materialized. In reality, Italian practice continued to stick to the old formalism, and only toward the end of the eighteenth century did some of the Italian architects advance to a new composition. Quite different was the development in France. Here the doctrine of functionalism came to the surface about two decades later than in Italy, but simultaneous with its emergence French architects began to search for new patterns adequate to express the ideals of a revolutionary era.

One of the first to compose a treatise on architecture in the Renaissance, about 1460, was the architect-sculptor Antonio Averlino Filarete.[72] His book, *Trattato d'architettura,* centering about the description of the utopian city of Sforzinda, tells much of the survival of the Middle Ages in the Renaissance. Nevertheless, in his treatise we may also find the essence of Renaissance doctrine. Filarete stresses the importance of the proportions,[73] and in speaking of the Cathedral of Sforzinda, he points out how important is the relationship between the whole and the parts.[74] This emphasis on the proportions and the analogies he found between the human body and architectural performance,[75] were not simply derived from Vitruvius. The Renaissance most certainly would not have taken over these concepts had they not expressed its own aspirations. Filarete's designs, with their symmetry and emphasis on the center, follow the Renaissance pattern (elevations of the Cathedral,[76] of the Hospital,[77] and the church project for Bergamo[78]). Strict symmetry is also characteristic of his schemes for private buildings such as the Houses of A Nobleman, A Merchant, An Artisan.[79]

At the end of the fifteenth century there appeared a fantastic novel, *Hypnerotomachia Poliphili,* by the Dominican friar Francesco Colonna, which reveals the whole body of the compositional principles of the Renaissance. In the opinion of Colonna, one idea was to be of chief importance in all building: the harmonious integration of the elements in the structure. (Perhaps it was harmony with the universe itself that Colonna meant.) This the architect must consider his major goal; this must be his first concept, or the "preconceived" idea of the building; decoration is merely accessory and can easily be invented later.

Sopra tutto il solido integro conseruando, & cum luniuerso conciliato. Il quale solido chiamo tutto il corpo della fabrica che e il principale intento, & inuentione & praecogitato, & Symmetria dil Architecto, sencia gli accessorii bene examinato & conducto, Indica (si non me fallo) Ia praestantia dil suo ingiegnio, perche lo adornare poscia e cosa facile.[80]

When Colonna asks for harmony of the structure with the "universe" (*cum luniuerso conciliato*) there emerges already one of those contradictions which, centuries later, were to lead to the downfall of the Baroque system. For one can never combine, or, as he says, "reconcile" the integrality of the building with "universal" harmony. Either the building is complete within itself, or it forms a subordinate part of the "universe." In the preparatory stage of the Baroque system its destiny was already foreshadowed.

Colonna's most succinct statement is the laconic sentence: *Turpe e qualunque parte al suo principe non congruente.*[81] This means that the parts are to be subordinated to the main feature, which he called the *principe;* and further, that the parts must conform. A similar statement deals with the particular case of the entrance door: *Uno integro portale miro & conspicuo, & ad tutto lo aedificio proportionato.*[82] The postulates *proportionato* and *conspicuo* reflect the new Renaissance ideal. The *proportionato* was just as strange to the Middle Ages, as was the *conspicuo* to the classic ideal of undifferentiated beauty. The woodcut of the pyramid by his fictitious architect Lichas Libycus,[83] shows a "conspicuous" portal and harpies' feet of metal joining the obelisk to its base, *ambiendo ligavano lo infimo socco di uno grande Obelisco.*[84] A definite aesthetic function is assigned to each of the features. Nothing is more important to Colonna than the harmonization and integration of the parts, *gratificare lo obiecto cum lo obtuto.*[85] To obtain this result, Colonna recommends the two great panaceas of his epoch, proportionality and symmetry, *miranda & exquisita Symmetria,*[86] or, *La praeclara dispositione di Architectura, & la obstinata Symmetria.*[87] His Temple of Venus,[88] is given the form which promises the most perfect unity; it is designed on a circular plan, crowned by a mighty dome. Again we see the volutes which Brunelleschi had used on the lantern of the Cathedral of Florence to underline the structural design, and we see from Colonna's words how he favored the idea of tying the parts and establishing a correspondence between the inner space and the outer structure: *Cum consentanei illigamenti intrinseci & extrinseci congrui.*[89] Another passage conveys the same idea: *Alla congruentia della structura opportuna e la integritate dela harmonia,*

Imperoche omni cingibile ligamento intraneo, expostula el concincto extraneo.[90]
Most elucidating is the suggestion that the architect, after having conceived the
general form, "divide" the building into smaller elements: *Poscia licentemente
quello* [solido corpo] *inuento, Lo Architecto perminute diuisione el reduce . . .
dapo la inuentione la principale regula peculiare al Architecto e la quadratura.*[91]

One of the basic differences between Renaissance and Baroque was thought
to lie in the opposed principles of addition and division. Yet it is not enough to
look upon a colonnade with equidistant columns merely as the sum of the columns.
To grasp the significance of the composition we must take the entire colonnade as
a motif in itself. Thus, even in the extreme case of the Foundling Hospital at
Florence, the main point is not the "added up" arcade, but the vertical subdivision
of the front into differentiated stripes and the less conspicuous, yet very significant,
horizontal subdivision by doors and windows into compartments.

The Renaissance architects followed Vitruvius[92] in considering the human
body, by its proportions and the correspondence of the parts, as a perfect model:
*Imperò il sapientissimo maestro nostro al bene participatamente proportionato, e
decoramente vestito corpo humano assimiglia lo aedificio.*[93]

Indicative of the identity of the basic principles in the Renaissance and the High
Baroque are Tommaso Temanza's enthusiastic words on Colonna's remarks regarding the *congruentia della structura*.[94] This Venetian of the late eighteenth
century recognized in the precepts of the Renaissance friar the "most splendid
rule" which ultimately would lead to perfect unity.

Quì Polifilo accenna il più bel precetto, che dar possa un dotto, ed eccellente architetto,
in fatto dei Templi, ed è, che i legamenti o sian fascie, e cornici, che ricorrono, e
ricingono internamente le muraglia rispondano a quelli, che le ricingono esternamente;
onde l'opera riesca regolare, ed armoniosa, conseguendo così quella simplicità ed
unità, . . . in cui consiste la perfezione di tutte le cose.[95]

Such are the views set forth in Colonna's text, which Temanza termed "a
dream full of wisdom and mystery" (*sogno pieno di sapere, e assai misterioso*).[96]
In spite of Colonna's strange language, his meaning is clear. He offers a deep insight into the architectural thought of the Renaissance.

From Colonna's book we learn that the Renaissance had already added to the
ancient ideal of perfect numerical relations the concepts of the preëminence of one
part, the unification of all, and their integration into the whole. It is of great importance to grasp the difference between the two epochs, antiquity and the Renaissance.
I therefore want to add one more passage from Colonna which throws further
light on the ideals of the early Renaissance. This passage is clearer than Colonna's
usual odd mixture of Italian dialects and corrupt Latin. In speaking of the "super-
excellent" Hall with the Throne of the Queen he emphasizes that it was distinguished not only by the most "exquisite" measurements and forms, but also by

the correspondence of the parts and their convergence toward the center. The ideal of differentiated architectural values comes forth in the description of the Hall which

era piu de laltre subleuata per la locatione del throno della Regina. Per laquale cosa omni parte accuratissimamente di materia, di numero, di forma ad linea, & qualunque minima parte & locatione aequatissimamente, & allibella correspondeua, & cusi mutuamente la parte dextra cum la sinistra & de qui & deli cum exquisitissimo congresso conuenivano. Del quale superexcellente loco ciascuno alamento extenso era di passi uintiocto.[97]

The fundamentals of the new system are contained in the *Ten Books on Architecture* by Leone Battista Alberti. Like Colonna, Alberti asks for proportionality and "order":

All these things [ornament; rarity and beauty of the stone] are very noble in themselves; but they will make no figure if there is not care and art used in their composition or putting together: for every thing must be reduced to exact measure, so that all the parts may correspond with one another, the right with the left, the lower parts with the upper, with nothing interfering that may blemish either the order or the materials.[98]

Beauty is the "consent and agreement of the parts of a whole."[99] To attain it there is, according to Alberti, no better help than the proportions. Yet, for the Renaissance, proportionality was no end in itself, but rather the prerequisite of unity: "Let them bear that Proportion among themselves, that they may appear to be an entire and perfect Body, and not disjoynted and unfinished Members."[100]

Alberti's attitude does not differ widely from that of the late Baroque when he approves variety if coherence is not impaired by it. "Variety is without Dispute a very great Beauty in every Thing, when it joyns and brings together in a regular manner Things different but proportionable to each other."[101] In no case must the members appear "separate and divided from the rest of the Body."[102] To Alberti, the main thing is the whole, which he conceives in humanistic terms. Obviously depending on Vitruvius, he finds in the structure a simile of man's corporeality: "As the Members of the Body are correspondent to each other, so it is fit that one Part shou'd answer to another in a Building."[103] The "force and spirit of all the parts"[104] shall unify the structure to make it "one body."[105] Unity would be disturbed if the parts were not balanced. "Let those [ornaments] which are at equal distances on each side, be proportioned exactly alike."[106] The supreme rule which should govern the parts, however, is the principle of hierarchy. Here Alberti goes far beyond Vitruvius:

To every Member therefore ought to be allotted its fit Place and proper Situation; not less than Dignity requires, not greater than Conveniency demands; not in an impertinent or indecent Place, but in a Situation so proper to itself, that it could be set nowhere else more fitly. Nor should the Part of the Structure, that is to be of the greatest Honour, be thrown into a remote Corner . . . nor that which should be most private, be set in too conspicuous a Place.[107]

According to Alberti, ruling and subordinate parts should enter into perfect union, so that "nothing could be added, diminished or altered, but for the worse."[108] Perfect union is to Alberti the "quality so noble and divine," *cosa grande, & divina*.[109]

The very arrangement of Alberti's treatise reveals his viewpoint. His First Book is *De lineamentis,* or, in the translation by Leoni, "Of Designs"; the Second Book is *De materia,* "Of The Materials"; the Third Book, *De opere,* "Of the Work." The Fourth and Fifth Books are a continuation of the Third. The Sixth to Ninth Books deal with the embellishments; the Tenth Book with practical topics. Again, as with Colonna, decoration ranks last, composition first. And composition, or design (which in all probability is Alberti's *lineamenta*), is so extremely important, that the properties of the materials play a secondary role. It was not alone the late Baroque which trespassed against the nature of the materials, for Alberti proclaims in the first chapter of his First Book: "Nor has [the] Design any thing that makes it in its Nature inseparable from Matter" (*utiam tota aedificij forma et figura ipsis in lineamentis conquiescat. Neque habet lineamentum in se ut materiam sequatur*).[110] There is no doubt what Alberti meant by these words. Another passage makes his point clear: "We can in our Thought and Imagination contrive perfect Forms of Buildings entirely separate from Matter" (*seclusa omni material*).[111] The supremacy of design over matter appeared to the Renaissance and the Baroque as natural as it appears inconsistent to many people of our day.

Colonna's and Alberti's ideas on composition continued in all sixteenth-century treatises. Apart from technical topics, the largest space was devoted to the discussion of numerical relations. To many modern students these scholastic disquisitions have offered unsurpassed opportunity for minutiose, sterile research. Passages which reveal deeper artistic intentions of the architect-writers, and of the period itself, are quite rare in the treatises. One must look for them carefully if they are to be detected.

The concept of hierarchy is clearly formulated in Sebastiano Serlio's *Opere*.[112] The tendency towards unification appears both in his designs and text. Rusticated bands around the columns are a particularly characteristic feature of his "Doors."[113] The bands serve to tie the columns to the wall;[114] their shape reveals the disregard of the Renaissance for the properties of the material. In order to express supposed living forces the stone is treated as if it were flexible matter. The doors which Serlio devised in endless variations tell much of the feeling of the time. They are "dull" inventions[115] only to one who is exclusively interested in factual data and indifferent to those qualities which make of an object a work of art. Serlio allowed mural paintings in the interiors, but never on the outside where he felt they would disrupt the solid wall.[116]

Vincenzo Scamozzi's lengthy treatise seems at first glance to be merely a repetition of Vitruvius. But in expounding the Roman's categories, Scamozzi adds comments which are typical of the Renaissance and the Baroque. In defining *ordinatio* he speaks of ruling and subordinate parts, that is, of gradation.[117] The idea of concatenation underlies his explanation of eurythmy.[118] The concept of integration combining with concatenation is set forth in a remarkable passage in his Sixth Book.[119]

Palladio's ideal of configuration, which I have dealt with in the first part of this book, did not differ essentially from Alberti's. Thus, having become acquainted with the essence of the leading theories prior to about 1600 through both these men, let us go on to the doctrine of an influential architect of the late seventeenth century, Padre Guarino Guarini.[120] Guarini shares the views of the Renaissance; he refers to the authority of Vitruvius and agrees with his dictum on the necessity of careful proportioning: *Nulla architecto maior cura esse debet, nisi uti proportionibus ratae partis habeant aedificia rationum exactiones.*[121] Like Vitruvius, Guarini warns against blind obedience to the rules, and demands that the effect on the eye should be well considered.[122] The artists of the Renaissance and Baroque held Vitruvius in high esteem, because in many ways their feelings were like his own.

Guarini preferred, as did Alberti, beautiful arrangements to beautiful materials (*la materia non fa tanto bella la Fabbrica, quanto la bella disposizione*).[123] Balance and gradation must have meant as much to him as to his predecessors. The entrance door should be in the center and "not less ornate" than the other parts of the building; the windows should be arranged at equal distances; and the same number of rooms should be to the right as the left.[124] In this connection Guarini refers to Palladio—to him an authority, not a "classical" opponent.

In a remarkable passage, Guarini demands that over a void there should be nothing but a void, and over the solid nothing but mass: *Ogni vivo sia sopra il vivo, ed il muro sia sopra il muro.*[125] Here Guarini, who was a Baroque extremist, advances a view which had previously been expressed by Palladio, and later became so common among the French theorists of the eighteenth century. The demand that the *porte-à-faux*[126] must be avoided fits into the Baroque system, for void over void, mass over mass, warrants concatenation and unity. To the same end, Guarini recommended those continuous vistas in the interior which were extremely popular in the early eighteenth century; they came to be known as *enfilades,* while Guarini called them *incontramenti.*[127] (No doubt "mass over void" could be attacked because it is against solidity, but this argument would not hold good in the case of "void over mass.")

Predilection for concatenation manifests itself in Guarini's praise of Serlio's doors. He interprets the rustication of their columns as a means of tying them to the wall.[128] But the postulates of integration and gradation can hardly be found in his text. Was this a chance omission? Guarini's designs can provide the answer. They show that these two patterns did not mean much to him. On his church of San Filippo Neri, Turin (1714), as well as on other façades,[129] the apertures virtually dissolve the wall, and the overabundant decoration deprives the central portion of its predominance. Here the architect paid no heed to his own warning that the portal should be not less ornate than the sides. His designs clearly reveal that the disintegration of the Baroque system was progressing rapidly in his day. In Colonna's pyramid with its "wonderful and conspicuous portal"[130] the concept of superiority had been expressed unmistakably, and by the simplest means. In Guarini's entire work, as in the church of San Filippo Neri, the exaggeration of the hierarchical principle almost resulted in its negation.

I feel that it has been necessary for us to look back into the fifteenth century, for what happened in the eighteenth century could not easily have been evaluated without clarity on the vicissitudes of the Baroque system. Its latest and, for us, its most important stage could be treated only after discussion of the entire post-medieval development in Italy. Before we enter the century in which the most profound changes were to occur in architecture, a comment of Guarini's which fully reflects the thought of the Renaissance and the Baroque may be remembered: architecture should be an art which gratifies the senses; it should not be dominated by reason.[131]

Some Italian architectural publications of the latter eighteenth century differ fundamentally from all the treatises dealt with so far. The change which they reflect did not simply consist in a more scholarly attitude towards antiquity, derived from the increasing interest in archaeology. It rather meant a new attitude towards matter and pattern; it meant the transition from Baroque sensualism and animism to the spirit, or perhaps just the mood, of rationalism; from the Baroque ideal of hierarchical organization to the ideal of the rights of the individual. The new reasoning—it must be pointed out right here—was not to put an end to the *art* of building, although it influenced it to some extent.

The Italian architects were by no means as radical as were the Italian rationalistic writers. The latter rejected not merely traditional formality, but any kind of formal rule, convinced that the future belonged to a strictly functional architecture.

The Venetian Dominican Francesco Colonna had proclaimed the theory of the Renaissance-Baroque system; the Venetian Franciscan Carlo Lodoli was the first advocate of functionalism.[132] Lodoli himself left no writings behind him, but his lectures in a school for young Venetian nobles were taken down by Andrea Memmo and collected into a book entitled *Elementi di Architettura Lodoliana,*[133] published in Rome in 1786, twenty-five years after Lodoli's death. Two other sources which tell us of Lodoli's thought are the writings of Francesco Algarotti and Francesco Milizia. I believe it is best to present Lodoli's views chiefly on the basis of Algarotti's writings which came out when Lodoli was still alive. In his *Saggio sopra l'Architettura,*[134] Algarotti mentions that he often heard Lodoli discuss architectural topics, and this essay as well as his *Lettere sopra l'Architettura*[135] are particularly stimulating reading because he comments critically on Lodoli's views from the standpoint of a conservative. Algarotti is generally considered a brilliant but rather superficial writer and, because of his activities in the most diversified fields, as a dilettante. But he had discriminating taste, independent judgment, and attempted to be objective. He knew how to appreciate Lodoli, though he himself sided with the traditionalists. Thus he provides us not only with information about Lodoli's thought, but also gives a picture of the antagonistic currents of the period, whereas the Venetian patrician Memmo was a one-sided Lodoli partisan. Temporarily, Milizia also seems to have been a fervent adherent of the new doctrine. But it may be that sheer spirit of opposition caused him to inveigh against the old views. Altogether, Milizia had no firm conviction of his own. The writings of these three, Memmo, Algarotti, and Milizia, reveal that the Colonna-Guarini epoch definitely belonged to the past.

One is justified in calling Lodoli a revolutionary from Algarotti's characterization in the dedication of the *Saggio*. Lodoli appeared to him to embody the "philosophical mind" eager to penetrate to the last principle. Setting out to scrutinize architecture and to lay bare the very bases of all building, Lodoli began to feel that contemporary architecture was fundamentally wrong, *ella posa in falso*.[136] Algarotti saw in Lodoli's robust and at the same time fascinating argument a menace to the doctrine of Vitruvius which might become detrimental to classical building and contemporary as well.[137] Still more revolutionary than Lodoli's negative criticism were the novel ideas in which even Algarotti foresaw the possible rise of an entirely new art of building.

According to Lodoli, there were two ways in which to create a better and truer architecture and thus to overcome the past. In his first blast against the established system he declares:

In architecture only that shall show that has a definite function, and which derives from the strictest necessity. (Niuna cosa . . . metter si dee in rappresentazione, che non sia anche veramente in funzione.)[138]

Consequently, no useless ornament should be admitted (*niente ha da vedersi in una fabbrica, che non abbia il proprio suo uffizio, e non sia parte integrante della fabbrica stessa, che dal necessario ha da risultare onninamente l'ornato*).[139] Everything in contradiction to these principles should be condemned. They are the cornerstones of architecture (*abuso tutto quello, che tanto o quanto si allontana da un tale principio, che è il fondamento vero, la pietra angolare, su cui ha da posar l'arte architettonica*).[140] In his second commandment he observes:

Architecture must conform to the nature of the materials. (Tale esser dovrebbe l'Architettura, qualesi conviene alle qualità caratteristiche, alla pieghevolezza o rigidità delle parti componenti, a'gradi di forza resistente, alla propria essenza in una parola, o natura della materia che vien posta in opera.)[141]

When architecture will have attained these two great objectives—of being true to purpose and to matter—then only will it become honest and reasonable, and will be able to surpass all previous achievements:

Alle quali sostituirà quando che sia una Architettura sua propria, omogenea alla materia, ingenua, sincera, fondata sulla region vera delle cose, per cui salde si manterrano le fabbriche, intere, e in un fiore di lunghissima, e quasi che eterna giovanezza.[142]

That Algarotti had imbibed some of Lodoli's enthusiasm can be seen from the almost lyric tone of the last cited passage. This contains the friar's credo of the day to come when the glorious new architecture will arise and live on in perpetual youth, and calls to mind the dithyrambic effusions hymned by the prophets and protagonists of the Art Nouveau and the Secession with their slogan of *Ver Sacrum*.

It is to Algarotti's credit that he had the fullest understanding of the far-reaching significance of Lodoli's doctrine,[143] though he himself did not share these views.[144] Firmly rooted in the classical tradition, Algarotti resolutely defended it against the onslaught of his compatriot. There is, of course, no particular merit in maintaining tradition if one simply does not understand the new, as there is no merit in following uncritically a brilliant innovator. But even with Algarotti's understanding of Lodoli, he still felt that the realization of the new principles would bring a catastrophe in architecture. Nurtured in the *ancien régime* he feared for his beloved art "the most terrific consequences." His intellect grasped the great promise contained in Lodoli's thought, but his heart could not renounce what was to him supreme architectural beauty.[145]

Though he defended the traditional ways, he could not but admit their perplexing contradictions. It was not easy to meet the charge of Lodoli that in the past stone often had been shaped as if it were wood.[146] It was certainly absurd to have allowed a material to deny its own nature and use it to simulate another material. This was sheer masquerade or, to put it bluntly, a lie.[147] Yet Algarotti would not submit to this new self-confident and seemingly irrefutable theorem. Lodoli's disturbing criticism could not shake his belief in the old doctrine. An architecture which disguised the materials did not at all displease Algarotti.

Eschewing Lodoli's rationalism he held aloft once more the banner of the animistic concept of architecture. For support, he turned to the great authority of bygone times, Vitruvius, who had taught that architecture is a representative art. This view was shared by all who followed the Roman in spirit, Palladio among them who saw in architecture the "imitatrix" of nature.[148] To Vitruvius the "natural" primitive hut had been the model for all building.[149] It would be a mistake to consider the many eighteenth-century adherents of the Vitruvian log-cabin theory as rationalists. They still stuck to the time-honored animistic concept which related the structural elements to organic nature and wanted them shaped after plants, animals, or human forms. Algarotti also liked the old metaphors and spoke of the "skeleton" of the house,[150] and the "arms" connecting the supports of a bridge.[151] The capital was, of course, the *caput* to him.[152]

Algarotti, however, had still another reason to legitimize the forms which were so dear to him. Since wood could be carved more easily than stone, it offered greater facilities for embellishment, and the architect is justified in translating its forms into stone to obtain greater artistic perfection.[153] Algarotti's praise of wood finds its climax in the typically Baroque dictum: illusion is more beautiful than reality (*del vero più bella è la menzogna*).[154] Taking a position diametrically opposed to Lodoli, he found that the structure cannot be beautiful in itself; the ornaments beautify it.[155]

It was not given to Algarotti to follow the friar who intended to "purge" architecture from empty embellishments and illusionistic tricks.[156] In a letter to the architect Tommaso Temanza, on April 14, 1759, he wrote that he could not side with the "rigorists."[157] This manifests that as early as the 1750's the new program was already a topic of argument. Algarotti was in accord with the modernistic movement only insofar as he, too, declined to submit unconditionally to authority. Proof thereof is a passage in the early part of the *Saggio* written in 1756,[158] and a letter of October 5, 1758.[159] Nevertheless, he occasionally wondered whether the best way out of the dilemma might not be "drinking from the most pure fountains of Greece."[160] And he pondered over another problem of the time, whether the Italian design or the more comfortable French disposition was preferable. Apparently he had more respect for *Italiana correzione* than for the more modern French sacrifice of formality to convenience, which he contemptuously terms the *morbidezza oltramontana*.[161] Functionalism appeared to him morbid; formalism, however, right. Is it perhaps because the latter presupposes greater imaginative power? Algarotti found a jocular solution: he wished to live in a French house with a view of a Palladian structure.[162]

Andrea Memmo's presentation of Lodoli's doctrine differs from Algarotti's only in minor points. Though he censures the latter for having distorted Lodoli's views, in the main he tells the same story. He, too, finds that the friar was truly revolutionary;[163] that he was an enemy of authority, particularly of Vitruvius;[164] he disdained the ancients,[165] as well as the great masters of modern times, including Michelangelo and Palladio;[166] and was contemptuous of "popular" taste.[167] Lodoli opposed Baroque architects because they made of architecture a "plastic art."[168] Like him, Memmo ridicules those who find it safer to side with the official tenets.[169] Memmo, moreover, confirms that the dicta about function and representation were Lodoli's own,[170] and that the latter placed reason above all.[171]

In interior decoration, too, Lodoli wanted the design to be functional; for example, the furniture should be fitted to the form of the human body.[172] Memmo almost tires the reader by the endless repetition of Lodoli's opinions about the primacy of the material and the superfluity of decoration.[173] We learn from him that Lodoli's ideas became known as far back as the early 1740's,[174] and that Lodoli had put them into notes for a book. These were lost, as were the drawings which were made at his instructions.[175] About Lodoli's personality Memmo remarks that he set forth his theories with an enthusiasm bordering on frenzy, disregarding the criticism of the architects.[176] But, although Lodoli did not show a practical way from the past to the future, he was one of the highly interesting personalities in the Age of Reason who questioned the validity of the traditional principles and, if we can believe Abbate Angelo Uggeri, himself an architect, influenced architecture to some extent.[177]

Algarotti's writings reveal the crossing and overlapping currents of the Baroque, Romantic Classicism,[178] and the new "rigorism," or purism. It was a far cry from Alberti to Lodoli; from the principle of well-balanced organization of the parts to the goal of functionalism; from the disregard of the material—except for its sensuous beauty—to the strongest emphasis on its character. Yet Lodoli was not the protagonist of the architecture to come. He set forth astoundingly new principles, but did not provide answers to the questions, what architecture should look like, what should be its forms, and how the parts should be related to each other. We miss in his doctrine any suggestion as to the visualization of the new principles. Lodoli did not revolutionize architecture, and his doctrine itself did not bring about the architecture of the future. In believing that architecture could pass from formalism to functionalism, he missed the mark. The problem of the era seemed to him to lie only in abolishment of form. But the true problem was to find a new form able to express the changed attitudes. Some sound thought on functionalism was to play its part when a new form was developed, but only insofar as the architects struggled for form did they have a chance to renew the art of building.

The rationalistic outlook, we know today, did have some bearing on architectural development. Decoration was banned to a large extent after the second revolution, about 1900, and often, though not always, greater consideration was given to the "nature of the materials." But functionalism was not to become the exclusive ruler of architecture. The struggle for new patterns never ceased, the desire for form never died. Rationalism was only one factor in the profound change of architecture in the eighteenth century, and in no way the strongest.

Three little-known publications directed against the Baroque may be mentioned here. One is Teofilo Gallaccini's *Trattato sopra gli errori degli architetti,* published in 1767. The others are Antonio Visentini's *Osservazioni,* 1771, and Giambattista Passeri's *Discorso della ragione dell'architettura,* 1772. Gallacini's book had been written as early as 1621, but only appeared at a time when attacks on the Baroque were in fashion. Quite briefly, he was against any violation of the hierarchical order, and against the menace of disintegration.[179] Visentini branded the same defects as crimes against reason, while the rather superficial Passeri pleaded for *architettura regolata dalla ragion naturale.*[180] Though setting out from different principles, these writers held the same views on architecture, the one as an orthodox adherent of the basic rules of the Baroque system, the others as adepts in eighteenth-century rationalism. From this one may conclude that the inner contradictions of the Baroque system appeared in all of its stages, and that those who stood up to defend it were never able to do anything against the natural historical process, or to cope with fate.

Much can be learned about the change in architectural thought during the eighteenth century from Francesco Algarotti; still more from Francesco Milizia. Neither writer was an original thinker, yet each presents a different aspect of the transformation. In the fluent language of the versatile connoisseur Algarotti tells of the clash of a great and still powerful tradition with death-dealing new ideas. Milizia, too, could not quite get rid of the old trend of thought. Eventually, the modern ideas seem to have overtaken him, and though he himself was not deeply affected by them, his writings reflect the vehemence of the onrush against tradition.

Milizia has been labeled a typical classicist.[181] Certainly he was slightly affected by Romantic Classicism, that literary trend of wistful retrospection. But his personality was quite complex, at one time appearing as a stout defender of the Baroque, at another as an anticlassical purist. These contradictory attitudes no doubt sprang from his awareness of the growing disintegration of the Baroque. There were two ways to ward off the pending danger to architecture: one was the strictest confinement to the basic ideas of the old system; the other was in joining the rigorists. Milizia, alternately, became an ally of both parties. He was a victim of the contemporaneous unrest; his personality was "split" under the changing impact of the contending forces; he was, as he put it, "a heterogeneous compound of contradictions,"[182] or, as a malicious contemporary said, *il Don Chisciotte del bello ideale.*[183] He was not a leader who selected the most promising trend to emphasize. Standing at the crossroads, he recommended trying all ways. To protect architecture, he wanted to save it from "extravagance, license, and abuses," as the moralizing critics of the era put it; he wanted to free it from the symptoms of that disintegration which I consider to have been a part of the historical process. At the end of the Introduction to his *Lives of Celebrated Architects* he declares that his intention is to cure architecture.

Wherever the author has discovered faults, he can with safety affirm that they gave him pain; and if he has exposed them, it is only with a hope of preventing, if possible, their recurrence and increase.[184]

To Milizia *abuso* is, above all, excessive ornamentation.[185] Ornaments are deceitful parasites (*parasiti intriganti*).[186] Milizia spoke a straightforward language, quite different from the courtier Algarotti's elegant phrasing. Lavishness of decoration is not to the credit of a building,[187] he quietly states. He is opposed to any exaggeration,[188] and inveighs against the seventeenth century as the *secolo della bizzaria*,[189] contrasting it as the century of corruption, to the sixteenth, the century of correctness (*secolo della corruzione—secolo della correzione*).[190] Consequently, he is particularly hostile to Borromini.[191] He makes a stand against *bizzaria* because its "system" destroys the order and the forms: *La bizzaria fa un sistema distruttore dell'ordine e delle forme dettate dalla natura, costitutive dell'arte.*[192] Order to him is the concatenation of the parts.[193] Again and again he asks for unity, symmetry, and eurhythmy. Unity, he finds, is given when the parts are related to the whole[194] and subordinated to it.[195] The happy union—*l'unione felice*[196]—can be attained only by gradation.[197] He claims that the parts are not equal to all; that there is to be a dominant one (*oggetto principale*) to which the others lead,[198] and that the same compositional rules are valid both in architecture and in painting.[199] At all times, the principle of "economy," which to him means the preëminence of one part, has to be heeded.[200] Milizia's Baroque bias appears also in the demand that crude contrasts be avoided, and soft transition be aimed at (*addolcimento* versus *durezza*).[201] No doubt he still was an adherent of the Baroque system. He blames the exaggerations which might harm it, and some minor shortcomings (bays with chapels accompanying the main nave, which are confusing and rebel against unity, *in ribellione contro l'unità*).[202] In the same paragraph he explains further that unity does not exclude variety, but is disturbed by discrepancy (*discrepanza*). Such a discrepancy is found in an attic story above the main cornice, which appears to him as one structure over another.[203] He criticizes St. Peter's for being divided into too many parts,[204] and the façade of Sant' Andrea della Valle for having no relationship to its interior.[205] The portico of the Pantheon is to him a mere appendage insufficiently connected to the main body.[206]

Milizia's occasional conventional praise of Vitruvius may give the impression that he "accepted without question the doctrines and rules that Vitruvius propounded in the age of the Emperor Augustus."[207] Only, however, a superficial knowledge of Milizia can lead to such a conclusion. Hardly any man was so full of critical skepticism as Milizia. Though his feelings were toward the art of the

Baroque, intellectually he rebelled against tradition. Undoubtedly his vehement attacks were prompted by the slogans of the prophets and fathers of the French Revolution, and the alluring "back to nature" device. He thought that even the Greeks had gone astray by disregarding nature, and art had declined by imitating the Greek: *Da imitazione in imitazione l'arte si snatura.*[208] He railed at the despotism of authority—*dispotismo dell'autorità*[209]—and ridiculed the blind reverence for antiquity—*un cieco irragionevole rispetto per l'Antichità.*[210] Homer, Plato, Phidias, and so many others, Vitruvius not excepted, were to him just "cadavers"; their cult appeared absurd to him (*incensare Omero, Platone, Fidia . . . Vitruvio . . . e tanti altri cadaveri*).[211] Indeed, Milizia was no true classicist.

Milizia felt that the legacy of antiquity was exhausted. He believed that it made no sense to copy classical art, and that one could not revive it by the device of petty alterations. He knew that the popular idea of the invention of a new order of columns in the seventeenth and eighteenth centuries was nothing but transient pastime;[212] was aware that the agony of the classic art had come, and that revival was impossible.[213] He looked at the Gothic with great objectivity, without the disdain of the humanists, and without the sentimentality of the early nineteenth century. He disliked the unrest of the buttresses and pinnacles, but appreciated the boldness and impressiveness of the vaultings.[214] Of all the crosscurrents of his day the soundest, perhaps, was the new attitude toward nature. Seen from the twentieth century, there was much sentimentality and self-deception in it, yet it offered a way in which architecture could proceed to new goals. Milizia was among those who recognized the promise contained in modern landscape architecture. He sensed that there was something contrary to nature in the layout of the Baroque park, for nature does not know of eurhythmic arrangement, of parterres, or of straight canals.[215]

There were two additional trends to which he subscribed wholeheartedly, as we shall see, prevalent in French revolutionary architecture: the first that towards expressiveness, *l'architecture parlante,* and the second that towards grandeur. He asked for symbolic architecture—to him architecture was *linguaggio per disposizioni ingegnose e significative degli edificj*[216]—and for majesty of appearance.[217] Great masses, great forms, great "traits," great parts, are the ingredients of the works of good taste: *Grandi masse, grandi forme, grandi tratti, grandi parti sono gl'ingredienti delle opere di buon gusto.*[218] In particular, he disliked the alveolate interiors of the theaters.[219]

But again and again we find Milizia not firm in his views. In the *Dizionario* he wants the character of the structure to be expressed by its ornaments,[220] yet a few pages later he declares that sobriety and convenience only should direct the decoration.[221] In the *Principj* he goes a step further along the line of functionalism. He finds that architectural consistency requires that the proportions conform to the purpose of the building, and expects that the specific qualities of the materials be taken into account.[222] In *Dell'arte di vedere nelle Belle Arti del Disegno,* he demands that in architecture everything must be justified by necessity[223] and solemnly states that gratifying the senses is not to be the ultimate goal of the arts.[224] Again in the *Principj,* he condemns everything which is merely ornamental[225] and, plagiarizing Algarotti,[226] reproduces almost literally his version of Lodoli's functionalistic creed.[227]

Since the novel ideas Milizia set forth were not his own, it is no wonder that he contradicted himself so frequently. It did not take him long to remodel his views. He changed them almost from page to page, so that the *Principj* emerges as a book without any crystallized principles. After having proclaimed Lodoli's stern doctrine in the beginning, at the end he withdraws from the position of the rigorists. Now he declares complete abstinence from ornament is not good; if it were, a nude wall would be the most beautiful thing.[228] Since, in addition, he harps on the importance of symmetry and eurhythmy, proportions and decoration,[229] it is clear that his modernism did not derive from a deep conviction. Just as he bowed to the romantic at times, so did he bow to the rationalistic at other times. This explains his references to the first principles, the natural, the true,[230] or "the positive and eternal principles, derived from the very nature of things."[231] The preacher of freedom from authority[232] shifted helplessly from one extreme to the other and to all appearances was somewhat self-conscious, despite the revolutionary *élan* of his words. Altogether, Milizia's writings leave the impression that the ideas which, about 1750, were those only of Lodoli the solitary thinker and a few converts, now were well rooted and belonged to a large community of progressive minds. Already at about 1780 the torchbearers were out to spread the light which had been kindled by the vanguard of the mid-century. It was not long before Milizia's works were translated into French, Spanish, English, and German.[233] This is a further proof that the time was ripe for the new ideas. If functionalism itself did not find realization, at least the geometrical forms coming closest to it gained popularity. Milizia praised the suave forms (of the past),[234] but also extolled the modern rigid forms. The square in particular appeared beautiful to him for its simplicity: *Il quadrato è bello, come sono belle tutte le figure geometriche; sono belle per la loro semplicità.*[235] The entire late eighteenth century is mirrored in Milizia's writings; we find in them also the echo of the tirades of the French revolutionary orators. Milizia explains that the decay of Greek art was brought about when "the rich, the courtiers, the kings, became the arbiters of taste, instead of the philosophers."[236]

It is not an easy matter to decide whether Milizia acclaimed the principles of the rigorists to shock the reader, *pour épater le bourgeois;* whether the general spirit of insurrection or a sincere artistic conviction guided him. In conclusion, I should like to record some of his boldest critical attacks which made him many enemies in papal Rome. Two were directed against Michelangelo's "Moses" and "Pietà,"[237] another against his Porta Pia.[238] And a fourth was aimed at the overdecorated sacristy of St. Peter's (1775) by Marchionne. Milizia's description of the monuments of Rome was climaxed by a comparison of the sacristy with the Cloaca Maxima, vilifying the first, and glorifying the strict matter-of-fact character of the second. To him, the sacristy was the worst, the ancient sewer the best structure of Rome.[239] It is no wonder that soon he became an outlaw in the Eternal City.[240]

When Milizia expressed the hope that the salutary crisis, *la crisi salutare*,[241] would come before long, he apparently was not aware that it had already started in France.

In postmedieval times it had become more and more common for leading architects to express their ideas in writing. The great transformation during the eighteenth century can be fully understood only by paying due attention to the Italian theorems and the publications of the progressive French architects, just as the changes about and after 1900 are hardly comprehensible if one has not read Henry van de Velde, Otto Wagner, Frank Lloyd Wright, and Le Corbusier. Beside the architectural writings there are other, not strictly architectural, media which can help elucidate the architectural thought of a period as well as buildings can, or perhaps even better: decorations erected for only occasional use, including stage settings; designs made by architects without any prospect of execution; and the fantasy designs of architects. These different media are important because, to a greater or lesser degree, they are less subject to materials, the wishes of the patron, the chances of the site, etc. Architectural drawings, moreover, have come down to us almost unaltered. Their source value can hardly be overrated. In them the creative architect could say what he wanted. Theatrical decorations, which usually lag behind architectural designs, are nevertheless particularly instructive since they reveal how far the artists could go without becoming unintelligible to the public. Stage designs, of course, are always conditioned by technical factors. Fullest freedom of visualization of the artistic goals of a period belongs only to designs emanating from the unrestricted fantasy of the architect.

IX

GIAMBATTISTA PIRANESI

ANY PERIOD of extraordinary excitement will easily become a heyday for architectural fantasies. Just as the ecstasy of the early Renaissance was visualized by Filarete, and that of the High Baroque by the Bibbiena, so was the unrest of the eighteenth century visualized by Giovanni-Battista Piranesi. He had the same classical scene before him as those earlier architects. All started from similar models, but each took a different direction. What makes an artist is the way he transforms what he sees and experiences; architectural fantasies reveal the real trends of an era. Piranesi's etchings display, according to the masterly formulation of Henri Focillon, *une architecture à la fois impossible et réelle*.[242] Focillon, however, does not seem to be right in asserting that Piranesi did not belong to his era—*ce génie visionnaire, qui n'appartient pas à son temps*—or in saying with still greater emphasis:

L'art de certains maîtres semble étranger à leur temps . . . On est tenté de croire que, nés au hasard de l'histoire, ils ne doivent rien à l'enchaînement ordinaire des causes . . . Tel est Jean-Baptiste Piranesi.[243]

Piranesi would not have had such a tremendous influence on his and later generations, had his work not been timely.[244] He was not the only ecstatic of the period, as we already know, and shall know still better. One cannot say that an artist does not fit into his era. Perhaps he does not fit into the concept which we have formed of the time. For there stands his work; it tells its story of the period.

Piranesi's earliest work, the *Prima parte di Architetture* of 1743, already reveals his inclination for the great and the grand, for the extraordinary, and for unusual combinations. Most of the buildings in this publication are composed of traditional features, shown in serene bright daylight. They might well have been carried out, to stand among average Baroque structures. The "Mausoleo antico" might be cited as an illustration.[245]

In addition to architectural inventions, which according to Albert Giesecke were the fruits of studies in perspective in Piranesi's Venetian days, there are in the *Prima parte* a few etchings thoroughly different in subject matter and graphic treatment. Instead of stately buildings, they represent dilapidated structures; instead of sumptuousness there is picturesqueness; instead of clarity and precision a bold and free technique is applied. These new qualities reappear with still greater intensity in the Groteschi, or Capricci, which Giesecke with good reasons dates about 1745. No one who compares the two classes of etchings can fail to remark that within a short time the artist had undergone a deep change. Giesecke says that he has no explanation for this. The influence of Giambattista Tiepolo can hardly have been the reason, for Piranesi must already have known Tiepolo's designs when he worked on the etchings of the Mausoleo type. Nor was the sudden transformation of Piranesi's style brought about by the sight of the ruins of Rome, as one might suppose. I believe Jean-Laurent Le Geay's influence was responsible for Piranesi's new manner.[246] This winner of the French Grand Prix of 1732 had come to Rome in 1738, two years ahead of Piranesi, who had many contacts with the colony of French artists. It is most probable that Piranesi became acquainted with the works and ideas of Le Geay, who in his young years had won a great reputation. Piranesi appears to have adopted Le Geay's manner, but did not imitate him slavishly. He soon created highly original works, surpassing, perhaps, those of the older architect who, as we shall see, became an extremely influential teacher in Paris in later years.

The Plan of a great college (*Pianta di ampio magnifico Collegio*) is noteworthy for its composition. Formed by about a dozen concentric circles[247] it resembles the strictly geometrical arrangements which became common in France after 1760.

In the publication which is famous as Piranesi's greatest achievement, the "Prisons" of 1745,[248] neither antiquity nor architecture proper play any considerable role. I shall not comment on their pictorial or graphic qualities, for only their architectural content interests us. Rooms of tremendous dimensions are depicted. They are crammed with a great variety of nonarchitectural objects which visualize space by their contrasting directions and their different levels: poles, ropes, banners, beams, chains, ladders, etc. These objects produce a three-dimensional impression, but they are far from forming a unified whole. (Again, I have the architectural design in mind, not the pictorial representation with the binding floods of light and shadows.) The elements act against each other; each is a menace to all. It is a pandemonium of hostile forces; disorder and uproar are regnant. Thus the objects visualize and, at the same time, decompose space. Together with traditional features, the concept of unified and integral space has gone.

There is almost no consistency in the prison of plate IX, nor in the viaducts represented in a drawing now in the Kunsthalle, Hamburg.[249] The single features have broken loose from the whole. The Baroque cycle has come to its end. Its way had been from bodies to space, from space to chaos. Now, the task of architecture was to search for a way out of the cataclysm, to find a new form of coexistence of the parts.

We already know from many instances that excitement could be expressed within the hierarchic order of the Baroque. Piranesi, in the impetuosity of his youth, renounced the traditional order and arrived at chaos. He was not able to replace the old system by a new one in that moment of utter confusion. Thus, like other revolutionary spirits of the eighteenth century, poets of the German pre-Romanticism (*Sturm und Drang*), say, and some daring architects of the French revolution, he discarded order and strove for the extraordinary. The chaotic assemblage in the "Prisons" is beyond any order; extraordinary is the size of everything and the make-up of the whole. But to speak of the artist himself, exceptional also was his inventiveness and his fertility in devising these many prisons. Not only the quality, but also the quantity of his work reveals the overwhelming power of the force which inspired him. At the very moment when the rigorists gave up the old order in theory, he gave it up in fact. With this statement we must content ourselves, without searching for the reasons why all this happened at this particular time, and why it became manifest through men from Venice, which city Focillon, with the intuition of the great scholar, terms *la capitale de l'individualisme italien au dix-huitième siècle.*[250]

In the middle fifties of the century two compositions originated which Piranesi felt to be of particular significance: the "Vie Appia e Ardeatina" and the "Ancient Circus on the Via Appia." He assigned to them conspicuous places in his publications, and etched them twice in different sizes. The first etching appears as the second frontispiece in volume II of the *Antichità Romane;*[251] the second etching is used as a frontispiece in volume III.[252] Both reappear on a reduced scale and with slight alterations in the *Opere Varie.*[253] From the architectural viewpoint the main characteristics of the compositions are the overabundance of incongruous features and the lack of a definite plan of organization, particularly in the "Vie Appia e Ardeatina." Focillon speaks of *monuments funéraires de dimensions colossales, étagés les un au-dessus des autres.*[254] Piranesi built fantastic wholes out of classical features chosen at random and with little regard to topographical correctness or archaeological accuracy. He found in the designs an outlet to express his deep disquiet. These etchings present chaotic situations, reflecting the chaotic frame of mind of their author. Piranesi the artist reacted to the general feeling of uneasiness not less vehemently than Lodoli the writer.

Now let us turn to two publications of 1761 and 1765. I will begin with the latter, the *Parere sull' architettura.* This was composed as a dialogue between Protopiro and Didascalo, or, as we may call them by simply translating their names, the Novice and the Master. The Master represents tradition; he is a fictional friend of Piranesi, so to say, his voice. In the end he gets the better of the Novice, who represents a type already familiar to us, the rigorist. The dialogue not only helps us to understand Piranesi, but it also reflects the situation at Venice already known to us from Algarotti's and Memmo's comments. We learn from the *Parere* that the adherents of Lodoli must have been quite articulate in the Adriatic republic about 1760. In the city in which Italian Rococo painting had just reached its height, in the atmosphere of somewhat effeminate Venetian splendor, the stern doctrine of functionalism rose to significance for the first time. An analogous situation developed in France when revolutionary austerity succeeded the frivolity around Marie Antoinette. Such were the contrasts the eighteenth century brought with it—contrasts which could not end but in grave conflict.

The Master proclaims a dogma which makes all further justification of tradition superfluous: "Usage establishes law" (*L'uso fa legge*).[255] The Novice retorts: "But abuse doesn't" (*ma non l'abuso*).[256] Then the Master inveighs against the rigorists, using strong language quite up to the attacks of the Novice. While the latter brands ornaments as "impertinent additions to architecture," foreign to its very nature,[257] the Master scoffs at the rigorists whose principles would lead back to the most primitive type of dwelling: *a fare un edifizio secondo que' principj che vi siete posti in capo, cioè di far tutto con ragione e verità, ci vorreste ridurre a stare in tante capanne.*[258]

The modernistic Novice assails every kind of embellishment, particularly spirals, twists, and all broken lines.[259] He asks for smooth, unfluted columns without capitals and bases.[260] Only when architecture is freed from all fripperies may it rise again.[261] If there must be decoration, it should spring from the very nature of the structure.[262] The Master is afraid that by such purism the buildings would become "all equal, monotonous, and vulgar."[263] The viewpoint of the rigorists seems to him to be identical with that of Montesquieu who also was against lavish decoration:[264] *come il Montesquieu, ragionano i Signori rigoristi.*[265] To the last the Master extols the hierarchical Baroque order.[266]

In the text of *Della Magnificenza ed Architettura de' Romani* (1761),[267] Piranesi appears to be more modern than his Master of the dialogue. In this publication Piranesi takes his stand on the side of straight lines against curves, for the sake of "truth."[268] Deviating from straight lines and uprights seems to him the first sin;[269] the mingling or intertwining of the single features, the second step on the road to depravity. Intent upon defending the Romans, Piranesi charges the Greeks with these evil inventions.[270] He uses that bold and pretentious language which soon he was to impute to the Novice, the rigorist,[271] and preaches restraint in decoration as it was practiced by the Etruscan and Doric builders.[272] His idol is that nebulous "truth" which he, like so many others, believed to be attainable by copying nature.[273] He begins the display of Roman magnificence by discussing the *cloacae,* in particular the Cloaca Maxima,[274] the structural merits of which he cannot praise enough.[275] Long before Milizia, he recognized the specific beauty inherent in plain, utilitarian structures.

Or se avremo riguardo alla natura, ed al fine degli acquedotti dei Romani . . . chi mai non vi ritroverà tutta la bellezza propria ad un tal genere di fabbrica? E chi non la ritroverà nelle cloache, nelle quali sembra ch'ella piuttosto abbondi che manchi?[276]

To sum up: in 1765 Piranesi was more conservative than in 1761. His designs, too, became calmer in the course of the years, though the revolutionary element continued to play an eminent role in their composition.

The vignette above the title of the *Parere* shows a building composed in an unusual manner (fig. 75). The single features come from classical stock, but they are unrelated and thus deviate from conventional arrangement. The whole is an agglomeration of almost independent elements. (Focillon describes the building as *un édifice composite*,[277] hinting that it is composed of nonunified parts.) Another extremely interesting trait can be found in this design: the parts are disproportionate. Here the upper part of the center has definitely outweighed the lower; the balance of the parts is disturbed. Though the center is still accentuated, there is no gradation leading from one part to the other; there is no final climax, for all the elements, particularly the lateral obelisks and the columns flanking the entrance, do not conform to the upper central portion. How could Piranesi design this way while, in the very text of the *Parere* speaking of another building, he criticizes disproportion and discomposure? (. . . *non l'ingombro delle statue, ma la loro scompostezza, e la sproporzione di esse co' nicchj, con le basi ec. son ciò che toglie al tempio la vera cagione di lodarlo.*)[278]

The case of Piranesi is not exceptional. Discrepancies between the works and the words of architects are rather the rule. In writing, Piranesi still reflected inherited beliefs, in his designing he followed the period's dual trend toward dissociation and subsequent reorganization.

Several designs on the nine plates following the *Parere* are of the character of the vignette. They are obviously architectural fantasies, not pictorial compositions. Plates VI, VIII, and IX illustrate fantastic buildings without background or environment. These buildings, too, are *édifices composites,* consisting of a large number of heterogeneous, hardly related features. The continuity and consistency characteristic of Baroque structures here is missing. The lack of affinity between the parts is most conspicuous in plate IX,[279] representing a kind of temple front with a colonnade. Huge tablets with reliefs are set before the columns, cutting them virtually in two. A further menace to unity is the broad sculptured band which starts below the bases of the columns; then, interrupted by these tablets, the band rises to the attic, continues horizontally below the main cornice, drops down to the capitals, and at last stretches horizontally over the entire central part. The portion of the band which drops down to the capitals passes over the pediment and thus disrupts its continuity. The band, the tablets, and several minor features negate the principle of unification. They tell of the ardent aspiration towards innovation. As a reproof to those who cannot grasp the forms and therefore cannot understand the meaning of the composition, the artist inscribed on the attic the following from Sallust's *Jugurtha:* NOVITATEM. MEAM. CONTEMNUNT. EGO. ILLORUM. IGNAVIAM. This inscription in no way refers to the purpose of the building; it is the artist's proud boast of his invention.

Inscriptions on other plates likewise present Piranesi's personal point of view. Plate v contains a further defense of the modern, taken from the prologue of Terence's *Eunuchus:* AEQUUM. EST. VOS. COGNOSCERE. ATQUE. IGNOSCERE. QUAE. VETERES. FACTITARUNT. SI FACIUNT. NOVI. ('Tis but fair then for you to admit and allow the deed, if moderns do for once what their ancestors have done over and over.)[280] Indiscriminate copying is censored in the inscription on Plate VIII taken from Leroy, the editor of *Les Ruines des plus beaux monuments de la Grèce:* POUR. NE. PAS. FAIRE. DE. CET. ART. SUBLIME. UN. VIL. METIER. OU L'ON. NE. FEROIT. QUE. COPIER. SANS. CHOIX. If the compositions left any doubt about the revolutionary spirit of Piranesi, the inscriptions would certainly dispel it. We should of course keep in mind that Piranesi did not go beyond the negation of the old system. The time was not yet ripe for the next step.

The characteristics of the designs in the *Parere* reappear in the etching inscribed *Appartenenze d'antiche terme con scale che conducono alla palestra, e al teatro* (probably dating from the 1750's).[281] There are, once more, fantastic structures made up of incongruous elements: twin aedicules are superposed on multicolumned pedimented gateways. Only at closer inspection do we detect that these strange piles form the bases of piers from which arches rise. Piranesi was aware that the inconsistent combination of aedicules and gateways would not make sense, could they not be interpreted as parts of the piers. Thus, on second thought, he rationalized the pile of superposed structures in order to justify the weird composition. It seems that the idea underlying the design was not so much the definite concept of some building, but the vague concept of an entirely new order of disparate elements. There can be no doubt that the impressive composition emerged spontaneously from the depth of his artistic emotion. Whereas Guarini's "excesses" always remained within the framework of the Baroque system, Piranesi felt the urge to arrange the components in a new, free manner.

In the text of his *Apologetical Essay in Defence of Egyptian and Tuscan Architecture,* Piranesi once again appears as a defender of the Baroque system, especially of the hierarchical principle. He blames overdecoration by quoting Montesquieu: *Un édifice chargé d'ornemens est une énigme pour les yeux, comme un poème confus l'est pour l'esprit.*[282] Yet he makes clear that it is not simply "the multiplicity of ornaments that offends the eye," but such multiplicity as "for want of order and disposition troubles and confounds the eye." Or, more specifically:

The want of the *high* and *low* [his italics] which constitutes as well in art as nature a certain variety of degrees, and preeminence of merit, so that some parts appear principal, and others serve only to accompany the first.[283]

Piranesi's designs of chimneys in the Egyptian style seem to conform to the conservative text. They are strictly axially composed and the central portions are stressed.[284] Nevertheless, the chimneys have a strange unconventional look which cannot be accounted for merely by the use of the Egyptian features. In the particularly characteristic plates 5, 10, and 14 the central main axes are strongly marked, but the single features are unrelated: *Les ensembles ne manquent pas d'équilibre: ils manquent d'unité.*[285] The independence of the elements becomes still more apparent in plates 21 and 28.

Piranesi chose Egyptian forms at a comparatively early time. Egyptian forms became popular much later, in the nineties, when Napoleon battled on the Nile. Piranesi elected these rigid forms at a moment when Baroque composition was still the rule though movement, flexibility, etc., were no longer desirable. The chimneys are interesting instances of the Frozen Baroque. Piranesi remarks that he himself was the first to introduce the Egyptian forms into minor architecture: *le maniere Egizie . . . che prima ignote, o non curate nella piccola architettura, ho io il primo in essa introdotte.*[286] Yet he did not consider this revival as his chief merit. He was rather proud that he was able "to get out of the old monotonous track, and to present the public with something new in this branch."[287] What is true of the chimneys can also be said of two designs for wall panels, for the Caffè degli Inglesi.[288] These tripartite panels are symmetrical, and emphasis is laid on the central portion, but the whole composition is divided into neatly delimited compartments. Again the austere Egyptian forms are made use of. The chimneys remind us of the "frozen" decorations of Robert Adam. The two architects, who had become acquainted in Rome between 1750 and 1755,[289] held each other in high esteem.[290]

Piranesi did very little actual building. About 1765 he remodeled the church of Santa Maria del Priorato in Rome. Its entrance gate[291] and the façade[292] show the incoherent composition of the *Parere* designs.

X

THE THRESHOLD OF THE NINETEENTH CENTURY

PIRANESI SHARED the interest of his contemporaries in ancient forms, but he labored to get away from traditional composition. To free himself from the old formality he ventured on different experiments. In the Via Appia etchings he simply accumulated heterogeneous features. Yet the disorderly masses evidently did not satisfy him. He longed for some new order, based not on harmony and subordination, but on outspoken contrasts and individual liberty. By opposing forms of different characters and different sizes he dramatized the compositions and put an end to balance and coherence.

The "Prisons" were the dreams of an ecstatic who wanted the elements set free. They were the right medium through which the passionate protest against any bonds could rise. Piranesi protested against the old but made hardly any attempts to reach the goal of a new order of the constituents. What he offered in the chimneys was again the old forms and the old system, slightly modified by the new ideal of the free coexistence of the elements. His work had begun with a desperate outcry; it ended in tragic dissonance.[293]

Very soon Piranesi found a follower in a much younger Roman architect, Giuseppe Valadier. Valadier's buildings and a large number of his drawings of about 1790 reveal that he, too, wanted to achieve some new order of the elements. I see in him a follower of Piranesi, although in his works there is hardly a trace of the romantic mood of the Venetian master. He worked at a time when the revolutionary excitement had gone.

The drawings which will be discussed here are selected from a large number of designs kept in the Cooper Union Museum for the Arts of Decoration in New York. These drawings are said to be Valadier's. The question of the authorship matters little in this context. What is important is that the drawings can be dated and located from many inscriptions. They are undoubtedly Italian drawings of about 1790. Several are certainly stage designs; others, fantastic architectural projects.[294]

An analysis of several of these projects may reveal the kind of order aimed at by Valadier. In some the old patterns of centralization and gradation are still traceable, but not less distinct is the will to reform composition. On a gateway with the inscription P VI (Pius VI), lateral truncated cones with cylindrical finishings are far

112

more massive and consequently more conspicuous than the portal with all its embellishments (fig. 76). The wings of two palaces, the one with a cylindrical tower, the other with a domed rotunda in the center, are heavy blocks not inferior in weight to the central pile, although the latter is higher (figs. 79, 80). In these designs Valadier attempted to give equal importance to all the parts; in other projects his dislike for the old system of harmonious balance shows in quite a different way. The central towerlike portion of a building obviously planned as a memorial is tremendously oversized and out of all proportion with the low attenuated wings (fig. 78). A rotunda surrounded by colonnades is accompanied by outbuildings composed of arcaded structures carrying tall pyramids (fig. 81). The unity of the whole scheme has almost been lost by the incongruity of the masses. The memorial and the rotunda manifest the tendency of the parts to extricate themselves from the whole. Thus, compositionally, they resemble Sandys' Ickworth House. Discrepancies and incongruities within the single buildings occur often in the designs. They suggest that the components no longer felt at ease within the old order. The portal of a sepulchral monument carries a sarcophagus which is much bulkier than the whole structure below (fig. 77). Similarly, the superstructures of the Memorials to Louis XVI have about the same height as the templelike substructures (fig. 83). Both the memorial on the Greek-cross plan and that on a circular plan are reminiscent of the French experiments with form. A two-storied, domed casino (fig. 86) has a cylindrical core from which prismatic wings depart diagonally; a pedimented porch is inserted between two wings; a richly decorated pavilion (fig. 87) composed in a similar way. One building (fig. 88) has a multi-columned portico topped by a small temple and flanked by massive cubic wings. The tendency to combine incongruous features appears in the bell tower of a funeral chapel (fig. 84), although a perfunctory inspection would leave the impression of a Baroque character. Valadier's true intention is revealed in the inscription which characterizes the structure as "of mixed style" (*Campanile d'una cappella funebre in stile misto*). The architect had "style" in mind, and, most certainly, some new style.

Predilection for elementary geometrical forms is revealed in many features of the projects which have been discussed above. The forbidding character of the elementary forms is commensurate with the tendency to make the parts free. Greatest independence from the environment is achieved in cylindrical houses (figs. 89, 90) be it an old-fashioned one with statuary, columns, and large windows, or an austere modern one with plain walls, flanked by conical substructures and topped by a cylindrical belvedere. The cylindrical form played a large role also in theatrical decorations of the period, according to Rudolf Berliner,[295] who ascribes the invention of the "motif of the curved structure in the foreground" to Francesco Fontanesi. The motif is presented in Valadier's "Sepulchral Precinct" (fig. 82).

Particularly significant is Valadier's interest in what may be subsumed under the collective name of the withdrawing forms—pyramids, cones, and cylinders. These forms, as well as the sphere which was applied only by a few French extremists, are scarcely fit for practical use, but they are self-contained to a higher degree than cubes and prisms; the pyramid and the cone withdraw by their slope from the spectator who stands near to the base; the cylinder permits him to be close only to one vertical line; the entire sphere, only to one point. Valadier's hexagonal house (fig. 91) is an outstanding specimen of the tendency to retire from the environment. The sentimental interest in pyramidal and cylindrical structures of the past certainly played some role in reviving these forms. They were imitated chiefly because their forms were timely. The new formal aspirations account also for a novel method of handling the cubes—the terrace building. Terrace buildings were favored especially by some architects of the French revolution, as they are by architects of the twentieth century. This form was devised long before practical considerations became a factor. Valadier's inventiveness shows in several stepped buildings, such as a stepped tower and the casino with rusticated doors (figs. 85, 92).

Valadier came comparatively close to the goal which Piranesi had seen only dimly in the feverish visions of the "Prisons." The parts were at last allowed to play their role as individuals. Valadier's drawings were the products of a strong artistic will, not perhaps of cool reflection. They are calmer than Piranesi's fantasies, for Valadier had already won greater clarity. Lucidity and composure characterize his later achievements. The calm after the storm has come. Older and more serene, the patterns of independence lived on even in his late works to attest that the revolutionary efforts had not been in vain.

A selection of buildings erected by Valadier in the early nineteenth century may illustrate a few of the new patterns. The front of San Pantaleo in Rome, which was remodeled by him in 1806, presents a plain wall on which the pedimented door, the semicircular window above it, and a bull's-eye in the top pediment are almost the only features. He was rightly proud of the simple, refined arrangement. That such refinement meant much to him can be seen from his projects for the Teatro Valle in Rome (1819).[296] The first project shows oblong openings of different sizes on the second floor, alternating oblong and arched apertures on the ground floor. In the second project many reciprocities between the diversiform openings can be detected. These reciprocities would tell of the correlation of the stories even if the colossal order did not unify them in the traditional way. The bull's-eye of the gable is repeated in the row of bull's-eyes below the top story; the arches of the wings reappear in the central section of the ground floor and in the center of the second floor. In a third project Valadier tried out a further variant. He discarded the bull's-eyes and substituted a semilunette in the gable, thereby establishing some interrelation with the various arched openings below. This pattern of multiple response of different motifs had already been

applied by French architects prior to Valadier. We shall discuss this more extensively later.

The contrast between the colonnade in the center and the lateral flat walls also
plays a role in the front of the theater. A similar contrast marks the Villa Ponia-
towski in Rome: a broad five-part loggia above is opposed to a huge arched window and two small niches below. On the Villa nei pressi di Ponte Milvio varied
oblong panels make an original pattern. The narrow panels containing the windows are reinforced by medallions on top.[297]

Authentic designs by Valadier were published in *Raccolta di diverse invenzioni* [1796], *Progetti architettonici* (1807), and *Opere di architettura* (1833).[298]
They show how fond Valadier was in the years prior to 1800 of inventing strangely
shaped structures and unusual plans; and how much thought he gave, later, to
novel arrangements of the façades. In the *Raccolta* we find a pavilion on the
Greek-cross plan with the four arms protruding between quarter cylinders inserted in the angles. There is a circular pavilion surrounded by a colonnade and
topped by a round turret which seems to telescope from the lower structure. Two
more pavilions are designed on triangular plans. An observatory (*Specola*) (fig. 93)
presents a tall tower piled upon a two-storied house. The *Progetti* contain restrained and sound designs which have nothing in common with Baroque composition. In the "Pinacoteca" and the "Entrance of a Villa," Valadier pays his
tribute to the Egyptian fashion of the day and tries out the compositional possibilities of tomorrow. The "Coffee House" and the "Exchange" remind us of the
experiments with traditional forms made by Jean-François Neufforge, about which
we shall learn more in Chapter XII. The coffeehouse shows a high pedestal carrying statues on top of the roof; the exchange (fig. 94) consists of a wide substructure and a narrow superstructure. The "Palestra" and a country house are stepped
buildings of a type rather popular among French designers about 1800. A theater
with a semicylindrical audience hall projecting from the square body also appears
dependent on French models. Perhaps Valadier borrowed it directly from Neufforge, just as several German architects of the nineteenth century took it over
from the French. Stylistically, many of the *Progetti* resemble the designs of Soane
and Smirke, and still more those of Durand and Dubut. About 1800 architecture
in the different countries had reached a similar stage, although the development
leading up to it had been different in each. In artistic progress, at least within the
modern European scene, time seems to play a far greater part than space, or "race."

The "House on the Corso" illustrated in the *Opere* reveals the architect's efforts
to invent a new surface pattern with the help of alternating elements. Here the
effect is based on the interplay of diversiform openings and different-sized balconies. The relationship between the stories is visualized not perhaps by any tying
features, but merely by certain corresponding features. The arched and straight-
headed apertures of one floor respond to arched or square openings of the other

floors; the short balconies on the sides below answer the long balcony higher up. The center of the front is in no way emphasized; the more remote parts have come into prominence. This shifting of the accent from one exalted feature to a multitude of features seems to be very significant. Compositionally this house stands close to the Teatro Valle and other buildings discussed above. Valadier comments thoroughly on his intentions in the accompanying text. He still was an heir to the revolutionary ideal of an entirely new architectural form, but not a spiritless copyist like so many architects of the following decades.

Other Italian architects of the latest eighteenth and the early nineteenth centuries also were on the search for new patterns. The project for a theater by Vincenzo Ferrarese again presents the semicircular auditorium projecting from the cubic stage house. Milizia had much appreciation for this solution.[299] Antonio Rinaldi's Montagne Russe at Oranienbaum of about 1768 was a cylindrical pavilion from which three wings departed.[300] Rinaldi's project for the palace of Gatschina, of about 1770, was a curious agglomeration of prismatic and cylindric masses.[301] Even the very conservative Ottone Calderari did not remain untouched by the modern trends. The second court of his Palazzo Cordellina (1776) is remarkable for its heavy walls and the picturesque grouping of its masses.[302] Many works of Giacomo Quarenghi present daring mass effects, to name only the exchange in St. Petersburg, erected between 1784 and 1800, and the project of an observatory. The pattern of multiple response shows on the project of a concert hall.[303] The church at Great Packington, Warwickshire, which Giuseppe Bonomi carried out in 1790 is a severe cube with four squat corner towers unrelated to the main mass. The pattern and the shapes of the openings call to mind certain works of Valadier. The English patron must have found them acceptable.[304] On the front of the theater La Fenice at Venice, built by Giannantonio Selva in 1792, the upper central portion is markedly contrasted to the sides.[305] Luigi Cagnola designed a circular casino, and very original campanili.[306] The Cisternone at Livorno, completed by Pasquale Poccianti in 1809,[307] is not inferior to the boldest inventions of Ledoux. The grandiose theater project by Tommaso Carlo Beccega would have been built with heavy masses contrasted in size and shape.[308]

The Teatro San Carlo at Naples by Antonio Niccolini (1810) is a great work of art and a clear manifestation of the new compositional principles.[309] Each of its two stories is individually shaped and contrasted to the other in the strongest manner. The columns of the second floor antagonize the horizontals of the main cornice and the balcony. Relief panels and small niches under the balcony alternate in a free rhythm totally different from the scanning of the apertures above and below. Everything that was dear to Baroque builders is gone: concatenation, integration, and gradation; movement and flexibility. And yet, though each portion is self-contained, the whole is nevertheless a vigorous community. The same compositional principle of contrasted independent stories shows on Nicola Bettoli's Teatro Regio of Parma (1829).[310] Here the ground floor presents a colonnade, the second floor has five windows, the third a mullioned semicircular window. Such incongruity of the stories characterizes also the Cisternino, the second great structure which Poccianti erected at Livorno, a few years after the Cisternone;[311] its massive ground floor is disproportionately high compared with the low columned loggia above. Gino Mazzanti rightly observed the *mutato ritmo* of the structure.

After these attempts at a new surface disposition some noteworthy instances of modern spatial composition may be pointed out. Giuseppe Japelli's Caffè Pedrocchi at Padua (1816–1831) is a highly attractive specimen of a house consisting of juxtaposed blocks.[312] Maybe Japelli had learned much on his travels in England and France. Even those contemporaries who disliked the modernism of the building perfectly understood its peculiar character, censuring *l'unità offesa* and *il passaggio così brusco*.[313] The portico of Carlo Francesco Barabino's Teatro Carlo Felice at Genoa (1827) seems to come forth from the main block, while the latter itself emerges from the podiumlike ground floor.[314] Rodolfo Vantini's Porta Venezia at Milan (1826) consists of two tollhouses, each presenting a prismatic shape topped by a smaller prism.[315] Most interesting is the Barbetti house on the square Il Prato at Florence.[316] It is composed of an oblong block, to which two lateral half cylinders seem to be appended. However, these half cylinders are the projecting halves of two huge circular halls inserted in the square mass.

Down to the end of the eighteenth century Italy had not abandoned conventional compositions and conventional forms. The sporadic appearance of modernistic buildings about 1800 in all probability was due to the growing influence of France, just as many German architects were so inspired, to name only Heinrich Gentz, Friedrich Gilly and his pupil Carl Friedrich Schinkel, Peter Speeth, Leo Klenze, Georg Moller, and also the architectural publications of Schaeffer.[317] It is a well-known fact that Durand's textbooks were used all over Europe through many decades. And it might be interesting to learn that Pietro Nobile, the author of the austere church of San Antonio at Trieste,[318] who in his later years taught in Vienna, owned a copy of Ledoux's *Architecture* of 1804, which he donated[319] to the library of the Vienna Academy of Fine Arts.* Even two very late and very curious structures may be traced back to the most extravagant designs of French revolutionary architects: the tall dome which Alessandro superimposed on Pel-

---

* Incidentally, it was from this copy that my studies of Ledoux started more than thirty years ago. Nobile passed his knowledge of Ledoux's ideas to his colleague Josef Kornhäusel, as the latter's Schloss Weilburg (1821) seems to prove. Emil Kaufmann, *Die Kunst der Stadt Baden* (Vienna, 1925), figs. 31, 69.

legrino Tibaldi's church of San Gaudenzio at Novara,[320] and the fantastic pile of the Mole Antonelliana, begun by Antonelli in Turin in 1863.[321]

If all these works of the Italian *ottocento* were not directly dependent on French models, they were no doubt the fruits of the eighteenth-century revolution against convention. As long as one considers merely their classicizing features, one cannot grasp their meaning. But after having become acquainted with the new artistic trends that came to the surface in different countries in the Age of Reason, we can appreciate the historical significance of their achievements.

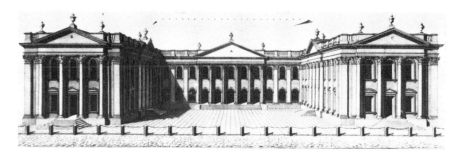

1. Gibbs, "Publick Building" at Cambridge (p. 7)

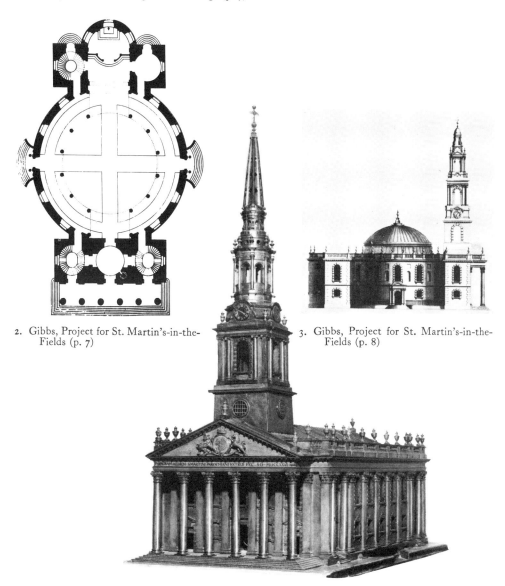

2. Gibbs, Project for St. Martin's-in-the-Fields (p. 7)

3. Gibbs, Project for St. Martin's-in-the-Fields (p. 8)

4. Gibbs, St. Martin's-in-the-Fields, Model (p. 8)

5. Ware, Wrotham Park (p. 10)

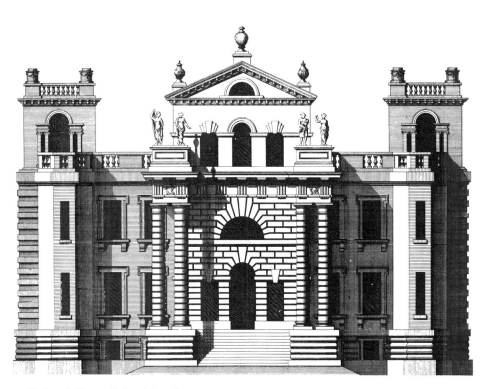

6. Vanbrugh, Seaton Delaval (p. 18)

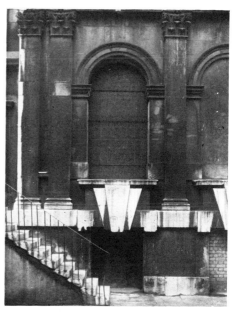

7. Hawksmoor, St. George's, Bloomsbury, Tower (p. 19)

8. Hawksmoor, St. George's, Bloomsbury, North Wall (p. 19)

9. Hawksmoor, Christ Church, Spitalfields, East Façade (p. 19)

10. Gibbs, St. Martin's-in-the-Fields, East End (p. 19)

11. Robert Morris, Structure Overlooking a Valley (p. 22)

12. Robert Morris, Bathhouse (p. 22)

13. Robert Morris, Square Summer Room (p. 22)

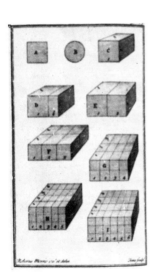

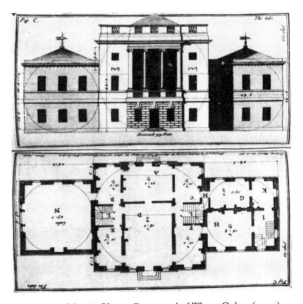

14. Robert Morris, Combination of Cubes (p. 25)

15. Robert Morris, House Composed of Three Cubes (p. 25)

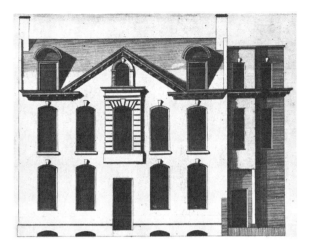

16. Anonymous, "Irregular" House, 1724 (p. 26)

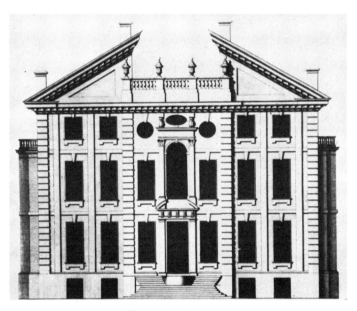

17. Archer, Roehampton House (p. 27)

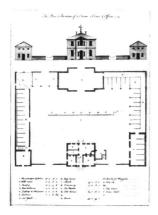

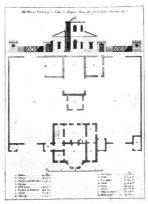

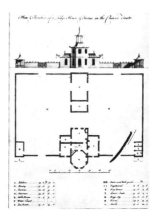

18. Lightoler, Farmhouse (p. 28)

19. Lightoler, Keeper's House (p. 28)

20. Lightoler, Lodge in the Chinese Taste (p. 28)

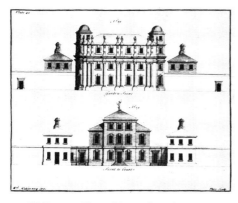

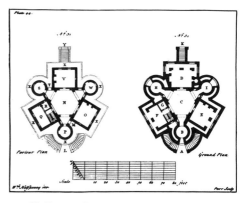

21. Halfpenny, House No. 29 (p. 29)

22. Halfpenny, House No. 31 (p. 29)

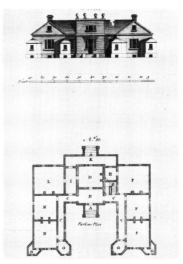

23. Halfpenny, House No. 27 (p. 29)

24. Halfpenny, House No. 10 (p. 29)

25. Dance, St. Luke's, Old Street (p. 31)

26. Paine, Gosforth Hall (p. 43)

27. Paine, Axwell Park (p. 43)

28. Paine, Stockeld Park (p. 44)

29. Thomas, Mirehouse House (p. 45)

30. Thomas, Mausoleum (p. 45)

31. Thomas, Surrey Chapel (p. 45)

32. Steuart, St. Chad's, Shrewsbury (p. 46)

33.

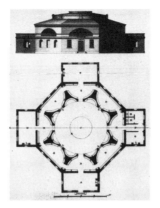

34.

35.

36.

37.

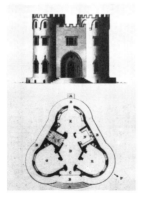

38.

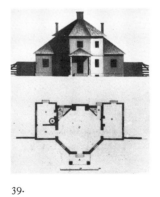

39.

40. Soane, Royal Palace, 1821 (pp. 51, 52)

41. Soane, Triumphal Bridge (p. 51)

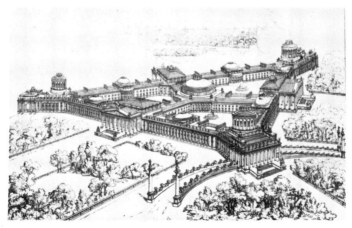

42. Soane, Royal Palace, 1779 (p. 52)

43. Soane, Mausoleum for Earl of Chatham (p. 53)   44. Soane, Bellevue Building (p. 53)

45. Soane, Castello d'Acqua, Wimpole (p. 53)

46. Soane, Monk's Tomb (p. 53)

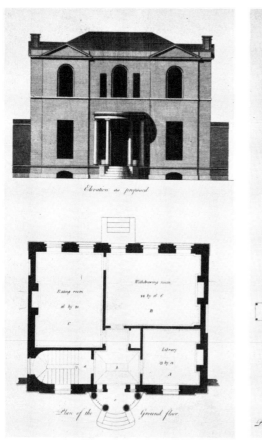

47. Soane, Parsonage at Saxlingham, first design (p. 56)

49. Soane, Rix House, Oulton (p. 56)

48. Soane, Malvern Hall (p. 56)

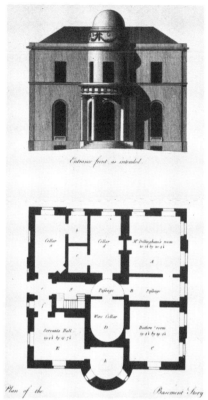

50. Soane, Circular Temple (p. 56)

51. Soane, Letton Hall (p. 56)

52. Soane, Dairy "in the Moresque Stile" (p. 56)

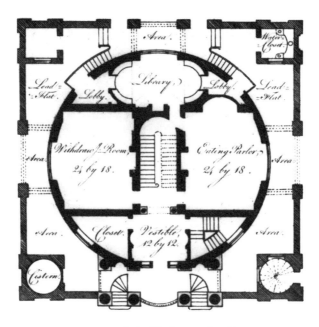

53. Plaw, Circular House, Lake Windermere (p. 64)

54. Plaw, St. Mary's, Paddington (p. 65)

55. Gandy, A Laborer's Cottage (p. 66)   57. Gandy, Two Cones as Lodges (p. 66)

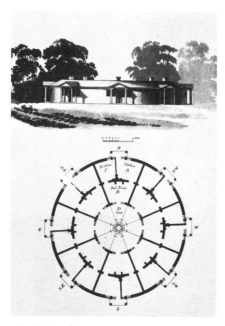

56. Gandy, Cottage of the Winds (p. 66)

58. D. Burton, Grove House (p. 67)

59. Jay, Albion Chapel (p. 67)

60. C. R. Cockerell, St. George's Chapel (p. 67)

61. Smirke, United Service Club (p. 67)

62. S. P. Cockerell, St. Anne's, Soho (p. 68)

63. Thomson, "Irregular" House (p. 69)

64. Goodwin, Gothic Villa (p. 69)

65. Goodwin, Lissadell Court, Park Lodge Entrance (p. 69)

66. Nash, Haymarket Theatre, Suffolk Street Elevation (p. 68)

67. Nash, St. Mary's, Haggerston (p. 68)

68. Nash, All Souls', Langham Place (p. 68)

69. Nash, Hanover Terrace (p. 70)

70. Nash, York Terrace (p. 70)

71. Nash, Cambridge Terrace (p. 70)

72. Nash, Ulster Terrace (p. 70)

73. Nash, Cumberland Terrace (p. 71)

74. Nash, Chester Terrace (p. 71)

75. Piranesi, Vignette (p. 109)

76. Valadier, Gateway (p. 113)

77. Valadier, Sepulchral Monument
(p. 113)

78. Valadier, Memorial Building (p. 113)

79. Valadier, Palace with Cylindrical Tower (p. 113)

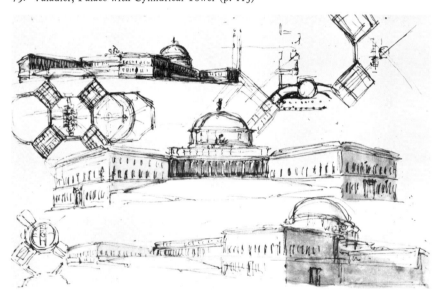

80. Valadier, Palace with Domed Rotunda (p. 113)

81. Valadier, Rotunda (p. 113)

82. Valadier, Sepulchral Precinct (p. 113)

83. Valadier, Louis XVI Memorial (p. 113)

84. Valadier, Bell Tower of a Chapel
(p. 113)

86. Valadier, Casino (p. 113)

87. Valadier, Pavilion (p. 113)

85. Valadier, Stepped Tower
(p. 114)

88. Valadier, Public Building (p. 113)

89. Valadier, Cylindrical House with Belvederes
(p. 113)

90. Valadier, Cylindrical House with Statuary
(p. 113)

91. Valadier, Hexagonal House (p. 114)

92. Valadier, Casino with Rusticated Doors
(p. 114)

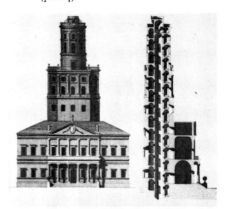

93. Valadier, Observatory (p. 115)

94. Valadier, Exchange (p. 115)

95. Hardouin-Mansart, Dôme des Invalides
(p. 129)

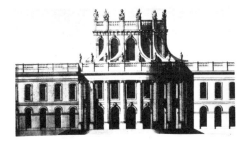

96. Boffrand, Malgrange (p. 130)

97. Soufflot, Ste. Geneviève with East Towers (p. 139)

98. Peyre, Academy (p. 143)

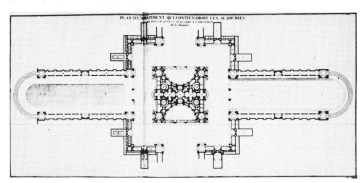

99. Peyre, Academy (p. 143)

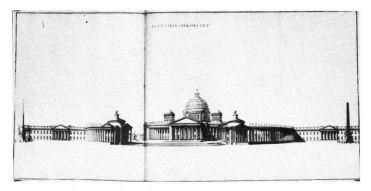

100. Peyre, Cathedral (p. 143)

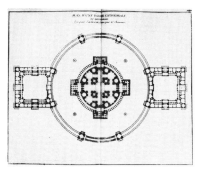

101. Peyre, Cathedral (p. 144)

102. De Wailly Odéon, First Project (p. 146)

103. De Wailly, Pulpit, St. Sulpice
(p. 146)

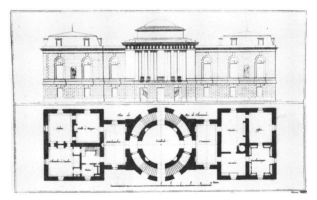

104. De Wailly, Montmusard (p. 146)

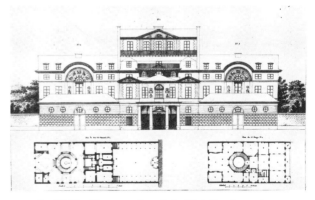

105. De Wailly, House on Rue de la Pépinière (p. 147)

106. Le Masson, Pavilion at Viarmes (p. 148)

107. Huvé, House at Meudon (p. 148)

108. Heurtier, Théâtre Italien, Rear Façade
(p. 149)

109. Le Camus, Halle au Blé (p. 149)

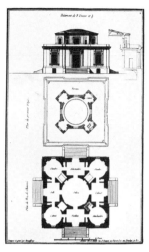

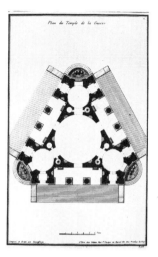

110. Neufforge, House on Nine-
partite Square (p. 151)

111. Neufforge, Temple
(p. 152)

112. Neufforge, Temple
(p. 152)

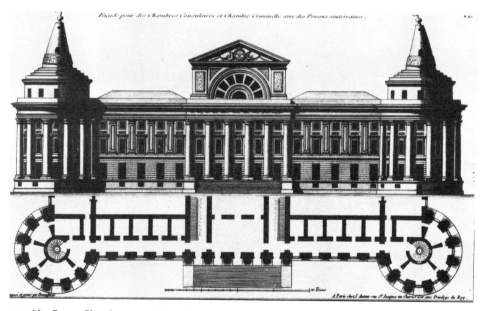

113. Neufforge, Chambres consulaires (p. 152)

114. Neufforge, Bathhouse (p. 152)

115. Neufforge, Town House (p. 153)

116. Neufforge, Prison (p. 153)

117. Neufforge, Sepulchral Chapel (p. 153)

118. Neufforge, Hôtel de ville (p. 153)

119. Neufforge, Maison de plaisance (p. 153)

120. Neufforge, Cemetery
Entrance (p. 153)

121. Neufforge, Sepulchral
Pyramid (p. 153)

122. Neufforge, Waterworks
(p. 153)

123. Neufforge, Fountain
(p. 153)

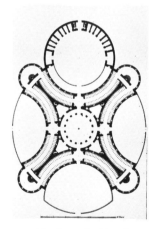

124. Neufforge, Stables, Plan
(p. 154)

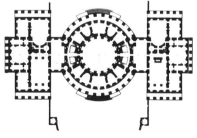

125. Neufforge, House for a
Prelate (p. 153)

127. Cuvilliés *fils*, Obelisk
(p. 154)

126. Cuvilliés *fils*, Prison (p. 154)

128. Cuvilliés *fils*, Commanderie (p. 154)

129. Cuvilliés *fils*, Retraite (p. 154)

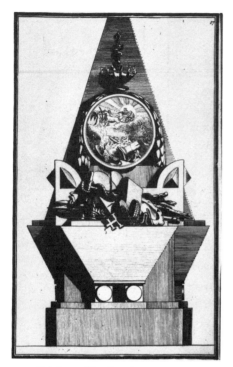

130. Delafosse, "Les Israélites" (p. 155)

131. Delafosse, "L'Asie" (p. 155)

132. Delafosse, "L'Amérique" (p. 156)

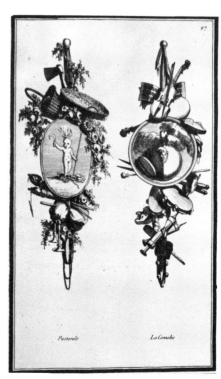

133. Delafosse, "Attributs pastorals" (p. 156)

134. Delafosse, "Origine du paganisme" (p. 156)

135. Delafosse, "L'Air et l'eau" (p. 156)

136. Delafosse, "Diverses vertus et diverses forces" (p. 156)

137. Delafosse, "Economie, silence, divinité, eternité" (p. 157)

138. Delafosse, "La Suisse" (p. 157)

139. Le Canu, Lighthouse (pp. 158, 263)

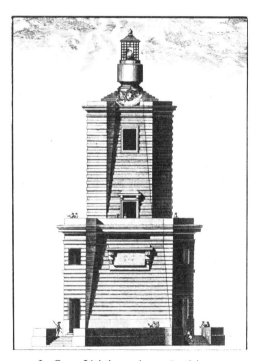

140. Le Canu, Lighthouse (pp. 158, 263)

141. Legrand and Molinos, Théâtre Feydeau (p. 158)

142. A. Aubert, Maison Deshayes (p. 159)

143. Poyet, Hospital (p. 159)

144. Poyet, Stables (p. 159)

145. Panseron, Beacon (p. 160)

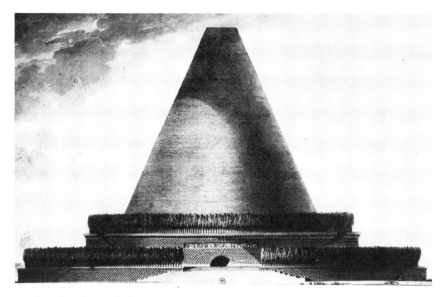

146. Boullée, Cenotaph (p. 161)

147. Boullée, Metropolitan Church (p. 161)

148. Boullée, Circus (p. 161)

149. Boullée, Library Hall (p. 162)

150. Boullée, City Gate (p. 162)

151. Ledoux, Entrance, Royal Saltworks (p. 163)

152. Ledoux, Barrière du Roule (p. 164)

153. Ledoux, Bellevue House (p. 164)

154. Ledoux, Barrière de la Santé (p. 164)   155. Ledoux, Jarnac House (p. 164)

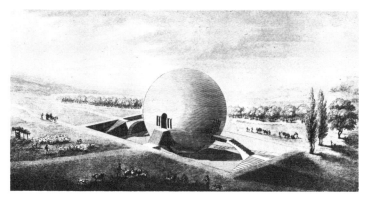

156. Ledoux, Shelter for the Rural Guards (p. 166)

157. Ledoux, Prison for Aix (p. 166)

158. Ledoux, House for Four Families (p. 166)

159. Gondoin, School of Medicine (p. 167)

160. Gondoin, Lecture Hall (p. 168)

161. Chalgrin, Senate Hall (p. 169)

162. Brongniart, Hôtel de Saint-Foix (p. 169)

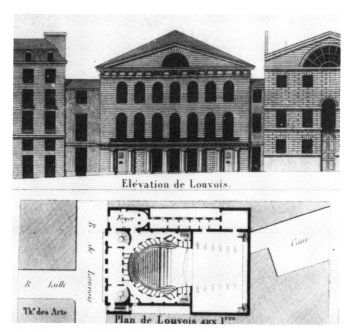

Elévation de Louvois.

R. de Louvois

Foyer

Cour

R. Lulli

Th. des Arts

Plan de Louvois aux 1res

163. Brongniart, Théâtre Louvois (p. 170)

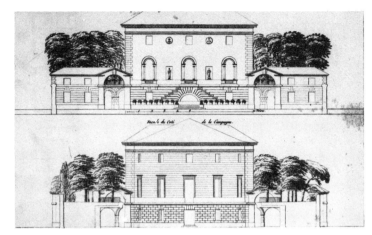

164. Belanger, House at Pantin (p. 170)

165. Belanger, Artois Stables (p. 171)

166. Belanger, Pump house
(p. 171)

167. Belanger, Opera House (p. 171)

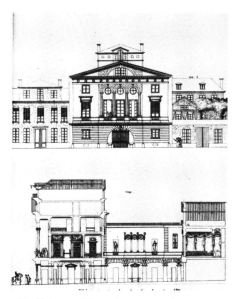

168. Belanger, House (pp. 172, 174)

169. Belanger, Slaughterhouse (p. 173)

170. Belanger, Slaughterhouse (p. 173)

171. Belanger, Three Houses (p. 173)

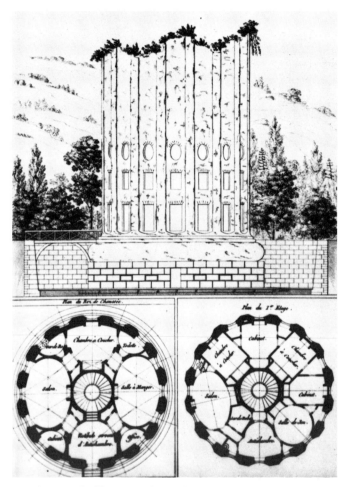

172. Demonville, House near Marly (p. 176)

173. Lenoir, Opera House (p. 176)

174. Desprez, Monument to Voltaire (p. 176)

175. Desprez, Stables at Haga (p. 176)

176. Desprez, Stables at Drottningholm (p. 176)

177. Desprez, Church (p. 177)

178. Desprez, Villa (p. 193)

179. Thomon, Exchange (p. 179)

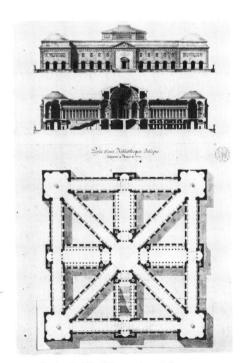

180. Paris, Public Library (p. 180)

181. Paris, City Gate (p. 180)

182. Paris, Bellêtre (p. 180)

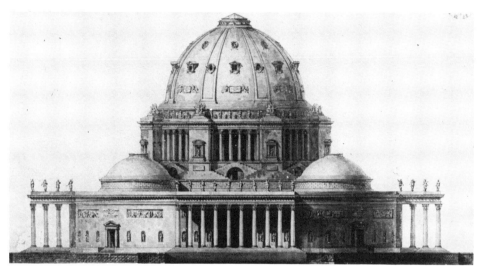

183. Paris, Cathedral (p. 180)

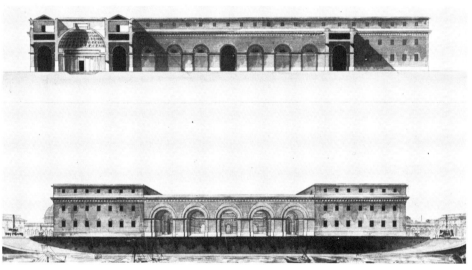

184. Réverchon, Customhouse (p. 182)

185. Réverchon, Château d'Eau (p. 204)

186. Ramée, Funeral at Nancy (p. 183)

187. Rousseau, Hôtel Salm (p. 183)

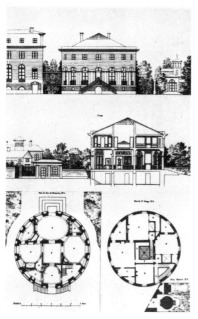

188. Henry, Vassale House (p. 184)

189. Sobre, Salle de spectacle (p. 184)

190. Sobre, Maison de Plaisance
(p. 184)

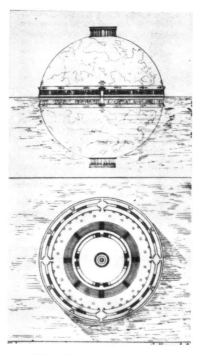

191. Sobre, Temple of Immortality
(p. 185)

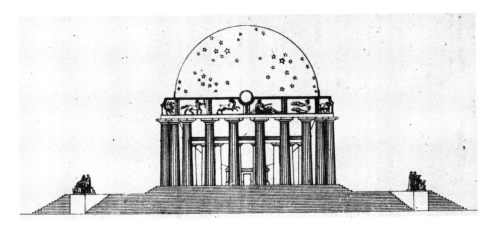

192. Vaudoyer, House of a Cosmopolite (p. 185)

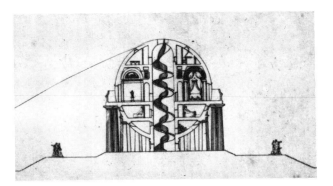

193. Vaudoyer, House of a Cosmopolite (p. 185)

194. Délépine, Monument in Honor of Newton (p. 186)

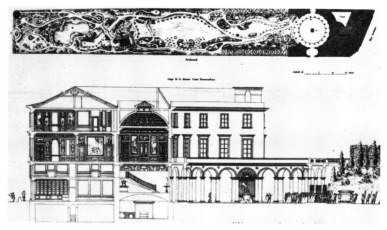

195. Lemoine, Beaumarchais House (p. 187)

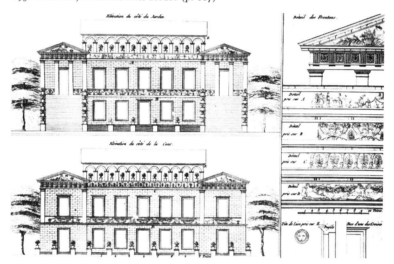

196. Bienaimé, Piau House (p. 190)

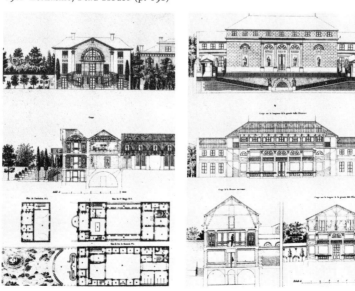

197. Olivier, Epinée House (p. 190)

198. C. Aubert, Institution Polytechnique (p. 191)

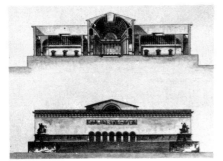
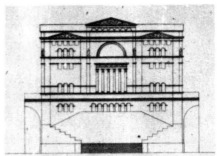

199. Bergognion, Bank (p. 191)   200. A. Gisors, Public Bath (p. 193)

201. Loison, House at Saint-Germain (p. 194)

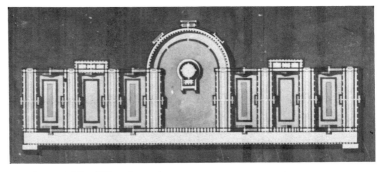

202. Bonard, Hôtel-Dieu (p. 195)

203. Baltard, Saint-Cloud (p. 196)

204. Héré de Corny, Chanteheux Pavilion (p. 197)

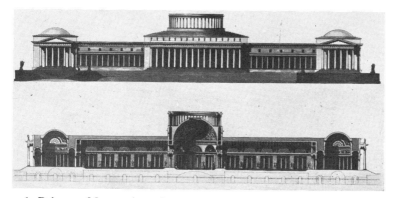

205. Granjean, Elysée (p. 197)

206. Delannoy, Museum (p. 197)

207. Moitte, Porte de Ville (p. 198)

208. Normand, Lighthouse (p. 198)

209. Lequeu, Rendezvous de Bellevue (p. 198)

210. Lequeu, Pompe à Feu (p. 204)

211. Sobre, Castle (p. 199)

212. Anonymous, Manor House (p. 199)

213. Damesme, Triumphal
Arch (p. 199)

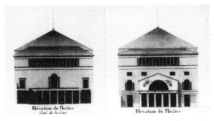

214. Demesme, Théâtre Olympique (p. 200)

215. Percier, Grotto (p. 204)

216. J.-P. Gisors, Hall of the Convention (p. 205)

217. J.-P. Gisors, Chambre des Deputés (p. 206)

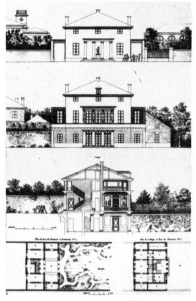

219. Durand, Lathuile House (p. 213)

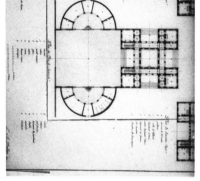

218. Dubut, House No. 14 (p. 209)

220. Durand, Temple décadaire (p. 213)

221. Mayeux, Mausoleum (p. 215)

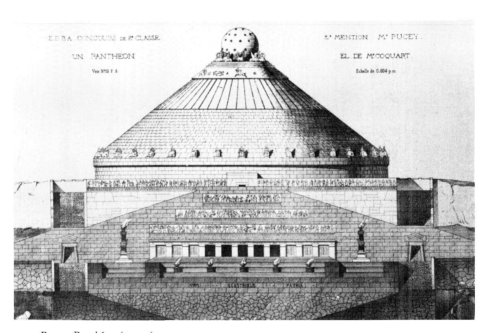

222. Pucey, Panthéon (p. 215)

PART III

FRANCE

FROM LEMERCIER TO SOUFFLOT

THE BAROQUE SYSTEM, which had originated in Italy, began to unfold in France much later, but it reached there such a high degree of accomplishment that from France, rather than from its homeland, it spread over Europe.[1] If we are to exemplify the system of the Baroque—not merely some typical traits of it—we are inclined to refer to Versailles rather than to any Italian performance.

Yet how can we assert that the Baroque system came nearer to perfection in the country renowned for its classical leanings than in Italy where the most luxuriant work was carried out? And was such higher perfection reached because balanced order agreed particularly well with the French national character? We know that the first great "national" style of France was the Gothic and soon shall see that certain new architectural concepts of the late eighteenth century found the most fertile soil in France. Both the system of the Gothic and that which arose in the revolutionary era were basically different from the Baroque system. Thus one can hardly derive the relative perfection of the Baroque system in France from the national character. Now, if it was not the specific national genius, what else may have caused the unparalleled unfolding of the Baroque system in France?

Italy, where the system had originated, necessarily became its principal battle-field. The French architects of the seventeenth century recognized its timeliness and transplanted it to France where it was accepted as a fully developed doctrine, and where its inner contradictions were less felt or, at least, less violently expressed. Even its last stage, the Rococo, was much tamer than the Italian late Baroque. The essence of every system is the struggle for the fulfillment of its basic ideas. The French architects had not "created" the Baroque system, but just took it over and thus were more prone to compromise and to conceal its inner contradictions. Consequently, what we see in seventeenth- and eighteenth-century France is, with all the excellence in the details and with all its refinement, nothing but the stage of a pseudo-achievement at which the Italians never connived. The latters' unyielding spirit altered and distorted the traditional forms in order to express the system in the strongest way. This led to the "extravagances" of Borromini and Guarini, and when the frantic efforts appeared to be hopeless, to the rebellious pronouncements of the rigorists with their battle cry, "Away from conventional formality and back to nature." The principles of composition hardly changed from the Louis XIII to the Louis XVI. There is not much difference between the Louvre Colonnade by Perrault and the buildings on the Place de la Concorde by Gabriel.* In the long run, of course, the system could not remain unaffected by its own weaknesses. But it offered a prolonged resistance against the disintegrating forces within itself. The consolidation of the architectural system had a parallel in the stabilized French monarchy about 1700.

In the late eighteenth century Italy and France changed roles. France became more active and leading in architecture. With unceasing ardor—and, one may well say, in a certain frenzy—the Italian architects had striven to attain the unattainable. So it happened that about 1800 Italian architecture fell into a state of exhaustion, into the stage of lethargic classicism. France had not gone through all the excitement of the struggles of the Baroque system. Yet under the superficial calmness of her "classical" art, the antagonistic forces strengthened. At last, the hollowness of the old system became apparent. It collapsed, almost suddenly, and a juvenile follower system rose into significance. The reaction against the rule of tradition was extremely violent.

One may well consider the French castle of the era of political absolutism, with its dependent outbuildings and the subjugation of the surrounding country, as the possibly purest embodiment of the Baroque system. All over Europe the architects looked at it as a perfect solution and copied it so frequently that perhaps more specimens of it can be found outside of France than within its borders.

With extraordinary energy Jacques Lemercier brought the Baroque system into appearance in the rebuilding of the castle of Richelieu in Poitou (1631). There is not a single part which is not in strict and marked relation to the other parts and the whole. In addition, the vast complex is intimately connected with the environment. Lemercier's intentions show very clearly in this castle while his churches—for example, that of the Sorbonne (1635–1653)—reveal rather his dependence on Italian models. The engravings of the castle by Jean Marot[2] manifest how strong the feeling for unification was in the seventeenth century. Marot renders the structure as it might appear from an opposite building through the wide opening of a door. The jambs of the latter act as a *repoussoir* as well as a framing of the prospect. Thus the engraver underlined architectural unity by pictorial means. The manor house was built on a square plan and surrounded by a moat. Its elevations were made up of features reappearing again and again in the symmetrical forecourt. Continuous lines effected the closest interrelation between the components.

In such masterly unification of house and garden hardly any Italian landscape architect equaled Lemercier. Italian Renaissance gardens were rather loosely related to the buildings. Their regularity just slightly foreshadows the later trend toward emphasized unity (Villa Medici by Annibale Lippi).[3] Eventually a broad

---

* All buildings, streets, etc., for which no location is given, are in Paris.

parterre separates the house from the park (Villa Aldobrandini by Giacomo della Porta, and the much later Villa Doria Pamphili by Gianfrancesco Grimaldi).[4] Italian casinos rise above the surroundings with an air of aloofness (Casino of Pius IV by Pirro Ligorio).[5] Sometimes the main building does not rule, even when it occupies a prominent position; the Villa d'Este by Pirro Ligorio, for example, looks merely like a terminating screen.[6] Already in the sixteenth century Delorme at Anet[7] and Du Cerceau at Charleval[8] had aimed at the closest relationship of house and garden. But Lemercier was the one who created the model pattern for most of the great country residences of the Baroque. The French manor houses of the seventeenth and eighteenth centuries reveal the compositional principles of the Baroque unobtrusively, but distinctly. French architects were careful to keep the basic ideas of the system unimpaired. In administrating the Italian heritage they were extremely conservative. They sensed the menace lying in exaggeration, and avoided all extravagance, at least in the exteriors.

In his *Desseins de plusieurs palais* (1652) Antoine Lepautre[9] presents three main types of manor house, the court type, the block type, and the wing type. What Lepautre has attained may be shown by comparing his designs with the Château de Madrid at Boulogne.[10] In this outstanding structure of the era of François I the idea of the fortified medieval castle had just been overcome. It was built on a strictly symmetrical plan with the main hall as the central piece. Du Cerceau praised the symmetry of the arrangement and particularly the interrelationship between the pavilions.[11] The castle seemed to him to be a well-integrated whole.[12] However, one who is acquainted with later developments will note the multitude of individual features reminiscent of medieval polyphony. Moreover, in Du Cerceau's own designs, published in his *Livre d'architecture*,[13] only timid attempts toward the introduction of the new system can be found.

Compared with the Château de Madrid, the designs of Lepautre are markedly advanced. The first house that he presents[14] is built around a square court as older castles were, but the corners are not stressed and the main accent is laid on the central pavilions. There is rivalry between the verticals and the horizontals, while in the plan the main hall dominates. A terrace is interposed between the house and the garden. Whereas at the Villa Doria Pamphili[15] the stairs leading from the house to the terrace and the stairs from the terrace to the park are inconspicuous, the broad stairs of Lepautre's house ostentatiously effect the unity of building and garden.[16]

Lepautre's second house (*Bastiment carré*) represents the block type.[17] A dome finishes the central hall, and wide stairs bind the structural mass to the surroundings. Numerous statues enliven the house. Jombert, the editor of a reprint of Lepautre's work, commented that the projections give variety to the structure and unify its parts,[18] while the podium effects the soft transition from the ground to the walls (*cet adoucissement*).[19]

The wish to tie the parts and to avoid all harshness shows also in the fourth house, a specimen of the wing type.[20] (Because of its double-curved aisles ending in deep wings one might speak of it as of the butterfly type.) The ornamental, organized plan and the plastic character of the body manifest a rather high degree of accomplishment in the Baroque system, within which, however, the germs of an early decay already lie. For plasticity is against the nature of stone, and ornamentation is against practicality. Jombert must have sensed the latent danger. To him, there was too much art and too little common sense in the design.[21]

The French "classical" period is said to have begun about the middle of the seventeenth century, in painting with Nicolas Poussin, in architecture with François Mansart. According to Anthony Blunt, the particular merit of the latter was to have "moved from Mannerism towards one of the subtlest and most sophisticated forms of classicism to which architecture has ever attained."[22] Blunt does not say what he understands by architectural Mannerism,[23] but occasionally deals with Mansart's classicism. Mansart, he finds, is a classicist because of his "static method of design,"[24] "his principle of rectilinearity,"[25] the "strictly classical coldness" of the moldings,[26] and the "contrast between the simplest geometrical forms."[27] But Mansart likewise is "classical" in "bringing all the various parts [of the castle of Blois] under a single continuous roof, the mass of which sweeps round with impressive simplicity,"[28] and in harmonizing the side chapels of Ste. Marie de la Visitation with the central space.[29] The porch of this church, however, is to Blunt not "a perfectly classical solution," for it "is not a complete and independent unit."[30] In all it appears to be hard to demonstrate Mansart's "classicism," here "static" and isolating, there "sweeping" and unifying.

Characteristic of Mansart's work is, in my opinion, that symmetrical grouping and that gradation which are typical of the entire Baroque system. These qualities show on the churches of the Feuillants (1624), Minimes (1636), and the Val-de-Grâce (1645), as well as on the castles of Blois (1635) and Maisons-Laffitte (1642–1650).[31] And one should not call the castle of Blois "classical" because "the form . . . is unbroken except for the central projecting pavilion."[32] You must not spirit away the central main feature of a structure and then judge the whole without it.

Blunt compares the castle of Beaumesnil, by an unknown architect, with Mansart's castle of Balleroy in Normandy (1626), and terms the latter "a design in many ways classical."[33] He finds Beaumesnil "an elaboration of conflicting masses, of tortuous detail and of broken silhouette"[34] and contradistinguishes "the unbroken flatness of wall, and a clarity of outline and mass" of Balleroy. Yet more significant than these differences is the compositional pattern common to both structures. In both the concept of the Baroque hierarchy is clearly expressed. At Balleroy, the multiplicity of features is a residue of the polyphonic architecture of the Middle Ages, with the difference that the single voices now are subjected to a hard and fast rule which assigns to each its place within the whole.

We must consider the whole also when judging the castle of Maisons-Lafitte. It certainly does not belong to the type of the Farnesina "in which the building is a free-standing block."[35] The engraving of 1785 by Rigaud, which Blunt illustrates, shows that the outbuildings stood at a distance from the *corps de logis*. However, let us not overlook the fact that in the composition the idea of correlation rules although there is no material connection between the structures. The projecting end pavilions of the main house are like arms pointing at the outbuildings. That "each pavilion taken separately is not symmetrical"[36] shows that Mansart wanted to emphasize their belonging together. By their asymmetrical form they are brought into mutual reference. The single feature can be understood only if we consider its role within the whole.

In the interior, Mansart did not care about the full reciprocation of the rooms on either side of the main axis. This becomes manifest particularly in the upper story.[37] Here the staircase disrupts the sequence of the rooms and the place which in later buildings was reserved for the *grand salon* is taken by the antechamber. Thus a room of secondary importance occupies the most prominent position.

In Maisons-Laffitte vestiges of medieval polyphony mingle with Renaissance details and Baroque composition. We should not speak of its "classical" character, also for the simple reason that the term "classical" is very vague. It might be useful to find a better term to distinguish the French production from the exuberant Baroque of southern and central Europe. Perhaps one might speak simply of the French Baroque. In any case it is better to avoid forcing an imaginary "classicality" on Mansart's works.

There are still remnants of the decorative variety of the Renaissance in the buildings of the early seventeenth century. It was Louis Le Vau who expressed, after the mid-century, the will of the Baroque system in the strongest way. His manor house at Vaux-le-Vicomte (1656–1660) has been severely criticized by competent scholars. Gurlitt censures the lack of unity;[38] Lemonnier reproaches the heaviness and tastelessness of the whole.[39] Blomfield objects that "there are too many breaks and returns and changes of motive . . . the garden front is clumsy . . . the intersection of the dome with the mansard roof is ugly." Le Vau is to him "a mere technician who is replete with details, but has not the power to combine them in one organic composition."[40] Brinckmann alone rates Le Vau's work very high because of its elaborate spatial disposition.[41] Beside this very noteworthy characteristic Vaux-le-Vicomte tells much of the aims and the fate of the Baroque system; it reveals the insolubility of the problems posed to it. Le Vau did not attempt to conceal its inner contradictions. Well aware of the impossibility of making the house and the garden each complete in itself, and at the same time subordinating to the greater whole, he laid the greater stress on the house itself. Like the entrance hall of the Laurenziana, this castle of Vaux reveals the creative force which lies in the struggle for a definite goal, even if this goal can never be attained. This is the historical significance of Le Vau's creation. Its disproportions and its lack of "charm"[42] are but trifling deficiencies. Le Vau visualized in it the supreme idea of the Louis XIV era: one part is to rule over the others, absolutely; and the ruled ones shall be tied, firmly and visibly, to the dominant one. After Le Vau had thus shown the objectives and the limitations of the Baroque system, nothing was left for the followers but to add refinement and elaboration, which in the end brought about invalidation.

The dome of Vaux has been said to prove the architect's bad taste.[43] But just by its oversize it claims to be the lord who has overcome the Fronde of the roofs, the chimneys, and the outbuildings. All the power which binds the land around goes out from it, all the roads converge at its feet. The house itself stands aloof, while the castle of Richelieu seems to coalesce with the environment. In the interior there is a firm core consisting of the vestibule and the salon; the other rooms are in perfect balance on either side.[44] The *enfilade* has become the axis second in importance. Mansart at Maisons-Laffitte let the staircase intrude into the sequence of the rooms. Le Vau, with the sovereign gesture of the great artist, relegated the stairs to inconspicuous positions beside the vestibule. He wanted to achieve his pattern at any cost. At Vaux, and later at Versailles, André Lenôtre attempted to visualize the basic ideas of the system in his sphere just as the architects did in theirs.

Some ten years after Lepautre's publication came out Le Vau started the Collège Mazarin, which today is the seat of the Institut de France (about 1660).[45] Lemonnier finds its plan "original"[46] although it closely resembles Lepautre's "wing type." There is similarity in that the central and side pavilions of the Collège, too, are distinguished by colossal orders and connected by two-storied segmental wings. But in the crescendo of the pedimented portico and the high dome the concept of hierarchy is more drastically visualized than in Lepautre's design. The Collège gives the impression of a self-contained entity. Its clumsy side pavilions bar the movement of the curved wings. Le Vau shunned the promiscuity of structure and surrounding as he had done at Vaux. His creed was that sharing the power means to lessen it. He would solve the problems of the Baroque system by favoring autocracy.

A similar tendency appears in Charles Errard the younger's church of the Réligieuses de l'Assomption in Paris (1670),[47] where the dome virtually overpowers the lower parts, or, as Jacques-François Blondel wrote, *toute cette masse générale anéantit le porche.*[48]

Here I wish to point out a particularity of the architectural process which might be termed the precocity of the architectural phenomenon. This means that the architectural transformation goes ahead of the corresponding and related changes in general thought and in social structure. In the late eighteenth century there was a revolution in architectural thinking long before the revolution proper broke out. Similarly in the seventeenth century the endeavors of Italian and French architects to set up a new architectural system came before Louis XIV established the new order in the state, and before the great metaphysical systems of the Baroque, Spinoza's theory of the all-embracing whole and Leibnitz' doctrine of the pre-established harmony, originated. The Renaissance in the arts was prior to the movement of the Reformation; and the architectural upheaval about 1900 preceded the political crises of the twentieth century.

Le Vau remained lonely in his strenuous effort. Not he, but Claude Perrault became the leader and teacher of the next generations. His manner agreed with the French taste better than Le Vau's intransigence. The latter's work represents uncompromising fanaticism; Perrault's, clarity and graceful reticence.

Perrault's Colonnade du Louvre (begun 1667) is a well-balanced structure no part of which carries the main accent.[49] For he believed that contrasts belong to painting and sculpture, but not to architecture.[50] The climax of the center is counteracted by the anticlimax of the row of columns. Whereas Le Vau did not want any part to compete with the center, Perrault allowed the rival elements to exist calmly side by side. He tuned down the latent conflicts and by doing so he harmonized the whole. This was the right way to please his contemporaries and the later French critics. Perrault became famous by what may be termed the Perrault compromise.

It was not just the result of intrigues, nor was it incidental that Perrault won in the Louvre competition. He was in line with the general taste of his country. His manner was still approved in the eighteenth century, as the comments of Jacques-François Blondel show. Blondel censured in the projects of the other competitors all "disparities."[51] He found fault with the designs of Bernini because of the lack of correlation between the whole and the parts,[52] the lack of unity,[53] and, on the other hand, the lack of differentiation between the stories.[54] His criticism of the project of Lemercier was similar, although the latter had aimed at better gradation by adding in the center and on the sides small pavilions to the large pavilions.[55] The façade by Jean Marot was to Blondel not reposeful enough,[56] that of Le Vau too full of discrepancies.[57] For the builder of Vaux enhanced the center and the end-pavilions of the river front in his usual strong manner.[58]

What the French liked was this: to express the ideas of both unification and differentiation distinctly, but without any exaggeration. Any abruptness was to be softened; the harsh exigencies of the Baroque system were to be reconciled to the refined national taste.

Perrault himself went through almost all the different stages appearing in the designs of his rivals, before reaching his own solution. Blondel tells of his first designs showing heavy crowning features on the old side pavilions, which lessened the effect of the central portion. To counterbalance them, Perrault on second thought devised a high dome in the rear above a chapel to be built between the Louvre and the Tuileries.[59] At last he conceived the actual front which presents the hierarchic principle mitigated by serene calmness. Blondel praised him for having put elegance and harmonious beauty above anything else.[60]

About 1670 a compromise was reached between the never quenched desire for the integral system and the national taste. Then came a period of lull lasting nearly a century. Historically, this period is of less importance than the preceding and following struggles. Its elaborate performances are very attractive and cherished by connoisseurs and people who pose as such. Here on uncontested ground they can show their taste, undisturbed by the pressing problems of growth and death. It is for the historian to see whether life was still going on under the surface in these in-between times.

One cannot discuss the second half of the seventeenth century without mentioning François Blondel although his buildings, including the refined Porte Saint-Denis (1672), are of little interest from the viewpoint of the general development. He did not make any real contribution to solving the problems which came up in his time. His bulky *Cours d'architecture*[61] contains just the rudiments of the Italian doctrine. Except for a few remarks on the importance of unity and clarity,[62] and some practical suggestions, it brings only endless discussions of the orders and numeral relations. How little the exemplary proportions meant in reality was later pointed out by Jacques-François Blondel, who discovered that the measurements of the Porte Saint-Denis deviate from the precepts given in the *Cours*.[63] All the lengthy discourses on the proportions, whether Italian or French, were, and today still are, the playground of people who have little feeling for artistic qualities and little understanding for the historical process, but wish to appear scholarly by the display of columns of figures, or, as Jacques-François Blondel put it in censuring François Blondel and Charles-Etienne Briseux, *d'affecter un air de sçavant . . . faire parade de théorie*.[64]

In the work of Jules Hardouin-Mansart the development from Lemercier to Perrault is repeated. The layout of the castle of Clagny (1676–1680)[65] may be compared to that of Richelieu, its *corps de logis* to Maisons-Laffitte. At Clagny there are still equivalent stories, and a vestige of the old polyphony can be detected in the features composing its roof. At Dampierre (1675–1683)[66] the outbuildings are not in direct contact with the manor house, but their forms refer to it distinctly.

At Marly (1680–1686) Hardouin turned to the manner of Le Vau.[67] Three characteristic features show here: first, the colossal orders which extinguish the differentiation between the stories; second, the comparative independence of the pavilions; third, the weakness of the axial relationship between house and park. In other words, at Marly Hardouin tried to emphasize the individual structures, just as Le Vau had at Vaux-le-Vicomte and at Rincy,[68] but cared comparatively little about the unification of house and park.

Hardouin's late works count among the glories of French architecture. Almost all marks of conflict are eliminated from them. The Grand Trianon (1687)[69] was created in the spirit of Perrault. It is calm like the Louvre Colonnade, but as a country retreat less majestic than the palace in the center of Paris. The Grand Trianon consists of two separate apartments. There were different solutions possible. The architect might have connected them by a dominating central feature, in the Baroque manner, or might have divided them completely as architects about 1800 would have done. Hardouin compromised, and inserted an insignificant hall between the apartments. Thus there is neither marked unification nor resolute separation. The result is perfect harmony, refined, attractive, but weak. The colonnade veils what is behind it. At Vaux, on the contrary, the exterior tells of the interior; the heavy dome and the bold projection of the front indicate the position of the salon.

Hardouin's irresoluteness shows also in the park front of the palace of Versailles (1680).[70] The critics who find it monotonous are right. There are no strong accents. Even the central projection is hardly perceptible from the distance. Also, the interior arrangement is less expressive than that of Vaux. The somewhat boring Galerie des Glaces is no more than a connecting corridor, without the binding power of Le Vau's salon.

The Chapel of Versailles (1699–1710) used to be considered Hardouin's greatest achievement.[71] It excels by the grace of its execution, but lacks the definite climax which was a main goal of all Baroque building. In this bright, well-balanced interior the rivaling main features, the altar and the tribune for the monarch, are submerged in the rows of supports. The chapel is a triumph of Perrault's style, and the dead end of the Baroque system. Perrault and Hardouin knew how to mantle its tragedy with brilliant elegance. Blomfield called Versailles "a gigantic failure."[72] Yet it was not the architect's failure, but the failure of the system, which could never attain perfection.

The Dôme des Invalides in Paris (1675–1706)[73] rises lonely from its environment (fig. 95). It lacks a broad base, without which its famous dome looks like a king without a realm. Originally, Hardouin had intended to add quadrant colonnades similar to those in front of St. Peter's in Rome.[74] The colonnades were to be terminated by pavilions with little cupolas. There may have been various reasons why the colonnades were not carried out. I believe it is not too hazardous to see in their omission the abdication of the old system.

Summing up, one can say that Hardouin acquiesced in the deficiencies of the system, while Vanbrugh and Hawksmoor were soon to raise their passionate protests against it by creating the most unorthodox designs.

When we turn our attention to the works of two famous pupils of Hardouin, some grave problems of art history face us, the problems of influence and dependence, and along with them the problem of change in the visual arts. One of these pupils was Gilles-Marie Oppenord, who is renowned for having been a protagonist of the Rococo. It matters little that most of his work was not "great" architec-

ture; for the principles of the latter direct all the tectonic arts. Obviously, Oppenord
was "influenced" by what he had seen in Italy in the 1690's. There he had witnessed
dissolution progressing rapidly, after the ideal of integrality had proved to be an
utopian goal. Side by side with structural disintegration and compositional incongruities went the opposite extreme of the coalescence of the formal elements. All
this derived, on one side, from the trend toward differentiation, and on the other,
from the trend toward unification and the interference of certain general ideas of
the era, such as the animistic conception of all things and the pantheistic yearning
for all-embracing unity, as well as that most powerful factor in Baroque art, the
fervent religiosity focused on the One above. Disintegration shows, for instance, in
the candelabra on plate xxx of Oppenord's *Oeuvres;*[75] incongruities, in the mixture of heterogeneous features composing the fountains on plates xlvii and
xlviii; coalescence, in the chandelier, plate vi.

Germain Boffrand, the second pupil of Hardouin, had never been in Italy, but
like Oppenord moved away from his master's manner and created designs full of
unrest. The predominance of the voids over the walls in many of his façades reflects the typically Baroque tendency toward the unification of outer and inner
space, which resulted in a conflict between form and practicality. For the wider a
house opens, the more it contradicts its purpose of sheltering and protecting. Boffrand's second, unaccepted project for the castle of Malgrange in Lorraine (1712)
appeared to himself of particular significance. It is indeed highly indicative of
the condition of architecture in the early days of the century (fig. 96).[76] The
towering central mass is broken up by tall windows, plastic decoration, and
buttresses. The plan presents a bold innovation: four apartments depart diagonally
from the circular core. A parallel to the virtual interpenetration of inner and outer
space was the ever increasing use of huge mirrors in the interiors. Boffrand's upper
oval salon (1735) in the Hôtel de Soubise loses by the mirrors the character of an
independent volume unit and becomes virtually a unit in an infinite sequence of
rooms. Ascending bands of scrollwork efface the differentiation between the walls
and the vaulted ceiling.

In Boffrand's text we find very advanced views. He recommends that the
character of each structure should be visualized, so that the spectator will be impressed or pathetically moved. He asks for unity of character in addition to formal
unity, and praises "noble simplicity." This last concept was long firmly established
in France and was, so to speak, in the air; Winckelmann breathed it in only to
apply it to Greek art.[77] Boffrand's theory foreshadows that *architecture parlante,* or
"narrative" architecture, which was expected to tell both the purpose and the character of the building and soon was advocated by many writers and builders.[78]

Still farther than these pupils of Hardouin went Just-Aurèle Meissonnier, who
was born in a region of the most exuberant Baroque, in Piedmont. His project for

Saint-Sulpice of Paris (1726) points back to the production of his native country.[79] He even surpassed Oppenord in overdoing the pseudo-organic character of small objects, such as candlesticks, inkstands, etc.[80] Most noteworthy are those decorative designs in which symmetry and centralization are given up and unbalanced elements oppose each other. The fragmentary character of the elements is particularly significant.[81] These Rococo designs were the true precursors of the architectural revolution to come.

The Rococo masters proceeded on lines which were very different from the line of Hardouin. They were not "influenced" by him and did not duplicate his works. The general trend of thought was of greater importance in forming them than the achievements of an individual. And yet, Hardouin's brilliant but restrained elegance and the most fanciful Rococo works had much in common. One who looks beneath the surface can observe in both the decay of the system. While the older master tried to conceal it, the younger ones were not afraid of extreme "solutions." Those who still believe in the "creation" of styles by individuals appear to be wrong. Every artist is the servant and the exponent of the ideas of his time. The discovery of supra-individual "styles" has been one of the most momentous achievements of our discipline. We should not go back to the more primitive concept of individual "creators." This must be said since many still cling to the obsolete view.

It is, of course, difficult to uncover the dominant trends of a period and still more difficult to perceive the forces behind them. But even though our endeavors to penetrate the mysteries of the historical process cannot reach definite answers, the attempt may help us to comprehend the development.

The reign of "classical" serenity continued down to the mid-century. Then, deep unrest overcame French architecture, similar to that which had brought about the frantic efforts of Borromini, Guarini, and the Bibbiena, led to the Lodolian utopia of pure functionalism and Piranesi's fantasies, and prompted the designs of those early English revolutionaries as well as Morris' doctrine of cubism, even affecting the work of the calm decorator Adam. The agony of the old system ended in chaos everywhere.

One who was aware of the actual unrest and the impending danger was Jacques-François Blondel, the greatest teacher of architecture in the eighteenth century. He still imparted to his students the traditional doctrine which centered around the demands for symmetry, proportionality, unification, integration, and gradation. But on some important points he began to develop new views. Anthropomorphic forms appeared to him inconsistent; rationality, he found, should rule in architecture—*la Logique de l'Art . . . qu'il paroît important de rétablir*.[82] To him not less than to Boffrand, "character" began to mean more than visual beauty, *simplicité* more than embellishments, atmosphere more than empty regularity.[83] All in all he was a traditionalist in sympathy with the modern trends. His lengthy publications are particularly interesting because they inform us about what was going on in French architecture after the mid-century. Blondel tells of the fashions of the day, of classicism, Gothicism, and the predilection for Oriental art, and the general incertitude about the right way. He tells of the revolutionary spirit of the young generation, of that *esprit de vertige* which had taken hold of them.[84] He understood that the deepest reason for the restlessness, the source of the various experiments, was the perennial antagonism of form and purpose, which once again was about to destroy the dreams of perfect solutions.[85] Thus he gave much thought to the grave problem of supremacy. Should aesthetic principles rule composition or should practical needs be considered in the first place? Blondel believed it was possible to present a workable formula. Yet what he found was at best a solution for him. In the light of history it was just another compromise.

In the early days of the Baroque system in France, the Perrault compromise had originated; in its latest days originated that of Blondel. The two compromises have nothing in common, for they have different points of departure. Perrault was intent upon reconciling formal antinomies. Yet he did not question the validity of the principles of the system. To him the only thing to do was to be the arbitrator between the rivaling claims of concatenation and gradation. He decided for a pattern of reconciliation. In Blondel's time formality itself was assailed by the rationalists, and the hierarchical pattern rejected by the believers in individualism. We know about this conflict from the discordance between Lodoli and Algarotti. There was no bridge between the contradictory views of the two Venetian theorists. Blondel did not quiet himself by leaving the question open. Though he defended traditional composition, he simultaneously developed a new concept of unity. Boffrand had remained within the sphere of aesthetic unity when he formed the concept of unity of character.[86] Blondel accepted this concept, but went beyond it in advocating *cette triple unité*[87] of practicality, solidity, and adornment.

The demands for *utilitas, firmitas, venustas* were nothing new. For centuries people had the illusion that these qualities could exist side by side, peacefully. The recognition of their incompatibility came with the general great awakening in the Age of Reason. Blondel was aware that any one-sided solution would make things worse. The disregard of function had led to the exaggerations of the Italian Baroque architects and the French Rococo masters, whom he condemned.[88] The disregard of form meant destroying art.[89] Therefore he recommended compromising. He found that the perfect appearance of a structure depended chiefly on how far the reconciliation between aesthetics and practicality could be attained: *C'est de cette conciliation que dépend l'accord général de toutes les parties d'un bâtiment.*[90] The gap between the formalistic and the rationalistic viewpoint could be bridged, if the higher triple unity was achieved: *L'unité consiste dans l'art de concilier dans son projet la solidité, la commodité, l'ordonnance, sans qu'aucune de ces trois parties se détruisent.*[91] The wording *se détruisent* reveals that the dogmatic slumber of centuries, the spell of the time-honored *utilitas-firmitas-venustas* formula, had come to an end.

Blondel made two concrete suggestions. Either formality should reign on the exterior, with practicality in the interior;[92] or the former should be applied to public buildings, the latter to private ones.[93] These suggestions manifest the weakness of his compromising. Every true solution should hold good in any case. What Blondel recommended had to a large extent become common practice in France in the course of time. Yet because it was he who formulated and taught this specific program of reconciliation, with the strongest emphasis, one may term it the Blondel compromise.

Anxious to test his views he designed two different plans for a palace, the one tending to formality, the other to practicality.[94] Moreover, he exemplified his theory of reconciliation by two projects of the architect François Franque. The plan of an "Abbot's House" carried out at Villiers-Cotterets in 1765[95] and the project for a manor house at Amiens[96] should show how formality could be achieved even on an irregular plot, or when practical regards were against it. Blondel was full of praise for Franque's solutions.[97]

The divergences of opinion apparent in Blondel's *Cours* were, according to himself, due to the fact that its completion took twenty years.[98] Yet the lack of consistency is characteristic in itself, reflecting the unrest and the incertitude of the period. It is a great document of its time, deserving the most careful study. In one of the most crucial moments of architectural history Blondel watched the development with deep concern.

Contrary to Blondel, Charles-Etienne Briseux was hardly affected by the newly arising problems. His *Architecture moderne*[99] and *Art de bâtir*[100] are practical handbooks containing a few aesthetic touches. Most plans of town houses in the first are conditioned by the smallness of the lots, and are rather uninteresting. Some plans in the second deviate from the typically Baroque disposition centering in the salon-vestibule group. In some instances the vestibules contain the staircases,[101] in others they are inconspicuous antechambers.[102] Occasionally the main axis of the house and that of the salon do not coincide.[103] Yet there are also a few plans following the traditional pattern, even on irregular lots, which remind us of Franque's efforts.[104] Before long, a profound change in the concept of the architectural body was to come about, after a long period of underground preparation. Yet in 1761 Briseux still designed his Temple de l'Architecture with definitely marked gradation, strictly observed correspondence of the parts, thoroughly pierced walls, and great plasticity.[105] The *Traité du beau essentiel*[106] contains a commentary on the old quarrel between Claude Perrault and François Blondel about the proportions, and lengthy discussions of the conventional categories of correspondence, harmony,[107] conformity of the building to the human body,[108] and so forth. The demand that the parts should be neatly set off, and yet combine into a well-rounded-off whole is a typically French interpretation of the Baroque.[109] Briseux still conceives the structure as an organic entity.[110] Of modern concepts only that of *noble simplicité* appears.[111]

Briseux's unoriginal and uninspired publication was rightly censured by the Abbé Marc-Antoine Laugier, who was a modernistic writer comparable to Carlo Lodoli. *M. Briseux vient d'imprimer magnifiquement un Ouvrage dans lequel il perd beaucoup de temps à prouver la nécessité des proportions,*[112] he said. Laugier's radicalism made him many enemies such as La Font de St. Yenne,[113] Charles Axel Guillaumot,[114] and Amédée François Frézier.[115] In the course of a controversy with the last he expressed the firm belief that some day an architect would arise destined to save architecture from all whimsicalities by discovering its eternal laws.[116] Characteristic of Laugier is his straightforward rationalism[117] and his disrespect for the masters of the past and the traditionalists.[118] He attempted to uncover the reasons why architectural works please or displease, and suddenly was "enlightened": *J'ai voulu pénétrer la cause de leur effet . . . Tout à coup il s'est fait à mes yeux un grand jour.*[119] He made a clear distinction between the super-fluous or incidental and the necessary or essential.[120] He believed that only the latter warrents architectural perfection and that naturalness and simplicity[121] alone can prevent the decay of the art of building.[122] To forestall such decay one should forsake visual beauty and aim instead at expressiveness and character.[123] This already was the mentality of romanticism with its predilection for the irregu-lar[124] and for productions of the past with outspoken character, such as Egyptian and Gothic works. While Laugier on one hand recommended "atmosphere," he advocated on the other the use of elementary geometrical forms.[125] Many French architects of the late eighteenth century shared his belief in geometrical composi-tion and strove to find new artistic solutions by combining the elementary forms in diversified manners.[126] We shall learn more about their endeavors later. They prove that in the Age of Reason architecture remained an art influenced, but not guided, by rationalism. Expressiveness and a new formality became the foremost goals. This development is foreshadowed in Laugier's theory, which was enthusi-astically received by the younger generation. We know about this from the last, posthumous publication of Jacques-François Blondel.[127] The great teacher himself appears to have been impressed by Laugier's *Essai, ouvrage plein d'idées neuves et écrit avec sagacité.*[128]

Lodoli and Laugier formed their views almost simultaneously and, we may assume, independently. Robert Morris went ahead of both with his modern views on form and composition. Yet he did not reach the far-going conclusions of the Venetian Franciscan and the Paris Jesuit.

Of Blondel's fellow architects, Jacques-Ange Gabriel was perhaps the most prominent and the most popular. Thanks to the conspicuousness of his main works, erected on outstanding sites of Paris, he became the best-known builder of the Louis XV period. His biographer Comte de Fels calls him *le grand maître de l'art français au XVIIIᵉ siècle*.[129] Unanimity reigns about the rank of Gabriel as an architect, but there is much diversity of opinion about the character of his art and the stages of his development. Fels observes that his work underwent some change in the course of the years. He finds the turning point in Gabriel's career about 1760, when Grecism began to permeate his former "national" manner.[130] Blomfield contradicts Fels, declaring that "there is no trace in the Petit Trianon of that pedantic neo-Greek motive which was to render the architecture of the early part of the nineteenth century so particularly dull." It rather "seems the expression of all the best and most characteristic qualities of pure French architecture."[131] Cox distinguishes four manners of Gabriel, each roughly corresponding to a historical period,[132] namely a Louis XIV, a Louis XV, a Louis XVI, and a "precursive Empire phase." The monograph by Gromort, however, indulges in oversimplification, denying any change of style in Gabriel's development—an astonishing fact, indeed, in the case of an architect who lived through more than eighty years. Gromort sees no stylistic difference between the Ecole Militaire, the buildings of the Place de la Concorde, and the Petit Trianon.[133]

The front of the Exchange of Bordeaux (1742) is Baroque in composition,[134] and so is the Ecole Militaire, which, of course, must be judged after the original project of 1750.[135] The imposing central pavilion of the latter is counterbalanced by the side pavilions. The verticals of the façade antagonize the horizontal wings and the screening walls in front of the lateral courts.

In planning the Place Louis XV (de la Concorde) in 1753, Gabriel made ample use of the projects of the other participants in the competition.[136] The general layout, climaxing in the dome of Contant d'Ivry's project for the Madeleine at the far end of the Rue Royale, is a Baroque composition. The colonnades of the two buildings on either side of the street, the building that became the Hôtel Coislin and the Garde-Meuble, since the Ministère de la Marine, remind us of Perrault's composedness. Already in these years, between 1750 and 1760, a deep-going change was preparing. Gabriel made the first, rather timid, steps in an entirely new direction when he erected some small fabrics about 1750; he achieved a mature specimen of the new manner in the Petit Trianon.

In 1750 Gabriel erected the Pavillon Français, one of the most attractive structures in the park of Trianon.[137] Not the tall French windows, but the massive wall and the horizontals of the cornice and the balustrade are the most conspicuous features. From the central circular room four short wings depart diagonally. Their movement seems to be abruptly stopped, quite different from the wings of Baroque structures which tend toward the environment. Similarly reticent is the Hermitage of Madame Pompadour at Fontainebleau (1749).[138] It is a square building with a flat roof, divided into a rusticated ground floor and a low attic. The façades show little relief.

In 1750 Gabriel designed the Pavillon du Butard, near Versailles.[139] The circular salon, inscribed into an octagon, is strongly oversized; the traditional balance of the plan had been lost. Much stress is laid on the solid wall. Above the side doors are sunk tablets, which originally were planned to receive sculptural decoration.[140] The first project shows a roof à la Mansart; the actual house, however, has a flat roof. These small structures represent preparatory stages of the fundamentally new form of the Petit Trianon.

The character of the Petit Trianon (1762–1764)[141] depends on the new form of the whole, but not on the conventional details.[142] The strictly cubical body is isolated from its surroundings in the most definite manner. The ground plan is informal, the roof flat, the decoration extremely reticent. There is no dominant part. Only in the differentiation of the stories you may find a reminiscence of former times. It has been said that the Petit Trianon marks Gabriel's third, Greek manner, inspired by David Leroy's *Ruines des plus beaux monuments de la Grèce* (1758).[143] However, it actually implies entirely new artistic goals. Here, Gabriel has surrendered to a new ideal of configuration. It proves his versatility that in advanced age he could not merely follow, but lead, the new trend. Yet one may just as well say that it proves the vigor of the new trend, when a mature "classical" master accepted it almost unrestrictedly.

Three projects for an entrance gate to the castle of Fontainebleau (1773) reveal how "modern" Gabriel was in his last years.[144] The main thing about them is not the details taken from antiquity, but the heaviness of the whole, the blocklike character, the predominance of the horizontals, and the independence of the parts. This is the last stage that Jacques-Ange Gabriel reached.

At this point I wish to discuss an interesting building, the composition of which represents that stage of the development between the Frozen Baroque and the "consolidated" architecture of 1800, to which, for example, the advanced works of James Paine belong:[145] the Arsenal of Le Havre, erected under Louis XVI by an unknown architect.[146] The entablature below the attic story and the main cornice bar energetically any upward trend; the horizontal grooves of the piers reveal that the concept of the "growing" supports was no longer influential. Each feature stands for itself; there is no rhythmic arrangement suggestive of movement. The attic shows features without any relationship to each other, square panels contrasted to semicircular windows. The lack of rapport becomes particularly manifest in the roof zone. One could cut off any feature from the roof without damaging the whole. In the center a clock turret rises, serving as the base of a monopteros. It looks as if it were put there haphazardly. The square-headed entrance door, running up to the entablature, tears the façade virtually asunder. Works of the Frozen Baroque lack liveliness, but are full of interrelationships which are missing on the front of the Arsenal.

The tendency to make the parts independent appeared already in much earlier works, for instance the west front of the church of Saint-Sulpice by Giovanni Niccolò Servandoni (1732–1745).[147] Yet the new manner is not easily recognizable in this early stage. Therefore I have demonstrated it first on the far more advanced Arsenal, which in addition can help us to understand Gabriel's latest manner. The narthex of Saint-Sulpice screens the building behind it. It is a unit for itself, and has no climax within itself. The towers—only that to the south is by Servandoni—are superimposed structures estranged from the body below; the roof balustrade severs them so markedly that they look like arbitrary additions. Often enough, Baroque church fronts, too, look like screens. However, their architects, disturbed by the discrepany of façade and body, strove after harmony and relationship between the parts. They tried to make a pictorial group out of the elements.

The novelty of Servandoni's narthex was recognized by contemporary and modern critics. Blondel admired its greatness; with all the acuteness of his vision he saw that from it there was a way which might lead into the future.[148] Laugier was dissatisfied with the work, although he grasped Servandoni's intentions. He censured its heaviness,[149] the lack of a climax, and the loose superposition of the towers.[150] Ledoux studied the church carefully.[151] Of modern critics, Gurlitt remarks the new handling of the masses (*ein Schaffen mit Massen, nicht mit gegebenen Formeln*).[152] Ward is fully aware of the epoch-making shape of the narthex:[153] "Servandoni broke with all the accepted rules of church design." Blomfield, always siding with tradition, shares the views of Laugier. He misses the centerpiece, the *avant-corps*.[154] Schneider sees in the front the end of the Baroque, the new composure, and the new grandeur.[155]

Of particular interest is the *Mémoire* by Pierre Patte about the best way of finishing the façade of Saint-Sulpice.[156] Patte makes various suggestions, all in the Baroque sense. He asks for a centerpiece to bridge the gap between the towers,[157] and recommends statuary at their base, which certainly would have effected a soft transition to the main mass.[158] He reports that Servandoni thought of a pediment in 1736, but abandoned the idea.[159] That means that Servandoni, after some hesitation, carried out the modern solution.

The church of Sainte-Madeleine, at Besançon, was begun by Nicole in 1746. Its façade presents a rhythmic group of openings, climaxing in the center. Yet the massiveness of the walls and the emphasis laid on the material are definitely "modern."[160]

The designs of Contant d'Ivry are full of discordant features. The church which he planned for the Royal Abbey of Panthémont in the Faubourg St. Germain, 1747, is composed of unrelated elements. The oversized porch is contrasted to the clerestory, the dome, and the lantern.[161] The dome is a plain, clumsy shell without ribs. The rivalry between the single features is still more conspicuous in the project for a town hall on the Quai Malaquais (1748).[162] There are odd discrepancies between the curiously shaped central dome and the lateral belvederes, and between the main mass and the appended wings. Blomfield says that this project, if it had been built, would have been "spoilt by indifference to scale in his orders."[163] This disregard of the proportions may be shocking to eyes accustomed to traditional harmony; yet, what means more to us, it is symptomatic of the basically changed attitude toward composition. Now, contrasts were preferred to harmonious balance, and in the end—in our century—one has come to find that buildings are "spoilt" by symmetry and "beautiful" proportions.

The best-known project of Contant is that for the church of the Madeleine, of 1764.[164] Blomfield rightly notices in it an "important deviation" from the "traditional French eighteenth-century type," for "at the west end, instead of the usual order above order, Contant stopped his nave abruptly and added beyond it a portico of a single Corinthian order. . . . The effect would have been questionable, as the portico had even less relation to the rest of the design than Soufflot's prodigious portico at the Panthéon."[165] It was the natural consequence of the new tendency toward setting the parts free, that the appended portico came into fashion. The dome of the church of the Madeleine would have been ribless like that of the abbey of Panthémont.[166] Under Napoleon, Contant's project was replaced by the Grecian temple of Pierre Vignon.

Several projects for stable entrances are distinguished by the forceful treatment of the stone. In them Contant combined traditional features in a bold manner. It was only one step from these designs to Ledoux's toolhouses.[167] Rustication, artificial rocks, stalactites, and other picturesque motifs appear in Contant's fountains,[168] a "Bâtiment d'Eau,"[169] and so on. Blomfield sees in similar features on the project for a town hall, designed by the brothers Slodtz for the Quai Malaquais, "strange examples of the fashion for the Romantic plus the Antique, which was gradually undermining the national architecture of France."[170] One may as well speak of features derived from the Renaissance—remember only the Luxembourg Palace—and, then, just wonder who was more "nationally" French, de Brosse or Perrault and his followers. Patte comments on the decoration of the Slodtzs as follows: *Pour rendre pittoresque sa décoration, on y a exprimé des quartiers de roche, dont la forme, sçavamment bisarre, auroit rélevé l'ensemble de ce morceau d'architecture.*[171] Incidentally, the loosely superposed bell tower of the Slodtzs' town hall resembles the clock turret of the Arsenal of Le Havre.[172]

In Contant's vestibule and staircase of the Palais-Royal in Paris (1763) the ornaments are clear-cut and neatly set off from the wall.[173] Contant, no doubt, was a precursor of the various trends which were to arise in the closing eighteenth century.

Jacques-Germain Soufflot in his youth was already much interested in the architecture of the past. After having been admitted to the Academy of Arts of Lyon in 1739, he read a paper on the proportions in architecture; two years later, he presented a comparison of Gothic and modern churches.[174] His Hôtel-Dieu at Lyon (1741)[175] may be regarded as a production of the Frozen Baroque. The horizontals prevail, the openings are poorly framed, the dome topping the flat roof is only weakly related to the extended body. The Loge du Change at Lyon (1747)[176] is the fruit of Soufflot's stay in Italy.[177] It reminds us of the Loggia of Brescia.[178] On the church of Sainte-Geneviève in Paris Soufflot's contemporaries noticed eclectic traits. Quatremère de Quincy wrote: *L'architecte y voulut mettre de tout,*[179] and Soufflot's pupil Brébion commented upon the architect's intentions: *Le principal objet de M. Soufflot en bâtissant son église a été de réunir . . . la légèreté de la construction des édifices gothiques avec la pureté et la magnificence de l'architecture grecque.*[180]

Soufflot's first project for the church (about 1757) is preserved in engravings by Bellicard.[181] It was Baroque in several regards. For the sake of a suave transition from the main mass to the dome, four pedestals were arranged around the base of the drum. The statues on the pedestals continued the upward movement of the columns of the porch, which was taken over by the columns of the drum and by the statue of the saint on top of the dome. The entablature of the drum consisted of projecting and receding portions. Soufflot was asked to add two towers to the east side (fig. 97),[182] by which addition the church came to resemble Baroque group compositions. In 1777 Soufflot planned the circular colonnade around the drum, which drastically severed the dome from the body.[183] Quatremère de Quincy, still thinking in terms of the Baroque, wrote about this colonnade: *Le péristyle . . . tend à diminuer l'effet de l'ensemble qui se trouve ainsi divisé, non pas en deux parties, mais en deux* tout [his emphasis] *dont chacun nuit à l'autre, ce qui donne l'idée de deux édifices indépendans.*[184] When in 1791 the church became the hall of fame of the nation and was named Panthéon,[185] further significant changes were made. Quatremère de Quincy "did away with the two towers . . . at the east end designed by Soufflot, and had the windows in the walls built up in order that all the light might come from above in the true manner of the antique."[186] It may be true that the windows were filled in simply for the sake of a "classical" skylight. But why were the towers removed and why was the tall lantern with the statue replaced by an inconspicuous cylindrical finishing?[187] These changes indicate that in the meantime Quatremère de Quincy had joined the ranks of the moderns, who preferred composure to movement, compactness to lightness, harsh contrasts to pictorial grouping. The alterations were applauded by his contemporaries.[188] From then on, the Paris Panthéon has preserved the austere aspect given to it in the French Revolution. Later, only a new lantern was added, similar to that of Soufflot.

Modern critics have been shocked by the discrepancy of classic features and bare walls. Ward finds that "the slender columns contrast painfully" with the solid mass[189] and regrets the "chilling aridity" resulting from the lack of openings.[190] Blomfield complains that Soufflot "lost his way in the catacombs of the Classic Revival," and censures Quatremère de Quincy for the "audacity to interfere to a disastrous extent with Soufflot's designs."[191] Mondain-Monval sees in

Soufflot *l'homme classique,* and the precursor of the nineteenth century.[192] He inveighs against those who transformed the edifice,[193] finds the art of the Revolution pedantic, dogmatic, heavy, and cold.[194] Nonetheless he senses the new in Soufflot's work, and rightly characterizes the Panthéon as a product of transition.[195] Heaviness and revivalism might be censured also in Soufflot's Rotonde in the park of Ménars.[196] However, we should not fail to remark its modernity in the forceful contrast between the smooth surface of its saucer dome and the rustication of the pilasters and the columns. The plainness of the works of about 1800 often has been explained with economic reasons. Yet the noblest shrine of the Revolution would hardly have been given such a sober appearance, had it not agreed with the taste of the time. It certainly would have been thriftier to leave the structure as it was, than to remove the Baroque features. Soufflot planned to finish the large square in front of the church with two quadrant buildings. The one, the Ecole de Droit, was carried out in 1771,[197] the other, the Mairie of the fifth district,[198] in the nineteenth century. The square and the streets leading to it could, of course, be laid out in different ways. Soufflot apparently was not hampered by any instructions nor by any older buildings and could follow his artistic intentions to the fullest.

From Bernini's Piazza di San Pietro to Vanvitelli's castle at Caserta,[199] from Lemercier's castle for Richelieu to Contant's "town hall" design it was customary to frame the square or the forecourt in front of a monumental building with low lateral structures. Thus the spectator felt as if he were being received with open arms. The Place du Panthéon differs in two regards. The quadrant buildings are, actually and formally, independent units; and they face the church itself, not the outer world. The whole complex has the character of a secluded precinct.

Outward show in behavior and costume were essentially Baroque, reticence in all circumstances characterized the post-Baroque, except the interlude of Romanticism. People of Baroque times liked to exhibit their feelings, people of the nineteenth century and still more in the twentieth have been reluctant to show their emotions. These different attitudes are clearly reflected in architectural schemes. The attitude underlying Baroque designs was extroversion; the resulting form was centrifugal. The attitude which created the Place du Panthéon was introversion; the resulting form, centripetal. In the following chapters we shall meet further introverted or self-centered schemes, a cathedral project by Peyre, Ledoux's ideal city, Belanger's Grand Théâtre des Arts, and Baltard's project for the castle of Saint-Cloud.[200]

We have learned about the deep-going change in architectural thinking in the mid-eighteenth century. Next, we shall see how the French architects born about 1730 reacted to the new trend of thought. These were the men whose extraordinary designs created on the eve of the Revolution mark the culmination of the architectural crisis in the Age of Reason.

XII

THE ARCHITECTS OF THE FRENCH REVOLUTION THE GENERATION OF 1730

MUCH HAS been done to elucidate the retrospective trends of the late eighteenth century. Yet its eclectic inclinations deserve far less attention than the signs which point to the future. We should not content ourselves with recording as many works as possible of the classic revival while omitting to investigate what was going on below the pseudoclassical surface. The most conspicuous features need not be the most significant ones.

Before discussing the achievements of the "generation of 1730," that is, the architects born between about 1715 and 1745, I want to outline briefly the new artistic ideals which rose with them. About 1750 many artists still held the Renaissance belief that architectural form is independent of the nature of the materials, or, as Alberti had put it, *Neque habet lineamentum in se ut materiam sequatur.*[201] However, the illusionism of the Baroque, its animistic tendencies, and its desire for perfect unification soon were to be things of the past. We know from the writings of Laugier and Milizia[202] that the appeal to the eyes now was considered to be less important than "character" and "naturalness." Buildings should no longer be like pictures, as Sir Joshua Reynolds still would have it, but should convey a moral, or stimulate sentiments. The spectator should be affected by the personality of the individual structure, but not by some impersonal "beauty." The intimate interrelationship of the parts, their right balance, and their concordance had been the foremost aims since the Renaissance. Carefully calculated proportions had been regarded as the best means to achieve these ends. Till after 1700 the theorists untiringly and minutely commented on the proportions and the critics based their judgments almost exclusively upon them. Hardly ever was an artistic doctrine more firmly rooted than that of the proportions. It means much that toward the end of the eighteenth century it was abandoned by all progressive minds. Yet one should not think that all formal aspirations were gone forever and the rule of a Lodolian functionalism about to start. The perennial competition between form and function went on. New patterns developed, influenced by the ideals of the rationalists, but dependent in the first place on the new concept of an individualistic organization. The independence of the elements could be well expressed by their simple repetition, or by dramatic antithesis. By and by the forms depending on the former ideal of unification, the flexible curves as well as the imitations of organic growth, were

141

superseded by forms which agreed better with the new ideal of configuration. The forbidding shapes of elementary geometry were found to be the most appropriate ones to satisfy both the individualistic feeling and the desire for modern patterns.

The changed attitude toward the material; the aim at a different effect on the spectator; the departure from time-honored, well-established patterns; the frantic efforts for the reorganization of the architectural whole and the consequent introduction of new forms—all these changes justify speaking of a revolution in architecture. The architects who played an active role in the great process of reorientation may be named the architects of the French Revolution, although they worked chiefly before and partly after the years of terror. It would be pedantic merely to consider as revolutionary architecture the production between 1789 and 1799, from the storming of the Bastille down to the Consulate. Indeed, many contemporaries spoke of an architectural revolution dating back to the 1760's.[203] Again, as in my monograph *Three Revolutionary Architects—Boullée, Ledoux and Lequeu,* my intent is to present the great transformation not only by analyzing a large number of designs, but also by quoting architects and critics of the period who seem to have been fully aware of the deep-going change.

In order to give a picture of architectural development between 1750 and 1800 one might group the architects according to their particular inclinations and distinguish between eclectics, or revivalists, who looked for inspiration from Egypt, classical antiquity, and the Middle Ages; romanticists, who wanted to give "atmosphere" and indulged in exaggerated dimensions and bold lighting effects; rationalists, who searched for basic rules, aimed at soundness and consistency, propagated the elementary forms and preached respect for the nature of the materials; reformers, who burned to establish a new order of the constituent parts. They all were fanatics carried away by the common desire of discovering a new means of expression. However, any classification would have a distorting effect, as traces of several or even all of these ideas can be found in each single work. Le Camus de Mézières was more of a romanticist in his writing, more of a rationalist in his building. Neufforge was an eclectic and a reformer, who used traditional forms in his novel compositions. Boullée was a rationalist and a romanticist. Ledoux, with his fascinating personality, was the greatest of all because he spoke every revolutionary idiom. Instead of attempting a more or less arbitrary classification it will be better to stick to the adopted plan of this book and to proceed from architect to architect, from work to work. French architects who worked mainly abroad, such as those who brought the modern French ideas to Germany, Scandinavia, and Russia, must of course be included in the discussion. The various aspects of the transition from the Baroque to the nineteenth century are the chief topics of this section, excluding any search for the latest reasons for the change as being beyond the scope of this investigation. Occasional remarks will intimate the forces behind the transformation.

The main works of Philippe de la Guêpière were the castles of Solitude near Stuttgart (1763-1767) and Monrepos near Ludwigsburg, Württemberg (1760-1767).[204] Their plans are variants of the traditional centralized arrangement. The salon at Monrepos is preceded by an oblong vestibule; at Solitude there is no vestibule, the center being occupied exclusively by the elliptical salon. The stiff decoration of both houses reminds us of the Frozen Baroque, but already the new concept of antithetical masses appears: central cylinders versus cubic wings, superstructure versus substructure. At Monrepos the attic story—*cet étage bâtard*[205]—intrudes between the dome and the main story. His project for a tomb presents the contrast of a colonnade with a heavy truncated pyramid on top of it.[206]

Marie-Joseph Peyre, a pupil of Blondel,[207] left behind him designs of considerable interest, which reflect the new compositional aims. In his text he reports his studies of the *thermae* of Diocletian and Caracalla, carried out with Moreau-Desproux and De Wailly.[208] To Peyre imitation of the ancients was a preliminary step. He was convinced that they could be surpassed.[209] The text which accompanies the engravings of his projects contains contradictory views inspired by the diverging trends of the era. Unity, beautiful proportions, and beautiful masses[210] still meant much to Peyre. On the other hand, he expressed a desire for novelty combined with simplicity,[211] and expected architecture to "impress the soul."[212] In his designs, however, he did not aim at simplicity and "character." These elevations show profuse traditional decoration, while the plans reveal that he wanted to make out of the classical details a composition entirely his own.

In his project for an "Academy Building" the center and the domed end pavilions are connected by concave colonnades, but they are entirely different in shape (fig. 98). The plan (fig. 99) presents an axial scheme.[213] Behind its somewhat playful arrangement we perceive the will to make the independent units form a pattern. The building stands in the center of a large square hemmed in by auditoriums, baths, a naumachia, a circus, and so on.

The "Cathedral" (fig. 100) is a circular structure with four porticoes.[214] It stands in the center of circular colonnades, to which two smaller buildings are adjoined: the palace of the archbishop and, diametrically opposed to it, the palace of the canons. Each of the two buildings could stand alone; the church, too, would not be impaired by their removal. Never could a Baroque complex endure such an amputation of its members. The colonnades seclude the sacred precinct from the outer world. This was the outspoken intention of the architect:

Les colonnades qui forment [l'enceinte magnifique], en éloignant l'église des embarras et du bruit, préparerait [*sic*], à l'exemple de quelques temples anciens, au respect que l'on doit avoir en y entrant.[215]

There is no better form to achieve such seclusion than the circle—this shy, withdrawing form which Valadier chose, also, for his "Sepulchral Precinct."[216] While the curved wings of the academy building still have in themselves something of the inviting character of Baroque compositions, the colonnades of the cathedral keep the spectator out.

The artistic meaning of the layout of the cathedral is clear (fig. 101). Peyre realized his intention although he had to compromise with the program which the patrons had asked him to carry out:

Je me suis assujetti dans la composition de ce morceau, au programme que l'académie avait donné. J'ai lié autant qu'il m'a été possible les deux palais, avec le plan général, par une enceinte magnifique, qui semble les réunir.[217]

Peyre does not name his patrons; maybe they were fictitious. Yet he certainly was not much hampered with regard for them. He designed the cathedral as great and as splendid as he wanted to have it. His "Chapelle sépulcrale" is an imitation of of the tomb of Cecilia Metella.[218] That he chose this particular model was, in all probability, due to the prevailing predilection for cylindrical form.

The church of the abbey of St. Blasien in Baden was built by Michel d'Ixnard between 1768 and 1779.[219] The hemispherical dome on top of the high drum has a strong competitor in the porch flanked by sturdy turrets. The architect was not interested in harmonic relations; he wanted to present the antagonism of heavy masses. For this reason a modern critic has found fault with the structure.[220] Yet one should not measure it by the gauge of Renaissance or Baroque standards. The concept of contrasted geometrical shapes shows also in the plan. The huge circular hall of the congregation is set against the narrow rectangular choir.[221] D'Ixnard's triangular "Maison de Plaisance" for Count Schoulenbourg—which, with its semi-elliptical porches in front of each side, calls to mind Laugier's invention of a triangular church[222]—stands in a circular clearing of the woods; the water basin in the center of the building is encompassed by a circular colonnade. The main façades of the castle of Coblence (1777) are Frozen Baroque.[223] The semicircular stable buildings show the predilection for elementary geometry.

Jacques-Denis Antoine also attempted to achieve the effect of independent elements. In his Hôtel des Monnaies (1768-1775) the central portion is slightly emphasized and the conventional tripartite rhythm of rusticated basement, main story, and mezzanine is still present.[224] But in the uninterrupted row of the windows all inequalities seem to be effaced. The court is richer in contrasts than the river front. The façade of the Hôtel de Fleury (1768) was composed of two equal pavilions connected by a lower wing as the subordinate center piece.[225] The pattern of reduplication which we see here means equality without monotony. It allowed for the later addition of a third pavilion without any damage to the aspect of the whole. Any extension of a Baroque building would have ruined its proportions and its rhythm. Soon Antoine passed to bolder arrangements in the portal of the convent of the Feuillants (1776) and the Mint of Berne (1789).[226] What makes the portal interesting is not the plain fact that once more classic features were made use of, but its oversize, or the incongruity between the portal and the whole. There hardly was a practical reason for making the portal so huge. The incongruity seems to have been just as intentional as were the discrepancies in many "irregular" English houses of the early century. The Mint at Berne (1789) consists of two independent blocks held together by the entrance screen. The main accent is on the top floor, which has the highest windows, while the mezzanine below has the smallest openings and the windows of the ground floor are of medium size. The conventional equilibrium has been reversed. Similar unbalance characterizes the project for the porch of Saint-Nicolas du Chardonnet, which exhibits a heavy attic surmounted by a pyramid.[227] (Top-heaviness has become a very common feature of buildings in our time.)

The three stories and the mezzanine of the theater (1763) projected by Nicolas-Marie Potain[228] are unified by colossal porches. Thus a huge lower mass is opposed to an attic story with tiny bull's-eyes. The result is striking disproportionality.

The theater at Bordeaux (1775-1780) by Victor Louis "has generally been regarded as inaugurating a new era in theatre design" because of certain improvements of the interior.[229] Externally it was modern, too, because it was "independent and isolated" and because of "the monotony of the nearly cubical mass."[230] The giant columns of the main front veil the gradation of the stories. Louis' Théâtre-Français (1787-1790) reveals still more distinctly that the sense for balance had been lost.[231] His arcaded fronts on the garden of the Palais-Royal (1784) present the uniform array of giant pilasters.[232] Neither in the vertical nor in the horizontal is there any vestige of the traditional rhythmization. This disposition was not the result of chance. Louis had developed very definite and very novel views about composition, as can be seen from his own comment in the *Almanach du voyageur à Paris*.[233] The concept of the repetition of equivalent elements underlies also his grandiose project of the Place Ludovise at Bordeaux (1783).[234] He planned fourteen cubic pavilions uniformly decorated with giant orders, on a semi-ellipse. Round arches connecting the attic stories would have achieved the effect of triumphal arches, from which thirteen streets were to start. (The streets were to be named after the thirteen United States of America.)

The court front of the Hôtel du Châtelet, Rue de Grenelle (1770), by Mathurin Cherpitel resembles Potain's and Louis' works with its high porch running up to the main cornice.[235] Very impressive is the vigorous treatment of the material. What Cherpitel had brought home from his Italian tour was not Greco-Roman refinement but the Italic predilection for crude stonework. The court reminds us of the achievements of the Tuscan Renaissance.

Having recognized certain major trends in French architecture after the mid-century we can appreciate the attainments of Charles De Wailly, who was a pupil of three great architects and became a great architect himself. Two of his teachers,

Jacques-François Blondel and Servandoni, are still well known today. The third, Jean-Laurent Le Geay, was held in high esteem by his contemporaries. Charles-Nicolas Cochin called him *un des plus beaux génies en architecture* and pointed out his extraordinary influence on students.[236] As we saw, even Piranesi seems to have changed under his spell. Le Geay, however, produced little and soon fell into oblivion. Modern critics have seen in De Wailly just one of the architects "who had travelled in Italy and who . . . hoped to reproduce in France, in terms as nearly identical as they could make them, the Temples of Rome and Magna Graecia."[237] Yet De Wailly was far more than merely a classicist. He surpassed Cherpitel in the handling of material, La Guêpière, d'Ixnard, and Peyre in the intensity of his search for new patterns.

De Wailly's interior decoration of the Palazzo Spinola at Genoa (1773)[238] was exuberant Baroque. But no Baroque traces could have been detected on the Odéon Theater in Paris (1779–1782)[239] or on the castle of Rocquencourt, which he rebuilt in 1786.[240] Nor were there any reminiscences of antiquity in the two buildings, except a few Tuscan columns of the former and a few Ionic pilasters on the latter. In both cases the basic idea was to present an elongated block with plain walls and unframed openings. Although the Odéon was connected with the neighboring buildings by arcades, its self-contained character remained unimpaired.[241] De Wailly had returned from Italy with a predilection for vigorous rustication and elementary shapes. When he rebuilt the castle of Rocquencourt he made the stone and brick show; only later were the walls covered with white paint.[242] De Wailly refrained from almost any decoration on the Odéon as well as on the Chancellerie d'Orléans in Paris.[243] It is significant that the *Encyclopédie* illustrated the Odéon as a noteworthy specimen of modern building.[244]

Yet De Wailly was not content with the merely negative attitude of renouncing all embellishments. He was eager for innovation, sometimes perhaps just for innovation's sake, more often with the definite goal of finding new patterns fitted to the seriousness of stone building. He was *impétueux, bouillant, altéré de modèles, devoré du besoin de connaître, d'étudier, de comparer,* as a necrologist characterized him,[245] and thus predestined to be a leading figure among the revolutionary architects.[246] A project for the Odéon presents a capricious superstructure on the roof and two curious "sentry boxes" on the balcony (fig. 102).[247] Innovation for innovation's sake appears also in the drawing of a pulpit at the Museum of the Cooper Union, New York, signed and dated 1789. It resembles De Wailly's pulpit at Saint-Sulpice (fig. 103), set on top of two flights of stairs which bridge the interval between two pillars, and goes back to suggestions of Jacques-François Blondel.[248] More remarkable than these whimsical inventions are two instances of his search for new methods in composition: the castle of Montmusard (fig. 104) near Dijon[249] and the group of buildings, including his own house, on the Rue de la Pépinière in Paris.

The plan of Montmusard reminds us in some respects of the castle of Solitude by La Guêpière. Evidently it was derived from the organic plans of the Baroque, but its basic idea was new. It consists of a central cylindrical body connected by very short wings to square end pavilions. The ground floor of the central body contains the vestibule with the curved stairs, its upper floor an airy *salon d'été,* that is, a double colonnade finished by a dome. Thus the center is markedly contrasted with the massive end pavilions in shape, but is approximately equal to them in size, having their width and depth, and differing only slightly in height. The whole composition is diametrically opposed to the Baroque principle, which demanded differentiation in size, or weight, and harmonization of shapes.

Soon De Wailly must have felt a certain inner contradiction in the rising new system at which he and his colleagues aimed. A perfectly individualistic architecture is impossible, for building is the physical combining of elements; wherefore aesthetic binding is almost inevitable. This difficulty was as insurmountable as were the contradictions within the Baroque system. Yet De Wailly was not one who easily gave in. He ardently strove to master the difficulty. So he came to devise a pattern with the help of which that inner contradiction of the individualistic system could, perhaps, be overcome. If he was not the first to try out the new pattern, he certainly was one of the first.

Three houses which De Wailly built on Rue de la Pépinière[250] between 1776 and 1779[251] reveal how he tackled the problem. The central house belonging to himself (fig. 105) was somewhat complicated in plan and elevation.[252] It consisted of a two-storied gateway, a three-storied circular vestibule with the staircase, and the five-storied rear house. Each lateral house was composed of a one-storied entrance building with porter's lodge and stables, a courtyard, and a four-storied apartment house in the rear. There was a great variety of features on the fronts, but there was no formal continuity between them. Only their relative positions intimated the unity of the whole. They appeared again and again all over the entire group, in different sizes and occasionally modified in shape. We detect the motif of the triangular pediment on top of the central rear house and twice on the gateway—on the hindmost plane high up, large, and single; and on the foremost plane on a lower level, small, and duplicated. The motif of the semicircular niche with sculptural decoration shows in the top pediment in the rear, and far bigger and somewhat altered on the two small lateral houses; at last it finds a weak repercussion in the arch of the central window of the gateway. The great depth of the side niches corresponds to the echelon arrangement of the whole group. All these reciprocities in no way affect the shapes of the single units, each of which could stand alone without looking incomplete. No feature is dominant. One has the higher position, but is small; the other is lower, but larger. The greater weight of the one is compensated by the joined effect of several smaller ones. I will speak of such variegated repetition of different motifs as the pattern of multiple response.

De Wailly's plans for the layout of Port-Vendres in the foothills of the eastern Pyrenees (1780) were not so grandiose as a necrologist saw them,[253] but they present a remarkable instance of plain juxtaposition of houses arranged in parallel rows on both sides of the castle. The latter is of the horseshoe type and evidently of Baroque descent; the obelisk in front of it accentuates the main axis of the entire group. The side houses, however, are of equal standing to the wings of the castle. This Place Louis XVI reminds us of the composition of Louis' Place Ludovise.

In his latest years De Wailly followed with much interest the discussions about measures which could give the Panthéon a "more solemn and more dignified character."[254] He suggested the dome being taken off, not so much for reasons of solidity, but because he felt that a dome fitted a church, not a national monument. He wanted it replaced by an open circular colonnade so that the sky and the clouds could be seen through the intercolumniations, for the sake of picturesqueness.[255] He, too, was affected by the romantic currents, just as he had accepted much from classic art. Yet, what made him great was his effort to find new timely patterns for the free coexistence of the independent elements.

The main characteristics of the Odéon, the "four-square sobriety"[256] and the energetic treatment of the material, show also in the works of Ennemond Petitot, a pupil of Soufflot. His Casino at Parma is a heavy cubic mass with a flat roof.[257] The Vénerie Royale (Hunting Lodge) at Colorno is likewise finished with a flat roof behind a balustrade.[258] Massive rusticated piers run up through the two stories. The project for a "Pont Triomphal" presents in the midst of the bridge a columned gateway topped by a heavy cylindrical pedestal carrying a quadriga.[259] The effect of the whole is derived from the contrast of the airy gateway and the bulky crowning.

The Pavillon à l'Italienne (fig. 106) of the Abbaye de Royaumont at Viarmes, Seine-et-Oise, which was built by Louis Le Masson between 1785 and 1789,[260] is a next of kin to the Odéon. In its original state it was a sturdy block with much emphasis on the horizontals and the stonework. The windows were unframed and varied in shape from large and small oblongs to semicircular lunettes and bull's-eyes. The west front opened in a triple arcade flanked by low rectangular side lights, an interesting enlargement of the Palladian motif. Aubin-Louis Millin illustrated the house in his book in connection with the adjacent Gothic church. The latter alone interested him, and he had no appreciation for the greatness of Le Masson's design.

The plainness and nobility of Italian country houses must have impressed Jacques-François Blondel's pupil, Jean-Jacques Huvé. This can be seen in the massive mansion of President d'Hormois, in Picardy (1780), and the architect's own house at Meudon (fig. 107).[261] Not a single Grecism shows on these structures.

The Théâtre Italien (or Favart) (1782) by Jean-François Heurtier,[262] a pupil of Le Geay, also was of "four-square sobriety." Eight giant Ionic columns—two of them engaged in the wall—were the only decoration of the massive block. Critics of 1800 pointed out that it was destitute of all ornament[263] and praised it for being entirely isolated.[264] An outstanding achievement was the rear of the theater (fig. 108) on the Boulevard des Italiens.[265] Its façade showed four large oblong openings on the ground floor, seven tall arched windows on the second floor, and seven small square windows on the mezzanine. The rows of unframed apertures contrasted effectively with each other because of the different sizes and shapes of the openings. Heurtier laid the strongest emphasis on the horizontals: the balcony of the second floor, the thin cornice under the mezzanine, the main cornice, the balcony running all along the massive attic story, and the top cornice. The almost complete lack of traditional decoration, as well as the lack of vertical members, is noteworthy. Still more remarkable is the accentuation of the flat wall. As a whole the front is very plain. And yet there is an enormous tension all over the surface, produced chiefly by the unequal intervals between the rows of windows. This façade of 1782 belongs to the most mature accomplishments of the revolutionary architecture. It comes close to twentieth-century works. Yet this mere similarity alone would not make it worthy of remark, it has its merits in itself. Its greatness becomes apparent when we compare it with the trivial adjacent houses.

De Wailly and Huvé were deeply impressed by the severity of the plain country houses of Italy. Not too long before them another ardent admirer and student of southern architecture had reacted quite differently to what he had seen in the peninsula. Gabriel Pierre Martin Dumont, traveling companion of Soufflot, had not been attracted by the austerity and consistency of Italic building. He was, rather, interested in the ancient ruins and composed fantastic etchings in the manner of Le Geay and Piranesi.[266] On the other hand he liked to make plans out of a variety of elementary shapes just as Peyre did. His "Temple des Arts," 1746, and "Rendez-vous de chasse" are illustrated in his *Recueil,* to which Le Geay contributed several vignettes.[267] Dumont's compositions of ruins and his plans were typical of the intermediary stage between the Rococo and the consolidated architecture of about 1800.

Hardly any traces of romanticism can be detected in the designs of Nicolas Le Camus de Mézières. In 1769 he was entrusted to erect one of the most expensive Vauxhalls, the Colisée in the Champs Elysées, north of the Rond-Point.[268] It was a fanciful composition consisting of small elliptical, circular, and octagonal halls, and a huge elliptical circus. This plan was extravagant, but it was timely, for the elementary geometrical forms were in great favor in the late Louis XV period. Even Blondel praised another work of Le Camus, the cylindrical Halle au Blé in Paris (1763–1767, on the site of the present Bourse du Commerce), although it was a far cry from his own delicate and well-balanced designs to this sturdy and sober structure.[269] The criticism of a popular guidebook is, perhaps, still more significant. Georges-Louis Le Rouge in his *Curiosités de Paris* calls the Halle "an edifice worthy of the Romans," finding great merit in its novel form, its structural beauty, and the precision and cleanness of workmanship (fig. 109).[270] Also, when its open court was covered with a low wooden dome by the architects Legrand and Molinos in 1782,[271] it was still much admired.[272] Le Camus' Pagode de Chanteloup, erected between 1775 and 1778 upon the order of the Duc de Choiseul,[273] is a free transformation of oriental models. It is a stepped structure with neatly set-off stories. The two lower ones are circular, the upper five polygonal. The vigorous treatment of the stone arrests the eye.[274]

In the treatise *Le Génie de l'Architecture, ou l'analogie de cet art avec nos sensations* (1780), Le Camus appears as an adherent of the current trend of *architecture parlante*. He claims that nobody before him dealt with this topic: *Personne n'a encore écrit sur l'analogie des proportions de l'Architecture avec nos sensations ... C'est un sujet neuf à traiter.*[275] He discusses the proportions of the orders only cursorily, referring readers who might be interested in them to previous authors and to the then recent publication by Potain.[276] His exclusive interest is the individual character of the single features.[277] A few general remarks directed against profuseness of ornament and lack of consistency in decoration are all that he has to say about the Rococo,[278] which at that time already belonged to the past.[279] Occasionally he asks for equilibrium, symmetry,[280] the predominance of the central parts,[281] harmony and proportionality.[282] The general tenor of his book, however, is in accord with the views which had become modern since Boffrand. Its motto is: *Non satis est plaucuisse oculis nisi pectora tangas.*[283] "Unity" is to Le Camus not a formal category, but uniformity of character.[284] From the demand for character he derives the postulate of the emotional proportions: *L'ensemble doit donc avoir une proportion relative à ses différentes parties, au genre et au caractère qu'on veut lui donner.*[285] He believes that symbolic accessories are not sufficient.[286] The single forms and the masses themselves should be expressive:[287]

Ce sont donc les disposition des formes, leur caractère, leur ensemble qui deviennent le fond inépuisable des illusions. C'est de ce principe qu'il faut partir, lorsqu'on prétend dans l'Architecture produire des affections, lorsqu'on veut parler à l'esprit, émouvoir l'âme.[288]

Le Camus makes various suggestions as to how architecture could be animated.[289] He recommends contrasts of light and shade,[290] and effects derived from projections, recesses, and variegated skyline. All trifling details should be avoided.[291]

Le Camus' work stands at the crossroads of the Baroque, Rationalism, and Romanticism:

La véritable harmonie en Architecture dépend de l'accord des masses et de celui des différentes parties, le style et le ton doit se rapporter au caractère de l'ensemble, et l'ensemble doit être pris dans la nature, dans l'espèce et la destination de l'Edifice qu'on veut élever.[292]

These architects of the generation of 1730 which we have dealt with so far produced designs of a new type and yet, most of them, rather calm and sound. There were others who aimed at identical goals, but reacted to the rising new ideal of configuration in a more vehement way. Most of their daring projects could not be carried out. They are preserved only in fantastic drawings, in which the architectural revolution of the late eighteenth century climaxed. Personally these architects were by no means outsiders. Nearly all of them belonged to the upper ranks of the profession. Boullée and Ledoux were members of the Paris Academy, Delafosse an *agrégé* of the academy at Bordeaux; Cuvilliés *fils* and Desprez were court architects abroad.

With the zeal of a fanatic Jean-François de Neufforge, a Belgian-born pupil of Blondel, created a tremendous number of drawings, which were published with the approval of the Paris Academy under the title *Recueil élémentaire d'architecture,* in eight volumes and two supplement volumes with nine hundred plates, from 1757 to 1777. Neufforge availed himself almost exclusively of traditional forms. This distinguishes him from Boullée and Ledoux, who in their most advanced productions favored pure elementary geometrical shapes, and places him close to Marie-Joseph Peyre and De Wailly. The features taken from the past are of little interest in themselves, for our entire attention is attracted by Neufforge's compositional efforts. Unlike Valadier he did not content himself with jotting down his inventions in a sketchy manner, but worked them out methodically in plans and elevations. In his latest years he confined himself to presenting plans alone. The new organization of the constituents was his foremost interest.

In plan design Neufforge continued where Briseux had ended. He gave up Baroque formality and cared chiefly about practicality. In many of his plans the old scheme lingers on. Occasionally he modified it noticeably, inserting, for instance, the staircase between salon and vestibule and thus disrupting the continuous main axis.[293] Often he arranged the rooms in a free manner.[294] His originality shows in a square country house where each of the four porches is followed by a room of importance.[295] (Palladio's Rotonda had a dominant central hall.) In another country house an open loggia, a salon *à l'Italienne,* and an oblong gallery are arrayed on the main axis.[296] By and by Neufforge developed an extremely simple pattern which was to become very common in Ledoux's work: the square divided up into nine small squares (fig. 110).[297] This pattern, when freed of all reminiscences of the past, expresses the equivalence of the rooms in an almost perfect way. It means the definite rejection of the hierarchical principle of the Baroque.

Thoroughly different from these sober plans are others in which the architect operated with gigantic dimensions or fanciful shapes. The "Bâtiment de l'ordre composite" has porches on three sides, while the fourth is preceded by a huge circular court.[298] The court has a diameter of about 170 feet, the sides are 120 feet long. All this was not enough for Neufforge. He circumscribed the court with an outer square and put the chapel and various other rooms into the corners. When he created he must have been obsessed by the same *aveugle enthousiasme* which inspired Ledoux.[299] A church with an enormous circular choir annexed to a short nave recalls d'Ixnard's church of St. Blasien.[300] Several plans with out-of-the-ordinary shapes may have been inspired by Laugier's suggestions. The "Temple de la guerre" is designed on a triangular plan (fig. 111). The "Temple de trois arts" consists of three wings departing from a central circular room.[301] The "House of the Four Seasons" ("Bâtiment à représenter les quatre Saisons ou les quatre Eléments") is planned on a circle with four enclosed small circles in the midst of which there is not, as might be expected, a prominent room, but the circular staircase.[302] It is impossible to discuss here the great variety of Neufforge's schemes, still less to follow the traces his inventions left in the following development. I should like to point out only the noteworthy plan of a theater.[303] Its semicircular auditorium projects from the longer side of an oblong block. This scheme was handed down to the nineteenth century by Jean-Nicolas-Louis Durand,[304] and adopted by the German architects Georg Moller and Gottfried Semper. Moller's theater at Mainz and Semper's theaters at Dresden and Vienna were wrongly praised as original innovations.[305]

Geometrical forms play only a minor role in Neufforge's designs (fig. 112). Rich decoration makes them inconspicuous where they appear ("temple de la guerre, des Beaux-Arts, de la paix").[306] In conceiving his plans Neufforge had visions of contrasting masses. He achieved the contrasts by presenting incongruous shapes or discrepant sizes. His court building ("Chambres consulaires et chambre criminelle") is doubly interesting: classical features appear side by side with geometric shapes; the conventional scheme of a ruling center and dependent sides encounters the new concept of harsh discrepancies (fig. 113). The cylindrical side pavilions with conical finials are much higher than the pedimented superstructure above the main portico. Peripheral forces antagonize the central parts: architecture is in full revolution. Six projects of bathhouses are conceived in a similar way (fig. 114).[307] Most of them are designed on centric plans, either circular or square ones. The strange thing which happens is that by the sheer weight of the parts the centric compositions come out eccentric. (One might add, literally and figuratively.) The circular bath of plate xxiv is an airy columned hall under a heavy cupola, encompassed by massive segmental structures. The tendency to give greater weight to the peripheral parts is obvious; the idea of a new distribution of power underlies the plan. I should warn against a misunderstanding. Neufforge certainly did not seek to illustrate this new ideal. He created intuitively. It would be ridiculous to impute didactic purposes to him just as it would be ridiculous to assert that Bernini intended to visualize the Baroque principles on the colonnades of St. Peter's.

Striking disproportionality was to Neufforge a legitimate means of artistic effect. Conventional façades gain in interest by oversized, overheavy semicircular pediments.[308] Extravagantly high obelisks and pyramids tower over fountains, city gates, a chapel, or a town house (fig. 115).[309] Eventually the crowning features preponderate over the substructures. The pyramid topping a prison (fig. 116) is nearly the same height as the building itself, and the width of its base equals the width of the portico. The obelisk and the dome above a sepulchral chapel are higher than its porch (fig. 117). A type which is very common in our time but was uncommon in the eighteenth century is the stepped or terrace building. Neufforge invented many of them, as did Ledoux's pupil, Louis-Ambroise Dubut (Country houses;[310] Hôtel de ville, fig. 118; Château seigneurial;[311] Mausoleum;[312] Lighthouse;[313] Château de plaisance,[314] etc.). The basic idea of the stepped houses is the superposition of diminishing blocks or the presentation of discrepant sizes.

There were still other patterns by which the new ideal of the free coexistence of the parts could be expressed. The simplest was the juxtaposition of equivalent compositional elements (bays, in barracks and coach houses[315]), another the superposition of unrelated elements (church front of the Corinthian order,[316] resembling Servandoni's façade of Saint-Sulpice; Maison Champêtre[317]). A further possibility was to make the parts self-centered. In several tripartite houses by Neufforge each section is complete in itself, though the traditional centralization of the whole is still traceable (fig. 119).[318] The pattern of multiple response is rare in Neufforge's work. It appears on the entrance of a cemetery (fig. 120), in the alternating motifs of medallions, niches with sarcophagi, and obelisks topping the structure and flanking the door. It appears more distinctly on the pyramid of a burial place (*Sépulture*) (fig. 121), where the arched door is repeated in a semicircular window and niches, and the oblong, pedimented opening below in an oblong window high above, while panels with inscriptions correspond to each other. All the other trends of the period are secondary to the search for new patterns in Neufforge's *oeuvre*. Romanticism shows only in a few designs, such as the waterworks (*châteaux d'eau*) (fig. 122),[319] and the fountains (fig. 123).[320]

The supplement volumes of 1777 contain plans of diversified purposes, such as a palace, a courthouse, an exchange, an educational building, a monastery, a university, the home of a prelate, a castle, a town hall, an academy, an armory, a prison, a hospital, stables and so on.[321] In former times, architects erected churches, palaces, private residences, and fortifications, but they were seldom called in for utilitarian structures. Since the era of the French Revolution any type of building has been considered worthy of an architect's abilities. The plan for the house of a prelate (fig. 125) is similar to that of De Wailly's castle of Montmusard (fig. 104).[322] It is composed of a circular main hall linked by two short wings to the oblong pavilions. The castle which Neufforge designed is on an octagonal plan.[323] The town hall[324] represents an intermediary stage between Peyre's fantastic academy[325] and the sober office buildings of the nineteenth century. The stables consist of four segmental structures grouped around a circular court and turning their concave front to the outside (fig. 124). The ornamental character of this plan reveals that Neufforge was far from functionalism. It calls to mind the fanciful plans of Peyre, while the fantastic accumulation of incongruous features on a catafalque[326] shows that Neufforge's efforts ultimately tended in the direction of one of the most fascinating personalities of the revolutionary architecture, Delafosse. Before we discuss the latter's weird visions, let us look at the creations of an artist who spent most of his life in Bavaria, when the most luxuriant Rococo blossomed there.

François Cuvilliés *fils,* a pupil of Blondel, was an early romanticist. After his death many of his etchings were collected in a volume, *Ecole de l'architecture bavaroise,* together with works of other architects, most of them Germans.[327] Cuvilliés received his first training from his father, who had played an eminent role in the Bavarian Rococo. The main factor in the young man's career was his contact with French architects during his long stay in Paris between 1754 and 1768. If he did not meet Le Geay personally there, then the latter's etchings, which came out in the 1760's, must have become a source of inspiration to him. Of course, Piranesi's works may also have contributed to shape the young architect, whose designs are full of discrepancies and incongruities. The dome and the lantern of the project of the Solitude de Faley are far too big for the substructure.[328] The plan, too, is very curious: two short wings depart in an obtuse angle from the circular salon. The project for a gateway at Munich, Thalstrasse, is an odd mixture of a triumphal arch inserted in a plain house and surmounted by a fantastic bell tower.[329] The "Corps de Garde" is distinguished by compactness.[330] Rustication as a means of *architecture parlante* shows on the "Prison Criminel" (fig. 126), on the fountain terminating a square,[331] and on the "Obelisque avec fontaine" (fig. 127) dated 1772. Full of unrest are the "Pont couvert attribué au commerce" (1776),[332] the "Palais attribué à une Commanderie" (1774) (fig. 128), and the Hôtel de Ville.[333] The two last ones are stepped buildings of exaggerated magnitude. The "Pont dans le goût gothique" shows Cuvilliés *fils* as an eclectic,[334] as most romanticists were with their longing for remote times and regions. The transition from the Rococo to Romanticism can be studied in many interesting etchings of the two Cuvilliés. The desire for new compositional solutions led to such highly original designs as the "Retraite" (fig. 129).[335]

As a truly great, romanticizing design the project for a prison by Daubanton deserves to be mentioned. It carries on its front the date 1775 and is preserved in an etching, a copy of which is kept in the Bibliothèque Nationale of Paris.

Jean-Charles Delafosse is commonly regarded as an *ornemaniste,* for his chief accomplishments were decorative etchings. On the title page of his *Iconologie historique*[336] he names himself an architect first and a decorator second. In this investigation we need not differentiate between "major" and "minor" arts. The stylistic aspirations of any period appear in decorative designs as clearly as in buildings.

Geneviève Levallet[337] calls Delafosse "pseudo-antique" and sees in him an innovator because of certain classicizing traits in his designs.[338] She finds his decorative
works lacking grace,[339] his architectural projects *grandioses*.[340] She recognizes
rightly that the symbolic content of many of his designs was just a pretext for the
decorative schemes,[341] but defines his historical position too vaguely by assigning
him to the class of "Louis XVI artists."[342] Carl Linfert, writing in an intentionally
obscure style, attempts to delve into the depths of Delafosse's creations. He notes
manneristic traits in his designs,[343] and points out his exaggerations[344] as well as
certain expressionistic tendencies which remind him of Le Camus' doctrine.[345]
Linfert's main point is that the iconological contents affect the ornamental form in
a decisive yet unfortunate manner.[346] Overrating the importance of the iconological
intention he concludes that any essentially formal interpretation of Delafosse's designs must fail.[347] This view can easily be refuted. For the formal characteristics of
the designs with iconological pretensions appear also in those designs which have
no symbolical meaning. Most symbolic designs show very strange forms. Some of
them, however, are still Rococo, unimpaired by their iconological contents.

Whatever Delafosse's didactic purposes were, his artistic aims were the geometrization and monumentalization of the forms, and the elaboration of patterns
in which the single features were brought into rapport through antagonizing shapes
and sizes. In the case of Delafosse it is hard to decide which object was more important to him or which came first to his mind. I shall discuss the forms in the
first place, and his composition, secondly.

His "Sepulchral Monument"[348] is an assemblage of massive, oversized features
such as a prismatic base, a cylindrical body surrounded by statues of mourners, and
a hemispherical cupola topped by a tall column. Here the single features still serve
a practical purpose; they make up a real building. In general Delafosse cared little
about devising objects for practical use. He turned to decorative design because he
felt more free in this sphere. In the allegorical composition "Les Israélites" (fig.
130) he presents a truncated pyramid to which a lamp and a medallion framed by
a garland are affixed.[349] The medallion contains a symbolic painting with the sun
god, an angel, a boat on a river, a broken column, serpents, etc. Different objects
below the medallion certainly also have symbolic significance. Yet more puzzling
than their symbolism are their shapes. These objects, as well as the large base of
the whole, show odd plane and solid forms bordered by straight edges. The design
"L'Asie" (fig. 131) consists of two distinct portions, namely a table and various
objects on it—a picture with an Oriental landscape, a book with half-moons, and
others, to make the composition readable to the average spectator or to make it
interesting by being a little enigmatic.[350] For the time was not ripe for undisguised
nonobjective art. The table itself is far from being strictly functional. Delafosse,
most certainly, did not want to provide a design for a cabinetmaker. As he used
symbolism as a pretext for the entire design, so he used the table as a pretext for an

experiment with the form. He attempted to restore the features which former art had "organized" to their legitimate abstract character. Not all his designs show a similarly bold transformation of a practical object into a example of pure form. The table of the etching "L'Afrique" is far more consistent (in the Baroque sense, of course),[351] and that of "L'Amérique" (fig. 132)[352] is almost as ordinary a table as were those designed by other *ornemanistes* of the advanced eighteenth century, say Richard Lalonde.[353] It is somewhat stiff, yet well balanced, and shows traces even of the former animism. (Compare the "growing" legs of this table with those on the etching "L'Asie.")

From such novel interpretation of the traditional forms Delafosse proceeded to geometrical shapes. The body of one vase is a cylinder,[354] that of another a truncated cone.[355] Their unshapeliness may shock the eye accustomed to classical proportions and smooth contours. It was not caused by the inability of the architect to produce something "gracious"; he could well design in the pleasurable Louis XV manner (see the "Attributs d'amour,"[356] the "Attributs de musique,"[357] the "Attributs pastorals," fig. 133[358]). Ordinarily, he was averse to the old suavity and wanted to create something entirely new.

Still far from the goal of utilizable modern forms, Delafosse was already haunted by visions of new patterns. His belief in conventional composition was shaken. He felt the urge to visualize an ideal of configuration which widely differed from the ideal underlying Baroque designs. It was a tragic moment when the desire to reform made the artist forget practical needs while he was discarding the tenets of traditional composition. It was a great and crucial moment for architectural development, too. Unable to realize the new ideal in actual building he had to resort to decorative inventions. Many designs inform us about the new aims. In the "Origine du paganisme," for instance, he presents monumental forms, heavy and crude, and attempts bold contrasts (fig. 134). The desire for an original arrangement of the elements appears in designs which are assemblages of heterogeneous, yet still proportionate, features ("Tombeau antique,"[359] lectern,[360] clocks,[361] stoves,[362] candlesticks[363]). An excellent way to create an impressive whole, out of discrepant features, was to contrast them in size. The fountain of the etching "L'air et l'eau" is an exceedingly huge structure, as the little figures beside it show (fig. 135).[364] Its effect derives mainly from the disproportionality of the components. The shell on top of the segmental pediment is much larger than the latter itself, and the cascade below is relatively much smaller than either of them. These disproportions bring life into the composition and add significance to each feature. They have a definite artistic meaning. There is no doubt that they are indicative also of the painfully unbalanced condition of the era. Contrasted shapes produce no less interesting designs. In the etching "Diverses vertus et diverses forces," the prismatic base and the fluted truncated cone are opposed to the sphere on top (fig. 136).[365] In the design "Economie, silence, divinité, éternité," the three-dimensional objects above are set against the flat panel below (fig. 137).[366] (The easily understandable symbols in the medallions on the panel are: balances and compass; fish and locked heart; triangle in a circle; serpent.) Similar in composition are the designs "Naples,"[367] "Portugal,"[368] "Switzerland" (fig. 138).[369] A tomb presents an odd combination of statues of women mourners, a sarcophagus, and an obelisk; another a gigantic column, a truncated pyramid, and a statue over the entrance.[370] The "Palais de justice" is a terrace building with a domed cylindrical story rising from three stepped blocks.[371] A curious invention is a stove composed of chains, balls, and a quatrefoiled column on a square base.[372]

Finally, I want to point out the drawings of a church and a riding school (*manège*).[373] The colossal porch of the former is much higher than the stepped saucer dome. The high prismatic central feature of the latter is markedly contrasted with the low saucer domes on the sides. In both projects Delafosse makes lavish use of classical features, the general effect being derived from the massiveness and the magnitude of the structures. The artistic will that created these projects was to bring about one of the deepest transformations which architecture has undergone in all its history. The designs of Guarini, Meissonnier, Oppenord, and Delafosse were not the products of individual whims. They were neither absurdities, nor "abuses." Actually, they were links in an unending chain. There was only one step from the decomposition of the old to the rise of the new, from the Rococo to the Revolution. There was no gap between the Baroque and the so-called era of classicism; there was no sudden break. The work of Delafosse helps us to recognize the continuity of the development and the necessity of the historical process.

The designs of other decorators also reveal the new formal aspirations. Four vases by Jacques Beauvais are typical instances of the geometrization and monumentalization of classical forms.[374] Neufforge designed vases of stressed geometric character[375] which show that piecemeal composition known to us from his architectural projects. The "Vases rustiques" by Charles François Joly likewise present boldly altered traditional forms.[376] These transformations mark the end of a long and curious evolution. Previously, architects had attempted to give organic character to structural forms; now, they were out to reduce the animated forms of the Baroque to geometric shapes. As further instances of the repetrification of pseudo-organic forms, a design for balusters by Jean Thomas Hauer may be referred to.[377] Hauer was a Hungarian artist who had fallen under the spell of the French modernists during his stay in Paris and almost overdid the new manner. All these innovators had a flair for the things to come in tectonics, which the pedantic copyists of the ancients never had.

The tombs designed by Le Canu are accumulations of diversified elements which do not blend into the whole.[378] The discrepancies between the single features are striking. The flat surfaces of the truncated pyramids are contrasted to the plastic character of the urns, swags, etc. Two lighthouses by the same architect are still more interesting (figs. 139, 140).[379] The lighthouse with a single central entrance consists of a heavily rusticated substructure topped by a much higher, absolutely smooth, truncated pyramid. The antagonism of texture adds to the antagonism of size. Apart from two garlands there are no curves, only rigid straight lines. The lighthouse with two lateral doors is shaped very originally with alternating vertical and sloping walls. Michel-Ange Challe's "Cenotaph and Catafalque of Louis XV" are typical piecemeal compositions.[380]

Actual buildings were necessarily more restful than the inventions of Neufforge and Delafosse. Yet even the most moderate architects moved away from Baroque composition and aimed at new surface patterns and new ways in mass composition. The façades of Jacques-Guillaume Legrand's Hôtels Galliffet, Rue de Varennes (begun 1775), and Jarnac, Rue de Monsieur (prior to 1787),[381] were decorated with colossal columns. There are only few vestiges of differentiation and centralization on them. On the house at 6 Rue Saint-Florentin, which Legrand built together with Jacques Molinos (1792),[382] the bays of each story are equivalent; the corner pilasters combining the two main floors are inconspicuous. In order to avoid monotony the architects grouped the stories. The ground floor and the mezzanine, the two main floors, and the fifth floor with the *mansardes* are the three groups separated by balconies stretching all along the front. Here, just as on Heurtier's façade on the Boulevard des Italiens[383] and on the beautiful anonymous house at 4 Rue d'Aboukir (1797),[384] a pattern has been created based on the principle of equality. The Théâtre Feydeau (fig. 141), or Théâtre de Monsieur, by Legrand and Molinos (1788-1790) was an oblong block.[385] The rear facade was composed of two arcaded stories. The main front presented a loggia opening into seven arches above the three arches of the vestibule. This was again an attempt to achieve an original surface pattern. The convex outline of this facade paralleled the semicircle of the auditorium. This was a noteworthy innovation to which Legrand himself wanted to draw attention: *La forme circulaire du plan s'annonce au dehors de la façade par une légère courbure qui rappelle la forme des théâtres antiques.*[386] He referred to ancient models in order to legitimate his own plan, which actually had little in common with them. Legrand and Molinos finished the old Halle aux Draps on the Place des Innocents with a barrel roof (1785).[387] Saint-Victor in 1809 praised its "elegant simplicity."[388] In 1791 the two architects projected a "Pritanée" on the Place de la Bastille, a Museum, and a Palais National on the site on which the later church of the Madeleine was built.[389] In the Palais National they wanted not merely to produce a copy of the Roman Pantheon, but to emphasize the contrast of the oblong entrance hall with the huge rotunda of the assembly rooms.

In 1804 Molinos erected the Morgue in Paris as an oblong block with unpierced walls,[390] decorated only with four Tuscan pilasters and two sarcophagi on the roof which concealed the chimney flues. Visitors entered a dimly lit vaulted hall. On each end, to the right and left, two columns and glass panes separated the hall from the small rooms in which the unknown dead were exposed on black marble tables. Light fell into these rooms from the height of their cupolas. There was the contrast between the coffered vault of the central hall and the cupolas, which opened toward the sky, and there was the contrast between the darkness in which the living moved and the pale light in which the defunct lay. These contrasts show how great the revolutionary architecture could be in all its simplicity.

The Maison Deshayes (fig. 142) on the corner of the Boulevard de la Madeleine and Rue Caumartin, by André Aubert,[391] was famous because of its roof garden with all sorts of playful things such as truncated columns, triumphal arches of trellis, pyramids, sham ruins, Chinese bridges over an artificial rivulet, etc.[392] The form of the still extant house is highly original. The corner is shaped as a semi-circular recess into which a somewhat lower cylindrical tower is inserted.

Bernard Poyet was one of the most talented students of De Wailly.[393] Through-out the years his main goal was grandeur, which he strove to achieve by elementary forms and forceful contrasts. On the Callet house, Rue du Montparnasse (1775), he contrasted the broad substructure of five bays with the superstructure of three bays, and the plane front of the building with the curved side walls of the court.[394] In 1785 he submitted to the Academy of Science a project for a hospital (fig. 143) on the Ile des Cygnes near the Champ de Mars.[395] He had conceived a rotunda for more than five thousand patients, with radiating halls connected by circular corri-dors containing offices and staff rooms. The diameter of the whole was to be about eight hundred feet.[396] In the center of the innermost court the chapel was to be situated, in the form of a monopteros without a cella (colonnade à jour), so that the patients could attend the holy service from their beds when the doors of the halls were opened. The exterior would have resembled the Colosseum, with a significant difference: Poyet contrasted the three-storied cylindrical pile with its rows of arched windows to a massive substructure of bigger diameter.[397] The Academy approved of the novel form, but was against the enormous size. The architect Legrand was enthusiastic about the beauty of the plan and the imposing form.[398] He liked the simplicity of the exterior and the practicality of the interior disposition.[399]

These designs were original and sound, and so were the Royal Stables (fig. 144) which Poyet built on the Rue Saint-Thomas du Louvre shortly before the outbreak of the Revolution.[400] In contrast to the stables of Chantilly,[401] with their Baroque pomposity, they were extremely plain and yet artistically effective. The high portal framed with rustication ran up to the third story, virtually tearing the front apart. Besides this mighty doorway there was nothing but blank wall, cornices, and windows. An interesting pattern resulted from the different sizes of the windows.[402] A massive attic completed the whole.

In 1798 (Revolutionary year VI) Poyet designed a 312-foot column in honor of the victories of the nation, to be erected near the Pont-Neuf. This *monument colossal*[403] was meant to consist of a rusticated substructure, a circular colonnade

("Temple de la Victoire") as the base of the column, and a tripod on top for a flame. Poyet dreamed even of an illumination from the inside on festival occasions. Bonaparte liked the project, but the Council of Five Hundred was against its execution.

In 1806 Poyet was asked to add the Corinthian portico to the sober walls of the Palais-Bourbon (Chambre des Députés).[404] He had to yield to the fashion of the day. Now the architects were against him. Brongniart ridiculed the aged ex-revolutionary: *M. Poyet pense que le lieu des assemblées du Corps législatif doit être regardé comme le Temple des Lois et qu'un fronton est ce qui désigne essentiellement un temple des autres édifices publics.*[405] In 1808 a parapet was added to the pediment which had annoyed the modern minded.

If we compare the "Rendez-vous de chasse" by Pierre Panseron[406] with the castle of Solitude by La Guêpière and the church of St. Blasien by Ixnard,[407] we note how fast the change in architecture had come and how deep it went. The two edifices in southern Germany still show something of the traditional gradation and are finished with upward-pointing domes. Panseron's work reveals the beginning of the principle of the equivalence of the parts by the four cubes placed in the corners of a square. The *salon à l'italienne* rising in the center is an upright, horizontally terminated cylinder, which looks like a foreign element amidst the four cubes. Panseron's design for a beacon is a product of romantic exaltation (fig. 145). The picturesque treatment of the details and the manifold contrasts between the parts call to mind certain designs of Neufforge and Delafosse.

The rear façade of the concert hall adjoining the house of the Duc de Laval, Boulevard du Montparnasse, which Jacques Célérier built in 1774,[408] may have been the model for the semicylindrical main front of the Théâtre Feydeau by Legrand and Molinos. In 1786 Célérier set a low wall in front of the circular stables of the Hôtel de l'Infantado, Rue Saint-Florentin (1786),[409] thus obtaining the effect of a cylinder emerging from a square substructure. He presented a highly interesting surface pattern on the Théâtre de l'Ambigu Comique (Boulevard du Temple, 1785), and imparted to the Théâtre des Variétés (1807) a blocklike character by adding a parapet behind the pediment, much as was done on the Chambre des Députés a year later.[410]

Boullée and Ledoux, the central figures in French revolutionary architecture, can be dealt with in this book only by outlining those chief traits of their *oeuvres* which are indicative of their historical position and their artistic ends. An extensive study of their accomplishments requires far more space than can be assigned to them in an investigation aiming at the comprehensive display of the transition from the Baroque to the nineteenth century. Therefore I made up a separate monograph, *Three Revolutionary Architects—Boullée, Ledoux and Lequeu,*[411] presenting their biographies and illustrating almost all of their works as well as the biography of Lequeu with a large selection of his designs. This monograph discusses also some outstanding architects and writers related to them as teachers or critics, namely Boffrand, Jacques-François Blondel, Laugier, Le Geay, and Viel de Saint-Maux, and contains a great many selected passages from the writings of all of them, which provide a deep insight into the trends of the era.

To appreciate the work of Etienne-Louis Boullée we must concentrate on the drawings which he bequeathed to the nation and which are kept in the Bibliothèque Nationale in Paris. Made in the 1780's and 1790's, they reveal his artistic goals and they manifest his talent. The few buildings which he carried out differed only little from the common run of classicizing houses. His manuscript treatise, "Architecture-Essai sur l'Art," also deposited in the Bibliothèque Nationale, reflects the ideas which had guided him. Many statements of his are extremely elucidating and deserve to be recorded, though a complete reprint of his text would hardly be worthwhile.

There are, of course, many traces of classicism in Boullée's drawings too. What distinguishes his temples, museums, triumphal arches, circuses, tomb pyramids, cenotaphs (fig. 146), etc. from the designs of the many narrow-minded copyists, is the boldness with which he handled the conventional forms and the skill with which he brought the old features into novel combinations.[412] If carried out, many of his projects would have surpassed in grandeur the achievements of the ancients. The works of the Greeks were outstanding in their refinement; the inferior Roman productions lacked such refinement, and were rather big than great. Boullée did not care about refinement, so it would not make sense to compare his inventions with Greek works, for one cannot compare works of intrinsically different character. Yet he knew better than the Romans how to free himself from the Hellenic models. Whether he applied traditional forms or whether he made use of the elementary geometrical shapes, he created designs more vigorous, more imposing, and more original than the Roman structures with their magniloquent imitation of Greek models.

The Pantheon in Rome presents the somewhat awkward addition of a columnar porch to a bulky rotunda. The piecemeal character of the composition is so obvious that some students believe the porch and the rotunda to have originated at different times. Boullée's "Metropolitan Church," on the contrary, presents the great concept of masses which rival each other and yet constitute one whole (fig. 147).[413] Even the most fervent admirers of the Colosseum can hardly overlook the fact that its stories resemble each other to such a degree that the general aspect is rather monotonous. Boullée's circuses do not consist of several rows with repeating features. He presents in them the powerful contrast of two differently shaped stories, and in addition opposes high columns like Trajan's to the sweeping horizontal lines of the massive cylinders (fig. 148).[414] Also, when using old features he was an artist in his own right. His "Triumphal Arches," too, are rather independent of classic models and very impressive in their original shapes. The halls of the Roman thermae presented assemblages of petty, though oversized, features. Vastness should not be taken for artistic greatness. Time has done away with their empty decoration, so that today the picturesque ruins impress the spectator more deeply than the former pomposity could have done. The "Library Hall" of Boullée (fig. 149) equals his circuses in grandeur. Its single features form into larger units, beside which they themselves have only very little significance. The coffers, the books on the shelves, and the columns bring some unrest into the hall. But the decisive compositional elements are the barrel vaulting, the colonnades, and the book stacks. These greater units strongly contrast with one another. The comparatively low colonnades are squeezed between the mighty vaulting and the three rows of stacks. From this arrangement a tremendous tension becomes apparent between the disparate elements. Boullée's inventions are unimpaired by the triviality of romanticizing architecture. Boullée never designed log cabins, thatched huts, artificial ruins and the like, nor did functionalism play any role in his works. He was an artist throughout, always conscious that form must be the architect's ultimate goal. He experimented successfully with the elementary geometrical forms which in occidental building had never been used to any extent prior to the mid-eighteenth century. He was not less successful in realizing the modern compositional principles. Juxtaposition of equivalent elements is seen in his city gates (fig. 150), forceful antithesis in the library façade, with the gigantic globe set against the bare wall.[415] All his fantastic projects reveal that his main concern was the whole rather than the details.[416] Above all he longed to create in fullest freedom. This shows in a statement of his which applies to artists dependent on models of the past as well as to writers borrowing their topics from others, "Ce n'est pas en se traînant sur les traces des autres qu'un auteur parvient à se faire distinguer dans les beaux-arts."[417] His work was far more than the end of the old; it was more than mere negation and protest. It was a beginning.

Boullée shared the fate of Ledoux. Their works, as well as the entire movement of revolutionary architecture remained unnoticed in their country.[418] Biographies of Ledoux came out in France only after he had been rediscovered abroad. Boullée's work was referred to quite briefly, by Henry Lemonnier in a lecture which was printed later, wherein he discussed the "megalomania" of early romanticism in a general way.[419] On this occasion he disparaged Boullée's inventions and expressed the view that there was nothing remarkable about the architect, except that he had been a member of the Institut de France since its foundation.

Claude-Nicolas Ledoux was a frontiersman, at home both in the old country of tradition and in new regions which he was one of the first to explore. With these words I summarized the view which I had formed on his historical position in my book *Von Ledoux bis Le Corbusier* (1933), which contained the first monograph on this outstanding architect.[420] He still appears to me to be the foremost exponent of the great transformation during the late eighteenth century. In the works which he created in the short span of about twenty years, classical and Baroque features showed side by side with features which have become common only in our own era. He was no mere copyist even when he applied conventional details; as a rule he combined them in some remarkable new manner and often altered them significantly. He was most certainly a seer of future development when he presented cubic masses, bare walls with frameless apertures, flat roofs, and above all entirely new compositional patterns. We have detected similar traits in the works of many of his contemporaries.[421] This means that Ledoux belonged to a group of progressive builders and that his works were not whimsicalities, but the products of a general, important movement. The view that a new continuity began about 1800 underlay my book; its title may have been misunderstood by some reviewers who believed that I wanted to intimate a direct filiation. In discussing Hardouin's followers in the present investigation I have put down my opinion about the comparatively small role of the individual in the general development.[422] However, I would not go as far as Heinrich Wölfflin did, who suggested an art history without names. He doubtless was right in believing that no one individual alone can account for a development. Yet we are able to understand the latter better after we have concentrated on the *oeuvres* of each single artist, just as we can comprehend the lifework only through preliminary analysis of the single works. Evidently the inductive method, which is the only legitimate procedure in art history, was also the method of Wölfflin. He started from observations, not from a theory. In writing, however, he skipped the preliminary stage of his thinking, perhaps for the sake of an appealing presentation, and set forth his historical concept while using the works of art merely as illustrations.

Many of Ledoux's buildings were not too different from the commonplace structures designed by many of his contemporaries. For example, the Palais Montmorency, built in 1770, displayed the traditional features of a heavy, rusticated basement, a main and an attic story unified by mighty columns, and a crowning balustrade surmounted by statues to make the transition to the sky less abrupt. The basic ideas of unity, of perfect equilibrium, and of the differentiation into dominant and subordinate parts were clearly visualized. In the Palais Thélusson, his largest and most splendid residential commission, built in 1780, the old system showed even more distinctly.[423] The main axis went from the imposing rusticated triumphal arch that served as the entrance to the estate, through the main building and the rear courtyard, and was terminated by a graceful belvedere set at a somewhat higher level. The house itself was of austere grandeur.

The larger part of Ledoux's executed work presented the familiar motifs of the classical revival. He appears to have appreciated the dignified repose of classical structures, as can be seen in many of his private residences and in the fine entrance portico (fig. 151) which he built in 1776 for the Royal Saltworks at Arc-et-Senans near Besançon.[424] The grotto in the rear of the portico is an interesting example of

early romanticism. The antagonism of smooth ashlar and rustication in the Salt
Magazine (Salle des Bosses) shows his skill in exploiting his raw material.[425]

Nevertheless, Ledoux was not too fond of features taken from antiquity. In the
perspective view of his ideal city we do not observe merely certain deviations from
the traditional classical forms in the central House of the Director and all the minor
buildings. We are particularly attracted by three structures showing how he
struggled to achieve a new compositional pattern. The courthouse, to the west, is
a Greek-cross building emphasizing the interpenetration of two blocks. The public
bath, to the northeast, has blocks coming forth from the cylindrical core. The
parsonage, to the east, presents the same pattern still more forcefully with its porticoes emerging from the rotunda and the latter rising from the low cubic substructure. Eventually Ledoux warned against copying blindly, and he chose to
modify the old forms in ever-changing ways in his best known achievements, the
tollhouses (Les Barrières) in Paris erected between 1784 and 1789.[426] These were
distinguished by the forceful treatment of the stone, the variety of their shapes, and
above all the grandeur of conception. (Four are still extant.) The contemporary
engraver who took the Barrière du Roule (fig. 152) as the background of his picture
showing the tragic return of Louis XVI from Varennes, fully grasped the monumentality of Ledoux's plain, tall structure. The house planned for the Parc de Bellevue presents a combination of heterogeneous elements, in which the single parts,
no longer welded into an indivisible community, have gained full independence
(fig. 153).[427] The crowning belvedere and the stairs are only loosely appended to
the body.

Ledoux's project for the Barrière de la Santé (fig. 154) is almost free from
classical reminiscences.[428] Its mass is compiled of elementary geometrical shapes, the
prismatic podium, the prismatic body, the horizontal semicylinders over the entrances, and a cylindrical belvedere capped by a hemisphere. Out of the turmoil of
the Revolution emerged the calmest and purest geometrical forms. The Jarnac
house (fig. 155) was, apart from some minor antique features, a simple cube with
an emphasized cornice and frameless openings.[429] Its sturdy podium resolutely
severed the building from its surroundings and made it look more modern than
houses of the type of Legrand's Hôtel Jarnac. Even when Ledoux dispensed entirely
with traditional features, he did not create a merely matter-of-fact architecture. For
instance in the project of a "House for a Writer" he repeats the basic motif of the
plain cube in the podium, body, and four belvederes, and thus obtains an aesthetic
effect of considerable interest and strength.[430] The cube appears here as the formative element. Robert Morris's bold concept was realized in Ledoux's design. Particularly striking patterns, which in the twentieth century have become very popular, were those of interpenetrating masses and of volume intruding into mass. Both
appeared as early as 1770 in the house of the dancer Mlle. Guimard.[431] Projects like
this must have startled eighteenth-century people. It is small wonder that Ledoux

complained about lack of understanding. To us, however, this early cubism looks quite familiar.

The church which Ledoux planned for his ideal city was full of contradictory reminiscences.[432] Its plan was the Greek cross, which Renaissance builders had liked so much. The portico and saucer dome followed antique prototypes. But one should not worry about the sources of the single features. Important as it is to explain works of art by comparison to their predecessors, it is still more important to ask not merely whence they come, but whither they lead. The significance of the walls of Ledoux's church with their solid unbroken masonry lies in the fact that they rigorously isolate the interior from the outer world. They announce the new individualism and the new self-sufficiency which begin to replace the contradictory Baroque trends toward coherence and expansion. The basic concept of the ideal city of Chaux, which Ledoux intended to build around the Royal Saltworks at Arc-et-Senans, was that of a self-centered entity.[433] The concept of self-sufficient isolation was also the generating idea behind the project of the Panarétéon, a sanctuary for the worship of the virtues.[434] The edifice is a free-standing mighty cube. Statues are placed against its upper wall, unlike Baroque sculptures seemingly "growing" out of the wall. This apposition of sculpture is an excellent illustration of the isolating system. In furniture, the separation of ornament and *fond* was often stressed by using contrasting materials, such as brass on dark wood. The *appliqué* technique was extremely popular under the French Empire. Like the Panarétéon many other buildings in the ideal city were to be devoted to the realization of the ideals of the Enlightenment such as the house of brotherhood, the house of peace, etc.

Many of Ledoux's inventions were daring experiments testifying to his restless will for innovation. A comparatively mild instance is the circular "House for a Broker."[435] On its second floor are plainly juxtaposed unframed windows; above, a spectral-looking arcade. In the gables lurk those symbols of bygone times, Palladian windows. Much bolder is the "House of the Surveyors of the River," set astride its rushing waters.[436] This mighty and impressive structure cannot be understood from a formal viewpoint alone. Though it was created by the desire for elementary forms contrasted with each other in the strongest manner, it was also created to satisfy the romantic wish for enhancement. It embodies one of the most characteristic postulates of romanticism, the wish to make the building speak, to make it express its meaning, to create *architecture parlante*.[437] Many architects have met this requirement simply by affixing easily understandable symbols to their structures, the caduceus of Aesculapius to medical buildings, the Orphic lyre to theaters. Ledoux, however, wanted to give the structure such a form that it would tell its story by itself. The Surveyors' House is a grandiose symbolization of nature made serviceable to man.

Besides the cube, the cylinder, and the pyramid, Ledoux experimented even with the sphere. His "Shelter for the Rural Guards" (fig. 156) is an extreme production of revolutionary undauntedness.[438] A modern critic has seen in this spherical house and in the few similar experiments by other architects the expression of the moral and mental instability which, he believed, started in the French Revolution.[439] Perhaps he overlooked, on the one hand, the high artistic qualities of these spherical houses and on the other, the fact that the vast majority of Ledoux's projects were structures of stressed static character, solidly resting upon the ground. These sound designs were not less symptomatic of the complex era than the more fantastic ones. There was a great beginning about 1800, in architecture and in other fields. Out of the vagueness and weirdness of the revolutionary ideals emerged not only the *code civil* and a new social order, but also a new, consolidated architecture.

Highly interesting are such projects as the Lauzon House,[440] and the prison for Aix-en-Provence (fig. 157).[441] The former presents a façade in which the old proportionality and the old equilibrium of the stories has been replaced by a free disposition of the openings; it is, moreover, an instance of a stepped or terrace building. The four façades of the prison are full of tension resulting from the insertion of an exceedingly broad stretch of naked wall between the two rows of tiny windows. A further noteworthy attempt to achieve a new surface pattern shows on the "House of the Art Dealers."[442] The pattern of multiple response is presented in the Saiseval buildings,[443] in which Palladian motifs, porches, and double flights of stairs reveal that the three houses are conceived as a group, and on the "Commercial Building"[444] projected for Rue Saint-Denis, with the repetition of gables, arches, and belvederelike superstructures on the different houses.

The doctrine of functionalism, which fascinated many in the Age of Reason, found an adherent in Ledoux—but only in theory, not in practice. He himself believed that there was no "art" in his plain design of a grange: *tout . . . est motivé par la nécessité*.[445] Yet even in this design we can detect an almost sophisticated pattern of contrasts between the various openings, and between the openings and the wall. It must be almost impossible for architecture to escape the perennial human urge toward form. Creating patterns, consciously or unconsciously, is the intent of every artist. The type of his patterns, or the system, is given to him by the ideal of configuration prevalent in his time. The revolutionary patterns were in accord with the new ideal of independence.

Two final examples may be cited to point out the meaning of the new architectural system. One is the first project for a "Discount Bank," made upon request of the Minister of Finance, Jacques Necker, in 1788.[446] We need not dwell on the cubic form of the three buildings of which the plan consists. It is more important to remark that each is a perfect unit in itself. There is not a single line in any of them that refers to its neighbors or makes contact with them. Baroque buildings were composed organically; here is inorganic juxtaposition. The second example (fig. 158) is the "House for Four Families."[447] There is no interrelation between its openings and, again, each of the four blocks could well stand alone. There is no superimposed climax, no pageantry, but there is the dignified pattern of equivalent units. From front, rear, or either side, one can get the idea of the whole, and each aspect would be equally satisfying. How different this is from Baroque structures conceived as pictorial compositions to be viewed from a single vantage point, and modulated according to an all-pervading hierarchical order. The ideal of individualism ushered in by the Revolution permeated every subsequent performance, struggling against traditional patterns in the nineteenth century, dominating almost indisputedly in the twentieth.

In the dawn of the nineteenth century two architect-critics, Goulet and Viel de Saint-Maux, vehemently censured the "gigantic and fantastic" projects of the modernists.[448] Goulet's blame of their "heaviness and lavishness of ornaments" seems to have been directed as much against artists of the type of Peyre and Neufforge as against Boullée and Ledoux. The still more acrimonious Viel assailed the two latter for having brought about "a true revolution" in architecture, blaming quite explicitly the modern incongruities and discrepancies. Viel originally had sided with the moderns, as can be gathered from his *Lettres*. In these and in the somewhat later *Principes* we see him fully aware of the fact that in his days architecture was in a stage of "incertitude" and going through a deep crisis. In *Décadence* he is an open enemy of Boullée and Ledoux, jealous of their achievements and their successes.

Several architects of the generation of 1730 are commonly considered as typical neoclassicists. Yet in their works the modern principles also can be detected behind the veil of conventional features.

Jacques Gondoin, a pupil of Blondel, erected the Ecole de Médecine et de Chirurgie between 1769 and 1776. He was just back from his travels in Italy, where he had met Piranesi, and England, where the climate had not agreed with him, as he wrote in a letter to M. de Marigny, alluding, perhaps, to the artistic atmosphere rather than to the atmospheric conditions.[449] The School of Medicine at once made him famous (fig. 159).[450] Quatremère de Quincy declared it the most classical work of the eighteenth century,[451] and ever after it was praised as an outstanding accomplishment of revivalism. Later, when imitations fell into discredit, it was regarded as the embodiment of a fad, and nothing else.[452] But it was far more than a copy, as both the entrance front on the Rue des Cordeliers (today, Rue de l'Ecole de Médecine) and the interior of the lecture hall show. The entrance front is built up of contrasts: the open colonnade in the center is set off against the lateral arches; the oblong central panel of the upper story is contrasted with the many windows on either side of it; and the two stories in their entirety oppose each other. The façade presents an attempt to arrange the parts in a new manner. It was valued accordingly by Gondoin's contemporaries. Legrand reports that the public was aware of the novelty of the structure and that the architects recognized in it the majestic character of Roman architecture, changed in a peculiar way, deprived as it was of all superfluous decoration, with an almost Greek simplicity. It appeared great to them, not because it resembled ancient models, but because of the disposition of the masses.[453] Legrand also observes that in it the whole "system" of the architecture of the past has been abandoned. Although the adherents of tradition were shocked by the lack of recesses and projections and by the straight, unbroken cornices, public opinion decided for the new "system" and the edifice was extolled as the masterpiece of modern French building:

Un style d'architecture si pur, si simple, et si différent de ce qu'on bâtissait alor . . . Tout le système de la vieille architecture française fut renversé par cet exemple inattendu, et les partisans de la routine furent stupéfaits de voir une façade sans pavillons, sans avant-corps au milieu, sans arrière-corps, et dont la corniche suivait d'un bout à l'autre sans rasant [ressaut] ni profil, contre l'usage reçu en France, et dont les Contant, les Gabriel, les Soufflot venaient de donner de si récens et si dispendieux exemples dans l'Ecole militaire, dans la Madeleine, et dans la nouvelle Sainte-Geneviève. Cependant l'opinion publique se prononça en faveur du nouveau système, la critique se tut, et l'Ecole de chirurgie fut proclamée par tous les gens de goût, le chef-d'oeuvre de notre architecture moderne.[454]

Jacques-François Blondel and Amaury Duval also appreciated the merit and the modernity of Gondoin's building.[455]

It reveals the discriminating sense and the keen vision of these contemporaries that they recognized the new system. They did not merely see the classic details; they fathomed the depth of the transformation. Comparing Gondoin's achievement with the Louvre colonnade of Perrault, the architect Goulet censured that famous work of the seventeenth century because its substructure impaired the effect of the row of columns above.[456] Thus he stigmatized as a deficiency that gradation which had been most important to all builders of the Baroque.

The lecture hall of the School of Medicine has been described as a portion of the Colosseum covered by the vaulting of the Roman Pantheon.[457] Seeing the single parts alone, the modern critic disregards the composition. The chief characteristic of the hall is the opposition of a half cylinder to a quarter sphere. The walls are bare, for any embellishments would impair the great concept (fig. 160).

The project for the prisons opposite the entrance of the school is great and plain.[458] Again the elements—the bare walls, the columned niche containing a fountain, the relief panel, the windows—are contrasted with one another. The upper story is disproportionately low. Of the whole project the fountain alone was carried out under Napoleon (1806) in a somewhat altered form.[459] It was a poor fragment deprived as it was of the flanking massive walls with their interesting arrangement of openings. The new pattern of oblong windows on the attic story, bull's-eyes below the cornice, and tall arched doors would have shown, as well, a certain refinement.[460]

The works of Jean-François Chalgrin and Alexandre-Théodore Brongniart reveal the increasing role of the fashion of classicism after 1800. The reaction against the revolutionary ideas had come rather fast. But these ideas were strong and sound, and infiltrated all the works of the traditionalists, although they could not gain the upper hand at once. All through the nineteenth century they had to be disguised in garments borrowed from the past.

Chalgrin was a pupil of Servandoni and Boullée.[461] His mansion for the Duc de Saint-Florentin (Rues Saint-Florentin and Rivoli, 1767)[462] belongs to the type of Antoine's Hôtel de Fleury. Its sobriety reveals the taste of the early revolutionary period. The porch of Saint-Philippe-du-Roule (1768-1784) is a massive block preceded by four Tuscan columns supporting a heavy pediment. Legrand and Saint-Victor felt that Saint-Philippe, and other churches too, should be freed from the adjacent houses, and they believed that this had been Chalgrin's intention.[463] We know that isolated churches became common in the nineteenth century. The greatest reticence in decoration and a fanciful plan are the distinctive traits of the Pavillon de Musique de Madame, at Versailles (1781).[464]

Chalgrin's first project of the Arc de Triomphe de l'Etoile (1806) was rich in classicizing features, especially columns and statues. The artist obviously had passed from revolutionary austerity to the decorative schemes of the *style Empire*.[465] But upon the request of Napoleon and the advice of the architect Fontaine he had to modify his project[466] and to give to the arch the severe aspect which it has preserved till today.

Chalgrin's dislike of traditional composition became apparent when he was called in to remodel the Palais du Luxembourg. Soufflot had already suggested, in a letter of 1776, that the space between its projecting pavilions be filled in with extra apartments, for practical and aesthetic reasons.[467] Chalgrin, too, proposed in a report of 1803 certain changes in order to eliminate what seemed to him too much differentiation of the masses.[468] The assembly room of the Senate (1804) presented the effective contrast of a vaulted niche for the chairman to the large main hall, which was lighted only from the top of its vaulting (fig. 161).[469]

Brongniart, a pupil of Blondel and Boullée,[470] built a *pavillon de plaisance* in Rue de Provence for the Duc d'Orléans in 1773.[471] Its plan calls to mind the extravagant manner of Peyre. The house was cylindrical, the courts elliptical, most of the rooms circular. The craving for innovation characteristic of the time appears in this layout. The next works were more composed; Baroque reminiscences and modern traits mingled in them. The plan of the once famous Hôtel de Saint-Foix, Rue Basse-du-Rempart (1775) was a square divided into nine compartments (fig. 162). The wings stretching toward the street were only loosely attached to the main mass, not organically combined with it in the Baroque way. When in 1798 the house was remodeled, the staircase was removed to the central square.[472] In the Dervieux house, Rue Chantereine (1778) Brongniart inserted the staircase between the entrance hall and the salon.[473] The latter protruded as a semicylinder from the garden front.[474] To all these houses the architect applied giant orders, and so he did on the Maison Bondy (Frascati), Boulevard Montmartre, of 1771, the Masserano house, Rue Plumet (1787),[475] and the Hôtel Monaco, Rue Dominique (1774).[476]

The Couvent des Capucins (1781), which later became the Lycée Bonaparte and to-day is the Lycée Condorcet, was far more modern with its smooth walls and its sparing decoration.[477] Its oblong court was surrounded by galleries of Tuscan columns supporting terraces in front of the rooms of the second floor. The third floor walls receded still more. The stepped stories presented an interesting specimen of vertically withdrawing form.[478] The structure was held in well-deserved esteem about 1800.[479] Several private houses built by Brongniart in the late 1780's were of the greatest reticence: the house of Mlle. de Condé, Rue de Monsieur (1781),[480] the Archives des Chevaliers de Saint-Lazare, Rue de Monsieur (1787), and the Maison Chamblin, Rue Plumet (1789).[481]

The front of the Théâtre Louvois (1791) was extremely sober (fig. 163). Tuscan columns carried the balcony above the ground floor; the second and third stories showed nothing but rows of equal-sized, frameless, arched windows.[482] Brongniart had reached modern simplicity. But he evidently was not able to create a modern, appealing pattern, at least not on this theater front. He would, however, rank close to Heurtier, if one could prove that the façade of the neighboring house was designed by him. For this façade showed a novel, bold disposition of the window rows, and a high portal which ran up to the third floor and added a dramatic note to the composition.

At the end of his career the frustrated revolutionary, who had ridiculed Poyet's classical pediment on the Chambre des Députés, became a classicist himself. The main feature of the Paris Exchange (1808) is the Corinthian peristyle, which conceals the blocklike body.[483] The revolutionary ideal of simplicity seems to have been defeated by the new decorative fashion. Yet we should not judge by the surface; beneath it, the modern concept of geometrical architecture was alive.

The monograph on Contant's and Leroy's pupil, François-Joseph Belanger, by Jean Stern,[484] is a most valuable contribution to art history, although it was prompted in the first place by the author's interest in the liaison of the architect with one of the *grandes impures,* Sophie Arnould. Many of Belanger's houses were of the square type of which Gabriel's Petit-Trianon is the best-known specimen: the pavilion in the garden of the Hôtel de Brancas (about 1770),[485] the house projected for Mlle. Arnould (1773),[486] Bagatelle, built for the Comte d'Artois (1777),[487] a house owned by the Carmélites, near Beauvais,[488] and another carried out at Pantin (fig. 164) for the American de la Ballue (or Battue) (1785).[489] This last house had a semicircular court front, along which the driveway ran, so that coaches could enter on one side of the house and leave on the other without turning. A low semicircular structure terminating the court contained the stables and coach houses; its roof was transformed into a terrace garden. On the rear façade of Bagatelle the circular salon projected as a half cylinder.[490] The main house of the Folie Saint-James at Neuilly was an oblong block (1777).[491] The stables of the Comte d'Artois (Rues du Faubourg-Saint-Honoré and Neuve-de-Berri; 1778) were plain, massive buildings (fig. 165).[492] Very remarkable were the pump houses[493] often referred to, erroneously, as works of the engineers Perrier—the Pompe à feu de Chaillot (Passy) on the Quai de Billy (1781),[494] and the Pompe à feu du Gros Caillou (fig. 166), on the Quai des Invalides (1786).[495] Both were sturdy blocks with heavy rustication, which looked to people about 1800, "very elegant."[496] About 1900 the Pompe de Chaillot was considered not only useless, but also "aesthetically unsatisfactory," and was demolished.[497] All these buildings show that Belanger with his predilection for geometrical shapes, clear-cut design, and aesthetically independent motifs of decoration was far ahead of conventional architecture.[498]

His projects for the Place du Carrousel, if carried out, would have been great achievements of civic art. Each plan presents a secluded precinct centered around a theater, which in 1781 would have been an opera house (fig. 167),[499] while in 1797 it was to be dedicated to all the arts as Temple d'Apollon or Grand Théâtre des Arts.[500] In particular the project of 1797 was distinguished by great severity and monumentality. The grandiose project made in 1777 for the reconstruction of the castle of Saint-Germain-en-Laye presents a huge cylindrical mass into which stepped, towerlike pavilions are inserted.[501] The drawing for a *Corps de garde national* shows a massive rusticated structure, that for a monument on the Pont-Neuf, a colonnade contrasted to a tall superimposed obelisk.[502] In general Belanger had not the ambition of other revolutionary architects to startle by bold effects and to create overdimensioned piles. Yet he was extremely interested in contriving original plan patterns, and, above all, imaginative surface patterns.

The court of the "Small Farm" carried out near Neuilly for a certain Castellane in 1791 was a large circle into which a small semicircular forecourt intruded. Instead of presenting my own comment on the artistic intention reflected in the plan, I want to quote the architect Goulet's views about the graceful composition of the *artiste architecte*:

L'architecte ingénieux a conçu son plan d'une manière large. Il a tracé sur le terrain un cercle de neuf toises de rayon pour faire une grande cour; il a laissé à la circonférence quatre ouvertures diamétralement opposées. L'une d'elles, beaucoup plus grande, fait la largeur d'une avant-cour, au moyen d'un demi-cercle qui pénètre le grand, et de deux pavillons aux deux côtés pour les remises et les écuries. Il a aussi élevé sur la circonférence du grand cercle une glacière d'un côté, et une laiterie de l'autre . . . Les deux planches . . . en représentent toute la grâce et la variété que l'auteur savait mettre à toutes ses compositions dans ce genre . . .[503]

Light and pleasant was the main front of the house of the Carmélites near Beauvais.[504] The ground floor opened into an arched loggia which proffered a mild contrast to the straight-headed upper loggia. There was almost no emphasis on the center nor any interrelation between the stories. The house which Belanger built for himself in the Rue Pigalle (1788) was similar in character.[505] There was much delicacy in it, and much serenity. The independent ornaments existed side by side, peacefully. The new concept of individualization appeared with great distinctness on the group of three contiguous houses in the Rue Saint-Georges (1788).[506] Each could very well stand alone, without any formal alteration being necessary. The lack of interrelation between the three houses is still more conspicuous in an early plan for them.[507] The group appeared to Goulet as a daring experiment, but he had the fullest appreciation for its sophisticated character.[508] Several minor structures in the courts of the two last-named projects were highly original and charming inventions.

The entrance to the garden of the poet Beaumarchais, near the Bastille (1789), was noteworthy for various reasons.[509] The relatively small portal was contrasted with the oversized relief figures and the oblong panel above. Here Belanger turned from his early delicate patterns to the forceful pattern of antithesis. Very interesting also is the way the sculptural decoration was treated. The statues on either side, representing Hercules and Minerva, were simply set against the wall. Baroque statuary was an integral part of architecture; now, the decoration was of the *appliqué* type particularly well known in minor objects of the Empire.

Besides the simple patterns showing on the houses discussed above, Belanger occasionally applied the refined and complicated pattern of multiple response. Its basic idea is the use of motifs which appear at different places on a building or on different buildings of a group, responding to each other and yet remaining independent. (The motifs become "themes" as soon as they "respond.") In Baroque composition all the features were related to the central axis and referred to each other by their shapes. Consequently, they were interdependent. They were parts of a continuous or coherent pattern. The isolated responding motifs appeal to memory rather than to the eye; they speak of unity, while Baroque features visualized it. The aesthetic significance of the isolated, responding motifs is that they suggest unity without the help of any ties, such as bands, giant orders, scrolls, and so on, and without the subordination of any feature to any other.

We have seen how Valadier experimented with his motifs on the Teatro Valle.[510] In one project he wanted to intimate the unity of the gable and the central portions of the structure, in another that of the gable and the side walls. Similarly, in the first plan for his own house in the Rue Neuve-des-Capucins (1787), Belanger applied bull's-eyes to the sides and to the rear of the loggia, while in the execution he replaced the lateral bull's-eyes by square openings corresponding with the squares of the ground floor (fig. 168).[511] No doubt artistic reasons prompted the different solutions, for practically one shape was as good as the other.

Further reciprocities on the house are the lunette in the gable echoing the shape of the entrance door, and the partial rustication of the gable reappearing on the front wall of the loggia. Thus there is mutual response between the gable and the ground floor, and between the gable and the loggia. Some Baroque reminiscences can be detected in the house. It was the product of a period of marked transition when a "pure style" was still less possible than in quieter times.

Much more refined and much less dependent on schemes of the past is the project of a slaughterhouse (about 1808).[512] Here (fig. 169) we see the Palladian motif high up on the tower and again on the ground floor; in between are triple arches. This arrangement, which can be expressed symbolically by P-T-T-P, reveals that P belongs to P and T to T. As the two Ts are inserted between the two Ps, it is also evident that all four motifs belong to one whole. If any other arrangement were chosen, for instance P-P-T-T or P-T-P-T, the building itself would appear incomplete. We remark moreover that there is a small distance between the lower P and the lower T, while the upper P and the upper T are far apart. It would, of course, have been possible to divide the front of the tower in a more regular way. Yet the greater distance gives more power to the lighter upper motifs. This is the new principle of compensation, or the lever principle, which superseded the former principle of the balance of equidistant symmetrical elements which were subordinated to one or several central features: s-c-s, or s-s-c-s-s, etc. (Incidentally, in twentieth-century design the lever principle was to play an enormous role.) For the sake of simplicity I have disregarded the rectangular openings on the tower and the arched windows of the wings. Further reciprocities and further compensations can easily be detected between them and the motifs discussed above.

In addition to the different weights and the different distances of the motifs, numerical relations enter into play. The rhythm of the openings on the tower, for instance, is 3 : 2 : 3 : 1 : 2. It is certainly enough to have demonstrated the principle, and not necessary to discuss all the combinations in detail. I want, however, to point out one more motif which signifies that the tower and the substructure belong together: the motif of the dentated cornice. The cornices on the tower naturally are shorter than the cornice running across the substructure. Therefore, two short cornices are set against the long one which for itself alone has far greater weight. Imagine how much artistic perfection would be lost if there were only one short cornice! It matters little that all the motifs are old, time-honored features; the modern arrangement counts more than the shape of the details. In the projects of several other slaughterhouses Belanger used the same or similar motifs for similar artistic ends. For example, in the group of three detached houses (fig. 171) standing in line, the three buildings are referred to each other by identical motifs. In the slaughterhouse with clock (fig. 170) the desire to create a pattern is still more patent.[513] In the original version the two roof turrets were finished by pediments; later, as can be seen in our illustration, the architect pasted on a sheet presenting three arches on each side instead of the pediments. Thus the response between the upper and lower portion, emphasized already by the reciprocities of the rectangular openings, became still stronger.

In a former essay I illustrated beside Belanger's slaughterhouse two similar Italian buildings after engravings by François Léonard Scheult.[514] The similarity lies only in the details. The two buildings in Scheult's version lack the refinement of Belanger's design; there is little interplay between their features, but rather a certain monotony. About 1800, new compositional principles came into being. These principles had far greater significance than the trifling variegations of the classical orders, which art history used and uses to record and comment upon, with superstitious awe.

Having dealt with some instances of multiple response on the surface, I shall discuss two instances of this pattern in space, such as we have met already in De Wailly's group of three houses and in Ledoux's Saiseval buildings. It shows with great distinctness in the court of Bagatelle.[515] Here the "Communs," named also "Bâtiment des Pages," consists of three units, the concave central structure, which includes the gateway, and two pavilions. The architect set off each unit markedly from the others, and yet wanted to intimate that they belonged together. To reach this end he repeated on the front facing the court the decorative motifs in different locations on each of them. And this was not all. The same motifs show also on the distant court front of the main house, with slight modifications. (The bull's-eyes are replaced by medallions, etc.)

The aforesaid house in Rue Neuve-des-Capucins (fig. 168) is another instance.[516] The interplay of the motifs takes place on the four walls enclosing the court with the result that the latter appears as a self-centered spatial unit, and the structures surrounding it are marked as belonging together. The repeating motifs are located on the court front of the main house (M), the front of the rear house (R), and the side wall connecting the two houses (W). (The engravings do not illustrate the second side wall; according to the plan it must have been similar to the first.) We see pediments above the side windows on the main floor of M, in the center of R, and above the fountain on the ground floor of W. Round arches show in the Palladian motif on the top floor of M, in the window on the top floor of R, and, tripled, on the second floor of W. Medallions are applied to the center of M (three), to the top floor of R (two), but none to W. This inequality is compensated by the other sculptural decoration: M has none, R has ornamental relief panels, W has niches with statues. The largest structure has the fewest embellishments, the smallest has most. The medallions intimate that M and R belong together, the statues and the panels suggest the community of R and W. A Baroque architect would have concentrated on one front, probably on that of the rear house, and distinguished it by a fountain or statuary as an eye-trap for people entering the court from the main building. Here, however, the four walls are equally important. The visitor will not be alarmed by the claim of a dominant feature to receive his whole attention. He will rather have the feeling of being sheltered in a secluded precinct. Wherever he turns he will find one motif or the other already familiar to him from the wall which he has seen first.

Various questions may arise about the pattern of multiple response. One may, perhaps, ask how far it was intentional. It certainly was neither more nor less "calculated" than any other decorative scheme. Or one may question whether there was anything like it at any other moment in art history. Let us keep in mind that all artistic motifs, all patterns, the individual works of art, the manner of each artist, the "styles," and the architectural systems result from unique constellations. The pattern of multiple response originated from the meeting of surviving traditional features with the trend toward individualization. Such a constellation will hardly ever occur again.

The pattern of multiple response remained rare. It was applied by a few outstanding architects in a few outstanding works. As a somewhat sophisticated concept it could hardly become common. Nor could it bring about the solution of the compositional problems of the period. It was an attempt to create something new, less forceful than other attempts of Boullée and Ledoux had been, but not less significant. When the traditional forms were superseded by the geometrical ones, it was not realizable any longer, whereas the simpler patterns of repetition and antithesis were to find even better fulfillment.

The analyses of a large number of revolutionary works and projects have enabled us to recognize the new trends in composition. As art historians we might be content with having seen the so-called era of classicism in a new light.[517] However, one who is not afraid to venture beyond the borderlines of our discipline will, perhaps, find out that a new general ideal was expressed by the new artistic patterns. The many weaker elements were no longer to be subjugated by the few stronger ones. And what is more, the elements could form a whole and yet remain free.

The principle of compensation was to play a certain role in romantic painting, and a decisive role in impressionist and post-impressionist painting. It is interesting to note that the most earthbound of all the arts, architecture, was the first to discover the great possibilities of unbalanced composition.

Belanger unremittingly strove to get away from the compositional schemes of the past. Nevertheless, all his designs are strictly symmetrical. He never achieved truly "irregular" architecture. The only exceptions are a few cottages belonging to his house at Santeny (1800); but the earlier structures in the park of the Folie Saint-James—a grotto with a temple front, a "Chinese" pavilion, a "Gothic" pump house—did not deviate from symmetry.[518] The manor house at Santeny presented highly interesting patterns on the narrow main façade and the extended side façades.

It would not be worthwhile to discuss at length the petty products of Romantic sentimentality, whether by Belanger or others. They have been dealt with sufficiently by several historians specializing in the Louis XV and XVI periods.[519] Just two somewhat famous, still extant fabrics may be pointed out. In 1771, the dilettante Racine Demonville shaped his country house in the garden Le Désert near Marly like a broken column (fig. 172).[520] Between 1783 and 1786, Richard Mique built the Hameau near Trianon for the queen.[521]

In creating original surface patterns Jacques Rousseau and Nicolas Lenoir "le Romain" were nearly as successful as was Belanger. Rousseau arranged the decorative motifs on the façade of the theater at Amiens (1778) in a charming, free manner.[522] The disproportionality of the stories adds to the interest of the design. His castle of Saint-Gratien near Amiens (1789) presents variegated features which discreetly respond to each other: "Le caractère composite de Saint-Gratien en est le charme."[523]

The front of Lenoir's opera house (fig. 173) near Porte Saint-Martin (1781)[524] was even more original than Rousseau's theater. He contrasted the three large arched windows of the main floor with the oblong relief panel above and the tiny windows on the sides. Another dramatic composition is the front of the Palais de Justice at Douai by Michel-Joseph Lequeulx (1784) with its variegated decorative motifs, especially its agitated center.[525]

Louis Jean Desprez was a pupil of Jacques-François Blondel and of Pierre Desmaisons, the rebuilder of the Palais de Justice and builder of the prison La Petite Force.[526] Desprez spent his last thirty years almost entirely in Sweden and found there recognition and understanding both from his contemporaries and posterity. The monograph by Nils G. Wollin informs us about the significant phases of his career, depicting the cultural background of the period and elucidating at length his development as an artist.[527]

In many of Desprez's designs symmetry and centralization lived on; for instance, in the project (fig. 174) of a funeral monument to Voltaire (1766),[528] and in the castle of Haga (1787).[529] The former with its accumulation of incongruous features is full of revolutionary unrest; the latter is calm and rather monotonous. However, the conventional schemes never satisfied Desprez. Again and again he attempted to make something new out of them. The overlarge central window on the third floor of the "Academy Building" planned for Stockholm disturbs the equilibrium of the whole.[530] (Its side lights are so narrow that one can hardly term it a Palladian window.) The huge portal of the stables at Haga (fig. 175) is definitely out of proportion.[531] The extrication of the central portion from the context of the whole is the most characteristic feature of the project for the stables of Drottningholm (1788).[532] The center is contrasted with the sides in texture, size, and shape, and contains strongly contrasted features within itself (fig. 176).

When I say that Desprez turned away from tradition I do not mean that he gave himself over to classicism and romanticism. These trends played a major role only in his theatrical decorations, which had to reinforce the stage performances and quite naturally tended in a literary direction. Eventually Desprez designed insignificant and ludicrous things of the sort which the sentimental landscape architects had brought into vogue. The chief interest of those battlemented turrets,[533] artificial ruins,[534] "Gothic" or "Antique" strongholds[535] does not lie in the romantic masquerade, but in the fact that they, too, were made up of artistic contrasts of elementary solids. It does not matter that Desprez availed himself of features of the past; what matters is what he made out of them.[536] Several designs reflect the romantic inclination toward grandeur and expressiveness, for example, the imposing staircase for a Russian castle[537] and many theatrical projects.[538]

Desprez's untiring efforts to reach new solutions reveal themselves in the projects for the castles of Riddarholmen[539] and Haga.[540] At Haga he began like his Swedish predecessor, Tempelman, with a scheme derived from Palladio's Rotonda, but ultimately devised a perfectly circular, self-contained building. Desprez's biographer censures the architect for having lost sight of the purpose of the house.[541] Desprez, I believe, simply disregarded practicality, like other revolutionary architects in their most personal productions. He was a creative artist with higher goals. The aspirations of the functionalists did not go beyond providing shelter; they expected from a building no more than an animal expects from its den. The French revolutionaries, however, found in the functional doctrine merely an ally in their feud against the Baroque. Their final aims were, as we know from Ledoux's own words,[542] not building, but architecture.

Desprez renounced any kind of decoration in the projects of a church (fig. 177)[543] and the Botanical Institute at Upsala (1791).[544] A word may be said here about the frameless windows showing in these designs and many others. The Baroque framing, often very rich, had a double aesthetic function; it was a mediator between the solid masonry and the fluctuating space, and it established relationship between the single openings. The frame rounded off the window and at the same time integrated it into the whole context. In revolutionary buildings where the framing is missing, the wall becomes prominent and the apertures stand isolated in it.

Very diversified were Desprez's attempts to create new surface patterns. The still centralized project of a villa and the totally different project of a naumachia[545] are particularly remarkable in this regard. The main story of the naumachia presents a row of seven equidistant arched windows of equal size contrasted with the oblong panel above, the huge portal, and the three slits on each side of it. The Baroque synthesis has been superseded by the new antithetical statement. Of great interest are the architect's new ways in spatial composition. The Armfelt house at

Frascati (1791) is a prostyle temple with a second entrance in the rear.[546] Extra rooms looking like small appended buildings are added to each side façade. More vigorous are several projects which present the concept of interpenetrating masses: the central portion of the stables at Drottningholm is virtually an oblong block emerging from the wings;[547] the double auditorium consists of two semicircular audience halls with the common stage house between them;[548] the concert hall has the stage house inserted between the auditorium and an oblong hall.[549] The "Royal Theatre," intended, perhaps, for London (1789), would have been a very impressive pile.[550] Its audience hall would have projected as a mighty semicylinder from the oblong main mass, which was to house sumptuous staircases on each side. This plan calls to mind the theater plan by Neufforge which was often repeated in the nineteenth century.[551] The architects of the revolution knew how to achieve striking effects by the antithesis of different-sized or different-shaped masses. Rarer, but not less significant was the opposition of masses against voids. It shows in Desprez's second project for the Armfelt house (1792),[552] which resembles Ledoux's Tabary house.[553] The narrow, deep vestibule containing the stairs and opening into a huge Palladian motif is inserted between the two prismatic wings. The basic concept is that of a hollowed-out block or the contrast of mass and void.

The project of a Vauxhall was obviously derived from the Roman Pantheon.[554] Yet Desprez wanted to mark the unity of the discrepant masses; he applied tall arched openings to both the portico and the rotunda and let the outline of the latter's low-pitched conical roof repeat the triangular pediment. The side entrances, moreover, repeat the shape of the portal, the lateral square panels are reverberations of the square door and the panel of the basement, and the lunettes on the rotunda echo the mightier arches below. The pattern of multiple response was called in to bridge the gap between the disparate elements. It shows also on the gothicizing project for the cathedral of Skara.[555] The natural thing would have been to apply lancet windows all over the façade, exclusively. But Desprez introduced, besides the ogives, in different but in no way arbitrarily chosen locations, oblong windows and bull's-eyes. He did not simply want to design a "Gothic" church; he attempted to create a meaningful pattern. Here as in the Vauxhall the result is not thoroughly satisfactory. Yet in several structures dealt with previously—the Academy Building and the stables of Drottningholm and Haga—striking artistry and a strange new grandiosity are revealed, after we have grasped the compositional principle of their façades. This new compositional pattern remained rare; it was a unique achievement of its period, as unique as are all great performances of art.

Nicolas Henri Jardin developed the Pantheon scheme in an unusual manner. His project for the church for Frederick V at Copenhagen (1755) consists of a rotunda to which a portico in front, a portico in the rear, and two tower-like, two-storied lateral chapels are annexed. Thus the project of the Danish architect

Eigtved, which was Baroque in composition and decoration, was replaced by an agglomeration of independent elements. There are several other interesting designs in Jardin's plans for the church.[556] The sepulchral chapel (Rome, 1747) was planned as a pyramid rising from a massive substructure and flanked by four obelisks. The "Pont triomphal" (Rome, about 1748) has a cubic gateway in its midst. In 1792 Jardin became a member of the first class of the Paris Academy, defeating his competitor Ledoux.[557]

Jean-Baptiste-Michel Vallin de la Mothe transplanted the new heavy style to Russia. It shows in the church of Sainte-Cathérine (1760), the old Erémitage (1764), the gateway La Nouvelle Hollande (1765), and the Academy of Fine Arts (1765),[558] in St. Petersburg. Thomas de Thomon brought to Russia the refined pattern of two rostral columns flanking a low pedimented temple. The example set by Boullée's third project for the restoration of Versailles (1780) and followed in the designs for Exchange buildings by Pierre Bernard (1782), Max-Joseph Hurtault (an VI), Dumanet (an X) and Thomon (1801, 1803) (fig. 179), was realized by Thomon in his Bourse of St. Petersburg (1805).[559]

What the designs created by the architects of the generation of 1730, or, better, what the artistic movement which they represented meant to their contemporaries, can be seen from the *Avertissement* in Krafft's and Ransonette's publication, *Plans des plus belles maisons à Paris,* of 1801:

The revolution, which has taken place in the arts, and particularly in architecture, since the last twenty-five years in France, has been remarked by every man of taste . . . A passion for travelling, and progressive improvements have brought about in the art of building, and decorating public edifices very remarkable changes. The great number of private Houses, erected in the new parts of the town for opulent proprietors, who brought back with them from their travels in Italy, and other Countries the taste of Novelty, and a certain propensity of deviating from the old, servile method of Building, of freeing themselves from many received prejudices, operated a complete change in the outward features of architecture. . . . We look upon it as an important service rendered to society to publish, what may well be called the monuments of architecture regenerated in the nineteenth century, and those, which *towards the end of the eighteenth, have prepared this regeneration* . . . in order that the public may be enabled to follow the progress of the art, and judge of the improvements and variations it experienced through the many *changes of the different systems.* [My italics.]

I add the French version of the last sentence, because of its particular significance: ". . . afin que l'on puisse suivre aussi la marche de l'art, et juger de ses progrès, ou des variations qu'il peut avoir eprouvées en changeant de système."

The writer of this passage believed that the source of the "very remarkable changes" lay somewhere abroad, while in reality the desire for innovation was equally strong inside and outside France. The "passion for travelling" was in itself a symptom of the unrest of the era. The architects who had visited Italy brought back the forms which were in accordance with their own aims but not perhaps the forms of Borromini and Guarini. The daring inventions of Boullée and Ledoux, who had never been to Italy, originated on the soil of France. The critic of 1801 was too close to the events to be able to perceive thoroughly the wide ramifications of the modern movement. Like many later art historians he could not think of its origins except in terms of transplantation and adoption. But he understood that in the last quarter of the eighteenth century not merely a slight transformation, but a true revolution had taken place. He understood that the "regeneration" of architecture had come to pass "through the many changes of the different systems," and with prophetic intuition he realized that the eighteenth century had "prepared" the way for the future. Today it is rather easy to detect the revolutionary traits in nineteenth-century architecture. There were, on the other hand, many works by "revolutionaries," that look as if they were devised between 1800 and 1900. This is especially true of the *oeuvre* of the architect Paris.

Pierre-Adrien Paris, a pupil of Louis-François Trouard and Le Geay,[560] would not be counted among the revolutionary artists if we class him according to his political beliefs.[561] All through his life he kept allegiance to Louis XVI, whom he had served as first designer of the decorations for festive occasions, and when Boullée invited him to become a member of the new Institut National, he declined.[562] But in his work, which in general has a typical nineteenth-century character, the traces of the revolutionary movement are obvious. The walls of the "Bibliothèque publique" (Rome, 1773) (fig. 180) call to mind the austerity of the Odéon. Many of his decorations were fantastic combinations of incongruous features;[563] and so was the city gate (Rome, 1771) composed of a triumphal arch and two Trajan columns (fig. 181). The contrast of cubic and cylindrical masses is evident in the house at Vauclusotte,[564] the Foache house at Colmoulin (1793)[565] and the castle of Bellêtre (fig. 182).[566] The trend toward grandeur combines with the extravagant application of discrepant features in the cathedral project (fig. 183), which might have been designed in the late nineteenth century. Although Paris designed "Gothic" fabrics (the "Windmill")[567] and was an ardent admirer of antiquity, he nevertheless was against blind copying.[568]

In passing judgment on the nineteenth century we should not merely point out its shortcomings and its lack of originality. If we look below the surface we can recognize that it preserved and handed down to our own era the greatest concept of the revolution, the concept of composing in bold masses which no longer were subject to Baroque formality.

XIII

THE ARCHITECTS OF THE FRENCH REVOLUTION
THE GENERATION OF 1760

WE HAVE seen that in the first decades after 1700 a critical attitude toward the well-established formulas of composition had arisen among the English architects.[569] Somewhat later the Italian "rigorists," led by Lodoli, felt that architecture should be basically reformed.[570] Toward the end of the eighteenth century France developed a new type of architecture distinguished by positive artistic aims of a quite novel character. The new predilection for elementary forms and the new truthfulness to the nature of materials reveal the soundness of the French movement;[571] the endeavors to find new patterns tell of its artistic aspirations. The ideal of pure functionalism remained confined to theory, but was nevertheless an influential ally in the struggle for architectural individualism. The geometric forms and the respect for the properties of the material promised artistic results which agreed with the rationalism underlying the functionalistic doctrine far better than the anthropomorphic forms of the Baroque ever could have done.

Architectural development is a process of slow infiltration of a decaying old ideal of configuration by a rising new one. In the accomplishments of the leading architects of the generation of 1730 the depth of the revolutionary movement has become apparent and the strength of the new concept manifest. It remains to expose its breadth, which I shall do by presenting a selection of works by several architects born about 1760.

These architects, who received their training in the last decades of the eighteenth century, were the followers of the older revolutionaries rather than pioneers themselves. First, I shall illustrate instances of their predilection for elementary geometry, then deal with the reform of the ground plan and new surface patterns and spatial patterns. In this respect, with its changed attitude regarding the material, the architecture of the late eighteenth century foreshadowed that of the twentieth. After presenting some instances of the less important trend toward picturesqueness, which ties the revolutionary era to romanticism, and of the rise of nineteenth-century eclecticism, I shall comment on a few specimens of revolutionary interior architecture. In conclusion, the works of Dubut and Durand and their ultimate efforts to create a modern architecture will be discussed. In their *oeuvres* we shall recognize the artistic legacy of the eighteenth century.

181

Art in geometry

The predilection for elementary geometry was perhaps the most conspicuous trait of architecture about 1800. Classical features were applied, sometimes prodigally, at other times sparingly; in some of the most interesting designs they were entirely dispensed with. Emphasis on the simple solids, however, became common to almost the entire production. On Nicolas Claude Girardin's cubic Chapelle Beaujon (1784)[572] there is no embellishment except the reticent framing of the door, the cornice, and the meager decoration of the pediment.[573] It is noteworthy that this sober structure pleased his contemporaries extremely.[574]

In 1784, Thévenin built the still extant Queen's Dairy (Laiterie de la Reine) in the park of Rambouillet in the form of a small cube.[575] Again, as on the Chapelle Beaujon, the grooves are the only decoration of the wall. The ringed columns of the porch are inconspicuous beside the obtrusive rustication; they seem to form part of the wall. The segmental tympanum over the door mitigates the severity of the front. With the beautiful and characteristic interior I shall deal later.[576]

The Biteaux house (1795)[577] in the Rue des Trois-Frères, by Blanchon, was distinguished by the plainness of its square fronts, each of which contained a Palladian door, and two oblong windows. The main façade was finished by a frieze of triglyphs, the garden façade made effective by the textural differentiation of the stories with stone contrasted with brick. Someone who expects to find in every revolutionary work at least some excitement may hardly consider Blanchon's house as a revolutionary accomplishment, although indeed it is. The compactness of its body, its flat, forbidding walls, its clean outline and the loosely appended stairs reflect the thoroughly altered concept of architectural perfection.

The reputation of Olivier as one of the more fashionable architects of the 1790's was to live on in France, as we may learn from the novel *Les Dieux ont soif* by Anatole France, who places him beside Ledoux and De Wailly.[578] In the house built near Noyon for M. Vincents, Olivier's work shows him to be a modernist of the type of Blanchon.[579] Yet he did not succeed equally well in achieving a well-rounded whole. Like other architects of the Directoire and the Empire he applied some dry decoration, a relief frieze and relief panels, to his house. We shall deal later with other works of Olivier, of a different type and greater appeal.

The porch of the Hôtel-Dieu on the Place du Parvis-Notre-Dame, by Nicolas-Marie Clavareau (1804) was an instance of the disguising of novel geometric forms with pseudo-classical apparel.[580] Comparing it to the project of a customhouse (fig. 184) by Réverchon, which was awarded a medal in the 1780's, we become aware of what had been happening in the closing century. The basic formal ideal had not changed; both houses are sturdy blocks. But about 1800 architects no longer liked to present the elementary form in its crudity and nudity. The qualities of massiveness, austerity, and monumental simplicity which distinguish Réverchon's customhouse are veiled by classicizing features on the entrance of the hospital.

Having found instances of pyramidal structures designed by Neufforge, Le Canu, Boullée, and Ledoux, I have no need to present further examples of this type. Yet I want to point out two rather early designs with pyramids as the main motifs, in order to refute the common error that the pyramid became fashionable through the Egyptian campaign. In 1785 Fontaine was awarded the Grand Prix for a cenotaph in form of a pyramid standing in the center of a circle dotted with sixteen small pyramids.[581] In 1774 Michel-Ange Challe had designed a gigantic pyramid for the funeral of Louis XV in Notre-Dame.[582] Its blank face showed nothing but a brief inscription.[583] The undecorated form alone was intended to impress the spectator.

Another temporary decoration which still more clearly showed the novel predilection for plain solids was the Autel de la Patrie, erected by Belanger's pupil Joseph Jacques Ramée for the Fête de la Fédération on the Champ-de-Mars, July 14, 1790.[584] Most certainly this decoration for the first great celebration of the Revolution did fully conform to the taste of the time. It was used not merely on the first anniversary of the destruction of the Bastille, but again and again on other Revolutionary festivals, too.[585] The altar stood in the center of an oblong circus, which could be entered from the embankment of the Seine through a triumphal arch with three openings of equal height. At the far end in front of the Ecole Militaire, a tribune for the king and the National Assembly was erected. (The layout of the circus was made by Célérier.)[586] The altar table of cylindrical shape rose above a low truncated pyramid. Cubic blocks were added to the four corners of the pyramid, carrying tripods and adorned with symbolic reliefs. The basis of the whole was a circular platform.[587] For the funeral of the soldiers fallen at Nancy, September 1790, the cylindrical altar table was replaced by a sarcophagus (fig. 186).[588] When in 1813 Ramée laid out Union College at Schenectady, New York, he once more made a cylindrical feature—the isolated Rotunda—the center of the whole composition.[589] The Autel de la Patrie is as characteristic of its era as were the many nonpermanent triumphal arches of the Baroque. It manifests that the modern elementary forms could be understood by the public and were appreciated by them. From Ramée his son Daniel may have inherited his admiration for Ledoux's accomplishments. He collected engravings after the latter's works and brought out the second edition of his *Architecture* in 1847.

Participating in a competition of the Academy, Jean-Nicolas Jomard composed an "Elysée" of receding cylinders topped by a truncated cone.[590]

Both the isolated whole cylinder and the half-cylinder projecting from the wall were very popular about 1800. We find the latter once more on the river front of the Hôtel Salm (at present the Palais de la Légion d'Honneur), erected by Pierre Rousseau between 1782 and 1785 (fig. 187).[591] In the front on the Rue de Lille and in the court[592] the architect stressed the heaviness of cubic masses. The central porch in the court visualizes cubic volume.

The architect Henry was a specialist in projecting half-cylinders. He applied them to the Intendance des Ponts et Chaussées, Rue Saint-Lazare, (1788)[593] and the Maison Lakanal, Rue du Mont-Blanc, (1795)[594] in a way very similar to the garden front of Brongniart's Hôtel Bourbon Condé.[595] One might remark that the convexity of the central portion was nothing new. Yet there is a difference between the Baroque and the revolutionary feature. In the Baroque the bays usually were gentle undulations of the wall.[596] Now, the bays detached themselves abruptly from the wall, thus producing the impression of a smaller body interpenetrating the larger one. Previously the walls were thoroughly pierced by huge windows; now the stonework was emphasized, making the cylindrical feature become more conspicuous. The complex of the Maison Lakanal is very interesting in another aspect, too. Where the narrow entrance passage widens into the forecourt, the walls recede in quarter-cylinders finished by spherical vaultings.[597] That means that the elementary form is visualized not only in mass, but also in volume.

Henry's Vassale house, Rue Pigalle, (1788) was a full cylinder with a conical roof (fig. 188).[598] The architect did not worry about the practical disadvantages of the circular plan. He instead made experiments with diversified shapes in the interior. The vestibule is an oblong with an added semicircle, the bedroom an oblong with a semielliptical addition and an alcove, the salon is an ellipse, the boudoir a half-ellipse, and the dining room is octagonal. The antechamber in the center of the house is the only square room.

The kiosk on the Boulevard du Temple by Bricard (1795) was also a circular structure.[599] This small building was called Paphos, but apparently was not devoted to the cult of Venus, as the name would imply. It served harmless entertainments, including a café and a hall for dancing. Through the peripheral arcades the interiors received ample light and the visitors could enjoy the view of the garden.

Perard de Montreuil, a pupil of Moreau-Desproux and Boullée, built the Rotonde du Temple (1788) on a rectangular plan with semicircles added to the short sides.[600]

A plan greatly resembling the Palais National by Legrand and Molinos was adopted by Ledoux's pupil Jean-Nicolas Sobre, when he designed a theater ("Salle de spectacle") in a Grand Prix competition (fig. 189). Here the main structure is a massive cylinder with bare walls. The general layout of the "Maison de plaisance," to which the theater was to belong (fig. 190), is the product of a fanatic of geometry. The structures are arranged along concentric circles and on their diameters. Sobre's design of a "Chapelle consacrée à la Trinité" won him a second prize.[601] To this circular building three porches are added, filling the corners of an imaginary circumscribed triangle. The surrounding yard is enclosed by an enormous outer circle.[602] When in 1791 Sobre gave to the shop windows of the Cour Batave the shape of half-cylinders, he drew public attention to this innovation, as we learn from a remark in Landon's *Annales du Musée*.[603] Segmental windows were becoming popular on private houses, and the motif of projecting semicylinders finally passed from the Old to the New World. Still today it is as common on the brick fronts of Boston, Massachusetts, as it is in the streets of Brighton, Sussex.[604]

Like Boullée and Ledoux, Sobre was bold enough to experiment with the most nontectonic form, the sphere. His "Temple of Immortality" was devised as an airy monopteros on top of a hemisphere (fig. 191).[605] The latter would have been mirrored in a surrounding lake, so that the impression of a total globe would have been achieved. Sobre planned to lay a belt of reliefs with the signs of the zodiac around the equator and to enliven the surface by a delicate sketchy design suggesting a map. Inside there was to have been an amphitheatrical audience hall under a starred cupola. The furnishing—an altar and benches—and the decorative accessories, such as statues and a frieze, would have somewhat impaired the majesty of the pure sphere. The almost empty globes of Boullée's Newton Memorial, Ledoux's cemetery at Chaux, and Lequeu's Temple de l'Egalité and Temple de la Terre are far more impressive.[606]

One may look at the strange idea of a spherical building from various viewpoints. One may recognize in it the unbridled will of innovation, the will to create something extraordinary, or one may blame its lack of "soundness."[607] One may find the motivating force behind the curious invention in a predilection for elementary shapes or one may point out that the sphere represents the "withdrawing" form in the most perfect manner and thus is most suitable to express the idea of self-contained individualism. To Houel, the sphere was the perfect symbol of equality; Ledoux praised it as an excellent means to express sublimity.[608] Since time immemorial the sphere has been to mankind the symbol of eternity. It appealed quite particularly to the architects of the Revolution, who were artists enough to forget about practicality, when they aimed at grandeur or at form.

From the artistic side alone we should judge the "House of a Cosmopolite" (1785) planned by Antoine Laurent Thomas Vaudoyer in Rome (figs. 192, 193).[609] This design with its suavity is similar rather to Sobre's temple than to the grandiose spheres of Boullée and Ledoux. The upper half of Vaudoyer's sphere, emerging from a circular arcade, is adorned with stars. A contemporary critic had the right understanding for the delicate composition when he likened it to a madrigal.[610] Like Ledoux in the Shelter for the Rural Guards,[611] Vaudoyer planned to create real lodgings in his sphere. Both architects subdivided the interiors into stories and the stories into single rooms.

The spherical "Temple de la Terre" (1790) by Jean-Jacques Lequeu ranks very high as a work of art, especially its interior.[612] Its lower half is encased in a cylindrical substructure adorned with hermae, while the upper rises from it like a dome.

Ledoux did not impair by any additions the pure form of his cemetery. He presented the solemn contrast of the dark hall to the still darker openings of the adjacent corridors. Lequeu devised the vault of his temple like the starred sky, adorned its walls with draperies and put a small terrestrial globe near the base. It may be that he took this last motif from Boullée's Newton Memorial, in which the sarcophagus is set against the immense void. However, he knew how to give to his composition a meaning of its own. The tiny terrestrial globe echoes the larger sphere in which it stands.

The projects of the hemispherical "Tombeau en l'honneur de Newton" (fig. 194) by Délépine, a pupil of Marie-Joseph Peyre, and the similar cenotaph to Newton by Labadie (1800) might well have been carried out.[613] Great and impressive, they rest firmly on their massive substructure and are conceived on an almost human scale. Their radii are about twice the height of the cypresses surrounding them, whereas their prototype, the Newton Memorial by Boullée, is eight times the height of the trees planted around it.

Boullée, Vaudoyer, and Lequeu founded their spheres solidly in cylindrical substructures, Sobre made his temple seemingly float on the water, Ledoux gave his cemetery the soil as a basis. None appears to have forgotten that architecture is an earthbound art. That the idea of spherical houses, like all the other fantastic projects of the revolutionaries, resulted from the restlessness of the period, is obvious. The spheres of the revolutionaries do not need any rational justification. Their significance lies in their creators having, in them, reached the realm of pure artistic invention. Whoever wishes architecture to remain an art will be thankful to those who set themselves so high a goal. For as long as there are such architects, everyday building, too, will move on higher levels.

New ways in planning.

After the three-dimensional structure has formed in the architect's imagination, he may put down his vision in a sketch, as a help to his memory or to test the presumable effect. However, the first step toward realization and the very first precise, full statement of his intentions is the ground plan. Eighteenth-century plans indicate whether the architect still followed traditional formality, whether he searched for a new form, or whether he was exclusively intent upon a functional disposition. Almost without exception some pattern, be it the most humble and the most inconspicuous one, appears in the elevation. The plan, however, can be affected by the perennial desire for form, or can be absolutely unformalized, made only to satisfy commodiousness. The functional doctrine could find realization at least in plan design.

Of the plans of the revolutionary architects, some are of the unadulterated or nearly unadulterated Baroque type, many are of geometric character, others are purely functional. Of course, a plan hardly belongs strictly to one of these groups;

each has in it traits of two or all of them. In my classification each plan will be assigned to the group with which it has most in common.

Baroque plans were not infrequent up to 1800. There is no need to illustrate any of them. We may pass at once to some typical experiments with elementary geometric shapes, which were mainly of two kinds. There were architects who composed in the fanciful manner of Peyre's "Academy" project, Brongniart's house for the Duc d'Orléans, or Le Carpentier's Pavillon de la Bossière, Rue de Clichy, built in 1767 and after 1800 "belonging to an American of the United States,"[614] and there were others who tried to find more sober solutions. Instances of the first type were the house by Huvé, at Meudon,[615] and the Thamney (or, Tamncy) house, (1789) Rue de Provence, by Itasse.[616] These houses were composed of circular, elliptical, and polygonal rooms, symmetrically arranged on both sides of the salon-vestibule axis. The main feature of the house of the poet Beaumarchais, Boulevard Saint-Antoine, carried out by Paul Guillaume Lemoine "le Romain" in 1790, was a circular arcade set between the concave front of the house and the garden (fig. 195).[617] An instance of sober geometry was the plan of Henry's Intendance, which I have mentioned above. Here that subdivision of the square into nine smaller squares was anticipated, which in the last years of the century became very frequent. Old and new trends balance each other in many hybrid plans. The house built by the architect D'Orliane for himself (1777), Rue du Montparnasse, had the traditional main axis disrupted by the staircase; the single rooms were of almost equal status.[618] The Courmont house (1789), Rue de Suresne (Surène), by Chevalier, showed an arrangement somewhat similar to D'Orliane's house, and variform rooms which remind us of Itasse.[619] The architect Vavin's own house, (1790) Rue Notre-Dame-des-Champs, was modern on the outside, with its undecorated walls and loosely attached wings, but in its plan we see still the traditional core of salon and dining room.[620]

Most plans submitted for the Grands Prix of the 1780's were of experimental character. Louis-Alexandre Trouard combined triangle and circle in the plan of his college (1780),[621] in a way similar to Sobre's chapel, while in the same year Durand presented a hexagonal college.[622] Goust projected a circular monument with radiating aisles in 1785,[623] Tardieu a "Trésor Royal" on the nine-partite scheme in 1789.[624] The museums of Jacques-Pierre Gisors[625] and Delannoy,[626] both of 1779, were conceived as large buildings with four inner courts.

Of functional plans I want to illustrate two. In the Le Duc house (1788), Boulevard du Montparnasse, built by Louis Emmanuel Aimé Damesme, a faint trace of the old main axis is recognizable.[627] It led from the gateway across the court to the vestibule, but then was blocked by the staircase. The arrangement of the rooms was dictated entirely by convenience. In designing the Varin house (1797), Champs-Elysées, Charles Aubert had only practicality in mind.[628] The vestibule was very small; to its right the staircase was situated, to its left, the dining room.

The latter communicated with the salon, which no longer was in the center of the garden front, but shifted to the side. Beside it, also facing the garden, was the bedroom. Commodiousness now meant more than representation.

Two houses by Jean-Jacques Lequeu, the casino Terlinden at Sgrawensel[629] and the house of the Comte de Vouville, near Portenort, named Temple de Silence,[630] looked like ancient temples from the outside. The rooms were freely arranged, as well as could be done in these classicizing structures which had to satisfy the taste of the erudite.

Survey of the revolutionary patterns

The new interest in the elementary geometric forms, deeply rooted as it was in the general trend towards individualism, of necessity affected architectural composition in a far stronger way than interest in the ancient features did. Wherever these features were used they were merely additional decorations, and no longer the vivid expression of those animistic tendencies which originally had played a decisive role in their creation. The pseudo-classical forms about 1800 were all dry and lifeless. However, the geometric forms in themselves are also of only secondary interest. Any architect, planning or building, has permanently in mind the whole. To grasp his intentions and those of his era we must look at the entire composition; we must study the surface patterns and the spatial organization. A few general observations, derived from a great number of designs, may be made before entering into details.

New compositional patterns appeared in all designs of the period, whether classicizing features were used or whether the architect applied geometric forms. The basic principle ruling composition now was the concept of independence. In attempting to visualize this principle, the architects first strove to get rid of the standardized composition of the past. Proceeding on their way they found instead of the exclusive hierarchical scheme of the Baroque a great number of diversified solutions. The rising epoch of individualism was to be artistically as rich as its predecessor, if not richer. The following survey of the new patterns may help to recognize more easily the various attempts toward a new organization of both surface and space. It is of course as artificial as any classification which draws imaginary border lines.

We can distinguish in the designs of the revolutionary architects these principal patterns:

1. Repetition, which may be
   a) Reduplication, or the repetition of a motif without any alteration in shape or size.
   b) Juxtaposition, or the undifferentiated array of equivalent elements.
   c) Reverberation, or the presentation of one and the same motif in different sizes.

2. Antithesis, which can be expressed by
   a) Contrasts in texture.
   b) Opposition of different sizes, different shapes, or both.
   c) Tension between distanced elements.
   d) Compensation between elements of different weight.
   e) Interpenetration, which under the revolutionary (individualistic) system means that one feature seems to intrude into another, or even to tear it apart. (The term "interpenetration" has often been used to indicate the intermingling or coalescing of features in the Baroque, and has also been applied where one part seemed to grow out from another, like a protuberance.) The pattern of interpenetration (in the revolutionary sense) can be visualized either by the crossing of masses, or by volume (space) intruding into mass. Interpenetration was almost exclusively a spatial pattern. It played an important part in the nineteenth century, and like the other patterns of antithesis it plays a still greater role in our time.
   f) Reverberation. Obviously the pattern of reverberation has an element of antithesis. The patterns of tension and differentiated texture can be found chiefly on surfaces.

3. Multiple response, which uses patterns of repetition, or antithesis, or both together. Here the motifs composing the pattern respond to each other and thus become "themes." In addition, different subpatterns may enter the conversation, by means of adequate spacing, sizing, or numerical variegation.

Each of these patterns which I have found in the revolutionary production and some more which, perhaps, keener eyes will discover, are contrary to Baroque concatenation, integration, and gradation. The patterns of repetition, which visualize calm coexistence; those of antithesis, which reveal antagonism and rivalry between the elements and their reluctance to subordinate themselves to the whole; as well as multiple response, with the interplay of single forms, or better, their interlocution, all leave its independence to the individual motif. They can, naturally, avail themselves only of such forms which are apt to stand alone. There is no place in the new system for features which seek contact with others, such as volutes and all sorts of naturalistic motifs. We have met specimens of the patterns in the works of several prominent architects; a few more will be illustrated in the following systematic display taken chiefly from the *oeuvres* of minor masters.

The patterns are evident to any one who scrutinizes the works. It is left to every interpreter to explain the patterns from that principle which in his belief has given them their origin.

The similar development in the graphic arts may be remembered here. The Baroque had developed the technique of the mezzotint which allowed a perfect blending of masses by the complete elimination of all separating contours. This technique was given up abruptly about 1800; the artists turned back to engraving, with its clear delineation. A noteworthy symptom of the new trend towards individualizing representation was the fashion, which arose rather suddenly, of the silhouette, by which the most definite separation of object and environment could be achieved.

New surface patterns.

The chief decoration of the garden front of the Dervieux house (1774) by Brongniart was the array of five lunettes above the doors (three on the central projection and two on the sides).[631] When in 1789 Belanger added two symmetrical annexes, he repeated on them the openings in the same shape and size.[632] The front of Maison Fortin (1795), Rue du Faubourg St. Honoré, by Brunau was strictly symmetrical and showed the traditional gradation, in the vertical.[633] Yet the central features, a square window on the top floor and the entrance door, were not exalted over the side openings, but were without differentiation repeated in them. The façades of this house and the Dervieux house are instances of plain reduplication. An interesting hybrid was Brunau's Chenot house (1790), Rue de Provence.[634] It was composed of three zones, the ground floor with the lintel-topped doorway flanked by two semicircular windows, the second floor with a broad Palladian window in a rectangular frame, accompanied by two narrow windows, and the top floor with five square openings. Here we see Baroque axiality combining with a pattern of horizontal stripes.

Unrelated parallelism intermingled with some antithetical statements showed in Piau's country house (fig. 196) at Courbevoye (1797), by Pierre Théodore Bienaimé.[635] Its multi-arched attic story was contrasted with the two main stories with only five windows each. On either side of the central mass broad stairs led up to the second story terminating in four-columned pedimented porticoes. Thus the main body was opposed to the sides and the center deprived of its dominance.[636]

Almost absolute equality reigned in the house for M. du G—— projected near Malmaison by Charles François Mandar in 1792.[637] Its four façades were all alike; they presented three stories each with three equally sized windows. The same pattern of the nine-partite square reappeared in the plan. A small belvedere was superposed above the roof, a triangular pediment and a meager porch were added to the entrance front. On the four façades of another cubic house, built by Mandar at Sarcelles, pilasters and broad horizontal bands separated the almost equal compartments.[638] These houses are representative of the "gridiron" type—the pattern of uncompromising equality of independent parts or juxtaposition in every dimension. Such extreme regularity was bound to lead to monotony. Therefore the architects turned to the more stimulating patterns of reverberation and antithesis.

The Epinée house (1796) on the Rue de la Pépinière, by Olivier, presented a

semicylindrical porch of four columns carrying a terrace (fig. 197). The room behind the latter (*salle de jeu*) opened in a half-circle framed by a broad ornamental
frieze. Thus the semicircular outline of the terrace with its semicircular railing were
reverberated by the frieze and somewhat more subdued by the three concentric
circles into which the windowpanes were divided. The house was a remarkable
instance of combined surface and spatial reverberation.

The Institution Polytechnique, Rue Neuve de Berri (1798), by Charles Aubert
showed reverberation of a somewhat different type (fig. 198). The decoration of its
façade consisted of several groups of features. In the center these features—a semicircular lunette on top, a relief tablet and a statue in a niche below—were firmly
held together by Ionic pilasters. At the sides the same features appeared unframed
and isolated; the groups have disintegrated into their parts. The loose side features
faintly echoed the corresponding central features. On Thamney house, Rue de
Provence, by Itasse, the three huge lunettes over the entrances of the main house
were echoed by the small lunettes on the lateral mansards.[639] The pattern of reverberation was more frequent in spatial than in surface composition.

The patterns of antithesis were more robust than the patterns of repetition; they
became increasingly popular in the later stages of the new system, that is, in our
own time. Again, as in Renaissance and Baroque the system passed from calm beginnings to exaggerated self-representation. There were different ways to contrast
the stories of a house. One consisted in setting them apart by differentiation in
texture, another consisted in the application of features differing in size or shape.
Among the designs which were awarded Grands Prix between 1779 and 1789 are
several which show elongated fronts consisting of two contrasted stripes. On
Bergognion's "Banque Nationale" (fig. 199) the low ground floor with windows
is opposed to the windowless upper story. In addition, there are in the center the
contrasting motifs of an arcade below, a panel with a relief on the main floor,
and a semicircular window in the gable. Compositionally similar are the court-
houses ("Palais de Justice") of Pierre Bernard[640] and Catala[641] (both 1782), and
the treasuries ("Tresor Royal") by Bonard (1789)[642] and Tardieu.[643] On Réverchon's hippodrome (1784) the high, blank wall of the ground floor is interrupted by
three large arched doors in the center, whereas an arcade runs all along the second
story.[644] Bénard's Hôtel du Timbre, Rue de la Paix, built under Napoleon, showed
a façade rusticated in its lower half, smooth in the upper.[645] The archivolt of the
door intruded into the wall of the second story.

The Portal of the Charité, Rue des Saints-Pères, originally carried out in a
heavy Doric by Antoine, underwent a restoration by Nicolas-Marie Clavareau.[646]
His still extant façade presents unbalanced elements. The deep recess of the entrance
with its heavy vaulting is set against the three tiny windows above, and the plasticity of the columns and fasces below is contrasted with the flat upper wall. Krafft
had the fullest appreciation for the novel arrangement:

The exterior architecture is of the Doric order, the same as was there formerly; but the three crescents, over the arcade, have been added, and the whole front wrought anew, and restored. Fasces, with crowns, have been sculptured between the columns. The rest of this order is very regular, of a very fine proportion, the whole producing a wonderful effect. The merit of this restoration is due to M. Clavaraux [sic].[647]

In some "Gothic" fabrics for the garden of the castle of Botosky, near Amiens, Olivier operated with different materials and the contrasts of variform openings as well.[648] The house of the gatekeeper (Garde du Parc) presented a Palladian window with an ogival central arch, a circular, a semicircular, and an oblong window.

Further instances of contrasted shapes can be found on Gondoin's Ecole de Médecine, on the house of D'Orliane (oversized tablets versus small windows, on both),[649] and on the castle of Saint-Assise near Melun, by Sobre (semicircular window versus oblong openings).[650]

With the help of patterns of repetition and antithesis an aesthetic whole can be achieved, without the parts being tied to each other in form. The effects of reduplication, juxtaposition, and reverberation are rather weak; textural differentiation and opposition of shapes and sizes, however, contain the danger that the whole composed of antagonistic elements may seem to fall apart. A good method to attain the impression of wholeness was the distancing of the single features in such a way that a certain tension could be felt all over the surface, for tension represents the last moments of coherence before the breaking point is reached. Ordinarily, practical reasons were against such bold distancing of the apertures, therefore the pattern of tension was rather rare. But when it was applied, by Heurtier on the rear façade of the Théâtre des Italiens,[651] by Ledoux on the Prison of Aix,[652] the artistic effect was great. For the stimulus to relate the parts mentally has, perhaps, more power than the visual unification of the Baroque. In building as in speech, mere intimation is more effective than the full statement. The more one talks, the less one says.

All these patterns were to win full freedom only in our day. In the eighteenth century the conventional schemes still impeded their way, and so did the time-honored forms, which one could not discard at a moment's notice. Yet the tendency underlying the new patterns is almost always manifest behind the veil of tradition. In the "House of the Sculptor," Rue Saint-Denis (1784), by Bricard, the small, low wings were distinguished by stately Palladian windows, and their gables decorated with genii holding wreaths.[653] The main block, however, had nothing but square and arched windows. This means that the wings were no longer subordinate to the central mass. Their inferiority in size and position was compensated by rich embellishment, and the main accent was shifted to the sides. Similarly, on the Lauchere house (1801) at Chaillot, by Charles Aubert, there was a lonely entrance door on the ground floor and only a single window on the second, whereas on the gable the full-fledged Palladian motif appeared.[654] Against all rules of careful and consistent balancing, the garret obtained a preferential treatment. The remotest and humblest portion was compensated by additional decoration. A new order of the components, though far from being fully attained, most certainly was in the making. (Compare what has been said about compensation in the comments on Belanger's slaughterhouse, p. 173.)

The pattern of interpenetration is the most vigorous of all the patterns of antithesis. In our day we meet it chiefly in the third dimension, yet about 1800 it appeared often on the façades, symbolizing the antagonism of the elements. On the *salle de spectacle* belonging to the house of the Duc d'Orléans (1770) Brongniart placed in the wall behind the second floor terrace a semicircular window of the width of the porch. Thus the porch seemed to intrude from the lower zone into the upper.[655] Similarly, in the court of the Pasgnier house (1772), Rue de Bourgogne, by Trepsat the tympanum of the portal formed part of the second story.[656] In the project of a villa (fig. 178) Desprez made a central Palladian window trespass from one story into the next. This motif of the intruding portal soon became very common. Two Parisian instances occur in the Rue de Paradis[657] and the Rue Saint-Lazare.[658] In speaking of patterns, I have in mind ordinarily patterns of abstract forms, for example, the interpenetration of two cubes. Yet I would not exclude, on principle, patterns achieved by any kind of feature, for example, the intrusion of a door into the upper story, and the like.

The limits of the individualistic system were reached in the multiple response. Beyond it we can hardly imagine any order of unrelated elements, but only patterns of interrelationship, that is, patterns of a different system. Whatever objections are made to the category of multiple response, it helps to understand a number of compositions of a particularly high level.

Its intricacy may have been the reason both for its rare application and its rather late appearance on the architectural stage. Apart from Belanger's and Desprez's attempts, and, perhaps, the façade of Saint-Gratien by Jacques Rousseau, I found this pattern only after 1800. One of those architects who did not content themselves with the mechanical repetition of the exhausted classical features, but liked to experiment with the general arrangement, was Mangot. The entrance gate of the house at 14 Rue de Londres showed the antithesis of three horizontal stripes,[659] while the house itself presented an example of surface response.[660] Apart from the Palladian window, only motifs with exclusively structural significance were used, namely, rectangular and arched openings. It may be enough to refer to the illustration, leaving it, for once, to the reader to discover the various reciprocities in the façade.

Contemporaries did not lack appreciation for the complicated pattern. Legrand highly praised the "Plan d'un projet de bains publics" (fig. 200), by Chalgrin's pupil, Alexandre Gisors (Gisors *jeune*), which was exhibited in the *Salon* of the year XII.[661] He found it worthy of the name "Thermes de Napoléon." Here the themes were taken from the customary repertoire of triangular pediments, squares, arches, and cornices. Enlarging, grouping, and distancing were the means by which the motifs were brought to interaction without being submitted to a regnant motif.

The architect Loison tested the possibilities of both plain parallelism and the multiple response. His residence on the Rue des Fontaines (1801) presented the quiet coexistence of unrelated stories with differently shaped windows.[662] On the house which he built for himself at Saint-Germain (fig. 201), there were on the court façade only two themes, the cornice and the rectangular opening.[663] (The three lunettes formed a coherent group and thus were merely motifs, not themes.) The cornices showed three times, two long ones on the roof and above the sub-structure and a short one high up above the central windows. There is no need to enumerate all the respondences of the rectangles. I wish only to point out how one motif became a theme in several constellations. The small lateral windows on the third floor belonged first to the row of five windows under the main cornice. Yet, being set at a distance from the three central windows, they communicated also with the high windows below them. Finally, they responded to the similarly "hang-ing," richly-framed windows under the lower cornice. The garden façade was different: a relief panel replaced the short cornice, and so on.

The inn (*guinguette*) by Alexandre Frary (prior to 1807) was a twin house.[664] Frary established unity with the help of responding motifs. Again, there were only two themes, rectangular and arched openings. Very remarkable was the re-sonance of the squat arch of the doorway in the three narrow arches on each side of the ground floor, as well as in the single arches of the upper floor. Legrand noted both the discrepancies of the elements and the difficulty involved in the new compositional manner:

M. Frary a cherché dans cette composition à se rapprocher de ce style naïf plus difficile à saisir que l'on ne pense, et peut-être trouvera-t-on qu'il a employé beaucoup de moyens dans un si petit espace. Les deux pavillons y semblent étouffer la partie du milieu, et présentent en quelque sorte trois maisons pour une, ce qui nuit à cette unité précieuse dont nous trouvons l'exemple dans la plupart des palais d'Italie.[665]

Evidently Legrand, comparing this particular achievement with Italian works of the old school, did not like it. Yet he was aware of the essential characteristics of the new composition.

The guardhouse (Maison d'Arrêt) and its stables at Marseilles were carried out by Michel Robert Penchaud in 1820.[666] Each structure had only one theme, the round arch. The pattern resulted exclusively from the grouping, the varying sizes, and, perhaps, the alternation of plain framings with rusticated ones. Of all the instances which I have discussed, this latest was the poorest. When the variety of classical features was no longer wanted, the end of the pattern of multiple response seems to have come. The simpler patterns were fitter to survive in the geometric "style." Though the pattern of multiple response was a product of the new individualism, it appears to have been, at the same time, the heir—and perhaps the last heir—to the refinement of the Rococo.

Modern methods of spatial organization

Of the spatial patterns those of reduplication and juxtaposition were rare within single buildings, but rather common in large complexes. We have met them in the prismatic projections of Boullée's city gates and in the belvederes crowning Ledoux's "House of a Writer" and the "House of Four Families."[667] In speaking of larger complexes I want to recall the Place Ludovise by Louis,[668] and to point out several designs by winners of the Grands Prix. The "Lazaret" by St. Hubert,[669] and that by Moreau[670] (both of 1784), as well as the Hôtel-Dieu by Bonard (1787),[671] consist of arrays of pavilions with little emphasis on the central buildings. The plans, of which I illustrate that of Bonard (fig. 202), prove that a definite pattern was intended. They have an ornamental character like any Baroque plan, differing, of course, in that they visualize the new compositional principle instead of the old.

The appendage of one or two small blocks to a big one without formal interrelationship constitutes, in many cases, spatial reverberation. First attempts in this direction appeared in buildings which to some degree still depended on the Baroque scheme, but had the wings only loosely appended to the main house. Examples were Brongniart's Hôtel de Saint Foix,[672] Olivier's own house, Rue de la Pépinière (1799),[673] and Sobre's castle of Saint-Assise between Corbeil and Melun. The last was characterized by Krafft: "Les trois corps de bâtiment ne se tiennent que par les angles."[674] The appended porches, so common about 1800, also echoed the cubes to which they were fastened. From numerous instances, I want to cite the Gontard house (1799) at Frankfort-on-the-Main, by Nicolas Alexandre Salins de Montfort,[675] and Jean Villot's theater (1817) at Strasbourg.[676] Reverberation of a semicylindrical projection was not rare. On Maison Labottière at Bordeaux (1770–1773) Laclotte emphasized the half-cylinder by a railing and the balustrade above the main cornice.[677] On the somewhat later Maison Carrée, at Arlac, Dufart circumscribed the projection with a colonnade.[678] Similarly he screened off the corner of the Théâtre Français at Bordeaux (1793–1800).[679] On Ledoux's Hôtel Thélusson[680] and Desprez's project of a villa,[681] a semicircular colonnade reverberates the projecting central bay. Ledoux availed himself of the pattern of reverberation in other ways, too. He planned in the "Broker's House" a small cylindrical belvedere echoing the main body, and made in the Barrière de Reuilly the cylindrical core telescope from the cylindrical arcade, which rose from the drumlike podium.[682] A similar compositional concept underlies the attractive and original project for a theater by André-Jacques Roubo.[683] Lequeu's "Castle on the Sea" is a striking instance of reverberation with its circular tower building, circular substructure, and the cylindrical sentry boxes.[684]

Louis Combes' project for a national assembly hall (Palais de la Nation) on the Place de la Bastille (1789) belongs to the same category.[685] The circular structure was to be surrounded by a low colonnade. Its heavy saucer dome reminds us that the design originated in the heyday of the geometric mania. Soon the formal ideal of the revolutionary architects became the artistic slogan of the Revolution. When on August 14, 1793, the Convention deliberated on a competition, the architect Léon Dufourny proclaimed: "L'architecture doit se régénérer par la géométrie."[686]

In a similar way P. F. L. Dubois *aîné,* the nephew and pupil of Jacques-Denis Antoine, conceived the "Temple de la Gloire," which upon request of the Emperor was to be erected on the Place du Carrousel between the Louvre and the Arc de Triomphe, facing the Tuileries.[687] Again, a low colonnade would echo the circular body, the form of which reappeared in the drum of the dome and found a further echo in the background in the semicircular Orangerie closing the prospect. In spite of the overabundance of decoration the temple to Napoleon's glory would have been a great composition. In the park of M. Davelouis at Soisy-sous-Etiole Dubois carried out an icehouse surmounted by a circular hall for dancing topped by a circular kiosk, and a second icehouse having an Egyptian temple front and surmounted by a similar kiosk.[688]

The project of Louis-Pierre Baltard for the Temple of Glory on the Place du Carrousel, submitted to the emperor, but not carried out, presented the contrast of a vast circular colonnade to a small monopteros in its center.[689] Highly significant was Baltard's project for the castle of Saint-Cloud (fig. 203), because of its layout.[690] The outbuildings were to be arranged in a circle on the slope of the hill on top of which the castle stood, formally independent from each other, just as the entire self-centered complex was independent of the environment.

Mathurin Crucy, a pupil of Boullée, won in 1774 the Grand Prix with the project of a bath, in which he attempted to create something similar to the Roman *thermae.*[691] It resembled very closely the design of a bath, for which Joseph Bénard, Boullée's favourite student, was awarded a second prize in the same year.[692] Later Crucy turned to modern patterns. His "Corps de Garde" planned in the center of the semicircular portion of the Place Royale of Nantes (1788) was to be a cylindrical structure from which a small cylinder telescoped.[693] The fishmarket (Halle au Poisson, 1783) presented a semicircular colonnade on the entrance front, reverberated by the low cylindrical dome and the ramps leading to the embankment.[694] The Public Bath (1800)[695] consisted of a cubic mass and a loosely appended semicircular structure: "Ces deux parties de l'édifice ne parviennent pas, malheureusement, à s'accorder."[696] In planning the Place Royale, Crucy once more set geometric shapes side by side, without unifying them: "En fait, la place Royale peut être considérée comme la juxtaposition de deux places."[697]

There was merely one step from the presentation of incongruous elements to the stronger artistic qualities of self-assertion and competition. Only a few architects knew how to contrast the masses as vigorously as Ledoux had contrasted them in the "Director's House" at Arc-et-Senans,[698] the Hôtel Thélusson,[699] and the "House of the Surveyors of the River."[700] However, with less ability, minor masters also achieved artistic effects by opposing elements of different sizes or different shapes, or by dramatizing the structure by a seeming interpenetration of the masses.

Contrasting elementary shapes by differentiating them in size has become rather common in our day. The stepped or terrace building is nothing but the superposition of diminishing cubes. A very early and very curious instance is the Pavilion of Chanteheux by Héré (fig. 204). This project combines rich Rococo decoration with novel composition. Many further examples of this pattern are contained in much later Grand Prix editions: Bernier's barracks (1786), Lefèvre's school of medicine (1789),[701] the "Prison d'Etat," by Houssin,[702] the circular "Elysée," by Granjean (1799) (fig. 205), the "Prytanée," by Gasse (1800),[703] the "Brasserie" (1813) and a "Maison à Thiais" (1827) by Philippon.[704] When in 1801 Alexandre Gisors had to decorate the Palais-Bourbon for the celebration of Bastille Day, he showed how the façade could be "modernized." By superimposing a belvedere-like story he achieved a perfect stepped building. Landon found the decoration worthy to be illustrated in the *Annales* lest it fall into oblivion.[705]

The commonest way of contrasting different shapes was the contraposition of a cubic substructure to a cylindrical drum and a dome. The neat separation of the parts distinguishes the revolutionary pattern from previous similar designs. To this type belonged Moitte's cathedral (1781),[706] Moreau's cenotaph (1785),[707] and Lefèvre's library (1787).[708] Similar were Percier's "Monument destiné à rassembler les différentes Académies" (1786)[709] and the museum (fig. 206) by Delannoy (1779). In both, the dome and the drum were replaced by a hypaethral circular colonnade, much in the way in which De Wailly had planned to finish the Paris Panthéon. Delannoy concealed the basic form by a multitude of columns, thus mitigating the "discordancy"; Percier added obelisks to the sides for further contrast. For comparison's sake I want to point out two nineteenth-century churches based on the same compositional principle—St. George's (1811), Edinburgh, by Robert Reid,[710] and the Nikolai Kirche (1830), Potsdam, by Carl Friedrich Schinkel.[711] A contemporary critic disparaged St. George's: "When examined upon architectural principles, it presents a pile of discordancy very rarely to be met with."[712] The aspect of unrelated elements was still unusual at that time, and the grandeur of such "discordant piles" not comprehensible.

Goust opposed the radiating prismatic wings of his monument (1785) to the central rotunda and the circular colonnade.[713] With traditional features the effect of antagonistic elements could also be obtained. In his Porte de Ville (1779) Moitte contrasted the cubic mass to both the free-standing columns set against the wall and the barrel vault of the thoroughfare (fig. 207). Bourjot enhanced the huge rostral column of his Phare over the massive substructure.[714] Charles-Pierre-Joseph Normand planted the column of a lighthouse (fig. 208) upon a multistoried, stepped building.[715] This design, which won a prize in 1791, is remarkable not only for its dimensions, but also for the skillful counterpoising of the square and round masses. The slow, harmonious decrease of weight has a counterpart in the increase of decoration from the bottom to the top. Very forceful is the Phare by Claude-Jacques Toussaint, composed of an enormous cylindrical column with a truncated cone as a base and a truncated pyramid as a podium.[716]

Compensation, or the lever principle, shows in Lequeu's project for the Rendez-vous de Bellevue (fig. 209). At first sight it seems to be just an odd combination of antique, Gothic, and Renaissance features. Yet its composition is quite new, and extremely significant. The airy temple high upon the right tower is counterbalanced by the massive dungeon on the left.[717] Compensation was the main motif in all the "irregular" houses in England,[718] France, and all over Europe.

Of all the attempts to visualize the concept of individualism, the pattern of interpenetration was to be the most successful. It showed in interlocking blocks seemingly intruding into, or emerging from each other. Nineteenth-century buildings of this type were: Thomas Hamilton's High School at Edinburgh (1825),[719] Jan David Zocher's Exchange at Amsterdam (1840),[720] Carl Ferdinand Langhans' New Theatre at Leipzig (1867),[721] the Vienna Opera House by Siccardsburg and Van der Nuell (1861–1869), the Vienna Parliament by the Dane, Theophil Hansen (1873–1883),[722] to name only a few. It is not too much to say that it is a standard pattern of the twentieth century. One may consider Ledoux's "House with roof-terraces" as the archetype of this pattern.[723] It consists of a cubic body with four high pedimented structures inserted, or, shall we say, rammed, into it, and a rotunda emerging from it.

The same compositional concept underlies Besnard's pavilion in the Parc de Monceau, erected 1790.[724] Its disposition reveals the artistic intention with astounding clarity. The salon and the dining room, both large and high, intrude into the square plan. The vestibule and the billiard rooms are insertions of minor size and secondary importance. If we divide the plan along one of its main axes and think of one half as the section of a house, this house would appear as a stepped building. From this we may conclude that stepped buildings can be interpreted either as instances of reverberation or of interpenetration. Besnard's pavilion is one of the very few eighteenth-century works illustrated in Louis-Marie Normand's *Paris moderne,* which is devoted almost exclusively to works of the first half of the nineteenth century. This means that it appeared "modern" to Normand.

We can detect the pattern of interpenetration in a rudimentary form in Jacques Rousseau's Folie de Lamotte-Brebière (about 1770).[725] The plan follows the old axial arrangement with balanced sides.[726] But the principal rooms seem to intrude from either side into the main body. The elevation produces the same impression; by their shapes and by the different materials (stone versus brick) the rooms seem to tear the house asunder. There is that tension which keeps apart the elements, and, nonetheless, reveals that they belong together. Strange as it sounds, tension, or any pattern of antithesis, bears in it the intimation of wholeness. This "Folie" is thoroughly different from all previous French country houses. When Pierre Dubois found that the architect *montra peu d'originalité*,[727] it was because he saw the design from the viewpoint of 1900. It is, indeed, very similar to the common run of late nineteenth-century work, but it was something outstandingly new about 1770.

Very frequent was interpenetration of cubes and cylinders. The projecting half-cylinder was just one instance. Another possibility was that the cube receded in a semicircular niche, in which the cylinder stood, half enshrined in the block, half emerging from it. Again, I can exemplify by a design from Ledoux's *oeuvre*, the charming "House of the Treasurer,"[728] which combines the novel composition with the grace of the *ancien régime*. Another instance was André Aubert's Maison Deshayes.[729]

Sobre designed a castle on the Greek-cross plan (fig. 211) in the center of the "Maison de plaisance."[730] He filled the right angles of the cross with low quarter-cylinders, which seemingly emerged from the main block. This is the essence of the pattern of interpenetration and this makes its dramatic character: one shape seems forcefully to invade another or to deliver itself from being bound in the mass.

Finally, I want to illustrate with the anonymous design of a stately manor house dating, to judge from the costumes shown in it, from about 1780 (fig. 212). It presents a building of great beauty achieved by a combination of reverberating and stepped blocks.

Multiple response in space is particularly complex. The discussion of instances by De Wailly, Ledoux, and Belanger may be followed by an instance by Damesme. Yet first let us cast a glance at the beginnings of this pupil of Belanger[731] and Ledoux.[732] We have already commented on the functional plan of Damesme's Le Duc house (1788).[733] Although in arranging its interior the architect was concerned with practicality alone, he did not forsake art on the exterior[734] following, intuitively no doubt, the line of his masters' master, the line of the Blondel compromise. Contrasts of sizes and shapes created the pattern of the court front. On both façades of the house on Rue Richer (1793) the interplay between the openings was still more refined.[735] In the design of a triumphal arch (fig. 213) we see unrelated diversiform elements; a temple has been piled upon a gateway. Here are classic features, but instead of "classic" harmony, there is discrepancy and disproportionality. Legrand rightly called the strange composition a *tour de force,* pointing at both the incongruity of the parts and the lack of unification:

Ici le portique d'un temple sert de couronnement à la masse d'un arc de triomphe; et peut-être y voit-on trop distinctement deux monumens, au lieu d'un seul; peut-être la masse y paraît-elle trop alongée . . . on s'accoutumerait difficilement à voir le temple ainsi placé dans les airs . . .[736]

Since the days in which Piranesi had conceived the "Appartenenze d'antiche terme,"[737] in a very similar manner, many decades had elapsed. In the meantime, Ledoux had reached more satisfying solutions, because he had given up, in his projects at least, the traditional forms. Damesme, who still stuck to them, failed. The new composition demanded new forms.

The front of the entrance pavilion of the Théâtre Olympique, Rue de la Victoire or Chantereine (1796), was of a highly decorative character (fig. 214).[738] Here Damesme still had in mind gradation and centralization, but tried hard to achieve a modern pattern. He made the overarched Palladian door intrude into the gable. However, by affixing above it two relief figures (genii holding a lyre) and putting above the side entrances small Venetian windows, he deprived it of its dominance. The garret thus gained far more weight than would have been permissible in the Baroque hierarchy. The design, unsatisfying as a whole, reflects all the uncertainty of the era; "it does not properly belong to any order."[739] It resembles Empire work in showing a morbid attachment to the past and a naïve helplessness in attempting the new. The same can be said of a similar gateway by Sobre on Rue Basse-du-Rempart, with a Victory in the place of the genii and rosettes instead of the Palladian windows.[740]

On both the court and the garden façades of the Théâtre Olympique there were low, extended loggias, which closely resembled the bands of windows in our time, and which Ledoux so often had applied, on the hunting lodge,[741] the "Memorial in Honor of Womankind,"[742] the Hosten houses,[743] and so forth. Yet of greater interest than this feature is the loose arrangement of the openings. While the old equilibrium is still present, an attempt to create some original grouping is evident. There is no main accent on each façade, but several accents are scattered all over. This loose arrangement of scattered motifs can hardly justify speaking of multiple response on the surface, for each motif appears only once or twice on its wall. However, when we look at the court as a whole, we notice on the different walls the interplay of the motifs, such as Palladian windows, oblong apertures, and loggias. The surface motifs have become themes, in space. The themes indicate that the entrance pavilion and the main house belong together. Damesme's theater was highly rated about 1800. Several critics expressed their admiration,[744] and the Russian emperor, Alexander I, asked for its plans to have them copied in St. Petersburg.[745]

In the Brussels prison (1813)[746] Damesme imitated, or, one may say, plagiarized Ledoux's project for Aix.[747] Damesme's building was far less imposing than the masses of Ledoux; in surface arrangement, too, it lagged behind its model. Ledoux knew how to impart to the wall an expression of utmost tension by keeping the upper row of tiny windows and the lower one widely apart. Damesme changed the proportions only a little, but this was enough to make the whole monotonous. It is noteworthy that even this faint reproduction of Ledoux's unexecuted masterpiece was acclaimed by a contemporary writer. P. J. Goetghebuer praised its impressive simplicity: "L'aspect est imposant par la simplicité de son ordonnance et la solidité de ses membres d'architecture" and exalted "les grandes lignes de cette façade, qui par ses masses et par la forme des croisées, désigne assez sa destination."[748] Goetghebuer apparently ignored Ledoux's design.

Italicism and Romanticism.

Many French architects were impressed by the sight of the plain rural structures of Italy. Sharing the predilection of Cherpitel and de Wailly for the Italic,[749] they liked the stone buildings of the peninsula for their "naturalness" which was due to extreme simplicity and the undisguised exhibition of the material. The adherents of functionalism found models conforming to their taste on Italian soil. The theoretician of this group was Jean Rondelet.[750] His viewpoint appears both in his historical criticism and in his own doctrine. The latter reveals his unshakeable belief in the Lodolian faith.

En effet, c'est le mérite de la construction, qui constitue à tous les yeux le premier degré de beauté d'un édifice. . . . L'art de bâtir consiste dans une heureuse application des sciences exactes aux propriétés de la matière.[751]

In his criticism, however, Rondelet advocates a compromise between formalism and functionalism. He finds that the Egyptians were wrong because they were unwilling to sacrifice the real qualities of material and construction to appearance, and the Greeks were wrong because they violated consistency by shaping stone like wood.[752] Only the Romans found the solution of a consistent and aesthetically satisfying treatment of the stone, and knew how to combine practicality and beauty.[753] However, what Rondelet says of Roman building is to some extent true of all architecture. Form will never simply follow function; nor can it disregard it completely. The very nature of architecture consists in the compromise of form with function. Sometimes the one, sometimes the other, will play the more important part.

Rondelet's viewpoint agreed well with those French architects who were enthusiastic about Italic primitivism. In copying the rustic productions of Italy, they believed they could conform with both the French desire for form and the program of the functionalists. They did not care to join their compatriots who strove to create new patterns, but trusted to reach their goal by the easier way of imitation. In spite of this fact, their achievements, seen from the twentieth century, have a far greater appeal than those of the shallow classicists. Out of numerous instances of Italicizing structures, I should like to mention the house erected by Huvé at Meudon,[754] the Le Beau house, Rue Saint-Lazare (1801) by Moitte,[755] the Weibre house, Rue de Lille (1801) by Jacob.[756] Rustic work with only horizontal grooves gave repose and firmness to the Queen's Dairy, by Thévenin (1784),[757] and the court front of the house of the goldsmith Pierre Gouthière, at 6 Rue Pierre Bullet (about 1780).[758]

Not all of those who were inspired by Italian models became adherents of the sternest Italic. François Soufflot, called "le Romain," turned his attention to the Italian Renaissance. He was evidently impressed by the rusticity of the Italic, yet softened it by the introduction of some decorative Renaissance features and even by the reinstatement of the gradation of the stories. The country house at Belleville, of about 1790, which Soufflot owned, may be discussed here as an instance of Italicizing architecture, although his authorship is not absolutely certain.[759] Its ground floor was rusticated and contained as the only opening the lintel-headed door. The three arched windows of the upper floor were framed by Doric semicolumns; the row of balusters under the sill was divided into three parts by the pedestals of the columns. The discrepancy of the stories, especially the lack of interrelationship between door and windows, tell of the revolutionary contempt for the old "order." Two other houses by Soufflot show how Italicism and Italianism mingled. The Montholon house, on the Boulevard Montmartre (1786),[760] presented bare rusticated walls with horizontal grooves and simply cut-in windows, but the two main stories were held together in the center by engaged colossal columns. The d'Epinay house at Sceaux[761] was somewhat richer in decoration, and in it the traditional differentiation between the stories was emphasized. The huge entrance doors on the court and the garden fronts were variations of the Palladian motif. Whereas the latter, in its original form, represents a firmly united group with a dominating central and two subordinated lateral parts, Soufflot's version consists of three juxtaposed upright rectangles separated from the semicircular lunette above the central compartment by a heavy entablature. The transformation of the motif tells of the general change in composition.

Another architect who stood between the Italicists and the Italianists was Charles-Pierre-Joseph Normand. The Italic influence appears very distinctly in the substructure of his lighthouse (1791), already dealt with,[762] and a second project of the same year, the "Halle sur le bord d'une gare."[763] The layout of the latter is a grand instance of planning with independent geometrical elements. The elevation shows an impressive stepped structure consisting of heavy masses, the walls of which are pierced merely by low arcades. Normand's market (1792) is likewise planned on a plain geometrical pattern.[764] The addition of a sumptuous portico

shows that the sternness of Italicism no longer satisfied him. Several houses give
further proof that his way led from the strong and the new towards the weak and
the conventional. The storm had quieted down, and soon increasing attempts
towards the restoration of the old were made. We know that the same happened
in politics. In architecture, this retrograde process becomes manifest when we compare the Grands Prix of 1779–1789 with those from 1791–1806. The former are full
of revolutionary unrest and audacity; the latter show the ascent of impotent revivalism. Normand's "Maison isolée de toute part" (1792) was designed on the Greek-
cross plan, intimating the concept of interpenetrating blocks.[765] This plan made
possible the complete independence of the single rooms which the patrons had
required.[766] While the composition was still modern, several Italianizing features
crept in: the topping belvedere (which is an Italian, not an Italic, feature), the
framing of the openings, the rustication of the subservient ground floor, and the
rhythmic grouping of door and flanking windows. Another house by Normand,
built "dans les environs de D—," designed after an Italian model, came still
closer to the conventional centralized and rhythmic scheme.[767] Finally, I want to
point out a country house in which Normand returned to the Baroque wing type,
conforming to the wish of the patron, and another in which the old Baroque gradation reappeared, although somewhat effected by the novel principles.[768] In many
designs of his *Recueil varié* Normand seems to have copied both great and small
Italian houses, to name as only one instance that resembling Villa Medici in Rome.
In others, which may be his inventions or those of his contemporaries, we find certain modern patterns. A "Salle de spectacle" shows the amphitheater projecting
from an oblong block much in the style of the designs of Neufforge, Desprez, and
Durand.[769]

The great interest in Italic forms is reflected in the collection of designs which
François Leonard Scheult made during his stay in Italy between 1791 and 1793.[770]
Circumstances prevented him from publishing them immediately. His *Recueil
d'Architecture* came out as late as 1821, and a second edition in 1840.

In the plain country houses of Italy the revolutionary architects must have
found realized many of their own aspirations: the undisguised display of the raw
material, the emphasis on the unbroken walls, the unframed openings, the cubic
masses, the free interplay of the parts instead of the canonical "order." They could
hardly find there any help in solving their problems of spatial organization. But
the simple and yet extremely appealing method of contrasting huge bare walls with
small arched or square openings were a great source of inspiration to the revolutionaries. Even minor architects knew how to give their performances a touch of
greatness. Proof of this statement can be found in Normand's above-mentioned
"Halle," in the Stables by Tardieu (1788),[771] the "Orangerie" by Delagardette
(1791), and the "Arsenal de Terre," by Blanchon (1801).[772]

Italicism had its source also in the boundless yearning of the era after the extraordinary and the exotic. On the whole, revolutionary architecture may be looked at in two opposed aspects. Beside its great restraint and the positivism of its formal aspirations there was the vagueness of romanticism, affecting it as a secondary, far less important factor. The feeling for simplicity, the desire for new patterns and the new subservience to material were the sounder trends, which were to play the greatest role in the remote future. Yet for a while the romantic fashion imposed itself upon building, leading it somewhat astray. One should consider it not so much as a decisive influence in the development, but rather as a retarding factor unfavorable to the realization of the new formal will.

There was no contradiction in the parallel appearance of Italicism, Grecism, Gothicism, and the playful tampering with Oriental and Egyptian features. All this was the outgrowth of the sentimentality of the era, largely dependent on its literary interests. From this sentimentality originated that type of "Picturesque" architecture, which one might term Rousseauesque, tending towards the imitation of nature. The "thatched hut" had as little significance for the progress of architecture as any of the revivals had and was bound to become, before long, equally ridiculous. All these trends started with the trivialities of landscape architecture, and found their way into architecture proper only later. That picturesque architecture, from Swiss cottage to Gothic castle, finally occupied a vaster territory than the more restrained and more positive architectural trends, must be charged rather to the patrons than to the architects. There is no need to give examples of these whimsicalities which at the end of the nineteenth century became the most vulnerable targets for the "Second Revolution"—the revolution which resumed and continued the struggle of the modernists of the eighteenth century, and ushered in the twentieth.

At any rate, picturesque architecture, too, was part of the general protest against convention—a protest and nothing more. All those *fabriques flamandes* by Lefebvre (Lefèvre) and others,[773] the grottoes, like that by Percier (fig. 215), the *châteaux d'eau,* like that by Réverchon (1787) (fig. 185), offered but little opportunity for presenting reform ideas, though the new principles can be discovered again and again behind the various masquerades. This can be seen in the "Pagode" by Le Camus, built up in cylindrical and polygonal units,[774] or in the designs by Jean-Baptiste Kléber, who studied in the workshop of Chalgrin and became a famous general of the Napoleonic wars. His circular pigeonhouse at Etupes near Montbeliard was inserted between two prismatic stables,[775] the Swiss dairy showed a semicylinder set against an oblong block,[776] the "Moresque" pavilion a circular belvedere contrasted with the cylindrical body below (1787).[777]

Form rather than picturesqueness was the ultimate goal of Jean-Jacques Lequeu, whether he made "Gothic" and "Oriental" designs or used classic forms.[778] The project of a "Pompe à feu "(fig. 210) presents an extremely original surface pattern. Here the artist contrasts the sober triangle finishing the turret, the crenelated roofline of the body, the string of beads framing the semicircular pediment of the porch, and the edges sweeping down calmly.[779] There is both excitement and repose in the little edifice and there are reminiscences of the past in it such as the ogival window and the Tuscan columns. Yet above all there is the imprint of a searcher's mind which strove after the unprecedented.

The revivals were only an interlude in the drama of the architectural evolution. They were, perhaps, necessary, for men dazzled by the tremendous possibilities contained in the revolutionary discoveries needed to take breath before continuing on the new and arduous path. In their uncertainty they turned back to the vanishing past. The revivalists certainly deserve a more profound study than the mere recording of their works. Yet this cannot be done in an investigation devoted to the eighteenth century.

Interiors

Boullée did not have an opportunity to realize any of the great interiors which he had conceived. It was Jacques-Pierre Gisors, a pupil of Guillaumot and Boullée, who carried out two halls that became the models of nineteenth-century parliament building.[780] The project of a museum that won him the Grand Prix in 1779 had already manifested his inclination toward monumentality, particularly the interior with its vaulted cross-arms and the dome over their intersection.[781] The "Monument in Honor of the King," designed for the Pont-Neuf (1787), to face the statue of Henri IV, is remarkable for the manner in which he altered the Roman triumphal arch.[782] The massive upper portion is almost as high as the columns which carry it, and consequently is too weighty. The old equilibrium has been replaced by the contrast of unbalanced masses. This project has been erroneously ascribed to Belanger by the latter's biographer, Jean Stern.[783]

In 1793, Gisors had to transform the theater of the Palais des Tuileries, the so-called "Salle des Machines," into an assembly hall for the Convention Nationale. In this theater the orchestra and the stage had been on one of the short sides of the oblong hall. Colonnades ran along the other three sides, with small balconies protruding between the supports. The third floor had been a continuous open balcony.[784] The framing of the stage was particularly rich, with colossal Corinthian columns as the main feature.[785] In remodeling the hall from the bottom, Gisors created the archetype of the continental parliamentary assembly hall (fig. 216),[786] following in practical disposition an idea of Legrand and Molinos.[787] The latter had arranged the seats of the representatives on a semi-ellipse; Gisors designed a hemicycle, in the center of which the tribune and the desks of the chairman and the officials were placed. Yet still more noteworthy than the new practical arrangement, which deviated from the British type, was the spatial composition which Gisors presented.[788] If you want to provide sitting room for the spectators in an assembly hall, the simplest thing you can do is to erect balconies or galleries. The basic idea of Gisors, however, was to carve boxes out of the wall, so that a few comparatively small voids, differing in size and shape in the three stories, were opposed to the big void of the hall of the deputies. What Ledoux had planned in the cemetery of Chaux,[789] and executed on a modest scale in the chapel at Arc-et-Senans,[790] was carried out here in monumental dimensions; volume was set against volume. Gisors avoided any projecting features which might disturb the calmness of the flat walls, and counteract or weaken the contrast of the boxes and the main room. The painted (not sculptured) statues on the piers were added upon request of the patrons. In addition to the dominating note of antagonistic voids, there were the contrasts in shape between the hollowed-out cubes of the first and second story and the hollowed-out semicylinders of the third. The cubes echoed the volume of the main hall, while the semicylinders echoed the curved benches of the deputies. With such simple means Gisors attained extraordinary grandeur. Probably in composing he had already had a vision of the crowd filling the room. Our engraving shows how the excitement of the spectators added to the turmoil in the main hall. One might say that the uproar in the larger hall reverberated among the agitated groups in the boxes.

In order to appreciate fully Gisors' accomplishment let us think of earlier auditoriums. The old theaters with their multitude of small boxes—the columbarium type—lacked monumentality. The variform decoration and the spots of faces and colorful costumes blended into a pictorial whole. Ledoux, in Bésançon, preferred the amphitheatrical type, achieving in this way repose and monumentality.[791] Gondoin went a step farther in the School of Medicine, contrasting voids of different shapes within an all-embracing larger void.[792] Gisors finally set the voids side by side, without subordinating them to a larger common space. In the Hall of the Convention the voids were independent units, as were the cubic masses of revolutionary exterior architecture.

Ramée's Autel de la Patrie—the decoration which witnessed the first great celebration of the Revolution—and Gisors' hall, which witnessed its most dramatic moments, were only temporary structures, which soon fell into oblivion. Art history did not take note of them, although they were representative of the artistic aspirations of the era, and proved that these new aspirations were understood by the public. The altar manifested the predilection for elementary geometry, the Hall of the Convention manifested the new compositional ideals, in a unique way.

From 1795 to 1797 Gisors had to carry out in the Palais-Bourbon the hall of the Council of Five Hundred which later became the Chambre des Deputés (fig. 217).[793] Here the new type of parliamentary assembly hall reached its definite form. The rows of seats were arranged in semicircles. The wall facing the auditorium receded in the center in a vaulted niche sheltering the tribune. Light fell only from the top of the main room and the top of the niche.[794] A row of thirty-two Ionic columns screened the balcony for the spectators. To get the space necessary for the niche, the wall had to be moved toward the court by about eight feet. It would, of course, have been possible to set the tribune in front of the straight wall, but Gisors wanted the effect of contrasting voids, which was given up in later remodelings. On the exterior, the cupola of the niche was opposed to the blank wall and the appended portico.[795]

Alexandre-Jean-Baptiste Guy de Gisors (Gisors *jeune*) continued the line of Boullée and Jacques-Pierre Gisors. Landon illustrates his project for the Bibliothèque Nationale (*an* VII).[796] The vaulted main hall, lighted from above, was intended to have a length of eighty meters. It was accompanied by three vaulted stacks on each side and terminated by a semicircular niche containing a statue of Apollo. The surrounding grounds were to be laid out as a garden containing the little houses of the employees.

The concept of opposing voids of different shapes gave rise to two other important assembly halls. In 1801, Claude-Etienne Beaumont[797] designed the Salle du Tribunat in the Palais-Royal.[798] Here the semicylindrical niche of the tribune, finished by a coffered vaulting, was separated by a barrel-vaulted corridor from the domed, semicylindrical auditorium. The very plain noble color scheme added further contrasts. The walls, the columns, and the vaultings were white; the niche was draped with a green curtain with gold embroideries; the furnishings were of mahogany with bronze ornaments.[799]

The dramatic quality of the Hall of the Convention with its vigorous contrasts was never reached again, although the great hall of the Five Hundred was almost equaled in Beaumont's hall and in Chalgrin's assembly room for the Senate.[800] The fate of the Hall of the Senate demonstrates how the *élan* of the revolution was lost in the nineteenth century. Alphonse-Henry de Gisors had to enlarge it between 1836 and 1840.[801] His changes meant a definite weakening of Chalgrin's great composition.[802] He added obtrusive decoration and pierced the vaulting with tripartite lunettes. Thus he destroyed the romantic effect resulting from the single skylight.[803] By letting the tribune and the desks of the officials protrude from the niche into the auditorium, he gave up the strict separation of the two voids.[804] Architecture was on the decline, passing from grandeur, monumentality, and plainness to overabundance in decoration and lack of character.

The principles valid in exterior architecture appeared likewise in the interiors. The architects who applied them were applauded by their contemporaries. Landon commended Moreau for having put side by side small barrel-vaulted compartments within a large vaulted hall, in the project of a Colonne Nationale: "Ces voûtes intérieures, symétriquement disposées, *se grandiront* à l'oeil, *par la répétition de leur forme*" (my italics).[805]

Landon also praised Normand for having avoided, in the interior of his "Monument à la gloire de la Grande Armée," planned for the site of the old Madeleine, all projections and subdivisions that might impair the quiet grandeur so dear to the period: "Normand a donné une preuve de goût, en faisant dis-paraître les ressauts et les subdivisions toujours nuisibles à l'effet..."[806]

The semicircular niches so common in interiors about 1800 only seldom con-tained the statues for which they seemed to be destined. In my opinion, these niches were added for contrast's sake, as smaller voids opposed to a larger void. Only the later nineteenth century with its *horror vacui* believed that the niches had to be filled with sculptures. Jacques Rousseau added to the dining room of the Castle Saint-Gratien two shell-vaulted apses at either end.[807] These apses were separated from the main room by two slender columns. In the wall of one of these apses, two smaller niches were arranged, flanking the door.

Rousseau's columns screening the annexed end rooms from the main room were an anachronistic feature of the sort which in the case of Palladio's churches has been interpreted as the "Mannerist way of linking room with room," or, in the case of Adam's Kenwood library, as a truly Rococo motif. However, setting voids against voids abruptly became common practice in the revolutionary era. The anonymous architect of the Hotel Pinsot (about 1792), 4 Rue St.-Georges,[808] must have been particularly fond of elementary shapes. The court front of his house showed projecting twin semicylinders;[809] the door of the dining room was flanked by semicircular niches.[810] The small salon of Thévenin's Queen's Dairy is circular and has a coffered vaulting and niches.[811] The table with its round top and round foot echoes the lines of the room. The tiny salon is a masterpiece of refined artistry.

The legacy of the eighteenth century.

About 1800 the revolutionary excitement had calmed down and the chief ar-tistic goals of the revolution seemed to have been attained. The question arises whether the revolutionary endeavors had any lasting effect. Having learned about the artistic aspirations of the progressive architects of the closing eighteenth cen-tury, we can no longer content ourselves with contemplating the pale features of classicism alone. We want to find out whether the new ideas were to live on through the Empire and perhaps the entire nineteenth century. *Architecture civile* by Ledoux's pupil Louis-Ambroise Dubut can provide the first answer.[812]

The façades presented by Dubut look like typical nineteenth-century work imi-tating models of the past. At closer inspection, however, we remark that they con-tain most of the revolutionary patterns. By vesting these patterns with some tradi-tional attire, the architect struck the keynote of the nineteenth century. His work gives evidence that this century became heir to the ideas of the revolution. Dubut's publication came out in 1803, with a second edition in 1837. His inventions must have been exemplary even forty years after they had originated.

The decorative features of the past were of only secondary importance to Dubut, as a curious instance reveals. Using one and the same plan for his House

No. 2, he designed for it a "Gothic" and an "Italian" (Renaissance) façade.[813] Not satisfied with mere imitation, he created a novel pattern. He contrasted the single openings on one floor with the window groups of the other and gave the wall between the rows of windows a preponderant role. Thus the modern tension shows among the old features.

In his introduction Dubut laid down his views about decoration. He wanted it derived chiefly from the practical exigencies and the nature of the materials: "La décoration extérieure naît de deux choses principales, de la disposition du plan et de la nature des matériaux qu'on emploie . . ."[814]

This freedom from the past—from its principles, not from its forms—is characteristic of Dubut's work. The rear face of House No. 30[815] reminds us of Damesme's endeavors to get rid of the old schemes. Here Dubut deprives the center of its strength by shaping it differently in the three stories. There is, moreover, double reverberation, that of the arches and that of the rectangles.

The elements of Dubut's compositions are the plain solids. Sturdy free-standing blocks are seen, for example, in Houses Nos. 3 and 13;[816] spatial juxtaposition shows in House No. 14 (fig. 218),[817] which consists of four cubes and loosely annexed semicircular outbuildings. Obviously, this design comes very close to Ledoux's House for Four Families (fig. 158). It is not less obvious that it resembles typical nineteenth-century buildings. The juxtaposition of four equal blocks is extremely simple and extremely forceful. House No. 14 lacks the variety of Ledoux's design with its belvederes, connecting arcades, and the dynamic motif of the open stairs, with its bare walls and unframed windows foreshadowing the twentieth century. Its decoration rather links it to nineteenth-century Renaissancism. Ledoux's house manifests the radicalism of the revolution, Dubut's the conciliatory attitude of the era of the revivals. Both can help us to understand the way of post-Baroque building. Juxtaposition shows also in House No. 25 where four independent structures stand on the arms of a Greek cross, enclosing the central court.[818] The four corners are occupied by gardens. House No. 24 is a twin house and as such an instance of reduplication.[819] We may consider as cases of reverberation all the houses with belvederes superimposed to the main mass; for example, House No. 9,[820] the terrace buildings, House No. 41,[821] and the stepped cylindrical building, House No. 28, called "Maison pour un savant."[822] Opposition of cubic masses is the main motif of House No. 22, although its Baroque descent is obvious.[823] Interpenetration is very common in Dubut's work, to name for example only House No. 10, on the cross plan,[824] and House No. 21 on the enriched (stepped) cross plan.[825]

The years during which Dubut had studied in Italy after having been awarded the Grand Prix in 1797 left an unmistakable imprint on his work.[826] Without having seen Italian structures he could hardly have devised his Houses Nos. 6 and 12.[827] Yet he knew how to impart to his designs a modern touch by presenting new patterns. Notwithstanding all similarities to previous achievements, his creations have the modernity of 1800.

Far more influential than Dubut was Boullée's draftsman Jean-Nicolas-Louis Durand, by both his teaching and writing. His treatises, of course, do not provide the entire picture of nineteenth-century development. But they show the direction which architectural thought was to take after the decline of the Baroque. To conclude the present inquiry into eighteenth-century development, it will be enough to point out this direction. It is important to note that the views of Durand were shared by his contemporaries[828] and by the next generations. His publications were reprinted and translated, again and again.[829]

Durand was still a revolutionary. He stood up against the idols of the day, the models of classical antiquity, and opposed the Baroque as well. However, the attacks against the latter were only incidental, for the conviction of its obsoleteness was already general and Durand merely did not want to be considered out-of-date.[830] His main concern was to denounce the chief literary fashion of the time. Although as a rule very sober in his writing, he loses his temper when he thinks of the never-ending worship of classical features:

Ces ordres ne forment point l'essence de l'architecture; le plaisir que l'on attend de leur emploi et de la décoration qui en résulte est nul; cette décoration, elle-même, une chimère; et la dépense dans laquelle elle entraîne, une folie.[831]

The application of the classical orders seems to him just a bad habit, understandable, but regrettable.[832] Yet he also repudiates Laugier's rationalism with its tinge of romantic sentimentalism. In his opinion, both Vitruvius and Laugier were wrong.[833] For architecture has nothing to do with the proportions of the human body, nor with the forms of the primitive hut[834] which in spite of its crudeness is not at all "natural," but artificial. He is strictly opposed to any kind of "masquerade,"[835] and accuses the Greeks of being untruthful in their building, which deficiency, he adds, even Vitruvius had remarked:

Mais il paraît, par ce qu'en dit Vitruve en plus d'un endroit, que les Grecs, loin de s'assujetir à imiter cette cabane, prirent à tâche, au contraire, de masquer les parties de leur édifices qui pouvaient ressembler le plus aux parties de la cabane.[836]

Again and again, Durand expresses his contempt for any disguise of the essential parts of a structure: "Loin de présenter à l'oeil et à l'esprit quelques parties essentielles d'un édifice, on affecte constamment de les masquer, de les faire disparaître."[837] His attacks are directed not merely against Baroque and classical features, but against formalism of any sort. He declares that one should not care about single forms, nor "masses" as a whole, but only about "convenience" and "economy."[838] When he inveighs against decoration, he finds the antidote no longer in "noble simplicity." His only gauge is usefulness.[839]

Architecture, Durand finds, is an art of quite a peculiar kind. It must take care of the necessities of life.[840] A structure which shows what is needed and is built practically and economically will please.[841] Forms and proportions are unessential;[842] decoration is superfluous.[843] However, there is another kind of embellishment, namely the "natural one" which consists in the application of the materials in conformity with their qualities and purpose. ("La disposition des matériaux relativement à leur nature, et à l'usage des objets à la construction desquels ils sont employés.")[844] The "natural" decoration will prevent all deception:

L'on ne sera plus alors tenté d'abandonner cette décoration naturelle, satisfaisante, pour y substituer . . . l'apparence d'une construction imaginaire qui, n'étant pas la construction réelle de l'édifice, donne de celle-ci une idée fausse, lui ôte de son caractère au lieu d'y ajouter . . .[845]

In this context Durand praises "les édifices antiques . . . les belles fabriques répandues dans toute l'Italie, morceaux où la pierre, la brique, le marbre etc. Se montrent pour ce qu'ils sont . . ." Such "natural" architecture needs must please:

Nous sommes loin de penser que l'architecture ne puisse pas plaire; nous disons au contraire qu'il est impossible qu'elle ne plaise pas, lorsqu'elle est traitée selon ses vrais principes . . . Or, un art tel que l'architecture, art qui satisfait immédiatement un si grand nombre de nos besoins . . . comment pourrait-il manquer de nous plaire?[846]

This is the great *idée générale*[847] which should underlie any architectural concept. There can be no difficulty in designing façades which derive from plan and section.[848] Departing from his utilitarian "general idea" Durand for a moment believes he has found the most fitting forms in those of elementary geometry.[849] Yet comparing the geometric forms with those derived directly and solely from the nature of the materials and the practical purpose, he soon denounces them just as he has rejected the traditional forms:

On peut ranger les formes et les proportions en trois classes: celles qui naissent de la nature des matériaux et de l'usage des objets à la construction desquels ils sont employés; celles dont l'habitude nous a fait en quelque sorte un besoin, telles que les formes et les proportions des édifices antiques; enfin, celles qui, plus simples et plus déterminées, obtiennent chez nous la préférence, à cause de la facilité que nous avons à les saisir. Les premières sont les seules essentielles . . .[850]

Parallel to this line of thought, there runs another in Durand's texts, permanently intermingling with the former. Durand was full of doubt; he sensed that strict functionalism was a utopia. It is an oversimplification, to stamp him merely as a *constructeur*.[851] He felt that there was something wrong with pure utilitarianism, and understood that the "natural" forms must be modified in one way or another. So he compromised:

Les premières sont les seules essentielles; mais elles ne sont pas tellement fixées par la nature des choses, que l'on ne puisse y ajouter, y retrancher, en sorte que rien n'empêche d'y allier les deuxièmes, celles des édifices antiques: et, comme celles-ci varient beaucoup dans les édifices grecs qu'ont imités les Romains . . . on est libre de choisir entre elles les formes et les proportions qui étant les plus simples sont les plus propres, en apportant de l'économie dans les édifices à satisfaire d'avantage et l'oeil et l'esprit.[852]

At last he believed he had found the way out of his dilemma, by turning once again, to composition:

Le mot construction . . . offre donc seul une idée assez générale et qui convienne à tous les édifices. Mais puisque l'architecture est non seulement l'art d'exécuter, mais encore celui de composer tous les édifices publics et particuliers et que l'on ne peut exécuter un édifice quelconque sans l'avoir conçu, il faudrait qu'à l'idée de construction se trouvât jointe une autre idée générale de laquelle découleraient toutes les idées particulières qui doivent guider dans la composition de tous les édifices.[853]

The second "general idea" is "economy," which plays a strange role in Durand's theory. It serves as the back door through which, besides "simplicity," the old "symmetry" and "regularity" reënter.[854]

So it happened that Durand searched for a timely pattern and at last reached an extremely simple formula which he could teach his pupils in good conscience: "The elements of the structures may be put side by side or one above the other."[855] This precept manifests that Durand was imbued with the idea of the equal importance of the elements. To realize this idea, a sober plan of intersecting axes would be good enough:

Après avoir tracè des axes parallèles, équidistants, et coupé perpendiculairement ces axes par d'autres axes éloignés les uns des autres autant que les premiers, on place, à la distance d'autant d'entre-axes qu'on le juge convenable, les murs sur les axes, et les colonnes, les pilastres, etc., sur les intersections de ces mêmes axes; ensuite on divise en deux les entre-axes, et sur les nouveaux axes donnés par cette division, on place les portes, les croisées, les arcades, etc.[856]

This is a hard and fast rule which gives a large amount of independence to the elements, and yet does not forget the architectural whole. Durand, however, had not overcome all his doubts. Now he recommended starting composition from the whole (in the Baroque way), now he emphasized the significance of the parts. He says in the *Précis*: "Lorsque l'on compose . . . on doit commencer par l'ensemble, continuer par les parties, et finir par les détails."[857] But in the *Partie graphique* we read: "L'ensemble d'un édifice quelconque n'est et ne peut être que le résultat de l'assemblage et de la combinaison de parties plus ou moins nombreuses."[858] The words "more or less numerous" speak volumes. The closely knit pattern of the Baroque did not allow an arbitrary number of parts. Under the rule of individualism, however, you may add or remove as many parts as you like. Once more we see how Palladio's *uno intiero e ben finito corpo*[859] was superseded by the composition *ad infinitum,* which obviously meant a serious menace to the whole.

Jacques-François Blondel was the voice of the prerevolutionary era; Ledoux that of the revolution; Durand that of the rising nineteenth century. As teachers Blondel and Durand attempted to present a seemingly irrefutable doctrine, of which they themselves were not fully convinced. Ledoux, however, expressed in his book without regard and without restraint what never could be taught and never could be realized. Blondel and Durand spoke *ex officio,* Ledoux's voice came *de profundis.*

The writing of these three representatives of three architectural generations reveal how quickly the artistic change came to pass. Blondel faintly guessed what the future had in store. Ledoux was carried away by the general excitement which ended in political upheaval. In Durand's work, the new faith already has become a new doctrine, apparently self-confident, but inwardly weak. Ledoux's writing style reflects almost better than his designs the restlessness, longing, struggling, doubting of his era. Durand's style is concise, clear, and cool.

Boullée had much appreciation for his draftsman Durand.[860] The close cooperation of the two architects left unmistakable traces in the designs of the younger one. The predilection for elementary forms and the sense of monumentality were characteristic especially of Durand's early designs. His cylindrical "Temple décadaire" (1795) was to rise from a powerful substructure, and be crowned by a saucer dome (fig. 220).[861] Censers on pediments all around the building were intended to create atmosphere.[862]

The project for a college won Durand the Grand Prix in 1780.[863] The rules of the competition required that the college be designed on an equilateral triangle—a condition which in itself was characteristic enough. In this plan Durand's inclination toward geometrical subdivision showed itself. He inscribed within the triangle a hexagon, and filled the latter with a large central square—the court—and smaller squares and semicircles.

His contemporaries liked his novel compositions. In a competion of the Convention, the jurors were struck by the boldness of his "Temple à l'Egalité.[864]

According to the necrology by A. Rondelet, Durand carried out only one private house in Paris, the Maison Lathuile (fig. 219), Rue du Faubourg Poissonnière, in 1788.[865] This was one of those plain and yet refined buildings in which the Baroque pattern is almost completely abandoned. There is symmetry, and there are a few traditional features. But the former balance is superseded by the antithesis of differently shaped and differently sized openings.

Like Boullée, Durand had the feeling that the austerity of the new architecture ought to be softened in some way. Neither thought of additional ornaments but rather of the introduction of natural features, such as fresh green or water basins.[866] Inspired by Italian models, Durand recommended adding pergolas to houses.[867]

Durand's method of axial composition seems to be rather mechanical. He himself spoke of the *mécanisme de la composition*.[868] Nevertheless he was able to attain artistic effects on simple plans of intersecting axes through the means of repetition and antithesis.[869] The occasional use of classical features should not blind us from seeing his conscious attempts towards a new arrangement. The plates of the *Partie graphique* show those patterns of aggregated block-units which became common during the nineteenth and twentieth centuries, concealed by overabundant decoration in the former, openly displayed in the latter. A very elucidating statement of the twentieth-century search for new solutions reads as follows:

As the basic cellular unit of that larger unit the street, the dwelling-house represents a typical group-organism. The uniformity of the cells whose multiplication by streets forms the still larger unit of the city therefore calls for formal expression. Diversity in their sizes provides the necessary modicum of variation, which in turn promotes natural competition between dissimilar types developing side by side.[870]

Thus an architect of our time, Walter Gropius, tries to explain his experiments which closely resemble those of the visionaries of about 1800. The latter with their patterns of repetition and antithesis went ahead of our moderns. More than the similarities of single features, such as blank walls, flat roofs, and unframed windows, the similarity of compositional efforts reveals the affinity of the two periods. The attempts of our own time developed from the principles discovered in the eighteenth century in a consistent, though not always obvious, process.

It is not my intention to enhance earlier accomplishments by comparing them with later ones, or vice versa. Only the historical continuity should be pointed out. And to avoid the misunderstanding that I see only the modern side of Durand's work, I should like to discuss two of his designs which show the intermingling of the various currents.

The country house built for a certain Lermina at Chessy, near Lagny en Brie, is the first example.[871] Durand made three projects. One of the three plans is an oblong, subdivided into rectangles of various sizes. The arrangement of the narrow vestibule and the large dining room on the main axis is reminiscent of the Baroque scheme. The second plan presents a nine-partite square; the third, however, an entirely free arrangement. In it each room has the size and the location most convenient for its purpose; the inner communications are carefully worked out.

The project for a "Maison de Ville et de Campagne"[872] is a compromise between the nine-partite type and Baroque emphasis on the central parts. The three rectangles in the middle are broader than those on the sides. One of them projects in a semicircle toward the garden. At last, mention may be made of Durand's renowned *Recueil et parallèle des édifices de tout genre, anciens et modernes,* typical of that interest in the past which was to last through the entire nineteenth century.

In the Age of Reason a new architectural epoch began, with entirely new compositional ideals and, in the end, entirely new artistic forms. The nineteenth century, to be sure, still made ample use of forms borrowed from various sources. How the revolutionary patterns were engulfed in that deluge of forms can be seen already in the Grands Prix of its second quarter.[873] The great inventions of the revolutionaries were not imitated by the following generations, yet neither were they totally forgotten. We have seen Daniel Ramée republishing Ledoux's *Architecture* in 1847. In the same year Léon Vaudoyer remembered, if rather disapprovingly, *ces rêves plus ou moins brillants qui dénotent l'unique préoccupation de faire du neuf à tout prix.*[874] I conclude by illustrating two prize-winning designs of 1873 (figs. 221, 222), the mausoleum by Mayeux and the "Panthéon" by Pucey, both in the spirit of Boullée and Ledoux, and naming from a wide selection of others the "Nécropole" by Defrasse (1884),[875] which calls to mind the Mole Antonelliana at Turin as well as certain projects of Neufforge and Delafosse.

In analyzing a large number of works we have become aware that the elements of architectural composition began to be associated in a new way in the course of the eighteenth century. From observations made on buildings and projects we have reached the concept of architectural individualism. We did not borrow it from other fields and adapt it to architecture. The process of establishing a new order of the constituent parts went on for a prolonged period in several countries. It came to a climax in the endeavors of the French revolutionaries.

No set of forms, nor any definite, all-embracing formula, but the challenge to struggle for new forms and new patterns was the legacy of the Age of Reason. From the moment when a new ideal of configuration arose—a moment which of course can hardly be fixed in time—the battle for its realization began. There was no chance for it ever to attain perfect fulfillment. Yet from it sprang endless tentative solutions, such as at all times have made, and always will make, the life and the history of Architecture.

NOTES

PART ONE: ENGLAND

I. ENGLISH BAROQUE AND
ENGLISH PALLADIANISM

1. Colen Campbell, *Vitruvius Britannicus* (London, 1715), I, 3. I refer to a set of *Vitruvius Britannicus* volume I of which is dated 1715 and includes a royal privilege dated April. 8, 1715; vol. II, 1717; III, 1725. Other copies of volume I, dated 1717; II, undated; III, dated 1731, have partly different paginations.

2. *Ibid.,* I, 3; pls. 8, 9.

3. *Ibid.,* I, 3.

4. Wren Society (Oxford, 1928), V, 9; pls. II, III. Ralph Dutton, *The Age of Wren* (London, 1951), fig. 9.

5. Wren Society, VII, 250; pls. X, XI.

6. *Ibid.,* VIII, pl. VIII.

7. Campbell, *Vitruvius Britannicus,* I, 5; pl. 40. Dutton, *Wren,* fig. 69.

8. *Ibid.,* II, 5.

9. Robert Morris, *Rural Architecture* (London, 1750), fourth page of the introduction. Quoted below, Chapter II, p. 24.

10. Campbell, *Vitruvius Britannicus,* I, 5; pl. 44. Dutton, *Wren,* fig. 82.

11. Wren Society, XIV, pls. I–IV. Cecil Whitaker-Wilson, *Sir Christopher Wren* (London, 1932), ill. opp. p. 134, with date. *Journal of the Royal Institute of British Architects* XLIV (1937), ill. p. 733. Dutton, *Wren,* fig. 21.

12. Whitaker-Wilson, *Sir Christopher Wren,* ill. opp. p. 135. Wren Society, I, pls. XI, XII.

13. Christopher Wren, *Parentalia* (London, 1750), pp. 261, 262.

14. Sacheverell Sitwell, *British Architects and Craftsmen* (London, 1945), 3rd ed. (1947), fig. 77, Orangery. John Summerson, "The Mind of Wren," in *Heavenly Mansions* (London, 1949), demonstrates the "unimaginative" character of Wren's work, seeing even

in the City churches no more than "fancy controlled empirically, not intuitively."

15. Joshua Reynolds, *Discourses,* ed. Edmund Gosse (London, 1884), p. 247: "When I speak of Vanbrugh, I mean to speak of him in the language of our art. To speak then of Vanbrugh in the language of a painter, he had originality of invention, he understood light and shadow, and had great skill in composition. To support his principal object, he produced his second and third groups or masses; he perfectly understood in his art what is the most difficult in ours, the conduct of the background; by which the design and invention is set off to the greatest advantage. What the background is in painting, in architecture is the real ground on which the building is erected; and no architect took greater care than he that his work should not appear crude and hard; that is, he did not abruptly start out of the ground without expectation or preparation. This is a tribute which a painter owes to an architect who composed like a painter; and was defrauded of the due reward of his merit by the wits of his time, who did not understand the principles of composition in poetry better than he, and who knew little, or nothing, of what he understood perfectly, the general ruling principles of architecture and painting." Excellent modern comments on Vanbrugh's work can be found in Geoffrey Webb's introduction to vol. IV of *The Complete Works of Sir John Vanbrugh,* ed. Bonamy Dobrée (London, 1928), and Laurence Whistler, *Sir John Vanbrugh, Architect and Dramatist* (London, 1938).

16. Campbell, *Vitruvius Britannicus,* I, 5, 6; pls. 63–71. H. Avray Tipping, *English Homes* (London, 1928), Period IV, vol. II, figs. 1 ff.

17. Campbell, *Vitruvius Britannicus,* I, 5; pls. 55–62. Tipping, *English Homes,* figs. 106

ff. About the distinction between "pictorial" (one of Wölfflin's categories) and "picturesque" (a quality cherished by Romanticism), see note 237, below.

18. Tipping, *English Homes,* figs. 106, 126.

19. Geoffrey Webb, in his introduction to Gerald Cobb, *The Old Churches of London* (London, 1942), p. 13, doubts whether Archer was a pupil of Vanbrugh. About the latter's influence on Archer, see Geoffrey Webb, "Thomas Archer," *Burlington Magazine* XLVII (1925), 200–209, and Marcus Whiffen's *Thomas Archer* (London, 1950).

20. Campbell, *Vitruvius Britannicus,* I, 3; pls. 10, 11.

21. Wren Society, XVII, 84; pl. XL. Cobb, *Old Churches,* pl. LXXX. Whiffen, *Thomas Archer,* p. 29, provides the date. Dutton, *Wren,* fig. 104.

22. Campbell, *Vitruvius Britannicus,* I, 4; pls. 31, plan 33, elevation. Tipping, *English Homes,* Per. IV, vol. I, p. xxxiv; fig. XVIII. Albert Edward Richardson, *Introduction to Georgian Architecture* (London, 1949), ill. p. 21.

23. John Summerson, *Georgian London* (London, 1946), fig. XIII. Dutton, *Wren,* p. 96, pointing out Vanbrughian traits; fig. 106.

24. Wren Society, IV, 17.

25. *Ibid.,* XVIII, 188; pl. XIII. Sitwell, *British Architects* (3rd ed.), fig. 93. Dutton, *Wren,* fig. 115.

26. Wren Society, XVIII, pl. XV.

27. *Ibid.*

28. John Belcher and Mervyn E. Macartney, *Later Renaissance Architecture in England* (London, 1901), I, 8; figs. 8, 9. Wren Society, XI, pl. XLVI. Dutton, *Wren,* fig. 63.

29. James Gibbs, *A Book of Architecture* (London, 1728), pls. 16–23. Godfrey, *Architecture in England,* II, fig. 130. Cobb, *Old Churches,* pl. VIII. Summerson, *Georgian London,* p. 69; fig. IX.

30. Cobb, *Old Churches,* p. 13. Sitwell, *British Architects* (3rd ed.), fig. 96.

31. Gibbs, *Book of Architecture,* p. ii.

32. Banister Fletcher, *History of Architecture* (8th ed., London, 1929) ill. p. 711. Godfrey, *Architecture in England,* fig. 60.

33. Fletcher, *History,* ill. p. 751.

34. See p. 5 and note 10, above.

35. Tipping, *English Homes,* Per. V, vol. I, fig. 223; p. 183.

36. *Ibid.,* figs. 241, 242; p. 205.

37 *Ibid.,* Per. V, vol. I, p. xxxiii.

38. James Gibbs, *Rules for Drawing the Several Parts of Architecture* (2nd ed., London, 1736), p. 2.

39. Gibbs, *Book of Architecture,* p. xvii. Similarly, p. xi.

40. *Ibid.,* pls. 38, 39, 55, 56, 63, 64.

41. *Ibid.,* pls. 44, 67.

42. James Gibbs, *Bibliotheca Radcliviana* (London, 1747), pl. I. Godfrey, *Architecture in England,* II, fig. 119. Fletcher, *History,* ill. p. 748. S. Lang, "By Hawksmoor out of Gibbs," *Architectural Review* CV (1949), 183–190, discusses the genesis of the project.

43. Gibbs, *Bibliotheca,* p. 9; pl. I.

44. Gibbs, *Book of Architecture,* pls. 72, 79; 71, 80, 81.

45. Sitwell, *British Architects* (3rd ed.), p. 111. Richardson, *Introduction,* ill. p. 167. Christopher Hussey, "Twickenham," *Country Life* XCVI (1944), pp. 464, 466; figs. 2, 4. James Lees-Milne, *The Age of Adam* (London, 1947), fig. 38. Dutton, *Wren,* fig. 152, interior.

46. Gibbs, *Book of Architecture,* pls. 8–15.

47. *Ibid.,* p. iv.

48. Marcus Whiffen, "The Progeny of St. Martin-in-the-Fields," *Architectural Review* C (1946), p. 4. Summerson, *Georgian London,* p. 72, brands the placing of the steeple on the roof as "an act of insensibility." My aim is historical explanation rather than aesthetic criticism. Sitwell, *British Architects* (3rd ed.), fig. 97. Dutton, *Wren,* fig. 119.

49. William Kent, *The Designs of Inigo Jones, with some additional Designs* (London, 1727), pt. II, pls. 16, 17, 18, 19. Sitwell, *British Architects* (3rd ed.), fig. 20, presents a plan for a circular house by John Thorpe.

50. John Soane, *Lectures on Architecture . . . from 1809 to 1836,* ed. Arthur Thomas Bolton (London, 1929), Lecture XI, p. 176.

51. *Ibid.,* p. 175. Soane explains: "Too great a Variety of Parts and Movement in the exteriors of buildings, as well as in their plans, is to be avoided as much as monotony. Variety

may be carried to excess, by too many breaks and divisions, by a repetition of curves and undulating forms running into each other without proper repose."

52. Isaac Ware, *A Complete Body of Architecture* (London, ed. of 1756), p. 127.

53. *Ibid.*, p. 94.

54. *Ibid.*, p. 336.

55. *Ibid.*, p. 295.

56. Leon Battista Alberti, *De re aedificatoria libri decem* [1450], bk. VI, chap. ii: "Nos tamen brevitatis gratia sic diffiniemus: ut sit pulchritudo quidem certa cum ratione concinnitas universarum partium in eo cuius sint: ita ut addi/ aut diminui/ aut immutari possit nihil/ quin improbabilius reddat." The English translation is from the edition of Giacomo Leoni (London, 1726), VI, 3.

57. Ware, *Architecture,* p. 299.

58. *Ibid.*, p. 305.

59. *Ibid.*, p. 305.

60. *Ibid.*, p. 309.

61. *Ibid.*, p. 296, about the rooms: "Some, according to their use, are to be larger, and others smaller, yet that there be a proportion observed among them; a proportion of one to another"; p. 310, about doors and windows: "These must be carefully proportioned; first to the general aspect of the building, next to the stories, and lastly to one another"; p. 314, about ornaments: "In the first place, all ornaments must be made to bear a due and exact proportion both to the edifice in the whole, and to one another. The more they are enriched, the greater nicety and care are required; for these additional articles of decoration must, in the same manner, be proportioned to the parts, and to the whole."

62. *Ibid.*, p. 296.

63. *Ibid.*, p. 321.

64. *Ibid.*, p. 314.

65. *Ibid.*, p. 296.

66. *Ibid.*, p. 323.

67. *Ibid.*, pls. 32, 35, 39, 40, 45, 49, 51, 52, 53, 61.

68. *The Four Books of Andrea Palladio's Architecture* (Published by Isaac Ware, London, 1738), dedication.

69. *Ibid.*, advertisement.

70. Fletcher, *History*, p. 734. The comments in his *Andrea Palladio* (London, 1902) also are rather superficial. The thoughtless use of the term "Palladian" goes back to the eighteenth century. Pierre Patte, "Notice sur l'architecte Boffrand," reprinted in *Revue universelle des Arts* XVII (1863), 275, said of Boffrand: "Sa manière approche beaucoup de celle de Palladio."

71. Fritz Burger, *Die Villen des Andrea Palladio* (Leipzig, 1909), building on the thought of Jacob Burckhardt and August Schmarsow, presents an excellent interpretation of Palladio's compositional principles. Rudolf Wittkower, "Principles of Palladio's Architecture," *Journal of the Warburg Institute* VII (1944), pp. 102–122, VIII (1945), pp. 68–106, points out the "Mannerist" factors in several works of Palladio as well as his contradictory predilection for "sweet," harmonious proportions. In dealing with Palladio's villas one should pay attention to his art of grouping rather than to the way the individual blocks are handled.

72. Palladio (ed. Ware), bk. I, chap. i, p. 1.

73. *Ibid.*, bk. II, chap. xvi, p. 53.

74. *Ibid.*, bk. II, chap. xvii, p. 55.

75. The terms "concatenation" and "gradation" are taken from Morris, *Rural Architecture.* See note 202, below.

76. Palladio (ed. Ware), bk. I, chap. xx, p. 25.

77. *Ibid.*, bk. II, chap. xvii, p. 55.

78. *Ibid.*, bk. II, chap. iii, p. 41.

79. *Ibid.*, bk. II, pl. 31.

80. *Ibid.*, bk. II, pl. 34.

81. *Ibid.*, bk. II, pl. 43.

82. *Ibid.*, advertisement.

83. Tipping, *English Homes,* Per. V, vol. I, frontispiece.

84. *Ibid.*, fig. 207.

85. *Ibid.*, fig. 213.

86. *Ibid.*, p. 179. A. E. Richardson, *Introduction*, ill. p. 161. See Arthur Thomas Bolton, *The Architecture of Robert and James Adam* (London, 1922), I, 54, with note.

87. Rudolf Wittkower, "Lord Burlington and William Kent," *Archaeological Journal* CII (1945), 154; pl. I.

88. A. E. Richardson, *Introduction*, ill. p. 157. Fiske Kimball, "Burlington Architectus,"

Journal of the Royal Institute of British Architects XXXIV (1927), pp. 686 ff., interprets Burlington's departure from Palladio's composition as a return to Roman models. Rudolf Wittkower, "Pseudo-Palladian Elements in English Neoclassical Architecture," in *England and the Mediterranean Tradition*, ed. Warburg Institute (London, 1945), pp. 142–153, discusses the form of Venetian windows and quoined windows in Georgian architecture. His study of these surface motifs climaxes in the generalization of a dominant trend toward "flatness." My investigation is to show that in England and France architecture passed from Baroque spatiality and plasticity to new methods of enhancing the third dimension. About the transformation of the Palladian motif in the eighteenth century, see Emil Kaufmann, review of Geneviève Levallet-Haug, *Ledoux* (Paris, 1934), *Kritische Berichte zur Kunstgeschicht lichen Literatur* (1935), p. 95.

89. Wittkower, "Lord Burlington," p. 155. Cf. note 376, below.

90. The overarched Palladian motif in Villa Poiana (Palladio, ed. Ware, II, pl. 41; Georgii K. Lukomski, *Andrea Palladio*, Paris, 1927, pl. XCII) is exceptional in Palladio's work, and different from the eighteenth-century versions of this motif.

91. Tipping, *English Homes*, Per. V, vol. I, fig. 170 (north front); fig. 169 (south front).

92. John Woolfe and James Gandon, *Vitruvius Britannicus*, IV (London, 1767), pl. 79. Kimball, "Burlington Architectus," fig. 26. Oliver Sheldon, "York Assembly Rooms," *Architectural Review* XCVIII (1945), 119–121, with ills.

93. James Lees-Milne, "Lord Burlington in Yorkshire," *Architectural Review* XCVIII (1945), ill. p. 17.

94. Wilton bridge: Frederick Moore Simpson, *A History of Architectural Development* (reprint, London, 1932), vol. III, fig. 250. Sitwell, *British Architecture* (3rd ed.), fig. 134. Prior Park bridge: Tipping, *English Homes*, Per. V, vol. I, fig. XIV.

95. Palladio (ed. Ware), bk. III, pl. 10.

96. Campbell, *Vitruvius Britannicus*, III, 8.

97. *Ibid.*, III, pl. 37. A. E. Richardson, *Introduction*, ill. p. 142.

98. Campbell, *Vitruvius Britannicus*, I, pl. 24/25.

99. *Ibid.*, I, pls. 29/30; p. 4.

100. *Ibid.*, I, pl. 96/97; p. 7.

101. *Ibid.*, I, pl. 54; p. 5.

102. *Ibid.*, III, pl. 23/24; pp. 7, 8. Summerson, *Georgian London,* fig. XIX.

103. Campbell, *Vitruvius Britannicus*, I, pl. 23.

104. *Ibid.*, I, pl. 28.

105. *Ibid.*, I, pl. 95.

106. Palladio (ed. Ware), II, pl. 32.

107. *Ibid.*, II, pl. 40.

108. Campbell, *Vitruvius Britannicus*, III, pl. 53.

109. Palladio (ed. Ware), II, pl. 31.

110. *Ibid.*, II, pl. 43.

111. Campbell, *Vitruvius Britannicus*, II, 4.

112. *Ibid.*, II, pl. 87.

113. *Ibid.*, II, pl. 88.

114. *Ibid.*, III, pl. 29/30; p. 8. A. E. Richardson, *Introduction*, ills. pp. 140, 141. Thomas Ripley, *Plans, elevations and Sections of Houghton in Norfolk, the Seat of Sir Robert Walpole*, ed. Isaac Ware (London, 1735), presents the executed house, different from Campbell's project.

115. Palladio (ed. Ware), bk. II, pl. 35.

116. Campbell, *Vitruvius Britannicus*, II, 4; pl. 83/84.

117. *Ibid.*, II, 5; pl. 87.

118. *Ibid.*, III, pls. 98/99; p. 12.

119. *Ibid.*, II, pls. 81/82. *Dictionary of National Biography* (London, 1909), XI, 944, ascribes "Bramham Park near Leeds" to Leoni. Charles Henry Collins Baker, *Life of James Brydges, First Duke of Chandos* (Oxford, 1949), p. 302, assumes that Wood the Elder was employed there. But see Whiffen, *Thomas Archer*, pp. 37, 38.

120. Campbell, *Vitruvius Britannicus*, II, 4. Bramham Park was surrounded by gardens, so lack of space cannot have been the reason for its plan. Cf. H. Avray Tipping, *English Gardens* (London, 1925), figs. 35, 38, presenting the house and the interesting façade of the stables.

121. Campbell, *Vitruvius Britannicus*, I, 1.

122. *Ibid.*, I, 2.

123. *Ibid.*, II, 2.

124. *Ibid.*, II, 1.

II. THE FIRST OPPONENTS OF TRADITION

125. Edgar Sheppard, *The Old Royal Palace of Whitehall* (London, 1902), ill. opp. p. 100. Geoffrey Webb, "Vanbrugh," *Burlington Magazine,* XLVII (1925), p. 225.

126. Tipping, *English Homes,* Per. IV, vol. II, p. 141.

127. *Ibid.*, Per. IV, vol. II, figs. 194, 196, 198.

128. *Ibid.*, Per. IV, vol. II, figs. 211–217.

129. *Ibid.*, Per. IV, vol. II, p. 153.

130. *Ibid.*, Per. IV, vol. II, fig. 268.

131. *Ibid.*, Per. IV, vol. II, fig. 279. Sitwell, *British Architects* (3rd ed.), fig. 78. Webb, "Vanbrugh," p. 227, ill. B.

132. Tipping, *English Homes,* Per. IV, vol. II, p. 153.

133. *Ibid.*, Per. IV, vol. II, figs. 86–89.

134. *Ibid.*, Per. IV, vol. II, fig. 196.

135. *Ibid.*, Per. IV, vol. II, fig. 210.

136. *Ibid.*, Per. IV, vol. II, fig. lxiii.

137. Campbell, *Vitruvius Britannicus,* III, pls. 16, 17; p. 7. Tipping, *English Homes,* Per. IV, vol. II, figs. 251–260.

138. Campbell, *Vitruvius Britannicus,* pl. 20. Tipping, *English Homes,* Per. IV, vol. II, p. 278; figs. 404 ff.

139. Tipping presents a masterly description of Seaton Delaval. However, I believe he is not right in speaking of an "abstract feeling for related masses" (Per. IV, vol. II, p. 274), or the "interrelation of the masses" and the "suave centre" of the north elevation (p. 277). The antagonism of the parts is the most conspicuous characteristic of this elevation. Geoffrey Webb in Vanbrugh (ed. Dobrée), IV, xxx, xxxi, says: "Seaton Delaval is the logical conclusion of a series of experiments . . . the final expression of what we may call 'Heroic' architecture in England." This criticism, revealing a profound understanding of Vanbrugh's endeavors, leaves only the problem of locating them within the entire eighteenth-century development. Whistler, *Sir John Vanbrugh,* p. 267, sees

the discrepancies in Seaton Delaval, but in the sense of traditional aesthetics condemns them as "palpable errors." Nikolaus Pevsner, "Good King James's Gothic," *Architectural Review* CVII (1950), 117–122, sees in the plan of Seaton Delaval a renewed interest in the Elizabethan and the Jacobean.

140. Campbell, *Vitruvius Britannicus,* III, pls. 11–14. Tipping, *English Homes,* Per. IV, vol. II, pp. 295 ff. Whistler, *Sir John Vanbrugh,* p. 278, sees Vanbrugh as affected by Palladianism at Grimsthorpe.

141. Campbell, *Vitruvius Britannicus,* I, pls. 98, 99/100; p. 7. Dutton, *Wren,* fig. 136.

142. Harry Stuart Goodhart-Rendel, *Nicholas Hawksmoor* (London, 1924), pls. 31, 32.

143. John Britton and Auguste Charles Pugin, *Illustrations of the Public Buildings of London* (London, 1825), I, ill. opp. p. 94. Fletcher, *History,* ill. p. 748. Goodhart-Rendel, *Nicholas Hawksmoor,* p. 23; frontispiece; pl. 19. Cobb, *Old Churches,* fig. 33. Summerson, *Georgian London,* fig. 12. Thomas Pennant, *Some Account of London* (4th ed.; London, 1805), ill. opp. p. 175, presents the main and the Lombard Street façades.

144. Cobb, *Old Churches,* pl. XL.

145. John Woods, *Views in London, Westminster and their Vicinities* (London, n.d.), ill. opp. p. 184. Goodhart-Rendel, *Nicholas Hawksmoor,* p. 19; pl. 2. Cobb, *Old Churches,* pl. VII.

146. Goodhart-Rendel, *Nicholas Hawksmoor,* p. 21; pl. 15. John Summerson, "St. George's-in-the-East," *Architectural Review* XC (1941), ills. pp. 135 (west and south), 138 (east end).

147. James Peller Malcolm, *Londinium redivivum* (London, 1802–1807), II, 82.

148. Goodhart-Rendel, *Nicholas Hawksmoor,* pl. 22.

149. Goodhart-Rendel, *Nicholas Hawksmoor,* pls. 25–28. Cobb, *Old Churches,* pl. VII.

150. Tipping, *English Homes,* Per. IV, vol. II, p. xlii; fig. XXXVII. Goodhart-Rendel, *Nicholas Hawksmoor,* pl. 33. For Hawksmoor's activities at Oxford, see S. Lang, "Cambridge and Oxford Reformed," *Architectural Review* CIII (1948), 157–160,

151. Reginald Blomfield, *A History of Renaissance Architecture in England, 1500–1800* (London, 1897), II, 202. Sitwell, *British Architects* (3rd ed.), p. 98; fig. 85, twin towers, Oxford. Dutton, *Wren,* fig. 139.

152. Fletcher, *History,* p. 707. Godfrey, *Architecture in England,* II, 124. Cobb, *Old Churches,* p. 12, preface by Geoffrey Webb. Webb, however, in "Baroque Art," *Proceedings of the British Academy* XXXIII (1947), is aware of Hawksmoor's tendency toward the abstract.

153. [John Gwynn], *The Art of Architecture* (London, 1742), p. 14.

154. Malcolm, *Londinium redivivum,* III, 387. Ralph, Architect [sic], *A Critical Review of the Public Buildings, Statutes, and Ornaments, in and about London and Westminster* (London, 1783), p. 161, remarks on St. George's, Bloomsbury: "He (Hawksmoor) erred so much, that the very portico does not seem to be in the middle of the church; and as to the steeple, it is stuck on like a wen to the rest of the building." James Dallaway, *Observations on English Architecture* (London, 1806), p. 147, says: "His genius runs riot amongst steeples."

155. H. Avray Tipping, "Nicholas Hawksmoor," *Journal of the Royal Institute of British Architects* XXXIV (1927), p. 652.

156. Summerson, *Georgian London,* p. 76.

157. Tipping, *English Homes,* Per IV, vol. II, p. 155.

158. For Kent's dependence on Burlington, see Wittkower, "Lord Burlington."

159. Fiske Kimball, "William Kent's Designs for the Houses of Parliament," *Journal of the Royal Institute of British Architects* XXXIX (1932), 733–755, 800–807. Margaret Jourdain, *The Work of William Kent,* with an introduction by Christopher Hussey (London, 1948), figs. 16–26.

160. Tipping, *English Homes,* Per. V, vol. I, p. xx, with the following quotation from a letter of 1734: "There is a new taste in gardening just arisen, which has been practised with so great success at the Prince's garden in town, that a general alteration of some of the most considerable gardens in the kingdom is begun, after Mr. Kent's notion of gardening—viz., to lay them out, and work without level or line . . . and this method of gardening is the more agreeable, as when finished, it has the appearance of beautiful nature, and without being told, one would imagine art had no part in the finishing, and is, according to what one hears of the Chinese, entirely after their models of works of this nature, where they never plant straight lines or make regular designs."

161. Tipping, *English Homes,* Per. V, vol. I, p. 314; figs. 364–385.

162. Woolfe and Gandon, *Vitruvius Britannicus,* V (London, 1771), pls. 64, 65. Tipping, *English Homes,* Per. V, vol. I, fig. 369.

163. Woolfe and Gandon, *Vitruvius Britannicus,* V, pl. 66/67. Tipping, *English Homes,* Per. V, vol. I, fig. 364.

164. Woolfe and Gandon, *Vitruvius Britannicus,* V, pls. 3–8. Blomfield, *Renaissance Architecture,* p. 231; ill. opp. p. 232. A. E. Richardson, *Introduction,* ill. p. 156.

165. William Chambers, *A Treatise on Civil Architecture* (2nd ed.; London, 1768), p. 76. Summerson, *Georgian London,* p. 99, presents a good description of the Horse Guards, based on his aesthetic approach. (See n. 48, above.)

166. Edwin Beresford Chancellor, *The XVIIIth Century in London* (London, 1920), fig. 150. Pennant, *London,* ill. opp. p. 32.

167. See article in *Country Life,* April 15, 1933, pp. 388 ff. Albert Edward Richardson and C. Lovett Gill, *London Houses from 1660 to 1820* (London, 1911), pl. XXXVII.

168. Isaac Ware, *Designs of Inigo Jones and Others* (n.p., n.d.), pl. 43.

169. *Ibid.,* pl. 47.

170. Sitwell, *British Architects,* fig. 121. Jourdain, *Work of William Kent,* fig. 36. Cf. Kent's design for the South gate at Holkham, Wittkower, "Lord Burlington," pl. X, fig. 1.

171. Not less than the Horse Guards, Worcester Lodge refutes the ultrabrief statement of Hussey (Jourdain, *Work of William Kent,* p. 16): "As an architect Kent was uninventive."

172. Sitwell, *British Architects,* p. 128.

173. William Chambers, *Plans, Elevations, Sections, and Perspective Views of the Gardens and Buildings at Kew, in Surry* (London, 1763), pl. III.

174. Blomfield, *Renaissance Architecture,* II, 260.

175. Woolfe and Gandon, *Vitruvius Britannicus,* IV, pls. 1–4.

176. *Ibid.,* IV, pls. 26–29.

177. *Ibid.,* IV, pls. 75, 76.

178. Tipping, *English Homes,* Per. V, vol. I, p. 81; figs. 364–366.

179. Campbell, *Vitruvius Britannicus,* II, pl. 61/62.

180. *Ibid.,* III, pl. 29/30. Tipping, *English Homes,* Per. V, vol. I, fig. 87.

181. Tipping, *English Homes,* Per. V, vol. I, p. xxiii. See n. 95, above.

182. Robert Morris, *An Essay in Defence of Ancient Architecture* (London, 1728); *Lectures on Architecture* (London, 1734–1736); *Rural Architecture* (London, 1750); *Architecture Improved* (London, 1755).

183. Fiske Kimball, *The Creation of the Rococo* (Philadelphia, 1943), p. 216, attempts to demonstrate the dependence of the Petit Trianon on English models by referring to the vignette of the title page of Morris' *Select Architecture* (2nd ed.; London, 1757). This vignette, however, is a mutilated replica of an engraving which had first appeared in the *Lectures* (Lect. XIII, fig. G) and, of course, should not be used for comparison. Morris' original design, with its pediment and its pitched roof, is totally different from the horizontalism of the Petit Trianon.

184. Blomfield, *Renaissance Architecture,* II, 315, 316.

185. Morris, *Rural Architecture,* pls. 2, 3, 12, 30, 47.

186. Morris, *Architecture Improved,* pls. 4, 5, 6, 10, 11, 12.

187. Morris, *Rural Architecture,* pls. 25, 29. *Architecture Improved,* pl. 34.

188. William and John Halfpenny, Robert Morris, and T. Lightoler, *The Modern Builder's Assistant* [London, 1757], pl. 35.

189. Morris, *Lectures,* Lect. IV, p. 51.

190. *Ibid.,* Lect. IV, p. 55; similarly, pp. 57, 58.

191. *Ibid.,* Lect. VIII, p. 123.

192. Morris, *Rural Architecture,* sixth page of introduction.

193. Morris, *Lectures,* Lect. VI, p. 90.

194. *Ibid.,* Lect. VI, p. 89.

195. *Ibid.,* p. 93.

196. *Ibid.,* p. 81.

197. *Ibid.,* Lect. II, p. 30.

198. *Ibid.,* Lect. V, p. 65.

199. *Ibid.,* Lect. VII, p. 105.

200. *Ibid.,* p. 113.

201. *Ibid.,* Lect. VI, p. 88.

202. Morris, *Rural Architecture,* fourth page of introduction.

203. *Loc. cit.* Cf. quotation from Reynolds, note 15, above.

204. Morris, *Lectures,* Lect. XIII, p. 202.

205. Palladio (ed. Ware), bk. I, chap. I. Cf. quotation from Alberti, Part II, note 100, below.

206. Morris, *Lectures,* Lect. V, p. 74.

207. *Ibid.,* Lect. IX, fig. C; Lect. XI, fig. E; Lect. XII, fig. F; Lect. XIII, fig. G; Lect. XIV, fig. I.

208. *Ibid.,* Lect. IX, p. 145.

209. *Ibid.,* p. 138.

210. On figs. C, E, F, G, I.

211. Morris, *Lectures,* Lect. XIII, fig. G.

212. Morris, *Essay,* p. 17.

213. Wittkower, "Principles of Palladio's Architecture," 98: "This classicist . . . developed a system of hard and fast rules of harmonic proportions." Luigi Malaspina di Sannazaro, *Delle leggi del bello applicate alla pittura ed architettura* (Pavia, 1791), p. 180, shows a deeper understanding of what distinguishes Morris's thought from that of the common run of theorists: "Chi ha voluto stabilirne le regole dalle semplici leggi musicali, come i. Sigg. Ou[v]rard, Brisseux ed altri, chi dalla regolarità del cubo, come il Sig. Roberto Morris, e chi dalla perfetta commensurabilità, come l'Abbate Laugier." Morris, *Lectures,* Lect. IX, p. 147, reveals that to Morris the "IDEA" [his capitals] of the cube was of primary importance, the proportions derived from it, secondary. Critics who, in

studying the proportions, get lost in the maze of numbers cannot see the wood for the trees.

214. Morris, *Lectures,* Lect. V, p. 67.

215. *Ibid.,* Lect. VI, p. 97.

216. *Ibid.,* Lect. IX, p. 138.

217. *Ibid.,* p. 139.

218. *Ibid.,* Lect. VI, p. 93.

219. *Ibid.,* Lect. IX, p. 153.

220. Morris, *Essay,* pp. iv, xiii.

221. *Ibid.,* p. xviii.

222. *Ibid.,* p. 15. "The Bulk and Body of the Structure" is important, but not "the smaller Ornaments."

223. *Ibid.,* p. xxii: "The Eye can only survey, and is confined to a narrow limit; whereas the Ideas . . . imprint on the Mind a lasting impression."

224. *Ibid.,* p. xxiii.

225. *Ibid.,* p. 87. On this page we also find the censures: "So odd a Composition of Deformity . . . How irregular is it in the Disposition . . . in a direct Opposition to the Rules of ancient Architecture."

226. *Ibid.,* pp. 87, 90.

227. *Ibid.,* p. 88.

228. *Ibid.,* pp. iv, 88.

229. *Ibid.,* p. 88.

230. Campbell, *Vitruvius Britannicus,* I, pl. 81 with the date 1712, whereas the text says 1710. A. E. Richardson, *Introduction,* ill. p. 22. Whiffen, *Archer,* pp. 27, 59-61.

231. Campbell, *Vitruvius Britannicus,* II, pls. 52–55. For "Goose-Pie House" note 125 above. Kent, *Designs of Inigo Jones,* II, pl. 52/53; Kimball, "Burlington Architectus," fig. 9, illustrate the school of Sevenoaks.

232. Morris, *Essay,* p. 21.

233. Morris, *Lectures,* Lect. XI, p. 183.

234. *Ibid.,* p. 169.

235. *Ibid.,* p. 170.

236. *Ibid.,* pp. 144, 161, 172–175, 183, 188, 189, 191, 205, 210, 216, 217.

237. *Ibid.,* Lect. X, p. 161. About the changes in landscape architecture, see Nikolaus Pevsner, "The Genesis of the Picturesque," *Architectural Review* XCVI (1944), 139–146; "The Picturesque in Architecture," *Journal of the Royal Institute of British Architects* LV (1947), 55–61, with bibliography. Whistler, *Sir John Vanbrugh,* p. 224, sees in Vanbrugh "the father of landscape gardening." Some critics fail to distinguish between "picturesque," meaning an "agreeable Disorder," and "pictorial," that is, composed in the way painters compose. See also note 17, above.

238. Halfpenny, Morris and Lightoler, *Builder's Assistant,* pls. 40, 43, 51.

239. T. Lightoler, *The Gentleman and Farmer's Architect* (London, 1762), pls. 1, 2, 6.

240. Halfpenny, Morris and Lightoler, *Builder's Assistant,* pls. 54, 55, 56, 61. Abraham Swan, *A Collection of Designs in Architecture* (London, 1757), does not deviate from strict symmetry in his façades, but presents a few interesting plans (e.g., pls. 17, 18, 19).

241. William and John Halfpenny, *New Designs for Chinese Temples* (Four parts; London, 1750–1752); *Rural Architecture in the Chinese Taste* (London, 1752); *Rural Architecture in the Gothick Taste* (2nd ed.; London, 1752); *The Country Gentleman's Pocket Companion containing 32 Designs . . . in the Augustine Gothick Taste* (London, 1753). Similar designs in William Wrighte, *Grotesque Architecture* (London, 1767).

242. William Halfpenny, *The Art of Sound Building* (London, 1725), ill. opp. p. 1.

243. William Halfpenny, *A New and Compleat System of Architecture in a Variety of Plans and Elevations of Designs for Convenient and Decorated Houses* (London, 1749). His *Twelve Beautiful Designs for Farmhouses* (London, 1750) are more conservative.

244. Halfpenny, *New and Compleat System,* pl. 28.

245. *Ibid.,* pls. 42, 43.

246. *Ibid.,* pls. 44, 45.

247. *Ibid.,* pls. 18, 19, 20. Original plans also occur in William Halfpenny, *Six New Designs for Convenient Farmhouses* (London, 1751); *Useful Architecture* (2nd ed.; London, 1752, and later editions), esp. pls. 4, 11.

248. Halfpenny, *New and Compleat System,* pl. 33.

249. *Ibid.,* pl. 35.

250. *Ibid.,* pl. 17.

251. Blomfield, *Renaissance Architecture,* II, 246. Godfrey, *Architecture in England,* II, fig. 126.

252. Cobb, *Old Churches,* pl. VII. Summerson *Georgian London,* fig. X.

253. Blomfield, *Renaissance Architecture,* II, 246. Whiffen, "St. Martin-in-the-Fields," shares Blomfield's view.

254. Kent, *Designs of Inigo Jones* (1770), pl. 64/65, Wentworth Woodhouse. Alfred Booth, "The Architects of Wentworth Castle and Wentworth Woodhouse," *Journal of the Royal Institute of British Architects* XLI (1933), 61–72, with ills. Blomfield, *Renaissance Architecture,* II, 246. A. E. Richardson, *Introduction,* ill. p. 51.

255. Marcus Whiffen, *Stuart and Georgian Churches . . . outside of London* (London, 1948), figs. 11, 22, 46, 45 (cited in the sequence of my comments); Summerson, *Georgian London,* fig. XV. Geoffrey Webb, "John and William Bastard," *Burlington Magazine* XLVII (1925), 144–149, pl. IB. Further instances can be found in the beautiful etchings of Charles Clarke, *Architectura Ecclesiastica Londini* (London, 1820).

256. Blomfield, *Renaissance Architecture,* II, 223; ill. opp. p. 222.

257. Albert Edward Richardson, *Monumental Classic Architecture in Great Britain and Ireland during the 18th and 19th centuries* (London, 1914), fig. 11. Godfrey, *Architecture in England,* II, fig. 145.

258. Tipping, *English Homes,* Per. V, vol. I, fig. 139.

259. *Ibid.,* p. 114. A. E. Richardson, *Introduction,* ill. p. 161.

260. A. E. Richardson, *Monumental Classic Architecture,* p. 12; fig. 6. Summerson, *Georgian London,* fig. III.

261. For Seaton Delaval, see beginning of this chapter.

262. A. E. Richardson, *Monumental Classic Architecture,* p. 14. Blomfield, *Renaissance Architecture,* II, 251.

263. Reginald Blomfield, *A Short History of Renaissance Architecture in England, 1500–1800* (London, 1923), p. 192. George Cooke, *Views in London* (London, 1826), pl. 8. David Hughson [Edward Pugh], *London* (London, 1807), IV, ill. opp. p. 419. A. E. Richardson, *Introduction,* ill. p. 137.

264. Summerson, *Georgian London,* p. 47: "This uproarious joke." About the authorship, see Howard Colvin, "Fifty New Churches," *Architectural Review* CVII (1950), 191.

265. Goodhart-Rendel, *Hawksmoor,* pl. 22.

266. *Ibid.,* pls. 2, 31, 32. St. John Horsleydown, by an unknown architect (1732), also had a curious tower, topped by a tapering Ionic column. Pennant, *London,* ill. opp. p. 47. Nikolaus Pevsner, *London* (London, 1952), p. 58.

III. BELATED BAROQUE

267. Mowbray A. Green, *The Eighteenth-Century Architecture of Bath* (Bath, 1904), pl. II.

268. *Ibid.,* pl. III.

269. *Ibid.,* p. 74; pl. XLVIII. John Wood, *Description of Bath* (2nd ed.; London, 1765), II, 238.

270. Green, *Architecture of Bath,* pl. XI.

271. *Ibid.,* pl. XII.

272. *Ibid.,* pl. XIV.

273. *Ibid.,* pl. XIX.

274. *Ibid.,* pl. XXVI.

275. *Ibid.,* p. 41.

276. *Ibid.,* p. 45.

277. *Ibid.,* pl. XXXI.

278. *Ibid.,* p. 128; pl. LXXVIII.

279. *Ibid.,* p. 138. Mr. H. M. Colvin, Oxford, obliged me with the information on the Grammar School.

280. *Ibid.,* pl. LXXX.

281. *Ibid.,* p. 49.

282. *Ibid.,* pl. XXXIII.

283. *Ibid.,* p. 59.

284. *Ibid.,* p. 74.

285. *Ibid.,* pls. XLVIII, L.

286. *Ibid.,* p. 85; ill. p. 83. Richardson, *Introduction,* ill. p. 162.

287. Green, Architecture of *Bath,* pl. XLIV; p. 67, plans. Walter Ison, *The Georgian Buildings of Bath* (London, 1948), pp. 107, 133; fig. 22, plan, pl. 54b.

288. Marcel Fouquier, *Paris au XVIII°*

siècle (Paris, n.d.), p. 95. Charles Simond [Paul Adolphe van Cléemputte] *Paris de 1800 à 1900* (Paris, 1900), I, 242, with ill. and date.

289. See Part III, p. 159, below.

290. Emil Kaufmann, *Three Revolutionary Architects—Boullée, Ledoux and Lequeu, Transactions of the American Philosophical Society,* vol. 42 (1952), figs. 113-129.

291. Ison, *Georgian Buildings of Bath,* figs. 100b, 116b. Bryan Little, *The Building of Bath* (London, 1947), fig. 94.

292. R. G. Collingwood, *The Idea of History* (Oxford, 1946), p. 69.

293. Claude-Nicolas Ledoux, *L'Architecture considérée sous le rapport de l'art, des moeurs et de la législation* (Paris, 1804), p. 23.

294. Green, *Architecture of Bath,* p. 141; pl. LXXXII.

295. *Ibid.,* p. 149; ill. p. 147. A. E. Richardson, *Introduction,* ill. p. 191.

296. Green, *Architecture of Bath,* p. 200; pl. CXXX.

297. *Ibid.,* p. 201; ill. p. 188.

298. *Ibid.,* pl. XCVI. Ison, *Georgian Buildings of Bath,* p. 161; pl. 83. A. E. Richardson, *Introduction,* ill. p. 207.

299. Green, *Architecture of Bath,* p. 175; pl. CVII.

300. *Ibid.,* p. 159; pl. XCIX, Assembly Room. Whiffen, *Stuart . . . Churches,* p. 63; fig. 72, Hardenhuish Church.

301. Green, *Architecture of Bath,* p. 190; pl. CXVIII.

302. *Ibid.,* p. 165; ills. pp. 166-168; pl. CV. A. E. Richardson, *Introduction,* ill. p. 207.

303. Palladio (ed. Ware), bk. III, chap. xiii, pl. 9/10.

304. Robert Adam, *The Works in Architecture of Robert and James Adam* (London, vol. I, 1778; II, 1779; III, 1822; reprint London, 1931), vol. I, preface.

305. John Swarbrick, *Robert Adam and his Brothers* (London, 1915), fig. 34. Bolton, *Robert and James Adam,* vol. I, ills. pp. 17, 21. Lees-Milne, *The Age of Adam,* fig. 35.

306. Bolton, *Robert and James Adam,* I, ill. p. 83.

307. *Ibid.,* II, ill. p. 103.

308. *Ibid.,* II, 173, with ill.

309. *Ibid.,* II, 112-116, with ills. Lees-Milne, *The Age of Adam,* fig. 126.

310. Bolton, *Robert and James Adam,* I, 37, with ill.

311. Georges Gromort, *Jacques-Ange Gabriel* (Paris, 1933), p. 83; pl. XC.

312. Robert Adam, *The Works,* preface.

313. Bolton, *Robert and James Adam,* I, 157; ill. p. 159.

314. Campbell, *Vitruvius Britannicus,* V, pls. 25/26, 27/28. Blomfield, *Renaissance Architecture,* II, 261, with ill. Bolton, *Robert and James Adam,* I, ill. p. 159.

315. Bolton, *Robert and James Adam,* I, ill. p. 115.

316. Robert Adam, *The Works,* vol. I, pt. 4, pl. II. Bolton, *Robert and James Adam,* I, ill. p. 105.

317. Robert Adam, *The Works,* vol. I, pt. 2, pl. II. Bolton, *Robert and James Adam,* I, 317, with ill.

318. Robert Adam, *The Works,* vol. I, pt. 4, pl. IV. Swarbrick, *Robert Adam and his Brothers,* fig. 167.

319. Robert Adam, *The Works,* vol. II, pt. 2, pl. II. Swarbrick, *Robert Adam and his Brothers,* fig. 178.

320. Robert Adam, *The Works,* vol. II, pt. 5, pl. VI.

321. *Ibid.,* vol. I, pt. 4, pl. II.

322. Bolton, *Robert and James Adam,* II, 105, with ill.

323. Robert Adam, *The Works,* vol. II, pt. 2, pl. IV.

324. Bolton, *Robert and James Adam,* II, 278, with ill.

325. Emil Kaufmann, "Klassizismus als Tendenz und als Epoche," *Kritische Berichte zur Kunstgeschichtlichen Literatur* (1931), pp. 201-214.

326. Robert Adam, *The Works,* vol. I, pt. 1, pl. IV.

327. *Ibid.,* vol. I, pt. 5, pl. I.

328. *Ibid.,* vol. II, pt. 2, pl. III.

329. Bolton, *Robert and James Adam,* I, 13; ill. p. 15. The date is inscribed on the tomb.

330. *Ibid.,* I, 94.

331. *Ibid.,* I, 77.

332. *Ibid.,* I, 164. William Pain, *The Prac-*

tical Builder, (2nd ed.; London, 1792), in his preface, apparently alluding to Adam, finds that the recent "very great revolution" in architecture affected chiefly "the decorative and ornamental department."

333. Bolton, *Robert and James Adam,* I, pt. I, chap. iii.

334. Tipping, *English Homes,* Per. VI, vol. I, p. xv.

335. A. E. Richardson, *Monumental Classic Architecture,* p. 18.

336. Bolton, *Robert and James Adam,* I, 76–79.

337. *Ibid.,* II, 94; ill. p. 103.

338. Robert Adam, *The Works,* vol. II, pt. 5, pl. IV. Soane, *Lectures,* ed. Bolton, pl. 60. Bolton, *Robert and James Adam,* I, 31; II, 288. Swarbrick, *Robert Adam and his Brothers,* fig. 175. Swarbrick (p. 238) is right in asserting that "ancient precedent seems to have been a secondary consideration."

339. Robert Adam, *The Works,* vol. III, pls. 16, 17. Bolton, *Robert and James Adam,* I, ills. opp. pp. 82, 83.

340. Robert Adam, *The Works,* vol. I, pt. 3, pls. III, IV. Bolton, *Robert and James Adam,* I, 65ff., ills. pp. 68, 70. John Preston Neale, *Mansions of England* (London, 1847), I, first plate.

341. Robert Adam, *The Works,* vol. I, pt. 3, pl. V. Bolton, *Robert and James Adam,* I, ill. p. 71.

342. Robert Adam, *The Works,* vol. II, pt. 5, pls. I–III. Bolton, *Robert and James Adam,* II, ills. pp. 146, 153–155, with the date 1776; plan, p. 148.

343. Bolton, *Robert and James Adam,* I, 50; ills. pp. 41, 42.

344. *Ibid.,* I, 97, ills. p. 91; II, 263 ff., ills. pp. 264, 266, 268.

345. Tipping, *English Homes,* Per. VI, vol. I, fig. 181.

346. George Richardson, *The New Vitruvius Britannicus* (London, 1802–1808), I, pls. XLVII/XLVIII, XLIX/L. Bolton, *Robert and James Adam,* II, ills. pp. 198, 199.

347. Bolton, *Robert and James Adam,* II, 214, with ill., Charlotte Square. Robert Adam, *The Works,* vol. III, pl. 14; Bolton, *op. cit.,* II, 236, ills. pp. 237, 249 (University).

348. William Adam, *Vitruvius Scoticus* (Edinburgh, n.d.), pls. 13, 56, 58, 95, 115, 125, 160, in the sequence of my comments.

349. Tipping, *English Homes,* Per. VI, vol. I, p. 27; fig. 39.

350. A. E. Richardson, *Monumental Classic Architecture,* fig. 10, with date.

351. Tipping, *English Homes,* Per. IV, vol. II, fig. 57, with date.

352. A. E. Richardson, *Monumental Classic Architecture,* p. 14; fig. 9. *Introduction,* p. 53; ill. p. 187.

353. Woolfe and Gandon, *Vitruvius Britannicus,* IV, pl. 74. A. E. Richardson, *Introduction,* ill. p. 186.

354. Belcher and Macartney, *Later Renaissance Architecture,* I, 19; pl. XXX. A. E. Richardson, *Introduction,* ill. p. 198.

IV. THE SECOND CRISIS OF TRADITIONAL COMPOSITION

355. Tipping, *English Homes,* Per. VI, vol. I, fig. 435. Date, p. 276.

356. A. E. Richardson, *Monumental Classic Architecture,* pls. II, III; fig. 17.

357. Chambers, *a Treatise,* p. 8. Nikolaus Pevsner, "The Other Chambers," *Architectural Review* CI (1947), pp. 195–198, discusses Chambers's part in the introduction of the Oriental fashion.

358. Chambers, *Treatise,* p. 32.

359. Arthur Trystan Edwards, *Sir William Chambers* (London, 1924), pl. 33.

360. *Ibid.,* pl. 34.

361. Chambers, *Treatise,* p. 85; two plates (unnumbered). A. E. Richardson, *Monumental Classic Architecture,* pl. IX. *Introduction,* ill. p. 221. Sitwell, *British Architects* (3rd ed.)., fig. 135.

362. See p. 30, above.

363. Tipping, *English Homes,* Per. VI, vol. I, p. 347; figs. 532, 537.

364. See note 354, above.

365. Whiffen, *Stuart . . . Churches,* p. 59; fig. 78.

366. James Paine, *Plans, Elevations, and Sections, of Noblemen and Gentlemen's Houses* (London, 1767), pt. I, preface, p. ii.

367. Summerson, *Georgian London,* fig.

XXI. Middlesex Hospital also illustrated in Walter Harrison, *New and Universal History, A Description and Survey of the Cities of London and Westminster* (London, 1776), ill. foll. p. 53.

368. James Paine, *Plans, Elevations, Sections, and Other Ornaments of the Mansion-House, Belonging to the Corporation of Doncaster* (London, 1751), pls. VI, XX, "Banquetting Room." Richardson, *Introduction,* ills. p. 174 (façade), p. 175 (Ball Room).

369. Paine, *Gentlemen's Houses,* pt. I, pl. VIII/IX, Derwent Bridge; pl. X/XI, Trent Bridge.

370. *Ibid.,* pt. I, pls. XX/XXI, XXII.

371. *Ibid.,* pt. I, pl. XXVIII. Afterwards Melbourne, now Dover House, Whitehall.

372. *Ibid.,* pt. I, pl. XXXIX/XL.

373. *Ibid.,* pt. I, pls. LVIII, LIX. William Watts, *The Seats of the Nobility and Gentry* (Chelsea, 1779), pl. LXXVII, gives the date.

374. Paine, *Gentlemen's Houses* (1783), pt. II, pl. LXVII, plan, pl. LXV.

375. *Ibid.,* pt. I, pl. XXIX.

376. *Ibid.,* pt. I, pls. XLIII, XLIV/XLV, Stockeld Park; LIV/LV, Bywell. Prior to Paine. Burlington had designed a similar pattern of disconnected elements when he wanted to combine two gabled wings of the Jacobean mansion at Chiswick by a higher central part. See Wittkower, "Lord Burlington," pl. II, fig. 3.

377. William Hogarth, *The Analysis of Beauty* (London, 1753), chapter VIII.

378. John Piper, "The Gratuitous Semicircle," *Architectural Review* XCIV (1943) 112-113, points out and illustrates instances of semicircular windows, but disregards the patterns into which they combine with roundheaded windows or Palladian motifs.

379. A. E. Richardson, *Monumental Classic Architecture,* p. 28; pl. XV. Summerson, *Georgian London,* fig. XXXV. Helen Rosenau, "Dance the Younger," *Journal of the Royal Institute of British Architects* LIV (1947), 502-507, deals briefly with Newgate Prison.

380. Blomfield, *Renaissance Architecture,* II, 272.

381. A. E. Richardson, *Monumental Classic Architecture,* p. 29.

382. James Lewis, *Original Designs in Architecture* (2nd ed.; London, 1797), vol. I, pls. III, IV.

383. A. E. Richardson, *Monumental Classic Architecture,* fig. 23, pls. XI/XII, XIII. *Introduction,* ill. p. 218. Thomas J. Mulvany, *The Life of James Gandon* (Dublin, 1846), p. 14. Sitwell, *British Architects* (3rd ed.), fig. 143.

384. Woolfe and Gandon, *Vitruvius Britannicus,* V, pl. 74/75.

385. A. E. Richardson, *Monumental Classic Architecture,* fig. 28 (Four Courts), p. 26; fig. 26 (King's Inn). See James Malton, *A Picturesque and Descriptive View of the City of Dublin* (London, 1794), with aquatints.

386. John Preston Neale, *Views of the Seats of Noblemen and Gentlemen in England, Wales, Scotland and Ireland* (London, 1822), vol. VI, nos. 45 (Castlegar), 47 (St. Clerons), 59 (Bear Forest).

387. Jean-Baptiste Benoit Barjaud and Charles Paul Landon, *Description de Londres* (Paris, 1810), pl. 28. C. F. Partington, *Natural History and Views of London* (London, 1834), ill. opp. p. 21, named Melbourne House. Thomas H. Shepherd, *London in the 19th Century* (London, 1829), ill. opp. p. 146, Melbourne House.

388. A. E. Richardson, *Monumental Classic Architecture,* p. 35; figs. 37, 38. Summerson, *Georgian London,* fig. XXXIX. Dorothy Stroud, *Henry Holland* (London, 1950). Britton and Pugin, *Public Buildings of London,* II, 195.

389. Henry David Roberts, *A History of the Royal Pavilion, Brighton* (London, 1939), figs. 9, 10. G. Richardson, *New Vitruvius Britannicus,* I, 2; pls. VI, VII.

Semicylinders projecting from the corners show in George Richardson, *New Designs in Architecture* (London, 1792), pls. XXXII, Orangerie; XXXIX, Town residence, both projects. Holland's Wimbledon House, Surrey (1801, according to the *Dictionary of the A.P.S.*) presents a semicircular portico opposed to a blocklike mass. See A. E. Richardson and H. Donaldson Eberlein, *The Smaller English House of the Later Renaissance, 1660–1830* (London, 1925), fig. 28.

390. Thomas Rawlins, *Familiar Architecture* (London, 1768), pls. XVII, XLIV, XXXVIII, XLVI (cited in the sequence of my comments).

391. Eneas Mackenzie, *An Historical, Topographical, and Descriptive View of the County of Northumberland* (Newcastle-on-Tyne, 1825), II, frontispiece; and his *A Descriptive and Historical Account of Newcastle upon Tyne* (Newcastle, 1827), I, 302. Thomas Sopwith, *A Historical and Descriptive Account of All Saints'* (Newcastle, 1826), frontispiece. Plan, p. 95. Whiffen, *Stuart . . . Churches,* fig. 60; "St. Martin-in-the-Fields," ill. p. 5. The church had been badly damaged by fire when I saw it in 1947.

392. Charles Middleton, *Picturesque and Architectural Views for Cottages, Farm Houses and Country Villas* (London, 1793), pl. III, no. 10; pls. XI, XII, XIV.

393. Richard Elsam, *Essay on Rural Architecture* (London, 1803), p. 47; pls. 13, 15, 22, elevation, 23, plan, of Pettyward House.

394. G. Richardson, *New Vitruvius Britannicus,* I, 11; pls. XXXVI–XXXVIII, with the spelling Steuart. Neale, *Views,* V, no. 4, with ill. A. E. Richardson, *Introduction,* ill. p. 61.

395. G. Richardson, *New Vitruvius Britannicus,* II, 4; pl. XXVI.

396. The date is taken from a tablet above the entrance. Whiffen, *Stuart . . . Churches,* fig. 62.

397. Tipping, *English Homes,* Per. VI, vol. I, pp. 375, 379; figs. 575–577.

398. Walter Besant, *Survey of London* VI, *London in the Eighteenth Century* (London, 1903), ill. p. 178. Partington, *Views of London,* ill. opp. p. 157. Partington presents many lesser-known buildings of great interest. Shepherd, *London,* ill. opp. p. 80, King's Weigh House, Little Eastcheap.

V. ROMANTICISM AND REVIVALISM

399. Anthony Dale, *James Wyatt* (Oxford, 1936), pp. 28, 29, 118; ill. opp. p. 28. Neale, *Views* (2nd ser.; London, 1824), vol. I, with ill. (The copy used has no pagination). Reginald Turnor, *James Wyatt* (London, 1950), ill. p. 53.

400. Neale, *Views* (2nd ser.), vol. V, with

ill., Castle Coole; Dale, *James Wyatt,* pp. 82-84, 123; ill. opp. p. 82, Ashridge Castle.

401. Tipping, *English Homes,* Per. VI, vol. I, fig. 318. John Summerson, "James Wyatt," *From Anne to Victoria,* ed. Bonamy Dobrée (London, 1937), pp. 492–503.

402. Lees-Milne, *The Age of Adam,* fig. 152, shows only the main façade. G. Richardson, *New Vitruvius Britannicus,* II, pl. LXVI, plan.

403. Tipping, *English Homes,* Per. VI, vol. I, figs. 521 (north), 524 (south).

404. *Ibid.,* Per. VI, vol. I, fig. 527, plan.

405. Dale, *James Wyatt,* p. 111.

406. James Dallaway, *Anecdotes of the Arts in England; or Comparative Remarks on Architecture, Sculpture and Painting* (London, 1800), p. 117. Sitwell, *British Architects* (3rd ed.), fig. 173.

407. Dale, *James Wyatt,* pp. 46, 55, about the relationship between Wyatt and Carter. Incidentally, I regard as revolutionary designs only those aiming at new formal or compositional solutions, but not any whimsical accumulation of old features such as the project for a bridge over the Avon by a certain W. Bridges, with oddly shaped entrance buildings, dated 1793, *Journal of the Royal Institute of British Architects* XLV (1938), ill. p. 867.

408. John Carter, *The Builder's Magazine or Monthly Companion for Architects,* By a Society of Architects (London, 1774–1778), pls. XX, XXV, XXXIX, LXIV, LXXII, XCV, CXIV, CXXXVIII, CLII, CLV.

409. *Ibid.,* p. 7; pl. XIV, panels in Pompeian style.

410. *Ibid.,* p. 2.

411. *Ibid.,* pls. XIX, XXI, (Mausoleum), XXX, XLVIII (Insularium, LXXX (Villa Fennick), CXXII (Harmonic Pavilion), CLIV (Company's Hall).

412. *Ibid.,* pl. XXXV (Malt-house).

413. *Ibid.,* pl. XXXIX.

414. *Ibid.,* pl. CXIV (Printing house).

415. *Ibid.,* p. 27; pl. XLIX.

416. *Ibid.,* pl. LVIII.

417. *Ibid.,* pl. CXLIV.

418. *Ibid.,* pls. CLXXVII, CLXXX.

419. *Ibid.,* pls. LXXX, LXXXIII.

420. *Ibid.*, pl. LIX.

421. *Ibid.*, pl. CLI.

422. *Ibid.*, pl. CXLVIII.

423. *Ibid.*, pl. CXX.

424. *Ibid.*, pls. XXVII, XLII, LVII, CIII.

425. *Ibid.*, pp. XV, XXIII.

426. *Ibid.*, pls. LXXIII, XC.

427. *Ibid.*, pls. XLI, XLIV, CVI.

428. *Ibid.*, pls. CXXXVI, CXL.

429. *Ibid.*, pl. CLXVII.

430. *Ibid.*, pl. CXXXII.

431. *Ibid.*, pls. XXXVIII, LI, LXII, LXV, LXVI, CIV, CVIII, CX, CXIII, CXXVI, CXXX, CLX, CLXIII, CLXVIII, CLXXXI, CLXXXV.

432. John Carter, *Ancient Architecture of England* (London, 1795–1807); *Specimens of Gothic Architecture and Ancient Buildings in England* (London, 1824); etc.

433. William Robertson, *Designs in Architecture* (London, 1800), pls. 14 (Garden Seat), 20 (Mausoleum).

434. Arthur Thomas Bolton, *The Portrait of Sir John Soane* (London, 1927), pp. ix, x.

435. *Ibid.*, p. xvi. Cf. John Soane, *Designs for Public and Private Buildings* (London, 1828), p. 15. This is an augmented edition of *Designs for Public Improvements in London and Westminster* (London, 1827).

436. John Soane, *Description of the House and Museum on the North Side of Lincoln's-Inn-Fields, the Residence of John Soane* (London, 1830), pp. 30, 33, 40, 46, 52, 56. A more complete edition of the *Description* came out in 1835.

437. *The Works of Sir John Soane,* ed. Arthur Thomas Bolton (London, 1924), p. xxiv.

438. Soane, *Description* (1835), p. 10. Bolton, *Portrait*, p. 3.

439. Tipping, *English Homes*, Per. VI, vol. I, p. 339.

440. Harry Joseph Birnstingl, *Sir John Soane* (London, 1925), pl. 1.

441. A. E. Richardson, *Monumental Classic Architecture*, pl. XVIII.

442. *Ibid.*, pl. XIX.

443. *Ibid.*, pl. XVII, Lothbury angle. Birnstingl, *Sir John Soane*, pl. 5.

444. Arthur Thomas Bolton, *A Short Account of the Evolution of the Design of the Tivoli Corner of the Bank of England, Designed by Sir John Soane, 1804/5* [London, 1933], pp. 5, 6.

445. Soane, *Description* (1830), p. 15; (1835), p. 18.

446. *Ibid.* (1835), pl. XIII. In the engraving, *Designs for Public . . . Buildings,* pl. 4, the date 1822 is inscribed.

447. Soane, *Designs for Public . . . Buildings,* title page. Soane, *Works,* ed. Bolton, pp. xxxi, 1, 2, illustrating variants.

448. Soane, *Works,* ed. Bolton, p. 1. John Soane, *Sketches in Architecture, Containing Plans and Elevations of Cottages, Villas and Other Useful Buildings* (London, 1793), p. iv.

449. Soane, *Lectures,* ed. Bolton, Lect. VIII, p. 131.

450. Soane, *Description* (1835), p. 17. Dorothy Stroud, "Hyde Park Corner," *Architectural Review* CVI (1949), 397–399, with ills.

451. Soane, *Description* (1835), pl. XIII; *Designs for Public . . . Buildings,* pl. 4.

452. Soane, *Description* (1830), p. 32; (1835), p. 2, quotations from Marc Antoine Laugier, *Observations sur l'architecture* (The Hague, 1765), pp. v–xi, 152, 153.

453. Soane, *Sketches,* p. iv; pls. XXXVIII, elevation, XXXIX, plan. *Designs for Public . . . Buildings,* title page.

454. Bolton, *Portrait,* ill. opp. p. 22.

455. Soane, *Sketches,* pls. XL, Bellevue Building, XXX, hunting casino.

456. Bolton, *Portrait,* pp. 179, 413, 525.

457. Soane, *Lectures,* ed. Bolton, Lect. VIII, p. 131.

458. Soane, *Description* (1835), p. 8.

459. *Ibid.*, p. 26.

460. *Ibid.*, p. 34.

461. *Ibid.*, p. 25. John Britton, *The Union of Architecture, Sculpture and Painting Exemplified by a Series of Illustrations of the House and Galleries of John Soane* (London, 1827), illustrates the rooms and, p. 14, points out that the modernity of the internal arrangement is derived from "variety in the size and forms of rooms" and "striking views."

462. Soane, *Description* (1835), p. 26.

463. *Ibid.*

464. *Ibid.*, pl. IV.

465. *Ibid.*, pl. IV, dining room, library.

466. *Ibid.*, pl. VIII, dressing room.

467. *Ibid.*, pl. VII, study.

468. *Ibid.*, p. 15; pl. X, picture room.

469. *Ibid.*, p. 26; pl. XVIII.

470. *Ibid.*, p. 27.

471. *Ibid.*

472. These passages full of praise for Soane's work and his person may have been composed by Barbara Hofland. See Bolton, *Portrait*, p. 526.

473. Soane, *Description* (1830), p. 28.

474. *Ibid.*, p. 27.

475. Soane, *Designs for Public . . . Buildings*, pl. 26. Soane, *Works,* ed. Bolton, ills. pp. 103, 105.

476. Soane, *Lectures,* ed. Bolton, p. 118; pl. 55.

477. Soane, *Works,* ed. Bolton, ill. p. 71.

478. *Ibid.*, ill. p. 87.

479. *Ibid.*, ill. p. 88.

480. *Ibid.*, ill. p. 4.

481. *Ibid.*, ill. p. 23.

482. Soane, *Lectures,* ed. Bolton, Lect. VII, p. 114; similarly, Lect. VIII, p. 121.

483. *Ibid.*, Lect. XI, p. 174.

484. *Ibid.*, p. 175.

485. *Ibid.*, Lect. V, p. 90.

486. *Ibid.*, Lect. XI, p. 172.

487. John Soane, *Plans, Elevations, and Sections of Buildings Executed in the Counties of Norfolk, Suffolk, Yorkshire, Staffordshire, Warwickshire, Hertfordshire, et caetera* (London, 1788), p. 1.·

488. *Ibid.*, p. 8.

489. *Ibid.*, pl. 41.

490. *Ibid.*, pls. 7 (execution), 8 (entrance front as intended).

491. *Ibid.*, pl. 3 (Shottisham), 40 (Mottram).

492. Soane, *Sketches,* pls. XV, XVII, XVIII, XXII, XXVI, XXX.

493. John Soane, *Designs in Architecture* (London, 1778), pls. VIII, XII, XXII, XXIII, XXX. The *Dictionary of National Biography* says he later bought up and destroyed all copies that could be found of this earliest publication,

494. Soane, *Designs in Architecture,* pls. XVI, XIX, XXXV, XXXVII.

495. *Ibid.*, pls. XI, XXV, XXXIII.

496. Soane, *Works,* ed. Bolton, p. 20; ills. pp. 21, 22.

497. *Ibid.*, p. 83; ill. p. 85.

498. *Ibid.*, p. 16.

499. L'Abbé [Marc Antoine] Laugier *Essai sur l'architecture* (2nd ed.; Paris, 1755), p. 207.

500. Laugier, *Observations,* p. 186.

501. See p. 203, and Pt. III, note 621, below.

502. See pp. 6, 29, 50, above.

503. Soane, *Works,* ed. Bolton, ill. p. 22.

504. *Ibid.*, p. 83; ill. p. 85.

505. *Ibid.*, p. 93; ill. p. 89.

506. Soane, *Plans,* pls. 7, 8.

507. Soane, *Designs for Public . . . Buildings,* pl. 12. Soane, *Works,* ed. Bolton, ills. pp. 96, 100.

508. A. E. Richardson, *Monumental Classic Architecture,* p. 37, fig. 39. Donald Pilcher, *The Regency Style, 1800–1830* (London, 1948), fig. 71. Another noteworthy instance of consolidated architecture is the anonymous building at Cirencester, Gloucestershire, which now houses Lloyd's Bank (about 1780). See Horace Field and Michael Bunney, *English Domestic Architecture* (London, 1905), pl. XXII.

509. Soane, *Works,* ed. Bolton, ill. p. 27.

510. *Ibid.*, p. 128, with ill.

511. *Ibid.*, p. 130.

512. Birnstingl, *Sir John Soane,* pl. 23. Soane, *Description* (1830), pl. I.

513. Birnstingl, *Sir John Soane,* pls. 17, 19.

514. *Ibid.*, pl. 20.

515. *Ibid.*, pl. 29. Soane, *Works,* ed. Bolton, ills. pp. 76, 80.

516. Birnstingl, *Sir John Soane,* pls. 24, 25. Neale, *Views,* I, (1818), pl. 23, presents the original state of Tyringham House.

517. *Ibid.*, p. 19 .

518. T. G. Jackson, "The High Street of Oxford, and Brasenose College," *The Magazine of Art* XII (1889), 338; ill. p. 333.

519. I saw in the reform movement about 1900 a "Second Revolution" (*Von Ledoux bis Le Corbusier,* p. 50). Hans Sedlmayr, *Verlust der Mitte* (Salzburg, 1948), p. 102,

accepted both my concept and term, just as he accepted in this book to a very large extent my interpretations of the "First Revolution" in the eighteenth century.

520. Birnstingl, *Sir John Soane*, p. 20.
521. *Ibid.*, pl. 29.
522. *Ibid.*, p. 21. John Summerson, "The Case-History of a Personal Style," *Journal of the Royal Institute of British Architects* LVIII (1951), 88, remarks that Dulwich "with a greater freedom of proportion and a very striking freedom of composition . . . owes nothing to any building of Soane's time or of a considerable period previous to it."
523. Soane, *Works*, ed. Bolton, p. 79.
524. Soane, *Plans,* pl. 6.
525. *Ibid.*, pl. 14.
526. *Ibid.*, pl. 28.
527. *Ibid.*, pl. 38.
528. Soane, *Works,* ed. Bolton, p. 16; ills. pp. 21, 22.
529. *Ibid.*, ills. pp. 15, 16.
530. *Ibid.*, ill. p. 10. Birnstingl, *Sir John Soane,* pl. 25.
531. Soane, *Works,* ed. Bolton, ill. p. 24.
532. Soane, *Lectures,* ed. Bolton, pp. 5, 106, 107, 197.
533. *Ibid.*, Lect. VII, p. 114.
534. *Ibid.*, Lect. I, p. 16.
535. *Ibid.*, p. 21.
536. *Ibid.*, Lect. III, p. 44.
537. *Ibid.*, Lect. XI, p. 174.
538. *Ibid.*, Lect. III, p. 46.
539. *Ibid.*, Lect. XI, p. 167.
540. *Ibid.*, Lect. IX, p. 144.
541. *Ibid.*, Lect. II, p. 40. Bolton, in the 6th edition of the *Description* (Soane Museum Publications, no. 1, 1920), p. 54, refers to a certain "Father John." However, in my opinion, Soane fancied himself in the role of Padre Giovanni.
542. Soane, *Lectures,* ed. Bolton, Lect. VIII, p. 118; Lect. XI, pp. 166, 167.
543. *Ibid.*, p. 7.
544. *Ibid.*, Lect. XI, p. 173.

VI. THE END OF "SCHOLASTIC REGULARITY"

545. *Ibid.*, Lect. IV, p. 67; pl. 28.
546. *Ibid.*, Lect. IV, p. 70. Summerson, *Georgian London,* p. 239 (fig. LXXVI) de-

rives the lack of interrelationship from a "hasty decision." I see in it a stylistic symptom. Hughson, *London,* VI, ill. opp. p. 610.
547. Bolton, *Portrait,* p. 149.
548. The *Dictionary of Architecture,* Part XXII, R–S (Architectural Publication Society; London, 1887), p. 91: "Concrete was habitually and systematically used by Smirke; and to some extent cast iron in girders." Smirke's cubistic manner can be seen also in two little "Grecian" structures, St. George's, Brandon Hill, Bristol (1823) and the sepulchral church at Markham Clinton, Nottinghamshire (1833). See Whiffen, *Stuart . . . Churches,* figs. 101, 105.
549. Bolton, *Robert and James Adam,* vol. I, ill. p. 83.
550. Roberts, *Royal Pavilion,* fig. 9. Soane, *Plans,* pl. 8.
551. James Elmes, *Metropolitan Improvements* (London, 1828), ill. opp. p. 81. Partington, *Views of London,* ill. opp. p. 84. Summerson, *Georgian London,* fig. LXIII. Reginald Turnor, *Nineteenth-Century Architecture in Britain* (London, 1950), p. 26.
552. John Summerson, *John Nash* (London, 1935), p. 62, Casina, with ill. p. 97; pl. VI, Rockingham House.
553. Charles August Busby, *A Series of Designs for Villas and Country Houses* (London, 1808), p. 18; pls. 2, 16. Paul Reilly, *An Introduction to Regency Architecture* (New York, n.d.), ills. pp. 59, 60, Brighton houses. Cf. Antony Dale, *Fashionable Brighton* (London, 1947), pls. 4, 5.
554. Busby, *Series of Designs,* pp. 12, 13.
555. John Miller, *The Country Gentleman's Architect* (London, 1787).
556. John Crunden, *Convenient and Ornamental Architecture* (London, 1770). Summerson, *Georgian London,* p. 135. A. E. Richardson, *Introduction,* ill. p. 188.
557. Lightoler, *Gentleman and Farmer's Architect,* pls. 1–8.
558. David Laing, *Hints for Dwellings* (London, 1800), pls. 6, 27, 18, 26, diversified plans. C. Lovett Gill, *Regional Architecture of the West of England* (London, 1924), ill. opp. p. 77. *Plans, Elevations . . . of Buildings . . . Executed in Various Parts of England*

(London, 1818), pls. 52 (Devon villa), 17 (Customhouse). The latter is reproduced also in Richardson, *Monumental Classic Architecture,* fig. 54, *Introduction,* ill. p. 104; Britton and Pugin, *Public Buildings of London,* I, ill. opp. p. 53. Elmes, *Metropolitan Improvements,* ill. foll. p. 146, presents Smirke's alterations.

559. John Plaw, *Ferme Ornée, or Rural Improvements* (London, 1795), advertisement.

560. *Ibid.,* pls. 3, 7, 12.

561. *Ibid.,* pls. 5, 8, 11, 18, 20, 22, 28, 36.

562. *Ibid.,* pls. 6, 15, 24, 25, 27, 30, 34, 35.

563. *Ibid.,* pls. 16, 23, 24, 35.

564. *Ibid.,* pls. 18, 20, 22, 37.

565. *Ibid.,* pls. 14, 15.

566. Cf. Pt. III, notes 593, 845, below.

567. Plaw, *Ferme Ornée,* pl. 37.

568. *Ibid.,* pl. 32.

569. John Plaw, *Rural Architecture; or, Designs, from the Simple Cottage to the Decorated Villa* (2nd ed.; London, 1794).

570. *Ibid.,* pls. L, LI.

571. *Ibid.,* pls. XXV–XXX.

572. John Plaw, *Sketches for Country Houses, Villas and Rural Dwellings* (London, 1800), p. 3.

573. *Ibid.,* pls. 2, 8, 11, 13, 18, 19, 20, 21, 37, 38, 40, 41.

574. *Ibid.,* pl. 12.

575. *Ibid.,* p. 17; pl. 32.

576. *Ibid.,* pl. 40.

577. *Ibid.,* p. 3.

578. *Ibid.,* p. 5.

579. Summerson, *Georgian London,* p. 197.

580. Cf. p. 43, above. B. Sprague Allen, *Tides in English Taste, 1619–1800* (Cambridge, Mass., 1937), II, 231, adheres to the conventional view that the great change in eighteenth-century architecture consisted merely in a "revitalized classicism."

581. James Malton, *An Essay on British Cottage Architecture* (London, 1804 ed.), p. 19. His design no. 5, pl. 6, is an instance of "irregular forms"; his *Collection of Designs for Rural Retreats* (London, 1802) presents further significant specimens.

582. Robert Lugar, *Architectural Sketches, for Cottages, Rural Dwellings and Villas* (London, 1815), p. 3. Pilcher, *The Regency Style,* fig. 11, "An Ornamental Cottage."

583. Daniel Garret, *Designs and Estimates of Farmhouses* (London, 1747), introduction.

584. Joseph Gandy, *Designs for Cottages, Cottage Farms, and Other Rural Buildings; Including Entrance Gates and Lodges* (London, 1805).

585. See Dimitri Tselos, "Joseph Gandy, Prophet of Modern Architecture," *Magazine of Art* XXXIV (May 1941), pp. 251 ff.

586. Gandy, *Designs for Cottages,* pls. I, XIV, XVI, XVIII, XXII, XXIV, XXIX, XXXIV.

587. *Ibid.,* pls. XXV ("A Labourer's Cottage"), XXX ("A double Cottage"), XXXIX ("A circular single Lodge").

588. *Ibid.,* pl. XXXVI.

589. *Ibid.,* p. ix.

590. *Ibid.,* pls. XII, XIII, XXVIII, XXIX, XXX, XXXI, XXXII, XXXIV, XXXVII.

591. Joseph Gandy, *The Rural Architect* (London, 1806), pls. 9, 10, 11, 13, 14, 18, 20.

592. John Summerson, "The Strange Case of J. M. Gandy," *The Architect and Building News* CXLV (January 1936), 39, rightly rates Gandy as a "lesser architect." He traces his imaginative compositions (p. 41; ills. pp. 38, 39) back to "French designers such as Patte and Neufforge." I find great similarities to the designs in François de Cuvilliés *fils, Ecole de l'architecture bavaroise* (see Part III, note 328, below), such as pl. 24, "Jardin," by Caspert (?), pl. 88, "Commenderie," by Cuvilliés *fils,* pl. 121, "Avant-cour," by Cirillus J. Gasperi, pl. 152, "Palais" (anonymous). It would be a trying task to trace all the French and Italian sources, architectural as well as stage designs, which may have inspired Gandy's fantastic drawings, some of which are reproduced in John Summerson, *Heavenly Mansions* (New York. 1948), pls. XXXIII–XXXV.

593. Tipping, *English Homes,* Per. VI, vol. I, p. 326.

594. *Ibid.,* Per. VI, vol. I, pp. 321, 328; figs. 495–503. John Gage, *The History and Antiquities of Suffolk; Thingoe Hundred* (London, 1838), p. 304; ills. opp. pp. 304, 306.

595. Tipping, *English Homes,* Per. VI, vol.

I, p. 326. It matters little whether the plan of Ickworth was circular or elliptical. The chief characteristic of the house is the block-like form.

596. Plaw, *Rural Architecture*, pl. 26, plan; pls. 28, 29, elevations. See p. 64 above. Tipping does not mention Plaw's design.

597. Tipping, *English Homes*, Per. VI, vol. I, fig. 500, illustrates the plan of Ickworth.

598. William Fuller Pocock, *Architectural Designs for Rustic Cottages, Picturesque Dwellings, Villas, etc.* (London, 1807), pls. XXVI, plans, XXVII, elevation.

599. Lugar, *Architectural Sketches*, pl. XVI, Residence; *Villa Architecture* (London, 1828), pl. 29, Glenlee House.

600. Pilcher, *The Regency Style*, fig. 112, Grange Park. Peter Clarke, "James Burton," *Architectural Review* XC (1941), ill. p. 95, Double Villas. A. Beresford Pite, "The Work of William Wilkins," *Journal of the Royal Institute of British Architects* XL (1932), 127, describes Grange Park as the "ne plus ultra of English domestic Greek." Yet there were hardly any Greek models presenting, in addition to the front portico, lateral porticos seemingly emerging from the main mass.

601. Britton and Pugin, *Public Buildings of London*, vol. II, pls. 1, 2. Elmes, *Metropolitan Improvements*, p. 30; ill. foll. p. 48. Pilcher, *The Regency Style*, fig. 113.

602. Ronald P. Jones, "The Life and Work of Decimus Burton," *Architectural Review* XVII (1905), ill. p. 154. Humphry Ward, *History of the Athenaeum* (London, 1926), ill. opp. p. 36.

603. Elmes, *Metropolitan Improvements*, p. 101; ill. foll. p. 166. Summerson, *Georgian London*, fig. LIX. Cobb, *Old Churches*, fig. 5.

604. Elmes, *Metropolitan Improvements*, ill. opp. p. 125. Summerson, *Georgian London*, p. 220.

605. Elmes, *Metropolitan Improvements*, ill. opp. p. 110. Summerson, *Georgian London*, fig. LXXII.

606. Elmes, *Metropolitan Improvements*, ills. foll. pp. 96, 98, 110, 112.

607. Elmes, *Metropolitan Improvements*, ill. opp. p. 148, inscribed, Italian Opera House,

Haymarket. Summerson, *John Nash*, p. 216.

608. Summerson, *Georgian London*, p. 198.

609. G. Richardson, *New Vitruvius Britannicus*, II, pl. LXIV.

610. Elmes, *Metropolitan Improvements*, ill. opp. p. 163. Summerson, *John Nash*, p. 286.

611. Elmes, *Metropolitan Improvements*, ill. opp. p. 97. Summerson, *John Nash*, p. 285; pl. XV. Cobb, *Old Churches*, pl. XIX.

612. Pilcher, *The Regency Style*, end vignette. The quotation is from Summerson, *John Nash*, p. 227.

613. Summerson, *John Nash*, p. 72, plan, pl. III, elevation of Cronkhill house; pp. 235, 236; pl. XVI, Buckingham Palace.

614. Samuel H. Brooks, *Designs for Cottage and Villa Architecture* (London, 1840), p. viii.

615. G. Richardson, *New Vitruvius Britannicus*, II, pl. LXI.

616. See note 581, above.

617. See Emil Kaufmann, "Die Wandlung der Bildform bei Waldmüller," *Zeitschrift für Bildende Kunst* LXIV (1930), 209–216.

618. Francis Goodwin, *Rural Architecture* (2nd ed.; London, 1835), vol. II, ser. II, pl. 21, design 11 (Gothic Villa); pl. 29, design 13 (Italian Villa).

619. The same illustrations in Francis Goodwin, *Domestic Architecture* (2nd ed.; London, 1843).

620. See the maps in Elmes, *Metropolitan Improvements*, opp. p. 19; Summerson, *John Nash*, opp. p. 288; *Georgian London*, fig. 25. "The Regent's Park Terraces," *Country Life* CXIX (1946), pp. 250 ff., with map and ills.

621. Elmes, *Metropolitan Improvements*, p. 48; ill. foll. p. 48; Britton and Pugin, *Public Buildings of London*, vol. II, ill. opp. p. 234, name Nash as the architect; Summerson, *John Nash*, p. 191, names J. M. Aitkens as the builder. According to Ulrich Thieme and Felix Becker, *Allgemeines Lexikon der bildenden Künstler* (Leipzig, 1908), Aitkens exhibited a painting of Hanover Terrace in 1824. (This book will be referred to hereafter as "Thieme-Becker, *Künstlerlexikon*.")

622. Elmes, *Metropolitan Improvements*, p.

46; ill. opp. p. 50. Summerson, *John Nash*, p. 189; *Georgian London*, p. 166.

623. Elmes, *Metropolitan Improvements*, p. 48; ill. foll. p. 48. Elmes's view was shared by Summerson, in *John Nash*, p. 191. Britton and Pugin, *Public Buildings of London*, II, 233; ill. opp. p. 234.

624. Elmes, *Metropolitan Improvements*, p. 46; ill. opp. p. 50. Britton and Pugin, *Public Buildings of London*, II, ill. opp. p. 234. Summerson, *John Nash*, p. 189.

625. Elmes, *Metropolitan Improvements*, pp. 47, 48; ill. opp. p. 48. Summerson, *John Nash*, p. 190; pl. XI.

626. Elmes, *Metropolitan Improvements*, ill. opp. p. 24. Summerson, *John Nash*, p. 187; pl. XI.

627. Elmes, *Metropolitan Improvements*, p. 45; ill. opp. p. 24.

628. *Ibid.*, p. 68, without naming the architect; ill. opp. p. 98. Britton and Pugin, *Public Buildings of London*, II, 231. Summerson, *John Nash*, p. 197.

629. R. P. Jones, "Decimus Burton," ill. p.

113. Elmes, *Metropolitan Improvements*, ill. opp. p. 47, presents it as executed.

630. Elmes, *Metropolitan Improvements*, p. 79, not naming the architect; ill. opp. p. 27.

631. Summerson, *John Nash*, p. 195.

632. Elmes, *Metropolitan Improvements*, p. 23; ill. foll. p. 22. Summerson, *John Nash*, ill. p. 194. Sitwell, *British Architects* (3rd ed.), fig. 192. Pilcher, *The Regency Style*, fig. 135. The *Dictionary of National Biography*, under James Thomson, says he was the architect of Cumberland Terrace. See Summerson, *John Nash*, p. 195.

633. Elmes, *Metropolitan Improvements*, p. 67; ill. opp. p. 67. Summerson, *John Nash*, p. 196; *Georgian London*, frontispiece, with the name of Nash. Sitwell, *British Architects* (3rd ed.), fig. 193. Pilcher, *The Regency Style*, fig. 128.

634. See p. 24 and note 204, above.

635. Pilcher, *The Regency Style*, fig. 52. Reilly, *Introduction to Regency Architecture*, ill. p. 60.

PART TWO: ITALY

VII. THE ARCHITECTURAL SYSTEM OF THE RENAISSANCE AND THE BAROQUE

1. Wilhelm Bode, *Die Kunst der Frührenaissance in Italien* (Berlin, 1923), p. 42: "Daher bringt die Renaissance der Architektur im Quattrocento keine wirklich neue Kunst."

2. *Ibid.*, p. 43: "der wahre Schöpfer der Renaissancebaukunst."

3. *Ibid.*, p. 43.

4. William James Anderson, *The Architecture of the Renaissance in Italy* (3rd ed.; London, 1901), p. 17; pl. V.

5. *Ibid.*, p. 18.

6. *Ibid.*, p. 20.

7. Hans Willich, *Die Baukunst der Renaissance in Italien bis zum Tode Michelangelo's* (Berlin, 1914), p. 17ff.

8. August Schmarsow, *Gotik in der Renaissance* (Stuttgart, 1921), pp. 10, 30, 32. Julius Baum, *Baukunst und dekorative Plastik der Frührenaissance in Italien* (Stuttgart, 1920), p. XXV, plan.

9. Georgii K. Lukomski, *I maestri della architettura classica da Vitruvio allo Scamozzi* (Milan, 1933), p. 15.

10. Baum, *Baukunst und dekorative Plastik*, p. XXIV: "Renaissance . . . der anthropozentrischen Gestaltung im ganzen . . . Klarheit . . . Grossartigkeit . . . Einfachheit."

11. Charles Herbert Moore, *Character of Renaissance Architecture* (New York, 1905), p. 29.

12. Paul Schubring, *Die Architektur der italienischen Frührenaissance* (Munich, 1923), p. 22.

13. Moore, *Renaissance Architecture*, p. 31.

14. Carl Stegmann and Heinrich Gey-müller, *The Architecture of the Renaissance in Tuscany.* American edition, with a preface by Guy Lowell (New York, n. d.), vol. I, p. vi. Paul Frankl, *Die Renaissancearchitektur in Italien* (Leipzig, 1912), p. 3: "im ganzen stand Brunelleschi zur Tradition ablennend, ja Feindlich."

15. Adolfo Venturi, *Storia dell'arte italiana* (Milan, 1923), VIII, I, 96. Venturi is interested chiefly in the single features, the façades and the architectural bodies, but illustrates only a very few plans.

16. Cf. Part I, pp. 11-12, about the principles of the Baroque system.

17. Venturi, *Storia dell'arte,* VIII, I, fig. 54. Stegmann and Geymüller, *Architecture of the Renaissance,* ill. I, 7, plan and elevation.

18. C. Stegmann and H. Geymüller, *Die Architektur der Renaissance in Toskana* (Munich, 1885), I, 8.

19. *Ibid.,* I, 7.

20. Cornel Fabriczy, *Filippo Brunelleschi* (Stuttgart, 1892), p. 337: "Schon Brunelleschi wendet dort die Rustica . . . mit vollem künstlerischem Bewusstsein an; schon er stuft ihre Bossagen nach den Stockwerken ab." Willich, *Baukunst der Renaissance,* pl. VI. Venturi, *Storia dell'arte* VIII, I, fig. 98. The problem of authorship cannot be discussed here.

21. Willich, *Baukunst der Renaissance,* pl. II.

22. *Ibid.,* fig. 28. Baum, *Baukunst und dekorative Plastik,* ill. p. XXV, section, p. I, view.

23. Willich, *Baukunst der Renaissance,* p. 22: "Der frühe Stil, der von antiken Formen sich fast unabhängig hielt . . ."

24. Paul Zucker, *Die Baukunst der Renaissance in Italien* (Berlin, n. d.), II, 253, in dealing with some later works, uses the meaningful term "Verspannung."

25. Baum, *Baukunst und dekorative Plastik,* ills. pp. 72, 73, 74, Venturi, *Storia dell'arte,* VIII, I, figs. 111, 345, 712.

26. Baum, *Baukunst und dekorative Plastik,* ills. pp. 66, 68, 69. Venturi, *Storia dell'arte,* VIII, I, figs. 183, 281, 307.

27. Willich, *Baukunst der Renaissance,* p. 95. Baum, *Baukunst und dekorative Plastik,* p. XXI; ills. p. XVII (exterior), p. 119 (courtyard).

28. Baum, *Baukunst und dekorative Plastik,* ill. p. 29. Venturi, *Storia dell'arte,* VIII, II, fig. 578.

29. Baum, *Baukunst und dekorative Plastik,* ill. p. 36. Venturi, *Storia dell'arte,* VIII, II, fig. 514.

30. Zucker, *Baukunst der Renaissance,* fig. 188. Venturi, *Storia dell'arte,* XI, I, fig. 332. Corrado Ricci, *Architecture and Decorative Sculpture of the High and Late Renaissance in Italy* (New York, n.d.), fig. 60, Farnesina. Zucker, *Baukunst der Renaissance,* fig. 227. Ricci, *Renaissance,* fig. 148. Venturi, *Storia dell'arte,* XI, II, fig. 664, Caprarola.

31. Ricci, *Renaissance,* fig. 116. Venturi, *Storia dell'arte,* XI, II, figs. 62, 76.

32. *Enciclopedia Italiana,* XXVI, pl. XXXVII.

33. Erwin Panofsky, "Zwei Fassadenentwürfe des Dom. Beccafumi und das Problem des Manierismus in der Architektur," *Städel Jahrbuch* VI (1930), 70, points out the continuity and consistency of the development from the Renaissance to the early Baroque. About Mannerism as an architectural style, see Erwin Panofsky, *Idea* (Leipzig, 1924), pp. 39f. Ernst Michalski, "Problem des Manierismus in der italienischen Architektur," *Zeitschrift für Kunstgeschichte* II (1933), 88f., Hans Hoffman, *Hochrenaissance, Manierismus, Frühbarock* (Zurich, 1938). Nikolaus Pevsner, "Architecture of Mannerism," *The Mint* I (1946), 116–138. Richard Zürcher, *Stilprobleme der italienischen Baukunst des Cinquecento* (Basel, 1947). Anthony Blunt, "Mannerism in Architecture," *Journal of the Royal Institute of British Architects* LVI (1949), 195–201. Colin Rowe, "Mannerism and Modern Architecture," *Architectural Review* CVII (May 1950), 289–299. Here I may add that Vasari's Uffizi Palace at Florence, the most widely known example of Manneristic architecture, contains a novel type of staircase with three parallel arms, two ascending to a landing, the central third continuing upwards

in the opposite direction. Some authors believe this type to be a Spanish invention.

34. Baum, *Baukunst und dekorative Plastik*, ill. p. 84. Venturi, *Storia dell'arte*, XI, I, fig. 760.

35. Ricci, *Renaissance*, fig. 275. Zucker, *Baukunst der Renaissance*, fig. 270.

36. Ricci, *Renaissance*, fig. 277. Zucker, *Baukunst der Renaissance*, fig. 271.

37. Corrado Ricci, *Architettura barocca in Italia* (Stuttgart, n.d.), ill. p. 122. Albert Erich Brinckmann, *Die Baukunst des 17. und 18. Jahrhunderts in den romanischen Ländern* (Berlin, n.d.), fig. 82. Timon Henricus Fokker, *Roman Baroque Art* (Oxford, 1938), fig. 138.

38. Ricci, *Architettura barocca*, ill. p. 140. Brinckmann, *17. und 18. Jahrhundert*, fig. 129.

39. Cornelius Gurlitt, *Geschichte des Barockstiles in Italien* (Stuttgart, 1887), fig. 31. Ricci, *Renaissance*, fig. 166.

40. Ricci, *Architettura barocca*, ill. p. 14. Brinckmann, *17. und 18. Jahrhundert*, fig. 144. Fokker, *Roman Baroque Art*, fig. 215.

41. Ricci, *Architettura barocca*, ill. p. 33. Brinckmann, *17. und 18. Jahrhundert*, fig. 148. Fokker, *Roman Baroque Art*, fig. 226.

42. Baum, *Baukunst und dekorative Plastik*, ill. p. 23.

43. Ricci, *Architettura barocca*, ill. p. 30.

44. Gurlitt, *Barockstil in Italien*, fig. 150. Brinckmann, *17. und 18. Jahrhundert*, fig. 120.

45. Gurlitt, *Barockstil in Italien*, fig. 182. Werner Weisbach, *Die Kunst des Barock* (Berlin, 1924), ill. p. 146. Cf. Wolfgang Born, "Spiral Towers in Europe," *Gazette des Beaux-Arts*, ser. 6, vol. 24, pp. 233–248.

46. Ricci, *Renaissance*, fig. 164. Venturi, *Storia dell'arte*, XI, II, fig. 724.

47. Baum, *Baukunst und dekorative Plastik*, ill. p. 65. Willich, *Baukunst der Renaissance*, pl. VI. Venturi, *Storia dell'arte*, VIII, I, fig. 98.

48. Gurlitt, *Barockstil in Italien*, p. 82. Brinckmann, *17. und 18. Jahrhundert*, p. 33; fig. 8. Ricci, *Renaissance*, fig. 84.

49. See Chapter VIII, below.

50. Baum, *Baukunst und dekorative Plastik*, ill. p. 19. Willich, *Baukunst der Renaissance*, p. 161, rightly remarks that the front of Santa Maria Nuova, Abbiate Grasso (fig. 177), has, basically, nothing in common with San Andrea at Mantua (fig. 92). Venturi, *Storia dell'arte*, VIII, I, fig. 149.

51. Willich, *Baukunst der Renaissance*, fig. 88. Venturi, *Storia dell'arte*, VIII, I, fig. 135.

52. See note 39, above.

53. Ricci, *Architettura barocca*, ill. p. 6.

54. *Ibid.*, ill. p. 9.

55. *Ibid.*, ill. p. 33. Fokker, *Roman Baroque Art*, fig. 226.

56. Ricci, *Renaissance*, fig. 54. Venturi, *Storia dell'arte*, XI, I, fig. 286.

57. Willich, *Baukunst der Renaissance*, fig. 169.

58. Gurlitt, *Barockstil in Italien*, figs. 208, plan, 209. Ricci, *Architettura barocca*, ill. p. 26. Brinckmann, *17. und 18. Jahrhundert*, figs. 125, 126.

59. Willich, *Baukunst der Renaissance*, p. 29; fig. 29. Bode, *Kunst der Frührenaissance*, p. 45. Venturi, *Storia dell'arte*, VIII, I, 106; fig. 60.

60. Zucker, *Baukunst der Renaissance*, fig. 200, plan, pl. XII, perspective view. Venturi, *Storia dell'arte*, VIII, I, fig. 299.

61. Gurlitt, *Barockstil in Italien*, fig. 64. Ricci, *Architettura barocca*, ill. p. 8.

62. Zucker, *Baukunst der Renaissance*, pp. 194ff.; figs. 208, 209. Baum, *Baukunst und dekorative Plastik*, ills. pp. xxix, 6, 7. Ricci, *Renaissance*, fig. 37. Venturi, *Storia dell'arte*, XI, I, fig. 800.

63. Zucker, *Baukunst der Renaissance*, p. 178.

64. Gurlitt, *Barockstil in Italien*, p. 309; fig. 124. Ricci, *Architettura barocca*, ills. pp. 11, 39 (interior).

65. Zucker, *Baukunst der Renaissance*, figs. 203, 204 (plan). Baum, *Baukunst und dekorative Plastik*, ill. p. 106. Venturi, *Storia dell'arte*, VIII, I, fig. 316.

66. *Enciclopedia Italiana*, XXVI (1935), pl. XXXVIII.

67. Gurlitt, *Barockstil in Italien*, fig. 146; p. 359: "Seitlich ist ein übereck stehender Turm angefügt, der in keiner Linie mit der

Fassade stimmt, so dass an ihm sich die Pro-
file hart und unkünstlerisch totlaufen." Ricci,
Architettura barocca, ill. p. 14. Fokker,
Roman Baroque Art, figs. 109 (plan), 215.

68. Gurlitt, *Barockstil in Italien,* fig. 155.
Ricci, *Architettura barocca,* ill. p. 18. Brinckmann, *17. und 18. Jahrhundert,* fig. 119. Fokker, *Roman Baroque Art,* figs. 152 (plan),
153, Santa Maria della Pace; Ricci, *Architettura barocca,* ill. p. 22. Brinckmann, *17. und
18. Jahrhundert,* fig. 33 (plan). Fokker,
Roman Baroque Art, figs. 118 (plan), 223,
Sant'Andrea del Quirinale.

69. Ricci, *Architettura barocca,* ill. p. 21.
Enciclopedia Italiana, IV, pl. LXII.

70. Gurlitt, *Barockstil in Italien,* figs. 208
(plan), 209, pp. 513f. Ricci, *Architettura
barocca,* ill. p. 26. Brinckmann, *17. und 18.
Jahrhundert,* fig. 126.

71. In this stage there is no longer that
coalescence of the rooms of which Brinckmann, *17. und 18. Jahrhundert* (5th ed.),
pp. 76–79, speaks. Vincenzo Golzio, *Il seicento
e il settecento* (Turin, 1950), p. 10, plan.

VIII. ITALIAN THEORIES FROM
ALBERTI TO LODOLI

72. Otto Stein, *Die Architekturtheoretiker
der italienischen Renaissance* (Dissertation;
Karlsruhe, 1914), p. 61. Julius Schlosser, *Die
Kunstliteratur* (Vienna, 1924), pp. 112 ff.

73. *Antonio Averlino Filarete's Tractat über
die Baukunst nebst seinen Büchern von der
Zeichenkunst und den Bauten der Medici,* ed.
Wolfgang Oettingen (Vienna, 1896), p. 51.

74. *Ibid.,* p. 223.

75. *Ibid.,* pp. 56, 222, 259.

76. Michele Lazzaroni and Antonio Muñoz,
Filarete, scultore e architetto del secolo XV
(Rome, 1908), appendix with designs from
the Codex Magliabecchianus, pl. 3, fig. 2.

77. *Ibid.,* pl. 7, fig. 4. Filarete (ed. Oettingen), ill. p. 369.

78. Lazzaroni and Muñoz, *Filarete,* pl. 12,
fig. 6. Filarete (ed. Oettingen), ill. p. 465.

79. Filarete (ed. Oettingen), pp. 371, 381,
382.

80. Francesco Colonna, *Hypnerotomachia
Poliphili* (ed. princeps, 1499; facsimile ed.;

London, 1904), c II, recto. Similarly, c III,
verso: "disponere, & nell'animo definire" is
more important than the ornaments, "gli
quali sono accessorii al principale."

81. *Ibid.,* c II, r.

82. *Ibid.,* a VIII, r.

83. *Ibid.,* b II, v.

84. *Ibid.,* a VIII, v.

85. *Ibid.,* c II, r.

86. *Ibid.,* a VIII, v.

87. *Ibid.,* g VII, r.

88. *Ibid.,* n III, r.

89. *Ibid.,* n II, v.

90. *Ibid.,* n I, r.

91. *Ibid.,* c IIII, r.

92. Marcus Vitruvius Pollio, *De architectura
libri decem,* Bk. III, chap. I: "Namque non
potest aedes ulla sine symmetria atque proportione rationem habere compositionis, nisi
uti ad hominis bene figurati membrorum
habuerit exactam rationem."

93. Colonna, *Hypnerotomachia Poliphili,* c
VI, v.

94. *Ibid.,* n I, r.

95. Tommaso Temanza, *Vite dei più celebri
architetti, e scultori Veneziani che fiorirono
nel Secolo Decimosesto* (Venice, 1778), Vita
di Fra Francesco Colonna soprannominato
Polifilo, p. 23.

96. *Ibid.,* p. 1.

97. Colonna, *Hypnerotomachia Poliphili,* f
IIII, v.

98. Leone Battista Alberti, *De re aedificatoria libri decem* [1450], Bk. VI, chap. V. I
quote from *The Architecture of Leon Battista
Alberti in Ten Books,* translated into English
(from the annexed Italian edition of 1550 of
Cosimo Bartoli) by James Leoni (London,
1726), p. 8, v. The original Latin text puts
it more clearly: "accuratus in conponendo . . .
ordo et modus."

99. Alberti *De re aedificatoria,* Bk. IX,
chap. V. Alberti, trans. Leoni p. 85, r.

100. Alberti, *De re aedificatoria,* Bk. I, chap.
IX: ". . . inter se ita conveniant ut inde unum
integrum recteque constitutum corpus magis
quam divulsa et dissipata esse membra videan-
tur." Alberti, trans. Leoni, p. 12, r. Bartoli's
translation, "uno intero, e ben finito corpo"

(Andrea Palladio, I quattro libri dell'archi-tettura [Venice, 1570]) reappeared, twenty years later, in Palladio's *First Book* chap. I. See Part I, p. 36, note 205.

101. Alberti, *De re aedificatoria,* Bk. I, chap. IX. Alberti, trans. Leoni, p. 12, v.

102. Alberti, *De re aedificatoria,* Bk. VI, chap. V. Alberti, trans. Leoni, p. 8, r.

103. Alberti, *De re aedificatoria,* Bk. I, chap. IX: ". . . veluti in animante membra membris, ita in aedificio partes partibus re-spondeant, condecet." Alberti, trans. Leoni, p. 11, v.

104. Alberti, *De re aedificatoria,* Bk. IX, chap. V. Alberti, trans. Leoni, p. 84, r.

105. Alberti, *De re aedificatoria,* Bk. IX, chap. V. Alberti, trans. Leoni, p. 83, v. Bartoli translates "in congeriem et corpus" with "in una massa, & in un corpo."

106. Alberti, *De re aedificatoria,* Bk. IX, chap. VIII. Alberti, trans. Leoni, Bk. IX, chap. IX, p. 94, r. Bartoli translates "pariter colli-brabuntur" with "si bilanceranno."

107. Alberti, *De re aedificatoria,* Bk. I, chap. IX. Alberti, trans. Leoni, p. 12, r.

108. Alberti, *De re aedificatoria,* Bk. VI, chap. II. Alberti, trans. Leoni, p. 3, r. Simi-larly, Alberti, *De re aedificatoria,* Bk. IX, chap. V. Alberti, trans. Leoni, p. 84, v.

109. Alberti, *De re aedificatoria,* Bk. VI, chap. II. Alberti, trans. Leoni, p. 3, r.

110. Alberti, *De re aedificatoria,* Bk. I, chap. I. Alberti, trans. Leoni, p. 1, r. Bartoli's sympathy with Alberti's feeling comes forth in his translation: "Nè a il disegno in se istinto di seguitare la Materia . . ." The trans-lation of *lineamenta,* "Risse" (Leon Battista Alberti, *Zehn Bücher über die Baukunst,* ed. Max Theuer, (Vienna, 1912), seems too nar-row, as can be seen from the passage, 'we see that the same Design is in a Multitude of Buildings" (". . . eadem plurimis in edifi-ciis esse lineamenta sentimus.") Paul-Henri Michel, *La Pensée de L. B. Alberti* (Paris, 1930), p. 449f., takes *lineamentum* merely for "ground plan," although this meaning is insufficiently supported by his quotations.

111. Alberti, *De re aedificatoria,* Bk. I, chap. I, Alberti, trans. Leoni, p. 1 r.

112. Sebastiano Serlio, *Tutte le opere d'architettura,* ed. G. D. Scamozzi (Venice, 1584), III, 50: "tutte le cose che procedono ordinatamente, hanno un principale, & sol capo, dal quale dipendono gli altri inferiori." The wording of this passage supports my interpretation of Colonna's term *principe.* Cf. Chapter VIII, p. 90.

113. Sebastiano Serlio, *Extraordinario libro di architettura* (Lione, 1551). This book is inserted in *Tutte le opere* in place of the Sixth Book.

114. Serlio, *Tutte le opere,* IV, p. 148, v:: "Per esser parte nell'edificio lelegate con altre pietre." Other Italian architects applied rusti-cation to supports with the same intention, as did Ammanati in the courtyard of the Palazzo Pitti.

115. W. B. Dinsmoor, "The Literary Re-mains of Sebastiano Serlio," *Art Bulletin* XXIV (1942), 117.

116. Serlio, *Tutte le opere,* IV, 191, v.: "Non se conviene apertura alcuna che finga aria, o paesi: le quai cose vengono a rompere l'edificio."

117. Vincenzo Scamozzi, *L'idea della archi-tettura universale* (Venice, 1615), Bk. I, chap. II, p. 8: "L'ordine . . . è una regolata prece-denza, e sussequenza delle parti . . ."

118. *Ibid.:* "La venustà (da' Greci nominata Eurithmia) riguarda'l fine: & è un aspetto gratioso, e senza menda di tutto'l corpo: & una anessione, e proportione delle parti conueneuoli à tutto l'edificio . . ."

119. *Ibid.,* Bk. VI, chap. I, p. 2: "Questa voce ordine . . . nell'Architettura specialmente dinota un concerto, o componimento di varie cose proportionate e corrispondenti, & annesse insieme . . . perche tutte poste insieme fanno ordine intiero, e corpo, con le sue parti, e membra."

120. Guarino Guarini, *Architettura civile* (Opera postuma, ed. Bernardo Vittone; Turin, 1737), p. 87: "L'Architetto per ben ordinare i suoi disegni, non dovrà eccedere smoderata-mente in alcuna sua parte."

121. *Ibid.,* p. 5: "La bellezza delle Fab-briche consiste in una proporzionata con-venienza delle parti." In support of this state-

ment, Guarini refers to the passage from Vitruvius, *De architectura,* Bk. VI, chap. II, quoted in my text.

122. Guarini, *Architettura civile,* p. 6: "Per serbare le dovute proporzioni in apparenza, l'Architettura devesi partire dalle regole, e dalle vere proporzioni." Similarly, p. 157, about seemingly faulty proportions. Cf. Vitruvius, *De architectura,* Bk. III, chap. III, Bk. VI, chap. II.

123. Guarini, *Architettura civile,* p. 8.

124. *Ibid.,* p. 70: "non sia men ornata dell'altre parti."

125. *Ibid.,* p. 67. Cf. Palladio, *I Quattro Libri* Bk. I, chap. XXV: "sopra il vano sia il vano, e sopra il pieno sia il pieno."

126. Emil Kaufmann, "Die Architekturtheorie der französischen Klassik und des Klassizismus," Doctoral dissertation, *Repertorium für Kunstwissenschaft* LXIV (1924), p. 215.

127. Guarini, *Architettura civile,* p. 66.

128. *Ibid.,* p. 156: "Si legano in varie guise gli ordini; il primo, e più comune con pietre rustiche . . ." Serlio's Doors are mentioned, p. 157.

129. Guarino Guarini, *Dissegni d'architettura civile et ecclesiastica* (Turin, 1686), pls. 5, 10, 13, 15 (San Filippo), 27.

130. Cf. Chapter VIII, p. 90.

131. Guarini, *Architettura civile,* p. 3: "L'Architettura è un'Arte adulatrice, che non vuole punto per la ragione disgustare il senso . . ."

132. Cf. Joseph Michaud, *Biographie universelle* (Paris, n.d.), XXV. *Enciclopedia Italiana,* XXI. Schlosser, *Die Kunstliteratur,* p. 578. Michele de Benedetti, "Un precursore dell'architettura funzionale nel settecento," Abstract in *Actes du 12° Congrès internationale d'histoire de l'art, Bruxelles, 1930,* I, 225. Maria Luisa Gengaro, "Il valore dell'architettura nella teoria settecentesca del Padre Carlo Lodoli", *L'Arte* (1937), pp. 313–317. P. M. Bardi, "Il Socrate dell'architettura," *Stile* (June 1943), pp. 5–11. Emil Kaufmann, "Algarotti vs. Lodoli," *Journal of the American Society of Architectural Historians* IV (April 1944), 23–29. Annamaria Gabrielli,

"La teoria architettonica di Carlo Lodoli," *Arti Figurative* I (1945), 123–137. Massimo Petrocchi, *Razionalismo architettonico e razionalismo storiografico* (Rome, 1947), pp. 19–24.

133. Andrea Memmo, *Elementi dell'architettura lodoliana; osia l'arte del fabbricare con solidità scientifica e con eleganza non capricciosa* (Rome, 1786).

134. Francesco Conte Algarotti, "Saggio sopra l'architettura," (1756), in *Opere* (Leghorn, 1764), II, 53. Giuseppe Antonio Monaldini, *Vite de' più celebri architetti* (Rome, 1768), exploits Algarotti's exposition of Lodoli's theory.

135. Franceso Conte Algarotti, "Lettere sopra l'architettura," 1742–1763, in *Opere* (Leghorn, 1765), VI, 171–278.

136. Algarotti, "Saggio," p. 51: "E come è della natura sua (dello spirito filosofico) ricercare addentro le ragioni prime e investire i principj delle cose, ha preso a sottilmente esaminare i fondamenti dell'arte del fabbricare, e finalmente ha proposto quistioni, che non tendono a nulla meno che ad iscalzargli, e a mostrare ch'ella posa in falso."

137. *Ibid.,* p. 52: "Autore di tal novità è un Filosofo [in a footnote, Algarotti adds, "Il Padre Fra Carlo Lodoli"], da cui tanto più ha da temere la dottrina di Vitruvio, quanto che feconda d'immagini ha la fantasia, ha un certo suo modo di ragionare robusto insieme e accomodato alla moltitudine."

138. *Ibid.,* p. 62. Similarly, "Lettere," p. 209.

139. Algarotti, 'Saggio," p. 61.

140. *Ibid.,* p. 62.

141. *Ibid.,* p. 65.

142. *Ibid.,* p. 66.

143. *Ibid.,* p. 66: "Ed ecco il forte argomento, l'ariete del Filosofo, con che egli urta impetuosamente, e quasi d'un colpo tutta la moderna intende di rovesciare, e la antica Architettura."

144. *Ibid.,* p. 53: "Ora per render conto a me medesimo di una così importante quistione, ho brevemente disteso la somma degli argomenti che soglionsi da lui proporre, e

quasi lanciare contro all'Architettura, e insieme le soluzioni che vi ho credute le più convenienti."

145. *Ibid.,* p. 65: "una troppo terribile conseguenza . . . di dover condannare . . . tutti insieme gli edifizj così moderni come antichi, e quelli singolarmente che hanno il maggior vanto di bellezza, e sono decantati come gli esemplari dell'arte."

146. *Ibid.,* p. 65: "Di pietra sono essi fabbricati; e mostrano essere di legname . . . Perchè ragione la pietra non rappresenta ella la pietra, il legno il legno, ogni materia se medesima, e non altra?"

147. *Ibid.,* p. 66: "Niente vi ha di più assurdo, egli [Lodoli] aggiugne, quanto il far sì, che una materia non significhi se stessa, ma ne debba significare un'altra. Cotesto è un porre la maschera, anzi un continuo mentire che tu fai."

148. Palladio, *I Quattro libri,* Bk. I, chap. XX: "l'Architettura imitatrice della Natura."

149. Vitruvius, *De architectura,* Bk. II, chap. I.

150. Algarotti, "Saggio," p. 82: "la ossatura della capanna."

151. *Ibid.,* p. 82: "quelle braccia che formano le arcate del ponte."

152. *Ibid.,* p. 77: "I capitelli vi fanno come una testa." Here also, "Le base fanno un piede alla colonna."

153. *Ibid.,* p. 72: "Quella [materia—il legno] che potea somministrar loro un maggior numero di modanature, di modificazioni, e di ornati, che qualunque altra." P. 75: "Talmente che se la pietra vuol essere nelle fabbriche armonicamente tagliata scolpita e disposta; pigliar le conviene come ad imprestito gli ornamenti e le forme dal legno."

154. *Ibid.,* p. 91. Cf. Torquato Tasso, *Gerusalemme liberata,* II, 1592.

155. Algarotti, "Lettere," p. 210: "Gli ornamenti nell'Architettura hanno da abbellire la fabbrica, e mostrare insieme le parti essenziali, la ossatura di essa." According to Algarotti, the construction is not expected to speak for itself, but through the ornaments as its interpreters.

156. Algarotti, "Saggio," p. 60: "Dalle vane

diciture, per così esprimersi, e dalle fallacie dei Sofisti, intende di purgar l'Architettura."

157. Algarotti, "Lettere," p. 209: "cotesti rigoristi."

158. Algarotti, "Saggio," p. 59.

159. Algarotti, "Lettere," p. 182: "non istarvene all'autorità."

160. Algarotti, "Saggio," p. 58: "di bere ai purissimi fonti dei Greci."

161. *Ibid.,* p. 57.

162. Algarotti, "Lettere," p. 194.

163. Andrea Memmo, *Elementi d'architettura Lodoliana, ossia l'arte del fabbricare con solidità scientifica e con eleganza non capricciosa* (Zara, 1833), I, 34: "intorno l'architettura combatteva contro tutti."

164. *Ibid.,* I, 133, 151, 310.

165. *Ibid.,* I, 14, 169–175, 342.

166. *Ibid.,* I, 253–256, 261; II, 91, 92.

167. *Ibid.,* I, 16. Cf. II, 35, on people who applaud "quello che approvava la prima capra che conduceva il gregge."

168. *Ibid.,* I, 21: "ridussero l'architettura ad arte plastica."

169. *Ibid.,* I, 14, quoting the Marchese Poleni: "Sa che io devo sostener Vitruvio, e che ho fatta sull'architettura la mia pubblica confessione."

170. *Ibid.,* II, 16: "originalissime parole Lodoliane." Cf. II, 59.

171. *Ibid.,* I, 84, 342; II, 92, a passage which might have been written in the twentieth century: "col di fuori dovrebbesì sempre . . . indicar il di dentro." ("The outside should be indicative of the interior disposition.")

172. *Ibid.,* I, 84.

173. *Ibid.,* I, 27, 291–295; II, 55, 57, 67, 68, 70, etc.

174. *Ibid.,* I, 28.

175. *Ibid.,* I, 29: 118, 370; II, 3, 50.

176. *Ibid.,* I, 27: "enunciava la sua dottrina con un entusiasmo che confinava molto col furore . . . Fermo a fronte della persecuzioni di quei del mestiere."

177. *Ibid.,* II, 166: "Al Lodoli bastava l'avere promosso il dubbio, che si potesse anche nell'architettura far meglio che non si fece nel passato." Angelo Uggeri, *Journées pittoresques. Des edifices de Rome ancienne*

(Rome, 1800), IV, pt. I, ii: "enfin on avoua que le P. Lodoli ait renfermé un principe fécond en conséquences dans ces deux mauvais vers: 'Debbonsi unir e fabbrica e ragione, E sia funzion a rappresentazione.' " Niccolò Carletti, *Istituzioni d'architettura civile* (Naples, 1772), shows how a conservative architect-writer was affected by Lodoli's thought.

178. The term "Romantic Classicism" was coined by Siegfried Giedion (*Spätbarocker und Romantischer Klassizismus*, Munich, 1922), and adopted by Fiske Kimball ("Romantic Classicism in Architecture," *Gazette des Beaux-Arts*, February 1944, pp. 95–112.)

179. Teofilo Gallaccini, *Trattato sopra gli errori degli architetti ora per la prima volta pubblicato . . . per Giambattista Pasquali* (Venice, 1767), p. 18: "I disegni son male ordinati . . . quando le membra, che debbono essere le principali, e le Signore dell'Arte, son fatte soggette." Gallaccini, p. 45, advocates, "continuazione degli ornamenti . . . legame delle parti infra loro, e col tutto, e . . . uniformità."

180. Antonio Visentini, *Osservazioni* (Venice, 1771), p. 1, defends unity; Pp. 25, 31, 75, praises *ragione*. Giambattista Passeri, da Pesaro, "Discorso della ragione dell'architettura," *Nuova raccolta d'opuscoli scientifici . . .* XXII (Venice, 1772), 12, 19, 63.

181. Brinckmann, *17 und 18. Jahrhundert*, p. 105: "Der Klassizist Milizia . . ." Konrad Escher, *Barock und Klassizismus* (Leipzig, 1910), p. 51: "einseitiger puritanischer Klassizismus."

182. Francesco Milizia, *The Lives of Celebrated Architects, Ancient and Modern*, trans. by Eliza Cresy (London, 1826), preface, p. XVI. "Vita di Francesco Milizia, scritta da lui medesimo," *Opere complete di Francesco Milizia* (Bologna, 1826), I, p. xxxiv: "Sono un ammasso di eterogeneo."

183. Milizia, *Opere complete*, I, p. vii ("Vita").

184. Milizia, *Lives*, introduction, p. lxxi. "Saggio di architettura." *Opere complete*, IX, 115.

185. Francesco Milizia, *Dizionario delle Arti*

del Disegno, estratto in gran parte dall'Enciclopedia metodica* (Bassano, 1797), I, 3.

186. *Ibid.*, I, 166. Here also: "L'ornamento ha distrutto l'Architettura."

187. Francesco Milizia, *Principj di architettura civile* (Finale, 1781–1800), I, 10: "profusione d'ornati"; I, 85: "ornati . . . alla rinfusa."

188. Milizia, *Dizionario*, I, 25: "Piedestalli sopra piedestalli, colonne e colonnette, pilastrini e pilastroni. . ."

189. *Ibid.*, I, 111.

190. *Ibid.*, I, 114.

191. Milizia, *Principj*, I, 43. I, 90: "la peste nell'Architettura."

192. Milizia, *Dizionario*, I, 110.

193. Milizia, *Principj*, I, 316: "Ordine . . . una serie di parti contigue di un medesimo tutto, ciascuna legata alle vicine . . ." I, 317: "Ma, o rotta, o non mai formata la catena, le cose . . . ci divengono incomprensibili. . ."

194. Milizia, *Dizionario*, II, 282: "Unità richiede che tutte le parti d'un opera qualunque si riferiscan all'oggetto principale, e formino insieme un tutto *unico, semplice, e solo*" (Milizia's italics). Cf. *Principj*, I, 318.

195. Milizia, *Dizionario*, I, 62: "Le parti debbono essere subordinate al tutto."

196. *Ibid.*, I, 48.

197. *Ibid.*, I, 172: "Per esser *chiaro*, bisogna . . . distinguer cosa da cosa, parte da parte, e mettervi un ordine che una cosa porti all'altra, e da una gradatamente si passi ad un altra parte." I, 272: "La *gradazione* mette accordo fra gli oggetti differenti." (All italics by Milizia.) The concept of the Baroque hierarchy shows also in the term "progressione crescente," *Principj*, I, 328.

198. Milizia, *Principj*, I, 318. *Dizionario*, I, 279.

199. Milizia, *Dizionario*, I, 174, on pictorial composition: "Si può anche con un solo gruppo luminoso fissar l'attenzione. E parimente si possono disporre varj gruppi di lume subordinati fra loro, che lascino dominare l'oggetto più interessante."

200. *Ibid.*, I, 225: "Economia . . . fare spiccar su tutte [le parti] la principale."

201. *Ibid.*, I, 12.

202. *Ibid.*, I, 142.

203. *Ibid.*, II, 282: "Sul cornicione d'una casa innalzar un altro appartamento, è far una casa sopra l'altra."

204. Francesco Milizia, *Dell'arte di vedere nelle belle arti del disegno* (2nd ed.; Venice, 1786). I quote from the reprint in *Opere complete*, I, 276: "E stupendo è tutto l'esteriore mastino e tagliato in tante parti."

205. *Ibid.*, I, 277: "È una facciata menzognera." Similarly, I, 295.

206. *Ibid.*, I, 274: "è aggiunto, e l'aggiunta non lega bene col corpo principale."

207. Ronald Bradbury, "The Romantic Theories of Architecture of the Nineteenth Century, in Germany, England, and France" (thesis, New York, 1934), p. 8.

208. Milizia, *Dizionario*, I, 63.

209. *Ibid.*, I, 87.

210. Milizia, *Principj*, I, 45.

211. *Ibid.*, I, 45. Cf. Francesco Milizia, *Roma delle belle arti del disegno*, (n. pl., 1792). Reprinted in *Opere complete*, I, 481.

212. Milizia, *Principj*, I, 163: "L'invenzione di un tal Ordine è impossibile."

213. *Ibid.*, p. 46: "la nostra gloria, sarebbe la mera, e servile imitazione."

214. Milizia *Dizionario*, I, 236: "La foresta de'contrafforti che circondan l'esterno dà idea disgustevole di edificj appuntellati, e mostra tanta timidità, quanto al di dentro spicca l'ardire . . ." See also *ibid.*, I, 270.

215. *Ibid.*, I, 266: "La natura non conosce euritmie, nè livellamenti, nè parterri, nè bacini, o canali regolari."

216. *Ibid.*, I, p. VII. *Principj*, I, 382: "simbolizzare il genere del monumento." Cf. *Dizionario*, I, 154, on "character." About *architecture parlante*, cf. Part III, p. 150, notes 78, 275.

217. Milizia, *Dizionario*, I, 272, "grandiosità, stile grande." I, 217, criticism of "piccole forme."

218. *Ibid.*, II, 110.

219. *Ibid.*, II, 268: "I nostri teatri sono una specie di alveari." Claude-Nicolas Ledoux, *L'Architecture considérée sous le rapport de l'art, des moeurs et de la législation* (Paris, 1804), p. 219, holds similar views.

220. Milizia, *Dizionario*, I, 252: "ogni ornamento nasca dal carattere dell' edificio."

221. *Ibid.*, I, 255: "Sobrietà e convenienza sono i due essenziali ingredienti della decorazione."

222. Milizia, *Principj*, I, 274.

223. Milizia, *Arte di vedere*, I, 273: "in architettura tutto ha da nascere dal necessario." Similarly, *Roma*, I, 300.

224. Milizia, *Arte di vedere*, I, 216: "Il diletto della vista . . . non è il loro [delle belle arti] scopo finale." Cf. Guarini's opposing view, Part II, note 131, above.

225. Milizia, *Principj*, I, 38: "Tutto quello, che si fa per mero ornamento, è vizioso."

226. Cf. the quotation, p. 96, above.

227. Milizia, "Saggio," *Opere complete*, IX, 20; *Principj*, I, 39; *Arte di vedere*, I, 266: "Quanto è in rappresentazione, dev'essere in funzione." Uggeri, *Journées pittoresques, loc. cit.*, says: "Milizia n'étoit que l'écho de ces prédécesseurs . . . Laugier, Frézier, Lodoli." However, Giuseppina Fontanesi, *Francesco Milizia* (Bologna, 1932), leaves out of account two most important factors in the formation of Milizia's views, for she is hardly acquainted with the French theories of the period and ignores Lodoli and the movement of the *rigoristi*. Giulio Natali, *Idee costumi uomini del settecento* (Turin, 1916), p. 241, likewise unfamiliar with the Lodolian doctrine, simply sees in Milizia "un enciclopedista classicista."

228. Milizia, *Principj*, I, 320: "Semplicità non consiste nella privazione degli ornati, altrimenti un muro schietto sarebbe il più bello."

229. *Ibid.*, I, 9, 260, 314; III, 396. *Dizionario*, I, 237.

230. Milizia, *Principj*, I, 41, 42.

231. *Ibid.*, I, 24: "V'è bisogno di principj certi, e costanti dedotti dalla natura stessa della cosa. . ."

232. Milizia, *Dizionario*, I, 220: "L'artista . . . libero dal giogo dell'autorità, non ha altro maestro che la sua ragione."

233. See *First Proofs of the Universal Catalogue of Books on Art* (London, 1870), II, 1375.

234. Milizia, *Dizionario*, I, 2: "Chi non ama la dolcezza?"

235. *Ibid.*, I, 166. *Principj*, I, 267, a reference to the praise of elementary forms, expressed in Robert Morris, *Lectures on Architecture* (London, 1734–1736).

236. Milizia, *Dizionario*, I, 275: "Quando . . . ne giudicarono non i filosofi, ma i ricchi, i cortigiani, i Re, l'arte andò giù. . ."

237. Milizia, *Arte di vedere*, I, 179, 192.

238. Milizia, *Roma*, I, 437.

239. *Ibid.*, I, 480: "Questa descrizione delle fabbriche romane è dalla Cloaca Massima alla sagrestia si S. Pietro: dall'ottimo al pessimo."

240. Milizia, *Opere complete*, I, pp. xxviii, xxx.

241. Milizia, *Dizionario*, I, 126: "Dall'eccesso suole derivare un rimedio al male. Si aspetta questa crisi salutare." *Roma*, I, 481: "Guarirà: speriamolo."

IX. GIAMBATTISTA PIRANESI

242. Henri Focillon, *Giovanni-Battista Piranesi* (Paris, 1918), p. 190.

243. *Ibid.*, pp. 286, 307.

244. Richard F. Bach, "Piranesi—Style Maker," *Architectural Forum* XXXIII (August 1920), 68: "His record was written in every country." Grahame B. Tubbs, "Piranesi," *Journal of the Royal Institute of British Architects* LV (1948), 310–313, presents a survey of the architect's life and work.

245. Giovanni Battista Piranesi, *Prima parte di architetture e prospettive* (Rome, 1743), republished in *Opere varie di architettura* (Rome, anno VII repubblicano), "Mausoleo antico," pl. 3 (Henri Focillon, *Giovanni-Battista Piranesi, Catalogue raisonné de son oeuvre*, Paris, 1918, no. 14). The "free" style shows in the frontispiece; "Carcere oscura," pl. 2; "Vestiggi d'antichi edificj," pl. 5; "Ruine di sepolcro antico," pl. 6; "Ara antica," pl. 7; "Camera sepolcrale," pl. 16 (Focillon, *Catalogue*, nos. 2, 4, 5, 6, 16, 18); and in *Capriccj*, in *Opere varie*, pls. 24-27 (Focillon, nos. 20-23). Albert Giesecke, *Giovanni Battista Piranesi* (Leipzig, 1912), discusses, p. 11, *Prima parte*, p. 75, *Capriccj*.

246. Emil Kaufmann, *Three Revolutionary Architects—Boullée, Ledoux and Lequeu, Transactions of the American Philosophical Society*, vol. 42 (1952), figs. 8-12, illustrates etchings by Le Geay.

247. Piranesi, *Opere varie*, pl. 22 (Focillon, *Catalogue*, no. 121).

248. *Carceri d'invenzione di G. B. Piranesi, archit. vene[ziano]* (n. pl., n.d.); (Focillon, *Catalogue*, p. 12, E).

249. Piranesi, *Carceri*, pl. IX. Helmuth T. Bossert, "Phantastische Architekturen und Piranesi," *Wasmuth's Monatshefte für Baukunst* V (1920-1921), ill. p. 29.

250. Focillon, *Piranesi*, p. 13.

251. Giovanni Battista Piranesi, *Le antichità romane* (Rome, 1756), vol. II, pl. II. Focillon, *Catalogue*, no. 225. Focillon overlooked the date 1756 inscribed on a tablet in the lower center of the engraving. Bossert, "Phantastische Architekturen," ill. p. 38.

252. Piranesi, *Antichità Romane*, vol. III, pl. II. Focillon, *Catalogue*, no. 287. Bossert, "Phantastische Architekturen," p. 37, reproduces an *état* with a dedication to Charlemont. Focillon, *Catalogue*, p. 63, A.

253. Piranesi, *Opere varie*, pls. 17 (Via Appia), 18 (Circus). Focillon, *Catalogue*, nos. 124, resp. 125. Both are also inserted in *Lettere di giustificazione scritte a Milord Charlemont* (Rome, 1757), pls. II, III.

254. Focillon, *Catalogue*, no. 225.

255. Giovanni Battista Piranesi, *Parere su l'architettura* (annexed to *Osservazioni*, Rome, 1765), p. 9.

256. *Ibid.*, p. 10.

257. *Ibid.*, p. 10: "impertinenti attributi dell'Architettura. . ."

258. *Ibid.*, p. 11.

259. *Ibid.*, p. 10: "le spirali, le storte, le inginocchiate."

260. *Ibid.*, p. 11. This view is expressed in an ironical tirade by the Master.

261. *Ibid.*, p. 10: "L'architettura comincerebbe a risorgere."

262. *Ibid.*, p. 12: "Gli ornamenti debbono nascere da ciò che costituisce l'Architettura." This view shows in the Master's words.

263. *Ibid.*, p. 12: "Voi. sareste tacciati d'una monotonia d'edifizj ugualmente odiata dalle

genti . . . diventereste ordinarj, ordinarissimi."

264. Cf. the quotation, p. 110, below.

265. Piranesi, *Parere,* p. 15.

266. *Ibid.,* p. 15: "Distingua ciò che dee far la figura principale, da ciò che dee far quella dell'accompagnamento . . . costituisca fra gli ornamenti, come si veggono nella natura, i gradi, le preminenze, il più e 'l meno dignitoso. . ." In this passage "nature" is called in to support the hierarchical order.

267. Giovanni Battista Piranesi, *Della magnificenza ed architettura de' romani* (Rome, 1761).

268. Piranesi, *Magnificenza,* p. lii: "Si deduce, quanto sia meglio nell'architettura, quando la necessità non richieda altrimenti, il servirsi di linee rette, e perpendicolari, in vece delle curve, e ravvolte, le quali, benchè il più delle volte soddisfacciano agli occhj, nondimeno egli è difficile, che possano usarsi senza scapito dell'Architettura, ed anche della verità." Similarly, p. LI.

269. *Ibid.,* p. lxxxi: "trascesosi una volta dal perpendicolo, e dalle linee definitive di ciascun membro, qual è quella cosa, che sul esempio dei Greci gli altri non han creduto di farsi lecita?"

270. *Ibid.,* p. lxxxi: "Piacesse al cielo, che questa licenza di mescolare una parte coll'altra, fosse restata in Grecia. Ma a poco a poco si è introdotta in Italia con gran depravazione dell'architettura, ed anco a' dì nostri."

271. *Ibid.,* p. lxxxi; "quell'impertinente giro di linee."

272. *Ibid.,* p. xliv: "Laonde i Toscani credettero di dovere andar parchi nell'adornare la loro architettura, come anche i Dori. . ."

273. *Ibid.,* p. xlii: "Tutle le arti sono imitazioni della natura . . . non dee certamente andarne esente l'architettura, la quale parimente è nata dal vero. . ."

274. *Ibid.,* p. xiii.

275. *Ibid.,* p. xix. Cf. the quotation from Milizia, Part. II, note 239, above.

276. Piranesi, *Magnificenza,* p. xxiv.

277. Focillon, *Catalogue,* no. 969.

278. Piranesi, *Parere,* p. 15.

279. *Ibid.,* pl. IX, reproduced by Bossert, "Phantastische Architekturen," p. 33.

280. Publius Terentius Afer, *Eunuchus,* ed. T. L. Papillon (Oxford, 1877), prologue. In the etching, *vas* should read *vos.*

281. Piranesi, *Opere varie,* pl. 18. Focillon, *Catalogue,* no. 126. Bossert, "Phantastische Architekturen," ill. p. 34. Nikolaus Pevsner and S. Lang, "Apollo or Baboon," *Architectural Review* CIV (1948), ill. p. 276.

282. Giovanni Battista Piranesi, *Diverse maniere d'adornare i cammini . . . con un ragionamento apologetico in difesa dell'architettura Egizia e Toscana* (Text in Italian, English, French; Rome, 1769), p. 5.

283. *Ibid.,* p. 5.

284. *Ibid.,* pls. 10, 14, 18, 21, 24, 26, 28, 32. Pl. 5 is reproduced in Bossert, "Phantastische Architekturen," p. 40.

285. Focillon, *Piranesi,* p. 282.

286. Piranesi, *Diverse maniere,* dedication.

287. *Ibid.,* Ragionamento, p. 35.

288. *Ibid.,* pls. 45, 46. Pl. 45 is illustrated in Bossert, "Phantastisches Architekturen," p. 41.

289. Focillon, *Piranesi,* p. 68.

290. Piranesi, *Parere,* p. 13: "Sig. Adams [sic] . . . uno de'più giudiziosi Architetti de' tempi nostri."

291. Werner Koerte, "G. B. Piranesi als praktischer Architekt," *Zeitschrift für Kunstgeschichte* II (1933), fig. 4; p. 22: ". . . lauter Fragmente im gegenständlichen, lauter zerhackte Splitter im formalen Sinne, denen jegliche ornamentale Verbindung untereinander fehlt. . ."

292. *Ibid.,* fig. 5; p. 26: "Reiche Ornamentprofile brechen unvermutet ab, der Fries büsst streckenweise plötzlich sein Mäanderband ein. . ."

X. THE THRESHOLD OF THE NINETEENTH CENTURY

293. Giesecke, *Piranesi,* pp. 31 ff., and Rudolf Wittkower, "Piranesi's 'Parere su l'architettura,'" *Journal of the Warburg Institute* II (1938/39) 147 ff., deal with the changes in Piranesi's style, with particular regard to his writings. Wittkower, p. 154, contends that Piranesi's *Parere* designs "are in complete accordance with his theory." (Similarly, p.

157.) Yet Wittkower was bound to misunderstand Piranesi's new attitude as appearing in the text of the *Parere,* because he did not remark the ironies in the words of the Master, and believed the *rigoristi* to have been "Vitruvian-Palladian rigorists" or, one might say, classicists, whereas Piranesi, like Algarotti, meant the adherents of Lodoli's functionalistic theory. In 1765 Piranesi attacked the radical moderns, being himself no longer "a revolutionary modernist." The fantastic plan which Wittkower could not locate seems to be that of the *Ampio magnifico collegio.* (See note 247, above.)

294. Rudolf Berliner, "The Stage Designs of the Cooper Union Museum," *Chronicle of the Museum for the Arts of Decoration of the Cooper Union* (New York, August 1941), vol. I, no. 8, pp. 285–320.

295. Berliner, "Stage Designs," p. 311.

296. San Pantaleo: Heinrich Strack, *Baudenkmäler Roms des XV.-XIX. Jahrhunderts* (Berlin, 1891), pl. 100. Gustav Pauli, *Die Kunst des Klassizismus und der Romantik* (Berlin, 1925), ill. p. 159. *Enciclopedia Italiana,* XXIV, pl.°C. Elfriede Schulze-Battmann, *Giuseppe Valadier* (Doctoral thesis; Munich, 1939), pp. 25 ff. Teatro Valle: *Enciclopedia Italiana,* XXIV, pl. CXVIII. Arnaldo Rava, "Architettura teatrale, Il Teatro Valle in Roma," *Bolletino d'Arte* XXX (1936–1937), ills. pp. 411, 412.

297. *Enciclopedia Italiana,* XXXIV, pl. CXVII, with both villas.

298. *Raccolta di diverse invenzioni di no. 24 fabbriche* (Rome, n.d.) was published in 1796, according to André Michel, *Histoire de l'art* (Paris, 1921), VIII, chap. I, 202. Pls. 2, 10, 12, 15, 16, 18, 19, and 20 are signed "G. Valadier." *Progetti* and *Opere* appeared under Valadier's name.

299. Francesco Milizia, *Trattato completo formale e materiale del teatro* (Venice, 1794), p. 92; pls. I–VI. Brinckmann, *17. und 18. Jahrhundert,* p. 150, fig. 162, plan.

300. Ettore Lo Gatto, *Gli artisti italiani in Russia* (Rome, 1934–1943), II, pl. CXIII.

301. *Ibid.,* pls. CXXV, CXXCIII. *Enciclopedia Italiana,* XXIX, ill. p. 345.

302. Ottone Calderari, *Disegni e scritti d'architettura* (Vicenza, 1808), I, pl. XXII. The editor comments, p. 26: "L'altra facciata riesce pittoresca per l'apertura della sua loggia terrena, per l'innalzamento dei due fianchi, che torreggiano sul corpo di mezzo . . ."

303. Lo Gatto, *Artisti italiani,* III, pls. XXII, Exchange; XL, Observatory; XXX, Concert hall. P. 67, a contemporary praise of Quarenghi as "sagace distributore delle masse . . ."

304. Marcus Whiffen, *Stuart and Georgian Churches . . . outside of London* (London, 1948), figs. 76, interior, 80, exterior.

305. Elena Bassi, *Giannantonio Selva* (Padua, 1936), pls. 13, 15. *Enciclopedia Italiana,* XXXI, ill. p. 331.

306. Paolo Mezzanotte, "Luigi Cagnola," *Architettura e Arti Decorative,* (1927–1928), ills. pp. 344, 346.

307. Pauli, *Klassizismus und Romantik,* pl. I. *Enciclopedia Italiana,* XXI, pl. LXX.

308. Tomaso Carlo Beccega, *Sull'architettura greco-romana applicata alla costruzione del teatro moderno italiano* (Venice, 1817), pl. III.

309. Paul Klopfer, *Von Palladio bis Schinkel* (Esslingen, 1911), fig. 78. *Enciclopedia Italiana,* XXIV, pl. XXXIII; pp. 249, 758.

310. *Enciclopedia Italiana,* XXVI, ill. p. 387.

311. The Cisternone and the Cisternino are illustrated in Pietro Vigo, *Livorno* (Bergamo, n.d.), pp. 81, 85; Gino Mazzanti, "L'architettura di Pasquale Poccianti," *Liburni Civitas, Rassegna di attivita municipale* IV (Leghorn, 1931), pp. 117, 118. My quotation is from p. 127.

312. Brinckmann, *17. und 18. Jahrhundert,* fig. 158. Anderson, *Architecture of the Renaissance* (5th ed.), pl. LXXXVIII.

313. Pietro Chevalier, *Memorie architettoniche sui prinicipali edifizi della città di Padova* (Padua, 1831), pp. 24, 25. On p. 21, an aquatint.

314. Klopfer, *Von Palladio,* fig. 77. *Enciclopedia Italiana,* XVI, pl. XCV.

315. The date is from *Guida d'Italia del*

Touring Club Italiano, Piemonte, Lombardia, II, 77.

316. According to the map of Florence in *Atlante Geografico dell'Italia* (1844), the Barbetti house had not yet been built in that year. The map published by Stabilimento Chiari, Florence, 1847, names it "Diorama."

317. Carl Friedrich Schaeffer, *Collection de* *nouveaux bâtiments pour la décoration des grands jardins et des campagnes* (Leipzig, 1802).

318. Klopfer, *Von Palladio,* fig. 48.

319. The copy has the imprint: "Nobiles Widmung."

320. *Enciclopedia Italiana,* XXIV, ill. p. 990.

321. *Ibid.,* III, ill. p. 547; XXXIV, pl. VI.

PART THREE: FRANCE

XI. FROM LEMERCIER TO SOUFFLOT

1. Louis Hautecoeur, *Histoire de l'architecture classique en France* (Paris, 1943f.) is very useful for its illustrations and the many, though not entirely reliable, factual data, but contributes little to a better understanding of artistic trends. After so much excellent research in the field of Baroque art has been done in long decades statements like the following (II, 412) are rather astonishing: "Le baroque était une manifestation de l'esprit libertin, de la fantaisie individuelle."

2. Jean Marot, *Le Magnifique Chasteau de Richelieu . . . commencé et achevé . . . sous la conduite de Jacques le Mercier* (n. pl., n.d.). André Michel, *Histoire de l'art* (Paris, 1921), vol. VI, chap. IV, by Henry Lemonnier, fig. 121, from Marot's third plate without the framing. Reginald Blomfield, *A History of French Architecture from the Reign of Charles VIII till the Death of Mazarin* (London, 1911), II, pl. CXXXIII.

3. Georges Gromort, *Jardins d'Italie* (Paris, 1922), I, 9, plan.

4. *Ibid.,* I, pl. 67, plan; respectively, I, 15, plan.

5. *Ibid.,* I, 11, plan; 14, view.

6. *Ibid.,* I, pl. 55, plan; pl. 57, view.

7. William Henry Ward, *The Architecture of the Renaissance in France* (2nd ed.; New York, 1926), I, 144, 145; fig. 140. Marie Luise

Gothein, *A History of Garden Art* (New York, 1928), I, 407; fig. 325.

8. Gothein, *Garden Art,* I, 410; fig. 327. I, 411: "one coherent scheme."

9. Anthoine Lepautre, *Les Oeuvres d'architecture: Desseins de plusieurs Palais . . .* (Paris, 1652). I shall refer to the reprint by Jombert, with the *siège* of a castle as the first plate.

10. Jacques Androuet Du Cerceau, *Les Plus Excellents Bastiments de France* (Paris, 1576), I, pls. 16 (plan), 17, 18. Henry de Geymueller, *Les Du Cerceau* (Paris, 1887), fig. 101.

11. Du Cerceau, *Bastiments de France,* I, third leaf: "Et est ce bastiment couvert de plusieurs pavillons, entrelacez les uns aux autres, et le tout si bien symmetrié, tant en son plan, que enrichissemens, que, rien plus . . ."

12. *Ibid.,* third leaf: "Tout l'édifice n'est qu'une masse . . ."

13. Jacques Androuet Du Cerceau, *Livre d'architecture* (Paris, 1611). Du Cerceau was fond of experiments (Octagonal, circular and decagonal houses, pls. XXVIII, XXXV, XLIX). More noteworthy than these seem to me his attempts toward a new relationship of the parts.

14. Lepautre, *Desseins,* ed. Jombert, 2nd plate, ground plan; 4th plate, perspective.

15. Giovanni Giacomo Rossi (Io. Jacobus

de Rubeis), publisher, *Villa Pamphilia* (Rome, n.d.), 80th plate.

16. Lepautre, *Desseins,* ed. Jombert, 6th plate.

17. *Ibid.,* 10th plate, plan; 11th plate, view. The legend "Bastiment carré" is inscribed on the 13th plate.

18. *Ibid.,* p. 5: "Tous les retours que forment ces balcons avancez donnent une grande variété à l'aspect, et font union du tout avec les parties."

19. *Ibid.,* pp. 6, 7.

20. *Ibid.,* 24th plate, plan; 25th plate, perspective of the "Quatrième Bastiment." Reginald Blomfield, *A History of French Architecture . . . from 1661 to 1774* (London, 1921), I, pls. XXV–XXVII.

21. Lepautre, *Desseins,* ed. Jombert, p. 14: "Le corps du milieu est d'une grande solidité et décoration; et l'Art et le génie de l'Architecte y ont plus de part que l'utilité qu'on en pouroit tirer."

22. Anthony Blunt, *François Mansart and the Origins of French Classical Architecture* (London, 1941), p. 10.

23. Among the very few "Mannerist" details which Blunt points out (pp. 10, 13, 21, 25) are the obelisks of the Church of the Feuillants. Such obelisks were common all through the Renaissance. Mansart used them to counterbalance the central piece.

24. Blunt, *Mansart,* pp. 24, 64.

25. *Ibid.,* p. 57. Similarly, p. 40, in dealing with the Hôtel du Jars.

26. *Ibid.,* p. 57.

27. *Ibid.,* p. 26.

28. *Ibid.,* p. 51.

29. *Ibid.,* p. 23.

30. *Ibid.,* p. 25.

31. *Ibid.,* pls. 2a, 2c, 3c, 18, 20.

32. *Ibid.,* p. 26.

33. *Ibid.,* p. 47; pl. 16 a. Cecil Gould and Anthony Blunt, "The Château de Balleroy," *Burlington Magazine* LXXXVII (1945), 248–252, with illustrations.

34. Blunt, *Mansart,* p. 48; p. 16b.

35. *Ibid.,* p. 54; pl. 20a.

36. *Ibid.,* p. 57.

37. Léon Deshairs, *Le Château de Maisons* (Paris, n.d.). First plate.

38. Cornelius Gurlitt, *Geschichte des Barockstiles, des Rocco und des Klassizismus in Belgien, Holland, Frankreich, England* (Stuttgart, 1888), p. 75.

39. Michel, *Histoire de l'art,* vol. VI, chap. IV, p. 199.

40. Blomfield, *French Architecture* (1921 ed.), I, 58; pl. III.

41. A. E. Brinckmann, *Die Baukunst des 17. und 18. Jahrhunderts in den romanischen Ländern* (Berlin, n.d.), p. 197: "einer der grössten Raumbildner Frankreichs." Thieme-Becker, *Künstlerlexikon,* XXIII, 150, speaks of "Begründung des französischen Spätbarock als Weltstil."

42. Michel., *Histoire de l'art,* vol. VI, chap. IV, p. 200, quotation.

43. *Ibid.,* p. 199: "un des dômes les plus disgracieux."

44. Blomfield, *French Architecture* (1921 ed.), I, pl. II.

45. Begun about 1660, according to Brinckmann, *17. und 18. Jahrhundert,* p. 190. Blomfield, *French Architecture* (1921 ed.), I, pl. XII.

46. Michel, *Histoire de l'art,* vol. VI, chap. IX, by Henry Lemonnier, p. 553, "un plan original"; fig. 370.

47. Jean Marot, *Architecture françoise* ("Le grand Marot"), (Paris, n. d.), perspective. Blomfield, *French Architecture* (1921 ed.), I, pl. XXIII, elevation and section taken from the "Grand Marot."

48. Jacques-François Blondel, *Architecture françoise,* (Paris, 1752), Book V, p. 140. The recent reimpression (Paris, n. d.) has a slightly different pagination.

49. *Ibid.,* Book VI, chap. VIII, description and dates. Blomfield, *French Architecture* (1921 ed.), I, pl. XVII. The mid-eighteenth century was uncertain whether the lack of accents should be praised or blamed. Cf. La Font de Saint Yenne, *Le Génie du Louvre aux Champs Elisées* (Paris, 1756), second annexed letter.

50. *Les Dix Livres d'architecture de Vitruve,* ed. Claude Perrault (Paris, 1673), Book I, chap. II, p. 10, note 3.

51. Jacques-François Blondel, *Architecture françoise,* Book VI, p. 56: "disparités entre

les masses et les parties de la façade . . .";
ibid., p. 59: "disparité d'ouvertures."

52. *Ibid.*, p. 51: "des arrières-corps qui n'ont de rapport ni avec l'avant-corps, ni avec les pavillons."

53. *Ibid.*, p. 57: "défaut d'unité."

54. *Ibid.*, p. 57: "Il est essentiel de désigner d'une manière frappante celui [cet étage] qui est destiné à la résidence du Prince, en sorte que l'étage inférieur et le supérieur, ne paroissent faits que pour lui servir de soutien et de couronnement . . ."

55. *Ibid.*, p. 52: "une forme pyramidale.qui annonce quelque succès dans sa composition."

56. *Ibid.*, p. 53: "pas assez de repos dans l'ordonnance de cetta façade."

57. *Ibid.*, p. 58: "pas assez de rapport entre le tout et les parties."

58. *Ibid.*, pl. 13. P. 59: "Il faut éviter ce contraste."

59. *Ibid.*, p. 49: "pour que ces pavillons ne l'emportassent pas en prééminence sur le reste du bâtiment, il avoit élevé au dessus et derrière l'avant-corps du milieu, une espèce de dôme."

60. *Ibid.*, p. 46: "Perrault, en grand Maître, a crû devoir sacrifier la commodité à la beauté de l'ordonnance . . ." *Ibid.*, p. 41: "on ne peut porter trop loin (l'admiration) à l'égard de l'élégance de son architecture, du choix de ses ornemens, et du rapport heureux qui se rencontre entre certaines parties et l'ensemble de ce vaste Edifice." This conforms to the ideals of Claude Perrault, *Ordonnance des cinq espèces de colonnes selon la méthode des anciens* (Paris, 1683).

61. François Blondel, *Cours d'architecture* (Paris, 1675).

62. *Ibid.*, II, 784, 785.

63. J.-F. Blondel, *Architecture françoise*, Book VI, p. 45. Blomfield, *French Architecture* (1921 ed.), I, pl. XXII.

64. J.-F. Blondel, *Architecture françoise*, Book VI, p. 45.

65. Blomfield, *French Architecture* (1921 ed.), I, pl. LXVII; p. 182. Brinckmann, *17. und 18. Jahrhundert*, p. 312.

66. Brinckmann, *17. und 18. Jahrhundert*, p. 312; fig. 340. Ernest de Ganay, *Châteaux et manoirs de France*, V (1939), pl. 39.

67. Blomfield, *French Architecture* (1921 ed.), I, 199; pl. LXXX. Brinckmann, *17. und 18. Jahrhundert* p. 315. In using the architect's family name Hardouin instead of the adopted name of Mansart I conform to J.-F. Blondel, *Cours d'architecture* (Paris, 1771), I, 387, 434; III, lxxix, 236; IV, liii; etc.

68. Blomfield, *French Architecture*, (1921 ed.), I, 60; pl. IV.

69. *Ibid.*, I, 197; pl. LXXVIII.

70. *Ibid.*, I, 188; pl. LXXII.

71. *Ibid.*, I, 210; pls. LXXXVI, LXXXVII.

72. *Ibid.*, I, 189.

73. *Ibid.*, I, 202; pl. LXXXI.

74. M. L. R. [Georges-Louis Le Rouge], *Curiosités de Paris, de Versailles, Marly . . .* (Paris, 1742), II, 143; ill. opp. p. 138.

75. Gilles-Marie Oppenord, *Oeuvres* (Paris, n. d.).

76. Germain Boffrand, *Livre d'architecture* (Paris, 1745), pls. XIX, XX. The castle of Stupinigi by Juvara (A. E. Brinckmann, *Theatrum novum pedemontii*, Düsseldorf, 1931, p. 61; *Enciclopedia Italiana*, XXVII, ill. p. 193, XXXII, ill. p. 189) begun 1729, has a similar plan, but its elevations are calmer.

77. Boffrand, *Livre d'architecture*, p. 26: "Un homme qui ne connoît pas ces différens caractères, et qui ne les fait pas sentir dans ses ouvrages, n'est pas Architecte." P. 27: "Il faut dans un ouvrage suivre le même caractère depuis le commencement jusqu' à la fin, pour que toutes les parties soient relatives au tout." P. 8: ". . . on doit toujours conserver la noble simplicité . . ."

78. The term *architecture parlante* was used in an anonymous essay "Etudes d'architecture en France", *Magasin Pittoresque* (1852), p. 388, to characterize Ledoux's work. A more complete discussion of Boffrand's achievements and views and of *architecture parlante* is contained in Emil Kaufmann, *Three Revolutionary Architects—Boullée, Ledoux and Lequeu, Transactions of the American Philosophical Society,* vol. 42 1952), pp. 447, 514, 417, 520, 535.

79. Just-Aurèle Meisonnier, *Oeuvres* (Reprint; Paris, n.d.), pl. 108. Paul Klopfer, *Von Palladio bis Schinkel* (Esslingen, 1911), fig. 25. Michel, *Histoire de l'art*, VII, fig. 13.

80. Meissonier, *Oeuvres,* pls. 10ff., 42, 66ff.

81. *Ibid.,* pls. 32, 96. Cf. Fiske Kimball, "J.-A. Meisonnier and the Beginning of the 'Genre Pittoresque,'" *Gazette des Beaux-Arts* (1942), ser. 6, vol. 22, pp. 27–40, with ills.

82. J.-F. Blondel, *Cours,* IV, liv.

83. *Ibid.,* II, 229, 230, 373, etc. Blondel's aesthetics and some of his designs have been presented in my *Three Revolutionary Architects.* In the present book I add to my earlier comments some remarks on his attitude toward composition.

84. *Ibid.,* III, 159; IV, ix: "ces tours de force."

85. *Ibid.,* IV, lii: "cette indépendance et cette incertitude . . . dans la plupart des compositions de nos jours . . ." IV, 186: "la difficulté de concilier la distribution avec l'ordonnance . . ."

86. See also note 77, above.

87. J.-F. Blondel, *Cours,* I, 397.

88. *Ibid.,* I, 385.

89. *Ibid.,* III, 2: "Il est plus difficile qu'on ne pense ordinairement, d'observer dans un édifice, la sévérité qu'exigent les préceptes de l'Art, lorsqu'il s'agit de concilier la décoration . . . avec la distribution et la construction."

90. *Ibid.,* III, 2.

91. *Ibid.,* I, 398. Similarly, III, 394.

92. *Ibid.,* IV, 153: "des difficultés qui se présentent à l'Architecte, lorsqu'il s'agit de concilier ensemble la régularité des dehors, et la distribution des dedans . . ." *Architecture françoise,* Book I, p. 21: "simétrie . . . est aussi peu essentielle dans l'intérieur qu'elle est importante à observer dans les dehors . . ."

93. J.-F. Blondel, *Cours,* III, lix: "Mais lorsqu'il s'agit de quelque édifice public . . . l'ordonnance de leur décoration doit être exempte de toute espèce d'irrégularité . . ."

94. *Ibid.,* IV, 185: "Nous donnerons deux Plans faits pour le même Palais: dans le premier, nous avons sacrifié une partie des dedans aux dehors; dans le second au contraire, nous avons préféré la commodité intérieure à la beauté extérieure."

95. *Ibid.,* IV, 357; pl. XLVI.

96. *Ibid.,* IV, 360; pl. XLVII.

97. *Ibid.,* IV, 359, 361.

98. *Ibid.,* I, vi: "le Manuscript que je vous ai confié n'est que le résultat de vingt années de recherches; mais qui faites dans des temps différents . . . manquent peut-être de cette liaison nécessaire . . ." Also Jean-François Sobry, *De l'Architecture* (Amsterdam, 1776) presents a mixture of old and new views.

99. [Charles Etienne Briseux], *Architecture moderne* ed. Claude Jombert (Paris, 1728), also contains designs by J. Courtonne. Cf. Emil Kaufmann, "Die Architekturtheorie der französischen Klassik und des Klassizismus," *Repertorium für Kunstwissenschaft* LXIV (1924), esp. p. 201.

100. C. E. Briseux, *L'Art de bâtir des maisons de campagne* (Paris, 1752). I refer to the 2nd edition of 1761.

101. *Ibid.,* I, pls. 3, 7, 15, 20, 24, 40, 43, 51, 76, 83, 87, 89, 91, 93, 132; II, pl. 137.

102. *Ibid.,* I, pls. 27, 31, 35, 109, 126.

103. *Ibid.,* I, pl. 32.

104. *Ibid.,* II, pls. 142, 146.

105. *Ibid.,* I, frontispiece. Briseux comments on p. 16: "Le Pavillon du milieu doit . . . dominer . . . il faut faire cadencer [les avant-corps] avec les parties qui les réunissent . . ."

106. C. E. Briseux, *Traité du beau essentiel dans les arts* (Paris, 1752). The text is not printed, but beautifully engraved.

107. *Ibid.,* I, 51.

108. *Ibid.,* I, 13, 14.

109. *Ibid.,* I, 36: "Tout y est distingué, et cepedant tout s'y réduit à un." This is the old piont of view, as expressed for instance in Sebastien Leclerc, *Traité d'architecture* (Paris, 1714), p. 188: "Que les parties qui entrent dans la composition d'un Bâtiment doivent être faites l'une pour l'autre."

110. *Ibid.,* I, 71: "Il faut que les parties des étages supérieurs semblent naître des inférieurs . . ."

111. *Ibid.,* I, 69: "La noble simplicité est le vray caractère du Beau dans les arts . . ."

112. Marc-Antoine Laugier, *Essai sur l'Architecture* (2nd ed., Paris, 1775), p. 108. In the *Essai,* pp. x, xxxvii, 16, 262, Laugier admits having profited from L. G. de Cor-

demoy, *Nouveau Traité de toute l'architecture* (Paris, 1706). Yet the latter's views were far less advanced than his. More about Laugier in my *Three Revolutionary Architects,* pp. 448–450.

113. La Font de Saint Yenne, *Examen d'un essai sur l'architecture* (Paris, 1753). Cf. Emil Kaufmann, in *Repertorium* LXIV (1924), 202.

114. Charles Axel Guillaumot, *Remarques sur un livre . . . de M. l'Abbé Laugier* (Paris, 1768). *Essai . . . sur la beauté essentielle dans l'architecture* (Paris, *an* X) reveals Guillaumot as an admirer of Greek grandeur.

115. Laugier, *Essai,* pp. 253 ff.

116. *Ibid.,* p. 263: "M. Frézier doute qu'on trouve jamais un Architecte, qui réussisse dans l'entreprise de sauver l'Architecture de la bisarrerie des opinions, en nous en découvrant les lois fixes et immuables, ainsi que je le souhaite . . . mais je ne saurois me résoudre comme lui à en désespérer."

117. *Ibid.,* p. v: "La nouveauté des principes, la hardiesse des Critiques, tout me faisoit craindre pour le sort d'un Ecrit, où sans autres armes que celles d'une raison sévère, j'osis combattre des usages reçus, et des préjugés dominans." Marc-Antoine Laugier, *Observations sur l'architecture* (The Hague, 1765), p. 84 "qu'importe que ce soit une nouveauté, pourvu qu'elle soit raisonnable."

118. Laugier, *Essai,* p. 15: "En relevant les imperfections de cet édifice [S. Gervais, Paris], j'acquiers le droit de n'en épargner aucun autre, sans blesser l'amour-propre de qui que ce soit. Voilà pourquoi j'en parlerai sans ménagement." *Ibid.,* p. 186: "s'affranchir des chaînes du préjugé."

119. *Ibid.,* pp. xl, xli.

120. *Ibid.,* p. 10: "C'est dans les parties essentieles que consistent toutes les beautés; dans les parties introduites par besoin consistent toutes les licences; dans les parties ajoutées par caprice consistent tous les défauts." P. xl: "J'ai conclu qu'il y avoit dans l'architecture des beautés essentielles, indépendantes de l'habitude des sens, ou de la convention des hommes."

121. *Ibid.,* p. 22: "Tenons-nous-en au simple et au naturel; il est l'unique route du beau."

122. *Ibid.,* p. 5: "Tout semble nous menacer d'une décadence entière."

123. *Ibid.,* p. xl: "La composition d'un morceau d'Architecture étoit comme tous les ouvrages d'esprit, susceptible de froideur et de vivacité, de justesse et de désordre." Similarly, p. 2.

124. Cf. Part I, p. 65, above.

125. Laugier, *Essai,* p. 206.

126. *Ibid.,* p. 56: "Avec une légère teinture de Géométrie, il [l'Architecte] trouvera le secret de varier ses plans à l'infini . . ." Hautecoeur, *Histoire de l'architecture,* IV, 51 f., disregards Laugier's predilection for the elementary forms, and his ideas about city planning.

127. Jacques-François Blondel, *L'Homme du monde éclairé par les arts,* ed. Bastide (Amsterdam, 1774), II, 13: "La plupart de nos jeunes Architectes sont raisonneurs, et ne raisonnent pas . . . Parce qu'ils ont lu l'essai du Pére Logier [*sic*], ils se croient très-instruits." Blondel reprimands the young architects in whose reasoning he misses reason.

128. Jacques-François Blondel, *Discours sur la nécessité de l'étude de l'architecture* (Paris, 1754), p. 88. For more quotations from Laugier's writings see my *Three Revolutionary Architects,* pp. 448–450.

129. Edmond Comte de Fels, *Ange-Jacques Gabriel* (Paris, 1912), p. 199.

130. *Ibid.,* pp. 159, 201.

131. Blomfield, *French Architecture* (1921 ed.), II, 131.

132. H. Bartle Cox, *Ange-Jacques Gabriel* (London, 1926), p. 7.

133. Georges Gromort, *Jacques-Ange Gabriel* (Paris, 1933), p. 28: "L'oeuvre de Gabriel est entièrement homogène . . . nous ne voyons aucune différence de style entre l'Ecole Militaire . . . la place Louis XV . . . et le Petit Trianon."

134. *Ibid.,* p. 19; pl. I.

135. Fels, *Gabriel,* p. 74. First project of 1750, pl. IX.

136. *Ibid.*, pp. 56, 57, with date 1753; pl. II.

137. Gromort, *Gabriel*, p. 69; pl. LVI.

138. Fels, *Gabriel*, p. 149; pl. XXX, plan; pl. XXXI, *élévation*. Gromort, *Gabriel*, pl. LXXXVIII.

139. Fels, *Gabriel*, p. 165; pl. XXXVIII. Leigh French and H. D. Eberlein, *Smaller Houses of Versailles* (New York, 1926), p. 135.

140. Gromort, *Gabriel*, pl. CI, first project; pl. CII, second project.

141. Fels, *Gabriel*, p. 157. Gromort, *Gabriel*, pls. LVII–LXXXI; p. 68, plan.

142. Gromort, *Gabriel*, p. 28: "Même façon d'engager les colonnes sur l'angle."

143. Fels, *Gabriel*, p. 22.

144. *Ibid.*, p. 131; pls. XXVI, XXVII. Gromort, *Gabriel*, pl. LXXXVII.

145. Cf. Part I, pp. 43, 44, above.

146. Louis Dimier, *L'Architecture et la décoration françaises aux 18ᵉ et 19ᵉ siècles* (Paris, 1921), vol. III, p. 4, pl. XLIV.

147. Blomfield, *French Architecture*, (1921 ed.), II, 88; pl. CLXI. Klopfer, *Von Palladio*, fig. 26. Michel, *Histoire de l'art*, VII, fig. 14.

148. J.-F. Blondel, *Architecture françoise*, Book III, p. 40: "Ce monument . . . dont la grandeur annonce à nos Architectes François une route presque nouvelle, a excité plusieurs esprits de parti . . ." Cf. *Cours*, II, 209; III, 346.

149. Laugier, *Essai*, p. 175: "Je ne vois que des épaisseurs et des masses." P. 202: "Tout y est massif, dur, gêné, plat."

150. Laugier, *Essai*, p. 202: "Bien loin de former la pyramide, ce sont deux bâtimens quarrés mis l'un sur l'autre." Laugier noted the independence of the elements composing the front of Saint-Sulpice.

151. Claude-Nicolas Ledoux, *L'Architecture de Claude-Nicolas Ledoux* ed. D. Ramée (Paris, 1847), preface by the editor.

152. Gurlitt, *Geschichte*, p. 283.

153. Ward, *Renaissance in France*, II, 455.

154. Blomfield, *French Architecture* (1921 ed.), II, 112.

155. Rene Schneider, *L'Art français* (Paris, 1926), IV, 188: "C'est la fin des façades en bas-relief du style baroque, l'apaisement définitif des surfaces . . . la ligne universellement tendue, et le colossal." This passage is in accord with Charles Paul Landon, *Annales du Musée* (Paris, 1801–1809), VII, 87, signed "L. G." (Legrand).

156. Pierre Patte, *Mémoires sur les objets les plus importans de l'architecture* (Paris, 1769), pp. 342 ff. The Mémoire on Saint-Sulpice was written in 1767. Cf. Mae Mathieu, *Pierre Patte* (Paris, 1940), p. 122.

157. Patte, *Mémoires*, p. 343: "Sans cet accompagnement, les tours sembleront à jamais deux grands corps hors d'oeuvre, sans unité et rapport avec le tout ensemble. Ce n'est qu'un fronton . . . qui peut leur donner . . . une inhérence avec la masse totale de l'édifice."

158. *Ibid.*, p. 350.

159. *Ibid.*, p. 343. Pl. XXVI, fig. 1, shows another way to unify the towers, of which Patte (*Mémoires*, p. 351) disapproves. Emile Malbois, "Oppenord et l'Eglise Saint-Sulpice," *Gazette des Beaux-Arts*, ser. 6, IX (1933), 39, fig. 8, shows a balustrade with statutes between the towers planned by Oppenord.

160. Cornelius Gurlitt, *Die Baukunst Frankreichs* (Dresden, n.d.), I, 23; pl. 49.

161. Pierre Contant d'Ivry, *Les Oeuvres d'architecture de . . .* (2nd. ed.; Paris, 1769), pl. 20. René Schneider, in Michel, *Histoire de l'art*, VII, 27, censures Contant: "Il superpose sans bonheur le fronton triangulaire du portail . . . et la lourde coupole . . ." According to Brinckmann, *17. und 18. Jahrhundert*, p. 283, the church was carried out by Franque on the rue de Grenelle.

162. Pierre Patte, *Monumens érigés en France à la gloire de Louis XV* (Paris, 1765), pl. LII. Blomfield, *French Architecture* (1921 ed.), II, pp. 144, 186; pls. CLXXXII, plan; CLXXXIII, elevation.

163. Blomfield, *French Architecture*, (1921 ed.), II, p. 186.

164. Patte, *Monumens*, p. 126; pl. X.

165. Blomfield, *French Architecture* (1921 ed.), II, 144; pl. CLXXIX.

166. Patte, *Monumens*, pl. V, shows the dome with ribs and a different façade.

170. Blomfield, *French Architecture* (1921
167. Contant, *Oeuvres d'architecture*, pls.
29, 43, 71 left.

168. *Ibid.*, pls. 14, 71 right.

169. *Ibid.*, pl. 37.
ed.), II, 186.

171. Patte, *Monumens*, p. 204.

172. *Ibid.*, p. 204; pl. LIV.

173. E. Dupezard, *Le Palais-Royal de Paris*
(Paris, 1911), pls. 21 ff.

174. Jean Mondain-Monval, *Soufflot* (Paris,
1918), pp. 424, 523.

175. *Ibid.*, p. 85. Gurlitt, *Geschichte*, fig.
88. Rogatien Le Nail, *Lyon* (Paris, 1909), pl.
33.

176. Mondain-Monval, *Soufflot*, p. 524.

177. Dimier, *L'Architecture*, II, pl. LXXII.

178. William J. Anderson, *The Architecture of the Renaissance in Italy* (London,
1901), pl. XXVIII.

179. Antoine Chrysostome Quatremère de
Quincy, *Histoire de la vie et des ouvrages des
plus célèbres architectes du XI*e *siècle jusqu'à
la fin du XVIII*e (Paris, 1830), II, 341.

180. Mondain-Monval, *Soufflot*, p. 423, letter from Brébion, 1780. Jacques Guillaume
Legrand and Charles Paul Landon, *Description de Paris* (Paris, 1806), I, 110, note the
"légèreté gothique" of the interior.

181. Mondain-Monval, *Soufflot*, pls. II, IV.

182. Jacques Antoine Dulaure, *Histoire
civile, physique et morale de Paris* (Paris,
1821), V, 179.

183. Aubin-Louis Millin, *Antiquités Nationales* (Paris, 1790–1798), vol. V (*an* VII),
part LX, pl. VI, shows the east towers and
the windows. Philippe Sagnac and Jean
Robiquet, *La Révolution de 1789* (Paris,
1934), p. 300, engraving of the church with
the windows. Mondain-Monval, *Soufflot,* p.
472; pl. VI, drawing "Dessinée par Lequeu
sous les yeux de Soufflot." Bibliothèque Nationale, Paris, Ha 41, engraving by Lequeu,
dated 1781. Georges Lenotre [Louis Léon
Théodore Gossselin], *Les Quartiers de Paris
pendant la Révolution, 1789-1804* (Paris,
1896), part II, pl. 16, illustrates the Panthéon
in 1792.

184. Quatremère de Quincy, *Histoire,* II,

342. Here appears also the further criticism:
"On peut reprocher à la colonnade qui environne le dôme, de découper son ensemble
en deux masses, qui . . . en rompent l'unité."

185. Jean Rondelet, *Mémoire historique sur
le dôme du Panthéon français* (Paris, 1797),
pp. 6, 7. *Mémoire* (2nd ed.; Paris, 1814),
"Addition au Mémoire," pp. 5, 6, about the
changes made by Quatremère de Quincy. Cf.
the latter's *Rapport sur l'édifice dit de Sainte-
Geneviève* (Paris, 1791), p. 28, asking for
gravité, grands lisses.

186. Blomfield, *French Architecture* (1921
ed.), II, 140. Landon, *Annales*, X, 72.

187. Dulaure, *Histoire de Paris,* ed. L. Batissier (1865 ed), p. 476. Legrand and Landon,
Description, I, pl. 24, and Jean-Baptiste Maximilien de Saint-Victor, *Tableau historique et
pittoresque de Paris* (Paris, 1808), III, ill. opp.
p. 315, show the church after all these change;
Klopfer, *Von Palladio*, fig. 11, its present
aspect.

188. Legrand and Landon, *Description,* I,
111, note 1: "le bouchement des croisées et
autres suppressions avantageuses à l'ordonnance et à la solidité." The general predilection for solid walls shows in the precept of
Wilgrin de Taillefer, *L'Architecture soumise
au principe de la nature et des arts* (Paris,
1804), p. 216: "Les percées doivent être rares
dans les façades."

189. Ward, *Renaissance in France*, II, 461:
"There is, in fact, no inevitable relation between the dome, the peristyle, and the substructure, with whose solid mass the slender
columns contrast painfully . . . huge blank
walls not relieved by any features except the
doorways. . ."

190. *Ibid.*, p. 462.

191. Blomfield, *French Architecture* (1921
ed.), II, 139. Cf. also II, 198, about Quatremère.

192. Mondain-Monval, *Soufflot*, p. 106.

193. *Ibid.*, pp. 2, 3, 90 ("l'austerité jacobine"), 513.

194. *Ibid.*, p. 505: "un art pédant, raisonneur, dogmatique, lourd et froid."

195. *Ibid.*, p. 501: "L'art de Soufflot, lui
aussi, veut être un art de réforme. . ." P. 511:
"le caractère ambigu d'une architecture de

transition, qui tâtonne et cherche sa formule définitive."

196. Hautecoeur, *Histoire de l'architecture,* IV, fig. 91.

197. Saint-Victor, *Tableau historique,* III, 407, with the date 1772, blames the "innovation" of the curved fronts. Ill. opp. p. 404. Mondain-Monval, *Soufflot,* p. 463.

198. Klopfer, *Von Palladio,* fig. 14.

199. Albert Erich Brinckmann, *Die Kunst des Rokoko* (Berlin, 1940), pl. I.

200. Cf. Louis Pierre Baltard, *Paris et ses monuments* (Paris, 1803), chapter Saint Cloud, ill. p. 18.

XII. THE ARCHITECTS OF THE FRENCH
REVOLUTION: THE GENERATION OF 1730

201. Cf. Part II, note 110, above.

202. Francesco Milizia, "Dell'arte di vedere . . . ," *Opere complete,* I, 200: "E falso dunque che il belle arti del disegno abbiano fra gl'altri loro scopi quello della *illusione*" [Milizia's italics]. *Ibid.,* p. 216: "Ma tanta pena di osservazioni, di riflessioni, di criteri, di teoria, e di pratica per un semplice diletto della vista? . . . questo effetto non è il loro (delle belle arti) scope finale. . ."

203. J.-F. Blondel, *L'Homme du monde,* preface, I, xv, written by Bastide, the editor of Blondel's posthumous book: "Il (Blondel) espéra que des observations . . . pourroient insensiblement produire la révolution des idées et la perfection de l'art." From this passage as well as from others in Blondel's own writings we learn that this great architect already foresaw the coming architectural revolution, of which others spoke, before long, as of a fact. Pierre Patte, in the introduction to J.-F. Blondel, *Cours,* V (1777): "la révolution qui s'est faite depuis 20 ans dans le goût de notre Architecture." François Michel Lecreulx, *Discours sur le goût* (Nancy, 1778), p. 17: "Le goût de l'architecture a changé sensiblement depuis quinze ans, on a remarqué plus de grandeur, plus de hardiesse dans les compositions . . . On a fait le procès à la symétrie et à la régularité . . . Dans ce choc d'opinions, chacun a posé des principes différens." Charles-François Viel de Saint-Maux, *Principes de l'ordonnance et de la construction des bâtiments* (1797), p. 250: "Jamais, à la vérité, les arts n'ont éprouvé de plus violentes secousses que celles dont nous sommes les témoins, et l'architecture y a été soumise particulièrement." Charles-François Viel de Saint-Maux, *Décadence de l'architecture à la fin du 18° siècle* (Paris, an VIII—1800), p. 8: "L'esprit capricieux de ces deux artistes [Boullée et Ledoux] s'est emparé d'un grand nombre d'architectes . . . et a opéré une véritable révolution dans l'ordonnance des édifices." Jean Charles Krafft and N. Ransonette, *Plans . . . des plus belles maisons à Paris* (1801), introduction: "Tous les gens de goût ont remarqué la révolution qui s'est operée dans les arts et particulièrement dans l'architecture en France depuis environ 25 années." Taillefer, *L'Architecture,* p. 22: "elle [l'architecture] a subi en France une révolution presque aussi soudaine, que celle dans les opinions a été terrible . . . Point de stabilité ni d'unité dans les principes . . . Cet art, malgré l'incohérence de ses préceptes . . . a fait, il faut le dire, un grand pas vers le beau." Similar optimism speaks out of the hymnic words of Ledoux, *L'Architecture considérée sous le rapport de l'art, des moeurs et de la législation* (Paris, 1804), p. 86: "Les arts se réveillent; un nouveau jour commence." Modern art history, however, did not notice the architectural revolution. Charles du Peloux, *Répertoire biographique et bibliographique des artistes du 18° siècle français* (Paris, 1930), ignores Ledoux's only publication, *L'Architecture,* hinting vaguely at the architect's "divers ouvrages." Hautecoeur, *Histoire de l'architecture,* IV, contents himself with restating at length the current views on classicism, Palladianism, and romanticism, with certain modifications made necessary by the rediscovery of Boullée and Ledoux. Du Peloux, *Répertoire* (1940 ed.), does not list the non-French publications on Ledoux; Hautecoeur in presenting Boullée omits the unique biography of this architect. It is surprising that compilers of handbooks are not conversant with foreign research. In Gabriel Vauthier, "Ledoux et les Propylées de Paris," *Bulletin de la Société de l'Histoire de l'Art*

Français (1929), p. 68, Ledoux's projects are contemptuously dealt with as "chimères." See Kaufmann, *Three Revolutionary Architects,* p. 434, note 1, p. 474, note 2.

204. Solitude: Cornelius Gurlitt, *Geschichte des Barockstiles und des Rococo in Deutschland* (Stuttgart, 1889), p. 462; plan, fig. 159. Klopfer, *Von Palladio,* fig. 181. Monrepos: Gurlitt, *Barockstil in Deutschland,* p. 462; plan, fig. 158. Max Osborn, *Die Kunst des Rokoko* (Berlin, 1929), ill. p. 351, garden front. Brinckmann, *Kunst des Rokoko,* ill. p. 208, entrance front.

205. J.-F. Blondel, *Cours,* III, 235.

206. De la Guêpière, *Recueil d'esquisses d'architecture* (Stuttgart, n.d.), pl. 25.

207. Marie-Joseph Peyre, *Oeuvres d'architecture* (2nd ed.; Paris, 1795), "Notice sur la vie de M. J. Peyre," by his son Antoine Marie Peyre. The original edition is that of 1765.

208. *Ibid.,* p. 32.

209. *Ibid.,* p. 8: "Nous parviendrons peut-être à surpasser les anciens dans l'Architecture, mais nous n'y parviendrons qu'après les avoir égalés . . . et soigneusement imités."

210. *Ibid.,* p. 7: "l'union des formes"; p. 8: "les belles proportions et les belles masses."

211. *Ibid.,* p. 8: "du neuf accompagné de la simplicité."

212. *Ibid.,* p. 8: "La bonne Architecture produit sur notre âme, les affections les plus fortes; elle inspire la terreur, la crainte, . . . la volupté."

213. *Ibid.,* pl. 3. Brinckmann, *17. und 18. Jahrhundert,* fig. 289.

214. Peyre, *Oeuvres,* pl. 11. Brinckmann, *17. und 18. Jahrhundert,* fig. 290.

215. Peyre, *Oeuvres,* p. 29; pl. 12.

216. See Part II, pp. 113–114. A general remark concerning the method of art history may be made here. Hautecoeur, *Histoire de l'architecture,* IV, 226, speaks of the colonnades of the cathedral as of a "portique à la Bernin." Such superficial comparisons based on certain minor similarities are rather common. Ledoux, *L'Architecture,* p. 23, blamed their authors: "La plupart des hommes instruits ne jugent que lorsqu'ils comparent: compilateurs exacts, ils s'appuient sur tous les examples qui servent

de boussole." Obviously, the colonnades of the Piazza di San Pietro and those of Peyre are thoroughly different. The former depart from the front of the church approaching the visitor, the latter encompass the building at a considerable distance and without direct contact. From the first step of careful observation the historian should progress to the second step of questioning whether the difference in form is indicative of a difference in meaning.

217. Peyre, *Oeuvres,* p. 29.

218. *Ibid.,* p. 28; pl. 6. Emil Kaufmann, "Architektonische Entwürfe aus der Zeit der französischen Revolution," *Zeitschrift für bildende Kunst* (1929), ill. p. 39.

219. Pierre Michel d'Ixnard, *Recueil d'Architecture* (Strasbourg, 1791), pl. 10, with the date. Klopfer, *Von Palladio,* fig. 21, perspective view. Cf. Liese Lotte Vossnack, *Pierre Michel d'Ixnard* (Remscheid, 1938).

220. Klopfer, *Von Palladio,* p. 43: "ohne Rücksicht auf den Wohlklang dynamischer Verhältnisse."

221. d'Ixnard, *Recueil,* pls. 4, 5; 12, section.

222. Cf. Laugier, *Essai,* p. 207, and above, Part I, p. 57.

223. d'Ixnard, *Recueil,* pl. 26. Osborn, *Kunst des Rokoko,* ill. p. 348.

224. Jacques-Denis Antoine, *Plans . . . de l'Hôtel des Monnaies* (Paris, 1826), p. 7; pls. 7/8. Klopfer, *Von Palladio,* figs. 143, 144. Saint-Victor, *Tableau historique,* III, ills. opp. p. 759 (river façade), p. 763 (court façade). Hautecoeur, *Histoire de l'architecture,* IV, figs. 124–126.

225. J. Vacquier, *Les Vieux Hôtels de Paris,* ed. F. Contet (Paris, 1913), ser. 7, p. 18; pl. 41. Hautecoeur, *Histoire de l'architecture,* IV, fig. 123. This *hôtel* has become the Ecole Nationale des Ponts et Chaussées.

226. Cornelius Gurlitt, *Historische Städtebilder* (Berlin, 1903), IV (Bern, Zürich), pl. 14 (Mint). Lenotre, *Quartiers,* part IX, pl. 79; Hautecoeur, *Histoire de l'architecture,* IV, fig. 130 (Feuillans portal).

227. Carl Linfert, "Die Grundlagen der Architekturzeichnung," *Kunstwissenschaftliche Forschungen* I (Berlin, 1931), pl. 44a.

228. Louis Hautecoeur, "Projet d'une salle

de spectacle, par N.-M. Potain, 1763," *L'Archi-tecture* XXXVII (1924), 31–36, ills. pp. 33, 34. Hautecoeur, *Histoire de l'architecture,* IV, fig. 277.

229. Ward, *Renaissance in France,* II, 453; fig. 431. Charles Marionneau, *Victor Louis* (Bordeaux, 1881), ill. opp. p. 103.

230. Ward, *Renaissance in France,* II, 451, 453.

231. Alexis Donnet, *Architectonographie des théâtres de Paris* (Paris, 1857), p. 119; pl. 9. Klopfer, *Von Palladio,* fig. 53. Haute-coeur, *Histoire de l'architecture,* IV, fig. 135.

232. Dupezard, *Le Palais-Royal,* pls. 63, 64.

233. Louis is qouted in H. Prudent, "Victor Louis," *L'Architecte* I (1906), 28: "Les grandes façades en ligne droite, et l'uniformité des détails donnent à l'architecture un carac-tère de grandeur qu'on n'obtiendroit jamais par des variétés de masse . . . il a été con-venable de rendre très simple la forme générale du plan et de suivre une décoration absolument uniforme . . ."

234. Prudent, "Victor Louis," fig. 27. Camille Jullian, *Histoire de Bordeaux* (Bor-deaux, 1895), p. 571. The layout resembles that of the Place de France projected in 1609. See Blomfield, *Three Hundred Years of French Architecture, 1494–1794* (London, 1936), p. 41. Hautecoeur, *Histoire de l'archi-tecture,* IV, fig. 57.

235. Vacquier, *Hôtels,* ser. 7, p. 8; pl. 11. Michel, *Histoire de l'art,* vol. VII, chap. X, fig. 295. About Cherpitel's reconstruction of the church of Saint-Barthélemy, 1787, see Lenotre, *Quartiers,* pl. 25. Luc-Vincent Thiéry, *Le Voyageur à Paris,* Extrait du guide des amateurs, (8th ed.; Paris, 1790), I, xxxvii, says; "M. Cherpitel prouve qu'il est possible de faire quelque chose de noble et d'agréable sans le secours de colonnes, par une disposi-tion bien entendue des masses, par la pureté des profils . . ."

236. Charles-Nicolas Cochin, *Mémoires in-édits,* ed. Charles Henry (Paris, 1880), p. 141. More about Le Geay appears in my *Three Revolutionary Architects.* Cochin's sympathy with the modern trends shows in his "Sup-plication aux orfèvres," *Mercure de France* II

(December 1754), 182. Le Geay's spirit lives also in the architectural drawings of Hubert Robert. See Hermann Egger, *Architektonische Handzeichnungen alter Meister* (Vienna, 1910), I, pls. 50 (monument by Hubert, 1761); 51 (villa by Hubert).

237. Blomfield, *French Architecture* (1921 ed.), II, 195.

238. *L'Encyclopédie,* ed. Diderot and d'Alembert (Paris, 1777), Recueil de planches XII, part 6, "Architecture," four plates en-graved by Desprez. Louis Réau, "La Décora-tion du Palais Spinola," *L'Architecture* XXXVI (1923), 219.

239. Peyre *fils* (Antoine Marie Peyre), "Mémoire sur l'Odéon," in *Projets de recon-struction de la Salle de l'Odéon* (Paris, 1819), p. 5. Peyre *fils* does not ascribe to his father a major part in the erection of the Odéon. Thus we may follow Joseph Lavallée, *Notice historique sur Charles Dewailly* (Paris, *an* VII—1799), p. 39: "Cette salle porte non-seulement le genre, le caractère, le style, mais encore . . . les défauts mêmes de Dewailly."

240. Marquis de Girardin, *Maisons de plaisance françaises* (Paris, n.d.), p. 3; pls. 9, 10. Ganay, *Châteaux,* IV, pl. 76.

241. A. M. Peyre, *Projets,* first plate. Le-grand and Landon, *Description,* III, 92; pl. 29.

242. Girardin, *Maisons de plaisance,* p. 3. Hautecoeur, *Histoire de l'architecture,* IV, fig. 116.

243. J. Mayor, "Hôtel de la Chancellerie d'Orléans," *Gazette des Beaux-Arts* (August 1916), p. 335, 339. Ward, *Renaissance in France,* II, fig. 406.

244. *L'Encyclopédie, loc. cit.,* nine plates engraved by Bénard.

245. Lavallée, *Notice,* p. 12.

246. Cf. above, p. 132, Blondel's remarks about the young architects.

247. The original drawing is preserved in the Bibliothèque Nationale, Paris, Cabinet des Estampes. The Comédie française owns a similar drawing, signed and dated 1780. About De Wailly's technique I have found the following interesting comment in An-drieux, "Notice sur la vie et les travaux de

Charles Dewailly," *Mémoires de l'Institut National . . . ,* III, Histoire, p. 39:

> . . . jusqu'au temps de l'école de Lejay [*sic,*] les architectes se contentoient de tirer des lignes, et tout au plus de tracer des plans . . . et l'on ne pouvoit juger de l'effet de leurs compositions. Dewailly, au contraire, composa et exécuta ses dessins d'une manière large et pittoresque; aussi donna-t-il à son art un nouvel essor.

Evidently, Boullée, too, learned the new style in drawing from Le Geay. Hautecoeur, *Histoire de l'architecture,* IV, fig. 118.

248. Hautecoeur, *Histoire de l'architecture,* IV, fig. 207, illustrates the executed pulpit of Saint-Sulpice.

249. Jean Charles Krafft, *Recueil d'architecture civile* (Paris, 1812 ed.), pl. 27. (This book was reprinted under the title *Maisons de campagne* in 1849 and 1876. The original text was written by the architect Goulet, according to Michaud, *Biographie universelle,* biography of J. C. Krafft.) On p. 8, in the comment on the castle of Montmusard (Montumfard) there is a characterization of De Wailly:

> M. de Wailly était doué d'un génie fécond, et d'une imagination quelquefois exaltée. La plupart de ses compositions portent l'empreinte de l'originalité, mais toujours vaste et tendante aux plus grands effets, auxquels il sacrifiait souvent l'agréable, quelquefois même l'utile, ou au moins les commodités domestiques. Ce château nous paraît en fournir un exemple."

Elie Brault, *Les Architectes par leurs oeuvres* (Paris, n.d.), II, 188, calls the castle "Mont-Meudard près Dijon." Hautecoeur, *Histoire de l'architecture,* IV, fig. 114.

250. Jean-Charles Krafft and N. Ransonette, *Plans, coupes, élévations des plus belles maisons et des hôtels construits à Paris et dans les environs* (Paris, 1801), pls. 43, elevation of the group, pl. 45, the lateral house belonging to the sculptor Pajou.

251. *Ibid.,* pl. 44 shows the general layout. Hautecoeur, *Histoire de l'architecture,* IV, fig. 41.

252. Marcel Fouquier, *Paris au dix-huitième*

siècle (Paris, n.d.), ill. p. 42. Krafft and Ransonette, *Plans,* pl. 43.

253. Lavallée, *Notice,* p. 16. The date 1780 appears on the engraving of the obelisk in honor of Louis XVI, on the square of Port-Vendres.

254. *La Décade philosophique, littéraire et politique* XV (Paris, *an* VI), 537, "un caractère plus solennel et plus auguste."

255. *Ibid.,* p. 540, with engraving: "Les nuages qu'on apercevrait à travers les colonnes, et qui se marieraient à l'Architecture, présenteraient des effets pittoresques."

256. Ward, *Renaissance in France,* II, 411.

257. Emma Monti, "L'Art du 18ᵉ siècle français à Parme et à Colorno," *Revue de l'Art Ancien et Moderne* XLIX (1926), ill. p. 269.

258. *Ibid.,* L, ill. p. 35.

259. Augusto Calabi, "Two Documents on Stefano della Bella," *The Print Collector's Quarterly* XIX (1932), 43; pl. X.

260. Millin, *Antiquités,* vol. II, part XI, pl. 1; p. 3: "un pavillon à l'italienne, d'un assez mauvais goût, que faisoit bâtir M. de Balivière." Ganay, *Châteaux,* III, 50, Millin's engraving, pl. 81, the present state; p. 49, the name of the architect without the first name. I assume he was identical with the Louis Le Masson listed in Thieme-Becker, *Künsterlexikon.*

261. Krafft, *Recueil,* pl. 7, Hormois house with the date. *Ibid.,* pl. 13, Huvé's own house at Meudon, with a semicylindrical projection on the court façade. The latter is also in Paul Jarry, *La Guirlande de Paris* (Paris, 1931), II, 9; pl. 32. Hautecoeur, *Histoire de l'architecture,* IV, fig. 47. About Huvé's travels see Louis Serbat, "Le Voyage d'Italie et les dessins de l'architecte J.-J. Huvé," *Bulletin de la Société de l'Histoire de l'Art Français* (1924), p. 40.

262. Landon, *Annales,* X, 113; pl. 55. Saint-Victor, *Tableau historique,* II, 136; ill. opp. p. 136. Auguste Charles Pugin, *Paris and its Environs* (London, 1830), ill. opp. p. 24.

263. Saint-Victor, *Tableau historique,* II, 136. Pugin, *Paris,* p. 23.

264. Landon, *Annales,* X, 113: "Il a l'avan-

tage de présenter, dans son ensemble, une masse parfaitement isolée entre quatre communications publiques."; pl. 55.

265. Prieur, *Collection complète des tableaux historiques de la Révolution française* (Paris, 1798), II, pl. 86. Saint-Victor, *Tableau historique,* II, ill. opp. p. 749, differing slightly. Donnet, *Architectonographie,* p. 32; pl. 3. Charles Simond [Paul Adolphe van Cléemputte], *Paris de 1800 à 1900* (Paris, 1900), I, ill. p. 371; II, ill. p. 31.

266. Emil Kaufmann, "Etienne-Louis Boullée," *Art Bulletin* XXI (1939), fig. 6.

267. Gabriel-Pierre-Martin Dumont, *Recueil de plusieurs parties d'architecture de différents maîtres tant d'Italie que de France* (n. pl., 1767). In either house three wings depart from the central core. Dumont, *Parallèle de plans des plus belles salles de spectacle d'Italie et de France* (1763), also illustrates the Temple des Arts, Dumont's project for a theater, and Soufflot's theater at Lyon.

268. Georges-Louis Le Rouge, *Description du Colisée, élevé aux Champs-Elisées sur les dessins de M. Le Camus* (Paris, 1771). J.-F. Blondel, *Cours,* II, 290. [Bachaumont], *Mémoires secrets* (London, 1784), IV, 249. Hautecoeur, *Histoire de l'architecture,* IV, fig. 291, interior.

269. F. Blondel, *Cours,* I, 108: "Cet édifice intéressant est rémarquable par sa forme circulaire, et par la régularité de son apareil." Hautecoeur, *Histoire de l'architecture,* IV, figs. 75, interior, 76, exterior.

270. Georges-Louis Le Rouge, *Curiosités de Paris* (1771 ed.), I, 226. *Ibid.,* I, 223: "L'un des mérites de ce nouvel édifice, est sa forme nouvelle, qui est circulaire." I, 225: "la beauté des voûtes qui forment comme un seul trait circulaire: le tout en pierres et briques, et de la plus grande perfection." I, 224: "La section des courbes . . . offre aux yeux la plus grande propreté et précision."

271. Saint-Victor, *Tableau historique,* II, 181; ill. opp. p. 180. Krafft and Ransonette, *Plans,* pl. 109.

272. *Ibid.,* II, 182: "Il est peu d'édifices à Paris qui présentent, sous tous les rapports

d'ensemble et de détails, un aspect plus satisfaisant."

273. J. Vacquier, *Les Anciens Châteaux de France,* ed. F. Contet (Paris, 1931), ser. XII, pl. 11.

274. *Ibid.,* pl. 12.

275. Nicolas Le Camus de Mézières, *Le Génie de l'architecture* (Paris, 1780), p. 1.

276. *Ibid.,* p. 31. Cf. Kaufmann, *Three Revolutionary Architects,* p. 456.

277. Le Camus, *Le Génie,* p. 2: "une combinaison qui pût faire un tout caractérisé, capable de produire certaines sensations." P. 45: "Chaque pièce doit avoir son caractère particulier."

278. *Ibid.,* p. 53: "Toute forme étoit permise; pourvu qu'elle papillotât, on étoit content: point d'harmonie, point d'accord, point de simétrie."

279. *Ibid.,* p. 52: "Les ornemens ne doivent pas être prodigués . . . nous ne mettrons pas au nombre des ornemens ces masses vagues, baroques, qu'on ne peut définir, et que nous nommons chicorée: écartons ces extravagances gothiques, quoi-qu'il n'y ait pas encore une dixaine d'années qu'on s'en servoit."

280. *Ibid.,* p. 43: "Pour que l'oeil soit satisfait, un équilibre de dimension devient aussi indispensable, qu'une juste pondération pour qu'un corps vivant se soutienne." P. 47: "La symmétrie ou plutôt les répétitions et les vis-à-vis sont essentiels."

281. *Ibid.,* p. 48: "Ayez le plus grand soin que les milieux soient occupés par des objets principaux et du même genre . . . rien n'est plus choquant que les contrastes." P. 75: "C'est pour l'ordinaire celle du milieu qui doit pyramider et commander aux autres." ["Celle" means "cette élévation."]

282. *Ibid.,* p. 54: "Le *beau* n'est qu'un: . . . on ne le trouvera que dans la pureté des proportions et dans leur harmonie; le Génie seul peut y conduire."

283. From a poem of Père [François Marie] Marsy, according to the statement on the title page.

284. Le Camus, *Le Génie,* p. 63: "Il faut dans un édifice observer l'unité de caractère."

285. *Ibid.,* p. 75.

286. *Ibid.*, p. 61: "Ces accessoires serviront à désigner le caractère, mais ne lui donneront pas l'expression; cette empreinte distinctive est due à des qualités majeures que rien ne peut suppléer." P. 64: "C'est par le grand ensemble qu'on attire et que l'on fixe l'attention."

287. *Ibid.*, p. 71: "Ces masses, ces formes décident le genre, le caractère de la sensation."

288. *Ibid.*, p. 7.

289. *Ibid.*, p. 72: "donner de l'âme au dessin."

290. *Ibid.*, p. 15: "L'ensemble, les masses, les proportions, les ombres, les lumières ont servi de bases à nos combinaisons." P. 43: "Les jours, les ombres distribués avec art dans une composition d'Architecture, concourent à l'effet et à l'impression qu'on veut produire, ils déterminent la réussite."

291. *Ibid.*, p. 72: "Ce sont les masses, ce sont les corps et les avant-corps qui concourent à l'effet . . . par le moyen de la perspective, les avant-corps nous paroissent plus élevés que ceux qui forment le fond; alors ils ont l'avantage à nos yeux de se dessiner dans le vague des airs, et d'y tracer la forme de leur plan . . . Observons encore que tout édifice qui a un peu d'étendue, doit être coupé et interrompu par des hauteurs inégales . . . il faut qu'il présente aux yeux du contraste."

292. *Ibid.*, p. 56.

293. Jean François de Neufforge, *Recueil élémentaire d'architecture* (Paris, 1757–1780), pls. 188, 195. I can dispense with referring to the volume numbers of the *Recueil*, for the pagination is continuous. Arabic numerals were used in the volumes from 1757 to 1768; Roman numerals in the supplementary volumes issued from 1772 to 1780. According to Académie Royale d'Architecture, *Procès-verbaux*, ed. H. Lemonnier (Paris 1911 f.), VI, 304, VII, 218, Neufforge was authorized to put the approval of the Academy only on the first volume, but not on the later ones.

294. Neufforge, *Recueil*, pls. 169, 170.

295. *Ibid.*, pl. 189.

296. *Ibid.*, pl. 196.

297. *Ibid.*, pls. 242, 243.

298. *Ibid.*, pl. 526.

299. Ledoux, *l'Architecture*, p. 113.

300. Neufforge, *Recueil*, pl. 439. Here mention may be made of Neufforge's project for a circular royal library to be erected between the Louvre and the Tuileries, referred to in J. G. Wille, *Mémoires et journal*, ed. Georges Duplessis (Paris, 1857), I, 383.

301. *Ibid.*, pl. XLII.

302. *Ibid.*, pl. CLV.

303. *Ibid.*, pl. 469.

304. Jean-Nicolas-Louis Durand, *Précis des leçons d'architecture* (2nd cd.; Paris, 1809), II, pl. 16.

305. Cf. Thieme-Becker, *Künstlerlexikon*, vols. XXV, XXX.

306. Neufforge, *Recueil*, pls. 397, 399, 401.

307. *Ibid.*, pls. XIX–XXIV.

308. *Ibid.*, pl. 202.

309. *Ibid.*, pls. 118, 120, 122, 128, XII.

310. *Ibid.*, pls. 242, 246, 251.

311. *Ibid.*, pl. 377.

312. *Ibid.*, pl. XVII.

313. *Ibid.*, pl. XVIII.

314. *Ibid.*, pl. CLXIII.

315. *Ibid.*, pl. 332.

316. *Ibid.*, pl. 9.

317. *Ibid.*, pl. LXXI.

318. *Ibid.*, pls. 177, 179, 180, 202, LXX.

319. *Ibid.*, pls. LV, LVI.

320. *Ibid.*, pls. LXIII, LXIV, etc.

321. *Ibid.*, pls. CCLXII—CCC.

322. See above, p. 147.

323. Neufforge, *Recueil*, pl. CCLXXXII.

324. *Ibid.*, pl. CCLXXXIV.

325. See above, p. 143.

326. Neufforge, *Recueil*, pl. CLXXXV.

327. [François de Cuvilliés *fils*], *Ecole de l'architecture bavaroise* [Munich and Paris, 1769–1776]. The plate numbers given below refer to the handwritten pagination of the copy at the Avery Library, Columbia University, New York. The title page is pl. 1. For Cuvilliés' life see Thieme-Becker, *Künstlerlexikon*.

328. Cuvilliés, *Ecole de l'architecture bavaroise*, pls. 30, 31.

329. *Ibid.*, pl. 69.

330. *Ibid.*, pl. 33.

331. *Ibid.*, pl. 48.

332. *Ibid.*, pls. 256, 257.

333. *Ibid.*, pls. 88, 89.

334. *Ibid.*, pl. 268.

335. Collection of etchings by Cuvilliés *père* and *fils* in the Library of Congress, Washington, D. C. *Ornements divers et d'architecture* [Munich and Paris, 1738–1773], vol. IV, pl. 66, by the son.

336. Jean-Charles Delafosse, *Nouvelle Iconologie historique* (Paris, 1768), with 108 plates. *Style Louis Seize. L'Oeuvre de Delafosse. Iconologie historique. Reproduction intégrale de l'ouvrage du temps,* ed. Armand Guérinet (Paris, n.d.), ser. A, with 103 designs by Delafosse. I refer also to Guérinet's more easily available publication, although despite its misleading subtitle ser. A is not a reprint of the original work, but of Jan de Witt Jansz, *Algemeen kunstenaars Handboek . . . geinventeerd . . . door J. Ch. de la Fosse* (Amsterdam, n.d.). De Witt Jansz's edition is incomplete, its plates are reduced and show the designs inverted (left and right exchanged). The plates, moreover, lack the captions, and are of inferior graphic quality. Several plates are added, which were not included in the original *Nouvelle Iconologie historique.*

337. Geneviève Levallet, "L'Ornemaniste Jean-Charles Delafosse," *Gazette des Beaux-Arts* (March 1929), pp. 158–169.

338. *Ibid.*, p. 164.

339. *Ibid.*, p. 165.

340. *Ibid.*, p. 167.

341. *Ibid.*, pp. 159, 163.

342. *Ibid.*, p. 166: "du plus pur style Louis XVI."

343. Linfert, *Grundlagen,* p. 211.

344. *Ibid.*, p. 212: "delafossische Uebertreibung alles Plastischen . . . Monument-phantasien."

345. *Ibid.*, p. 217, note 1.

346. *Ibid.*, p. 215: "Ikonologische Grimasse der Form." "Die Ikonologie-Absicht musste zur Wirkung auf die Ornamentform kommen."

347. *Ibid.*, p. 216: "Eine 'formale Ursache' wird unbeweisbar und konstruiert ausfallen."

348. *Style Louis Seize. Les Dessins de Delafosse exposés au Musée des Arts Décoratifs. Donation David Weill,* ed. Armond Guérinet (Paris, n.d.), ser. E, pl. 31. Linfert, *Grundlagen,* pl. 42c.

349. Delafosse, *Iconologie,* pl. 17. *Style Louis Seize* (ed. Guérinet), ser. A, pl. 17.

350. Delafosse, *Iconologie,* pl. 28. *Style Louis Seize* (ed. Guérinet), ser. A, pl. 30.

351. Delafosse, *Iconologie,* pl. 29. *Style Louis Seize* (ed. Guérinet), ser. A, pl. 28.

352. Delafosse, *Iconologie,* pl. 30. *Style Louis Seize* (ed. Guérinet), ser. A, pl. 29.

353. *Style Louis Seize. L'Oeuvre de Lalonde,* ed. Guérinet (Paris, n.d.), pls. 22–25.

354. Auguste Schoy, *L'Art architectural, décoratif, industriel et somptuaire de l'époque Louis XVI* (Liège and Paris, 1868), part A, pl. 26, right, with the date 1771. (In the edition of Schoy bound in two volumes, I, pl. 26.) *Style Louis Seize* (ed. Guérinet) ser. C, *Cahiers de bronzes, vases, orfèvrerie, etc.,* pl. 78.

355. Schoy, *L'Art architectural,* part A, pl. 27, center bottom, 1771. (I, pl. 27.) *Style Louis Seize,* ser. C, pl. 51, center.

356. Schoy, *L'Art architectural,* part B, pl. 3. (I, pl. 72.) *Style Louis Seize,* ser. D, pl. 29.

357. *Style Louis Seize,* ser. D, pl. 31. The lower part of the plate has Louis XVI character.

358. *Ibid.*, ser. D, pl. 33. Similar emblems of arts and crafts in Delafosse, *Iconologie,* pls. 92, 93, 96–100.

359. Schoy, *L'Art architectural,* part A, pl. 64, 1771. (I, pl. 64.) *Style Louis Seize,* ser. B, *Cahiers d'architecture, mobilier, décoration,* pl. 57.

360. *L'Oeuvre de J. Ch. Delafosse* ed. Daumont (Paris, n.d.), vol. III, cahier T, second plate. Schoy, *L'Art architectural,* part C, pl. 2. (II, pl. 2). *Style Louis Seize,* ser. C, pl. 62.

361. Delafosse, *Iconologie,* pls. 84, 85. Schoy, *L'Art architectural,* part D, pl. 7, 1771. (II, pl. 34.) *Style Louis Seize,* ser. A, pl. 75; ser. D, in pls. 46 and 50.

362. Schoy, *L'Art architectural,* part D, pl. 20, 1776. (II, pl. 47.) *Style Louis Seize,* ser. C, pl. 46.

363. Schoy, *L'Art architectural,* part E, pl. 1, 1771. (II, pl. 59.) *Style Louis Seize,* ser. C, pls. 29, 30.

364. Delafosse, *Iconologie,* pl. 2. *Style Louis Seize,* ser. A, pl. 2, without figures.

365. Delafosse, *Iconologie,* pl. 66. *Style Louis Seize,* ser. A, pl. 66.

366. Delafosse, *Iconologie,* pl. 86. *Style Louis Seize,* ser. A, pl. 76.

367. Delafosse, *Iconologie,* pl. 35. *Style Louis Seize,* ser. A, pl. 38.

368. Delafosse, *Iconologie,* pl. 33. *Style Louis Seize,* ser. A, pl. 37.

369. Delafosse, *Iconologie,* pl. 37. *Style Louis Seize,* ser. A, pl. 40.

370. *Style Louis Seize,* ser. E, pl. 4. Linfert, *Grundlagen,* pl. 43a.

371. *Style Louis Seize,* ser. E, pl. 29.

372. *Style Louis Seize,* ser. B, pl. 39. *Delafosse* (ed. Daumont), vol. III, cahier S, pl. 4.

373. Gurlitt, *Die Baukunst Frankreichs,* I, pl. 25. Each drawing bears the signature of Delafosse.

374. Schoy, *L'Art architectural,* part A, pl. 29, 1760. (I, pl. 29.)

375. Schoy, *L'Art architectural,* part A, pl. 35, 1763. (I, pl. 35.)

376. Schoy, *L'Art architectural,* part A, pl. 76, 1774. (I, pl. 167.)

377. Schoy, *L'Art architectural,* part A, pl. 19. (I, pl. 19.)

378. Schoy, *L'Art architectural,* part A, pl. 63. (I, pl. 63.)

379. These two designs belong to the "Suitte de phares" in *Delafosse* (ed. Daumont), vol. III, cahier DD. Pls. 1, 2, 3 bear the engraved remark, "Le Canu inv."; pl. 4 is obviously by the same designer. The comparison with the tombs of Le Canu (see previous note) supports this attribution.

380. Michel-Ange Challe, *Description du catafalque et du cénotaphe érigés dans l'Eglise de Paris le 7 septembre 1774 . . . pour Louis XV* (Paris, 1774).

381. Galliffet: Vacquier, *Hôtels,* ser. 3, p. 7, plan; pls. 23, 24. Jarnac: Krafft and Ransonette, *Plans,* pl. 31, dates the house 1788. According to Vacquier, *op. cit.,* ser. 13, p. 1, pls. 1–3, it must have been built prior to 1787.

382. J. Vacquier, *Le Style Empire* (Paris, 1924), ser. 2, p. 12; pl. 19.

383. See above, pp. 148–149.

384. Vacquier, *Empire,* ser. 2, pl. 23.

385. Landon, *Annales,* VII, 63, signed "L. G.," i.e. Legrand: "érigé quelques années avant la révolution." Pugin, *Paris,* with ill. of the rear façade, opp. p. 122. Donnet, *Architectonographie,* p. 97, provides us with the date.

386. Alste Oncken, *Friedrich Gilly* (Berlin, 1935), pl. 43, Alfred Rietdorf, *Friedrich Gilly* (Berlin, 1940), fig. 100, presents a drawing by Gilly, showing the main front, which may have been derived from Célérier's concert hall (see below, p. 160). Landon, *Annales,* VII, 64; pl. 28. Jean Charles Krafft and F. Thiollet, *Choix des plus jolies maisons de Paris et des environs* (Paris, n.d.), pl. 145. Henri d'Alméras, *La Vie parisienne sous la Révolution et le Directoire* (Paris, n.d.), p. 126, ill. opp. p. 128.

387. Landon, *Annales,* XIII, 31, signed "L.G."; pl. 12.

388. Saint-Victor, *Tableau historique,* II, ill. opp. p. 256; p. 241 gives the date, 1787, and the remark: "Ce monument, composé d'une voûte en berceau, formant un demi-cercle parfait . . . présente, dans sa masse et dans ses détails, une élégante simplicité."

389. Armand-Guy de Kersaint, *Discours sur les monuments publics* (Paris, 1792), pls. 4 (Pritanée), 10 (Museum), 5–7 (Palais National). Ferdinand Boyer, "Projets de salles pour les assemblées révolutionnaires à Paris, 1789–1792," *Bulletin de la Société de l'Histoire de l'Art Français* (1933), p. 181; ill. opp. p. 174.

390. Landon, *Annales,* XI, 36; XII, pl. 28, elevation, section and plan. In XII, 63, Legrand states that Molinos alone built the Morgue. Alfred Delvau and Théophile Gautier, *Paris qui s'en va* [Paris, ca. 1860], pl. 16, etching of the interior by Léopold Flameng. Georges Cain, *Nouvelles Promenades dans Paris* (Paris, n.d.), ill. p. 149, interior. Pugin, *Paris,* ill. opp. p. 62. Musée Carnavalet, Paris, lithograph of the interior, by Delannoy. Cf. *Grande Encyclopédie,* article on "Morgue."

391. Luc-Vincent Thiéry, *Guide des étrangers* (Paris, 1787), I, 136. Fouquier, *Paris au 18ᵉ siècle*, ill. p. 93. Marcel Poète, *Une Vie de cité. Paris de sa naissance à nos jours* (Paris, 1925), *Album*, pp. 232, 269; fig. 272. Poète speaks of the Hôtel de la Haye, by [André] Aubert.

392. Adolphe Lance, *Dictionnaire des architectes français* (Paris, 1872), p. 34.

393. Thieme-Becker, *Künstlerlexikon*, states that he was a pupil of De Wailly.

394. Legrand and Landon, *Description*, IV, 38, with date; pl. 46. Krafft and Ransonette, *Plans*, pl. 37. In the text the date is 1775. Different spellings of the names Poyete, Calais, Galeau. Fouquier, *Paris au 18ᵉ siècle*, p. 117. Hautecoeur, *Histoire de l'architecture*, IV, figs. 70, plan, 71, elevation.

395. Armand Husson, *Etude sur les hôpitaux* (Paris, 1862), p. 28, with plan. Landon, *Annales*, XI, 59, signed "L.G."; pl. 27, plan, 28, elevation.

396. Landon, *Annales*, XI, 60, signed "L.G." In Legrand and Landon, *Description*, III, 80, Goulet states that the physician Petit had recommended a circular hospital with radiant aisles in 1772. But it is hardly to be doubted that Poyet must be credited with the artistic solution of the contrasting substructure and rotunda. A. Petit, *Mémoire sur la meilleure manière de construire un hôpital* (Paris, 1774).

397. Landon, *Annales*, vol. XI, pl. 28.

398. *Ibid.*, p. 59, "cette forme imposante...," p. 62, "la beauté de ce plan."

399. *Ibid.*, XI, 59: "Il est de ces idées heureuses qui plaisent par leur simplicité, et qui n'ont besoin, pour être senties et appréciées, d'aucun ornement étranger." XI, 62: "Tous les amis des arts, tous ceux que les grandes idées frappent, et qui s'enthousiasment à la vue du noble et du beau . . . ne peuvent que faire des voeux pour l'exécution de ce vaste projet."

400. Luc-Vincent Thiéry, *Almanach du voyageur* (Paris, 1784), p. 258: "sur les dessins de Poyet." Pugin, *Paris*, ill. opp. p. 50. *The Dictionary of Architecture*, ed. The Architectural Publication Society (London,

n.d.), vol. VI, attributes the stables to Poyet. Rietdorf, *Gilly*, fig. 77 (after a drawing by Gilly) differs slightly from Pugin. The stables were owned later by the dukes of Chartres (Orléans). Hautecoeur, *Histoire de l'architecture*, IV, fig. 34.

401. Cornelius Gurlitt, *Geschichte des Barockstiles in Belgien, Holland Frankreich, England* (Stuttgart, 1888) fig. 43.

402. Cf. the façades referred to in notes 265, 384, above.

403. Landon, *Annales*, I, 79; pl. 38.

404. Ferdinand Boyer, "Le Palais-Bourbon sous le Premier Empire," *Bulletin de la Société de l'Histoire de l'Art Français* (1936), p. 112. Legrand and Landon, *Description*, II, 71; pl. 44.

405. Quoted by Boyer, "Palais-Bourbon," p. 119.

406. Kaufmann, "Boullée," 217, fig. 5.

407. See notes 204, 220, above.

408. Krafft and Ransonette, *Plans*, pls. 41, plan, 42, rear façade, with date.

409. *Ibid.*, pl. 54, with date.

410. Théâtre des Variétés Boulevard Montmarte; Legrand and Landon, *Description*, vol. IV, pl. 33; Pugin, *Paris*, ill. opp. p. 110; Donnet, *Architectonographie*, p. 44; pl. 4. Ambigu Comique, Boulevard du Temple: Donnet, *Architectonographie*, p. 130, pl. 10; Poète, *Album*, p. 233, fig. 268, called "Théâtre des Variétés amusantes." I want to point out here two other theaters named Ambigu Comique, though they do not seem to be by Célérier. The one with a very original side façade was located between Boulevard Saint-Martin and Rue de Bondy. (Donnet, *Architectonographie*, pls. XXI, XXII. Pugin, *Paris*, ill. opp. p. 148.) The other, a severe cube was near the Porte Saint-Denis. (Segard and Testard, *Picturesque Views of Public Edifices in Paris*, London, 1814, ill. opp. p. 23. Lenotre, *Quartiers*, part IX, pl. 77.)

411. See Part I, note 299. Kaufmann, "Boullée," 212–227, presented the first biography of Boullée.

412. Kaufmann, *Three Revolutionary Architects*, figs. 16, 17, 30–33, 41, 42.

413. *Ibid.*, fig. 35.

414. *Ibid.*, fig. 21. In the present book I illustrate Bibliothèque Nationale, Ha 55, no. 22.

415. *Ibid.*, figs. 38, 39, city gates, 44, library entrance. In the present book I illustrate the gate, Bibliothèque Nationale, Ha 55, no. 32.

416. Etienne-Louis Boullée, *Architecture,* in *Papiers,* Paris, Bibliothèque Nationale, Fonds français, ms. 9153, fol. 48: "Nos émotions naissent du tout ensemble et non pas des détails."

417. *Ibid.*, fol. 110.

418. For their first biographies see note 411 above; my first article on them appeared in *Zeitschrift für bildende Kunst* LXIII, 1929, pp. 38–46. Soon the significance of Boullée and Ledoux was recognized by several critics, who, of course, suggested divers interpretations, and they were included in the surveys of Talbot F. Hamlin, Pierre Lavedan and Nikolaus Pevsner. Many periodicals made them known to the public, *Arkitektura, Kentiku Sekai,* 1934; *Deutsche Bauzeitung,* 1935; *Emporium, Forum, Parnassus,* 1936; *Beaux-Arts,* 1937; *Architectural Review,* 1941, 1949, 1952; *Burlington Magazine,* 1944. Very meritorious were the popularizations of Mrs. Helen Rosenau who had become interested in my biographies of Boullée and Ledoux and in the Lequeu illustrations presented in them as well. Yet my biographical article "Jean-Jacques Lequeu," *Art Bulletin* XXXI (1949), 130–135, appeared only shortly before her essay on Lequeu, *Architectural Review* CVI (1949), 111–116, and the Lequeu documents of the Bibliothèque Nationale escaped her attention, so she could discuss Lequeu merely in a general way.

419. Henry Lemonnier, "La Mégalomanie dans l'architecture," *L'Architecte* V (1910), 92–97.

420. Emil Kaufmann, *Von Ledoux bis Le Corbusier* (Vienna, 1933), p. 59. See my review of M. Raval and J. C. Moreux, *C.-N. Ledoux* (Paris, 1944), in *Art Bulletin* XXX (1948), 288–291.

421. Though Hautecoeur, *Histoire de l'architecture,* IV, 402, admits the general tendency towards sobriety and austerity in the works of the period, he believes that the simplicity of some designs of Ledoux had exclusively economic origins. I wish to answer this view by referring to Ledoux's project for the house of a writer and that for four families. These apparently were not thought of as dwellings for poor people. More important, however, is to note that in designs which were not made on commission the architect could speak out freely. He might have added, on paper, any number of columns and ornaments, if as an artist he had wished to. These and similar projects, never realized and hardly realizable, represent the most determined efforts to create a new artistic form.

422. See p. 131 above. Very few architects seem to have reproduced works of Ledoux. One was Damesme, who will be discussed in my last chapter. Another was Christian Frederick Hansen, whose projects for the jail at Copenhagen (1799) resemble closely Ledoux's prison project for Aix, while the building as carried out differs considerably. Cf. Jörn Rubow, "C. F. Hansen," *Artes* III (1935), 131–165, with ills.

423. Kaufmann, *Three Revolutionary Architects,* figs. 50, 51, Montmorency; figs. 77–79, Thélusson.

424. *Ibid.*, fig. 137. The portico may also be seen in the foreground of the view of the "ideal city."

425. *Ibid.*, fig. 142. The main entrance of the factory building leads to the "Fourneaux," the lateral entrance to the "Magasin des Sels" or "Salle des Bosses."

426. *Ibid.*, figs. 113–129.

427. *Ibid.*, fig. 60, "House with a belvedere," is compositionally similar.

428. Cf. *ibid.*, fig. 134, Inn Marceau.

429. Cf. *ibid.*, fig. 70, Hocquart house.

430. *Ibid.*, fig. 164.

431. *Ibid.*, fig. 93.

432. *Ibid.*, fig. 150.

433. *Ibid.*, figs. 140, 141. Emil Kaufmann, "Die Stadt des Architekten Ledoux," *Kunstwissenschaftliche Forschungen* II (1933), 131–160. See also my *Three Revolutionary Architects,* p. 474, note 2.

434. Kaufmann, *Three Revolutionary Architects*, fig. 152.

435. *Ibid.*, fig. 174.

436. *Ibid.*, fig. 198.

437. *Ibid.*, pp. 441. 514, 517, 518. Concerning *architecture parlante* see above, note 78.

438. See also my *Three Revoluionary Architects*, fig. 158, Cemetery.

439. Hans Sedlmayr, *Verlust der Mitte* (Salzburg, 1948), p. 98. Having myself pointed out the extraordinary significance of the revolutionary designs and interpreted them as symptoms of their period (*Von Ledoux*, pp. 11, 25, etc.), I certainly do not underrate what Sedlmayr terms *kritische Formen*. However, the large number of original and yet "normal" inventions reveals that the complex period with all its excitement was sound enough to bring about a true regeneration of architecture. In the Epilogue to his book Sedlmayr points out that my rediscovery of Ledoux became the starting point of his investigation into the formative forces of our era. Though he does not fully agree with my interpretation, he nonetheless adopts most of my concepts and observations, especially those of the new decentralization in composition—*Verlust der Mitte!*—(p. 145; in my *Von Ledoux bis Le Corbusier, p. 19, 60*), the abolition of the old aesthetic canons (151; *43, 60*), the increasing hostility to decoration (91; *44*), the new "mobility" of furniture (26; *53*), the altered relationship between structure and environment (26, 88; *16, 61*), the ideal of equality in architecture (63; *38*), the triumph of elementary geometry (27; *30*), the parallel phenomena in the graphic arts, particularly the fashion of the silhouette (84; *47*), the end of the Baroque anthropomorphisms and the new attitude towards matter (37, 82, 151; *46*), the coming up of new architectural tasks (15, 65; *38*), the new sense of commodiousness (38; *38*), the presentation of new forms long before new materials fitting them were found (98; *46*), the continuity of the development after 1800 (12, 100; *6, 61*), the struggle of antagonistic tendencies in the nineteenth century (65; *59*), the appearance of a new structural order behind the masks of the various styles (62; *58*), and the typically nineteenth-century thought that perfect solutions of the past should be the standards for all the future (65; originally set forth in my article in *Repertorium für Kunstwissenschaft* LXIV, 1924, 228.

440. Kaufmann, *Three Revolutionary Architects*, fig. 83.

441. *Ibid.*, p. 490, about the spatial composition of the prison.

442. *Ibid.*, fig. 177.

443. *Ibid.*, fig. 106.

444. *Ibid.*, fig. 107.

445. *Ibid.*, fig. 168. The quotation is from Ledoux, *Architecture*, (Paris, 1804), p. 49.

446. Kaufmann, *Three Revolutionary Architects*, fig. 103, illustrates the first project for the Discount Bank, fig. 104, the second.

447. *Ibid.*, fig. 188.

448. Krafft, *Recueil*, preface written by Goulet (see note 249, above):

> Several modern architects have thought they should transmit their names to posterity by becoming innovators. Their imaginations gave birth to gigantic and fantastic ideas which they represented upon paper; their draughts were distinguished for heaviness and a lavishness of ornaments devoid of taste. Fortunately for us, they will never succeed in subverting the taste inspired by the excellent models of our great masters, and notwithstanding all their efforts, we shall not lose sight of the two distinctive characteristics of works of architecture: *elegance and simplicity*. [Goulet's italics.]

Charles-François Viel de Saint-Maux, *Lettres sur l'architecture des anciens et celle des moderns* (Paris, 1787), I, 14: "Ils dédaignoient de consulter la nature, la raison . . ."; VI, 8: "Ce siècle . . . flotte encore dans une incertitude." *Décadence*, p. 7: "Les loix mêmes de la symétrie sont violées . . . des constructions gigantesques surmontées par des parties de petites dimensions . . . de foibles supports couronnées par de lourdes murailles . . . les ordres y sont dénaturés . . . les profils . . . y sont . . . en un discord complet avec l'ordonnance . . ." *Ibid.*, p. 8: "L'esprit capricieux de ces deux artistes . . . a opéré une véritable révolution dans l'ordonnance des édifices . . . l'ambition sans bornes, pour jouer un rôle dans la société, les fait publier partout, qu'eux seuls connoissent la grande manière . . . *qu'il faut se frayer de nouvelles routes.*" [Viel's italics.] *Ibid.,* P. 9:"Ce succès des novateurs, et qui est si funeste à tous les arts, n'aura de durée que celle de ce siècle qui touche à sa fin." Of course, the revolutionary movement was not created by Boullée and Ledoux alone. That the general unrest had got hold of many artists was noticed also by Pierre Patte, and François Michel Lecreulx and Wilgrin de Taillefer. (See note 203, above.) For more quotations from Viel's writings see my *Three Revolutionary Architects,* pp. 457, 458.

449. *Nouvelles Archives de l'art français* (Paris, 1878), p. 76. Letter of September 30, 1766: "L'air d'Angleterre m'étant absolument contraire . . . j'ai vu tout ce qu'il y a à voir." *Ibid.,* p. 45, about his travel to Italy.

450. Goulet in Legrand and Landon, *Description,* III, 64: "Ce monument fit la réputation de l'architecte;" pls. 18, 19. Similarly, "L.G." (Legrand) in Landon, *Annales* (1803), V, 119. Krafft and Ransonette, *Plans,* pls. 105, 106. Pugin, *Paris,* ill. opp. p. 48. Lenotre, *Quartiers,* part VIII, pls. 68, 70. Jean Adhémar, "L'Ecole de médecine," *L'Architecture* XLVII (1934), 105–108, with ills. Jacques Gondoin, *Description des écoles de chirurgie* (Paris, 1780), with engravings. Hautecoeur, *Histoire de l'architecture,* IV, figs. 119–122.

451. Quatremère de Quincy, *Histoire,* II, 332: "Un seul mot fera l'éloge de ce monument. Il est l'ouvrage le plus classique du dix-huitième siècle."

452. René Schneider, in *L'Art français,* IV, 206, and in Michel, *Histoire de l'art,* VII, 458, speaks contemptuously of "velléité archéologique," referring to the School of Medicine, the Odéon, etc. He confuses, fig. 130, Antoine's Charité with Viel's Hôpital Cochin.

453. Landon, *Annales,* V, 119, signed "L. G.": "Les gens du monde y virent un genre entièrement neuf . . . les architectes y reconnurent la majesté de l'architecture romaine,

dépouillée de ses riches superfluités et rapprochée de la simplicité grecque; grande par la disposition des masses . . ."

454. *Ibid.,* V, 119.

455. J.-F. Blondel, *L'Homme du monde,* II, 112: "Ne vous attendez pas à trouver ici les termes de l'art exactement à leur place . . ." II, 114: "M. Gondouin [*sic*] . . . a su se délivrer des entraves communes; en homme de génie, il a franchi les bornes, et créé un genre qui, dans le goût antique, offre néanmoins les découvertes intéressantes des Modernes." Amaury Duval et Alexandre Moisy, *Fontaines de Paris* (Paris, 1813), p. 23: "M. Gondoin partagera avec M. Soufflot la gloire d'avoir contribué à cette révolution en architecture . . . le passage du goût affecté au goût sévère."

456. Goulet in Legrand and Landon, *Description,* III, 65. Saint-Victor, *Tableau historique,* III, 582, copying Goulet's text; ills. opp. p. 579, exterior, p. 581, court.

457. Schneider, *L'Art français,* IV, caption of fig. 132. Adhémar, "L'Ecole de médecine," ill. p. 107. Hautecoeur, *Histoire de l'architecture,* IV, fig. 122.

458. Emil Kaufmann, "Boullée," *Art Bulletin* XXI (1939), p. 227, quotation from Gondoin; fig. 14.

459. Quatremère de Quincy, *Histoire,* II, 333.

460. Legrand and Landon, *Description,* vol. III, pl. 20, with the date 1806.

461. Note in *Papiers de Boullée,* Bibliothèque Nationale, ms. 9153, fol. 21. Antoine Chrysostome Quatremère de Quincy, *Recueil de notices historiques* (Paris, 1834), p. 2, 6, remarks that Chalgrin became a pupil of Boullée in 1755, and characterizes the period of Servandoni's later years thus: "Cette époque . . . étant celle d'une révolution dans le goût de l'architecture en France.

462. Simond, *Paris de 1800 à 1900,* I, 211, with ill. Poète, *Vie de cité,* III, 98.

463. Saint-Victor, *Tableau historique,* I, 492; ills., opp. p. 491, exterior; opp. p. 493, interior. Krafft and Ransonette, *Plans,* pls. 103, 104. Pugin, *Paris,* ill. opp. p. 114. Legrand and Landon, *Description,* I, 130: "Cette église qui pouvait être facilement isolée . . .

et qui sans doute avait été ainsi projetée par son auteur . . ." Similarly, Saint-Victor, *Tableau historique,* I, 494. Hautecoeur, *Histoire de l'architecture,* IV, figs. 101, interior, 198, exterior.

464. Krafft, *Recueil,* pl. 14. Ganay, *Châteaux,* V, 15-18, with ills. Hautecoeur, *Histoire de l'architecture,* IV, fig. 28.

465. J. D. Thierry, *Arc de triomphe de l'Étoile* (Paris, 1845), pp. 10, 25; pl. 22/1, the first design of 1806; 22/5, that of 1810.

466. Gustave Hirschfeld, *Arcs de triomphe et colonnes triomphales de Paris* (Paris, 1938), p. 49.

467. A. Hustin, *Le Palais du Luxembourg* (Paris, 1904), p. 18: "On peut pratiquer deux logements . . . et des petites pièces commodes . . . L'addition . . . ôtera cette dureté qui naît de la saille énorme des Pavillons sur le Corps de Logis du Fond." Plan, p. 19.

468. *Ibid.,* p. 21: "Ces pavillons donnent au Palais un renfoncement en arrière-corps, qui aux yeux des personnes de l'Art, est tout à fait désagréable. Ces deux ailes auraient l'avantage . . . de cacher ce défaut essentiel . . ."

469. Hustin, *Palais du Luxembourg,* pp. 18–21, with plan; ills. pp. 68, 69. Edouard Joyant, "Les Gisors," *Bulletin de la Société de l'Histoire de l'Art Français* (1937), p. 290, gives the date as 1804. Hustin, *op. cit.,* p. 66, quotes Chalgrin as speaking proudly of "le style grand et imposant" of the hall.

470. J. Silvestre de Sacy, *Alexandre Théodore Brongniart* (Paris, 1940), p. 8.

471. Krafft and Ransonette, *Plans,* pls. 29, 30, with the date 1770. Fouquier, *Paris au 18e siècle,* pp. 52, 53, reproduces Krafft's engravings. Sacy: 1773. Hautecoeur, *Histoire de l'architecture,* IV, fig. 33.

472. Krafft and Ransonette, *Plans,* pls. 5, 6, with the date 1775, names Happe as the rebuilder of the court and staircase; Legrand and Landon, *Description,* IV, 23 (pl. 39), names Sobre. Fouquier, *Paris au 18e siècle,* ill. p. 92. *The Dictionary of Architecture,* I, 153: "The Hôtel de Saint-Foix was long considered as a model." Sacy: 1779.

473. Krafft and Ransonette, *Plans,* pl. 7, with date, 1774. Sacy: 1778.

474. Krafft and Ransonette, *Plans,* pl. 66, no. 1.

475. *Ibid.,* Bondy: pl. 21, with the date 1781. Sacy: 1771. Masserano: pl. 39, with the date 1784. Vacquier, *Hôtels,* ser. 12, p. 1, pl. 1: 1787.

476. Krafft and Ransonette, *Plans,* pls. 69, 70, with the date 1784. Sacy: 1774.

477. Krafft and Ransonette, *Plans,* pl. 114 (1784). Legrand and Landon, *Description,* III, 51; pl. 12 (1781). Saint-Victor, *Tableau historique,* vol. II, ill. p. 139; p. 137 states that the friars moved in 1783. Hautecoeur, *Histoire de l'architecture,* IV, figs. 164, façade, 165, court.

478. Legrand and Landon, *Description,* III, 51: "Une grand cour entourée d'une galerie couverte en terrasse." For the "withdrawing form," see pp. 114, 143, 185.

479. *Ibid.,* III, 52: "Ce joli monument est fait pour ajouter à la réputation de l'architecte." "Saint-Victor, *Tableau historique,* II, 138, adopts Goulet's view; ill. opp. p. 137, court.

480. Krafft and Ransonette, *Plans,* pl. 61, with date. Vacquier, *Hôtels,* ser. 12, p. 2; pls. 4, 5, 7.

481. Krafft and Ransonette, *Plans,* Archives: pl. 65, with date; Chamblin: pl. 15, with date. Hautecoeur, *Histoire de l'architecture,* IV, figs. 159, court, 160, plan, 161, garden front.

482. Donnet, *Architectonographie,* p. 187; pl. 12 presents also the neighboring house. The date is from *The Dictionary of Architecture,* I, 152.

483. Pugin, *Paris,* ill. opp. p. 24. Klopfer, *Von Palladio,* figs. 134, 135.

484. Jean Stern, *A l'ombre de Sophie Arnould—François-Joseph Belanger* (Paris, 1930).

485. *Ibid.,* I, 18 ff.; ill. opp. p. 22.

486. *Ibid.,* I, 42; ill. opp. p. 40.

487. *Ibid.,* I, 64; ills. opp. pp. 64, 66. Vacquier, *Châteaux,* ser. 3, "Bagatelle," pls. 1, 2. Hautecoeur, *Histoire de l'architecture,* IV, fig. 30.

488. Krafft, *Recueil,* pl. 10. Hautecoeur, *Histoire de l'architecture,* IV, fig. 248.

489. Krafft, *Recueil,* pl. 2, plans and section, with date, 3, elevations. Hautecoeur, *Histoire de l'architecture,* fig. 172.

490. Krafft, *Recueil,* pl. 116. Stern, *Belanger,* I, ill. opp. p. 66.

491. Krafft, *Recueil,* pls. 99, 100. Vacquier, *Châteaux,* ser. 3, Sainte-James, pls. 1, 2. Stern, *Belanger,* ill. opp. p. 136. Girardin, *Maisons de plaisance,* pl. 41.

492. Stern, *Belanger,* I, 98; ills. opp. p. 100, plan, p. 102, elevation. Thiéry, *Almanach,* p. 257.

493. Stern, *Belanger,* I, 230–232.

494. Saint-Victor, *Tableau historique,* I, 502; ill. p. 503. Pugin, *Paris,* ill. opp. p. 132. Simond, *Paris de 1800 à 1900,* vol. I, ill. p. 487. Stern, *Belanger,* I, 230, with date.

495. Stern, *Belanger,* I, 231. Ville de Paris, Commission municipale du Vieux Paris, *Procès-verbaux,* 1902 (Paris, 1903), p. 48; ill. between pp. 76 and 77.

496. Saint-Victor, *Tableau historique,* I, 502, about the Pompe de Chaillot: "Un petit bâtiment carré d'une forme très élégante . . ."

497. Ville de Paris, *Procès-verbaux,* 1902, p. 50: "La suppression de la pompe . . . ne laisse aucun regret, pas plus au point de vue de l'usage économique qu'à celui de l'esthétique parisienne."

498. Stern, *Belanger,* II, 361, holds a different view: "Belanger est resté fidèle à la tradition du dix-huitième siècle." II, 363: "Belanger avait été . . . le dernier représentant du 18e siècle."

499. Stern, *Belanger,* I, 127; ills. opp. pp. 128, 120, after a drawing.

500. Lemonnier, "La Mégalomanie dans l'architecture," 96; fig. 10. Stern, *Belanger,* II, ill. opp. p. 144.

501. Stern, *Belanger,* vol. I, ill. opp. p. 88, with date.

502. Both Bibliothèque Nationale, Estampes, Ha 58, pp. 28, 29. However, the "Projet d'embellissement du Pont-Neuf" illustrated by Stern, *Belanger,* I, 233, was by Jacques-Pierre Gisors, according to the caption on Berthault's engraving reproduced by Joyant (see note 483).

503. Krafft, *Recueil,* p. 19; pls. 91, 92. Stern, *Belanger,* II, 157.

504. *Ibid.,* pl. 10.

505. Krafft and Ransonette, *Plans,* pl. 63, with date.

506. *Ibid.,* pl. 17. Legrand and Landon, *Description,* IV, 36, pl. 44.

507. Bibliothèque Nationale, Estampes, Ha 58b. Stern, *Belanger,* vol. I, ill. opp. p. 194.

508. Legrand and Landon, *Description,* IV, 35: "On y reconnaît l'art et le goût avec lesquels M. Belanger sait embellir toutes ses compositions." IV, 36: "Avec une réputation et des talents distingués, tels que ceux de M. Belanger, il est sans doute permis de se livrer aux élans de son imagination et de hasarder quelquefois des compositions qu'on peut appeler de fantaisie . . ."

509. Lenotre, *Quartiers,* part I, pl. 5. Stern, *Belanger,* ill. opp. p. 220. Fouquier, *Paris au 18e siècle,* ill. p. 99.

510. See p. 114, above.

511. Stern, *Belanger,* vol. I, ill. opp. p. 210. Foquier, *Paris au 18e siècle,* Ill. p. 75, execution. Engraving by Van Cléemputte, Bibliothéque Nationale, Paris, Cabinet des Estampes, Ha 58, p. 16.

512. Stern, *Belanger,* II, 218, 238ff., presents much data, but no comments nor illustrations. The construction of slaughterhouses in Paris began in 1808. Cf. Simond, *Paris de 1800 à 1900,* I, 176. François-Joseph Belanger, *Notes instructives pour MM. les Architectes et Entrepreneurs de l'ex-Gouvernement* (Paris, 1814), p. 10.

513. Bibliothèque Nationale, Estampes, Ha 58b, has the group of three slaughterhouses and the slaughterhouse with the clock.

514. *Art Bulletin* XXI (1939), figs. 18, 19, taken from François Leonard Scheult, *Recueil d'architecture dessinée et mesurée en Italie 1791–1793* (Paris, 1821). Often the name of the architect is spelled Séheult.

515. Stern, *Belanger,* I, opp. pp. 56, 64, 68, illustrates the original drawings, which differ from Krafft, *Recueil,* pls. 115 (plan), 116 (main house), 117 (Communs). The latter

are reproduced in Vacquier, *Châteaux,* ser. 3, Bagatelle, p. 3. Fouquier, *Paris au 18e siècle,* ill. p. 2.

516. Krafft and Ransonette, *Plans,* pl. 4, section; pl. 66, nos. 2, 3, court façades; and see note 511, above.

517. See Emil Kaufmann, "Klassizimus als Tendenz und als Epoche," *Kritische Berichte zur Kunstgeschichtlichen Literatur* (1931/32), 201–214, presenting a cumulative review of writings on eighteenth-century classicism.

518. Sainte-James: Krafft, *Recueil,* pls. 105, 106, (pavilion); 109 (grotto); 114 (pump house). Girardin, *Maisons de plaisance,* pl. 43, grotto. Santeny: Krafft, *Recueil,* pls. 12 (rustic huts), 32, 33, (mansion). Stern, *Belanger,* II, 156. Kaufmann, *Von Ledoux bis Le Corbusier,* ill. p. 26.

519. Fiske Kimball, "Les Influences anglaises dans la formation du Style Louis XVI," *Gazette des Beaux-Arts* (January 1931), 36–39. "Romantic Classicism in Architecture," *Ibid.* (February 1944), 95–112. The term "Romantic Classicism" was coined by Siegfried Giedion, *Spätbarocker und romantischer Klassizismus* (Munich, 1922). Ernest de Ganay, "Le Goût du moyen âge et des ruines aux jardins du 18e siècle," *Gazette des Beaux-Arts* (October 1932), 183–197. "Fabriques aux jardins du 18e siècle," *Revue dé l'Art Ancien et Moderne* LXIV (July 1933), 49–74.

520. Kaufmann, *Von Ledoux bis Le Corbusier,* ill. p. 26. Ganay, *Châteaux,* V, 12–15, pl. 11. Raymond Lecuyer and J.-C. Moreux, "Le Désert de M. de Monville," *L'Amour de l'Art* XIX (1938) 119–126. Oswald Sirén, Le Désert de Retz," *Architectural Review* CVI (1949), 327–332.

521. Georges Gromort, *Le Hameau de Trianon* (Paris, 1928), Léon Deshairs, *Petit Trianon* (Paris, n.d.), p. 12.

522. Dimier, *L'Architecture,* I, 9; pl. XXXIII. Hautecoeur, *Histoire de l'architecture,* IV, fig. 59.

523. Pierre Dubois, *Anciens Châteaux* (ed. Contet; Paris, 1932), ser. 13, p. 12, with date; pls. 35, 36.

524. Legrand and Landon, *Description,* p. 87. Thiéry, *Le Voyageur,* II, 234. Saint-Victor,

Tableau historique, II, 404; ill. p. 406. Jacques Antoine Dulaure, *Histoire de Paris* (1839 ed.), VII, ill. opp. p. 258; (7th ed., 1842: IV, 47). Krafft and Thiollet, *Choix,* pl. 146. Lenotre, *Quartiers,* pl. 76, presents the original state. Poète, *Album,* fig. 269.

525. L. Noé, *Architecture et sculpture en France* (Paris, 1894), V, *feuille* 46. Hautecoeur, *Histoire de L'architecture,* IV, fig. 180.

526. Nils Gustaf Wollin, *Gravures originales de Desprez* (Malmö, 1933), p. 15. *Desprez en Italie* (Malmö, 1935), p. 10.

527. Nils Gustaf Wollin, *Desprez en Suède* (Stockholm, 1939). Reviewed by Emil Kaufmann, *Art Bulletin* XXVIII (1946), 283–284.

528. Wollin, *Gravures,* p. 16; figs. 9-11.

529. Wollin, *Suède,* figs. 48, 49.

530. *Ibid.,* fig. 217.

531. *Ibid.,* p. 331: "Mais, telle une dissonance tranchante, le portail du saillant central, d'une hauteur disproportionnée, brise l'harmonie d'accord avec l'architecture environnante . . ."

532. *Ibid.,* fig. 79; p. 330: "la partie centrale qui, dans sa forme, manque de parenté avec le reste de la façade."

533. *Ibid.,* figs. 32, 33.

534. *Ibid.,* fig. 63.

535. *Ibid.,* figs. 177-179.

536. *Ibid.,* p. 306: "Pour avoir une juste compréhension de cette architecture nouvelle, il ne suffit pas de constater que tels ou tels ont été ses modèles, il faut aussi considérer l'ésprit naissant qu'elle exprime. Nous ne sommes plus en face d'une imitation, mais d'une création." In studying Ledoux's work I had reached the same conclusion (*Von Ledoux bis Le Corbusier,* pp. 40, 42.): "Im Grunde sind in seinem gesamten Oeuvre . . . die übernommenen Formen nebensächlich . . . Die Frage nach ihrer Herkunft im einzelnen kann nicht dazu beitragen, die künstlerische Absicht aufzudecken. Das Wesentliche ist, dass er einen von Grund auf neuen Aufbau versucht . . . die entcheidende, die Klärung bringende Frage ist nicht die des 'Woher?', sondern die des 'Wohin?'."

537. Wollin, *Suède,* fig. 213.

538. *Ibid.,* figs. 27, 31, 88.

539. *Ibid.,* pp. 144, 148; figs. 128–133.

540. *Ibid.,* pp. 63–66; figs. 43–46.

541. *Ibid.,* p. 66: "C'est là un exemple de l'inaptitude souvent frappante, non seulement chez Desprez, mais aussi dans toute cette période, à adapter la composition architecturale d'un bâtiment à sa destination."

542. Ledoux, *Architecture,* p. 15: "L'Architecture est à la maçonnerie ce que la poésie est aux belles lettres: c'est l'enthousiasme dramatique du métier . . ."

543. Wollin, *Suède,* figs. 253–255.

544. *Ibid.,* figs. 140–142.

545. *Ibid.,* fig. 261.

546. *Ibid.,* p. 139; figs. 116–120.

547. *Ibid.,* figs. 79, 82.

548. *Ibid.,* fig. 241.

549. *Ibid.,* figs. 242–244.

550. *Ibid.,* p. 112; figs. 100–102.

551. See pp. 152, 202.

552. Wollin, *Suède,* figs. 121–123.

553. Kaufmann, *Three Revolutionary Architects,* fig. 94.

554. Wollin, *Suède,* figs. 262, 263.

555. *Ibid.,* fig. 67.

556. Nicolas Henri Jardin, *Plans, coupes et élévations de l'Eglise Royale de Frédéric V à Copenhague* (n.pl., 1765). P. Lespinasse, "Les Frères Jardin," *Revue de l'Art Ancien et Moderne* XXVIII (1910), ills. p. 115., Eigtved's project; 117, 119, Jardin's. Hautecoeur, *Histoire de l'architecture,* IV, figs. 97. 98.

557. Academie Royale d'Architecture, *Procès-verbaux,* IX, 317. Cf. *Art Bulletin* XXX (1948), 291. Kaufmann, *Three Revolutionary Architects,* p. 476.

558. Louis Reau, "Un Grande Architecte français en Russie, Vallin de la Mothe," *Architecture* XXXV (1922), ills. p. 176, church and Erémitage; 174, gateway; 179, Academy. *L'Art russe de Pierre le Grand à nos jours* (Paris, 1922), p. 69, pl. 12, La Nouvelle Hollande, Academy.

559. For Boullée, see also Kaufmann, *Three Revolutionary Architects,* fig. 28. For Bernard: *Collection des prix que la ci-devant Académie d'Architecture proposoit et couronnoit tous les ans (1779-1789),* ed. Pierre-Louis van Cléemputte, (Paris, n.d.), Cahier XII, pl. 5. Hurtault: Athanase Detournelle, *Recueil d'architecture nouvelle* (Paris, *an* XIII), pl. 33. Dumanet: *ibid.,* pl. 29. Thomon: Landon, *Annales,* XI, 91; pl. 43; Thomas de Thomon, "Recueil des principaux monuments construits à Saint-Petersbourg," in *Traité de peinture* (Paris, 1809). Georges Loukomski [Georgii K. Lukomski], "Thomas de Thomon," *Apollo* XLII (1945), 297, with ill.

560. A. Castan, "Autobiographie de P.-A. Paris," *Ministère de l'Instruction Publique, Réunion des Sociétés des Beaux-Arts des Departements* (1885), p. 194. Georges Gazier, "P.-A. Paris," *Les Trésors des bibliothèques de France,* ed. Richard Cantinelli and E. Dacier (Paris, 1933), V, 48, spells it "Le Jay."

561. Alexandre Estignard, *P.-A. Paris* (Paris, 1902), Georges Gazier, "La Salle A. Paris au Musée de Besançon," *La Renaissance de l'Art Français* III (1920), 11–19; VI (1923), 127. Jérôme Brochet, "Adrien Paris," *Académie de Besançon, Procès-verbaux et Mémoires,* 1921/22, pp. 19-44.

562. *Catalogue generale des manuscrits des bibliothèques publiques de France,* Départements, vol. 33, Besançon II (1904), 875.

563. Wollin, *Suède,* figs. 235–239, 251.

564. Ernest de Ganay, "Pierre-Adrien Paris," *Revue de l'Art Ancien et Moderne* XLVI (1924), 258; ill. p. 259. Bibliothèque de la ville de Besançon, IX, no. 44.

565. Ganay, "Paris," 256; ill. p. 259. Bibliothèque de la ville de Besançon, IX, nos. 45, 46, 59, 66.

566. Bibliothèque de la ville de Besançon, IX, nos. 74–77.

567. Krafft and Ransonette, *Plans,* pl. 47.

568. Bibliothèque de la ville de Besançon, I, "Observations sur les frontispices des temples," after fol. LXXVII.

XIII. THE ARCHITECTS OF THE FRENCH REVOLUTION: THE GENERATION OF 1760

569. See Pt. I, Chap. II, above.

570. See Part II, Chap. VIII, above.

571. See Pt. III, pp. 166, 215.

572. Dulaure, *Histoire de Paris* (7th ed.) IV, 15: "un chef-d'oeuvre de goût."

573. Saint-Victor, *Tableau historique,* I, ill. p. 497. Simond, *Paris de 1800 à 1900,* ill. I, 396. Hautecoeur, *Histoire de l'architecture,* IV, fig. 201.

574. Thiéry, *Le Voyageur,* p. 171. Saint-Victor, *Tableau historique,* I, 496.

575. Vacquier, *Châteaux,* ser. 7, "Rambouillet," p. 8; pl. 13. Ganay, *Châteaux,* V, 53 (giving 1783 as the date of construction); pl. 78. Henri A. Longnon, *Château de Rambouillet* (Paris, 1909), p. 80. G. Lenotre [Louis Léon Théodore Gosselin], *Château de Rambouillet* (Paris, 1930), p. 107. Edmond Dauphin and Edmond Pascal, *Rambouillet* (Etampes, 1950), p. 47. All these name Thévenin as the architect. Hautecoeur, *Histoire de l'architecture,* IV, 91, is mistaken in naming Mique.

576. See n. 811, below.

577. Krafft and Ransonette, *Plans,* pl. 22, with date.

578. Anatole France, *Les Dieux ont soif* (147th ed.; Paris, n.d.), p. 353.

579. Krafft, *Recueil,* pl. 4.

580. Landon, *Annales,* IX, 93; pl. 43. Pugin, *Paris,* ill. opp. p. 108.

581. *Collection des prix,* ed. van Cléem putte, VI, pl. 4.

582. See Pt. III, note 380, above.

583. "Manibus Ludovici Decimi Quinti."

584. Lenotre, *Quartiers,* Part V, pls. 40, 41/42, with description. Spire Blondel, *L'Art pendant la Révolution* (Paris, n.d.), p. 88. Gabriel Mourey, *Livre des fêtes françaises* (Paris, 1930), ill. opp. p. 270. Edouard Drumont, *Fêtes nationales à Paris* (Paris, 1879), ills. passim.

585. Prieur, *Tableaux historiques,* I, pl. 39; I, pl. 43: "Pompe funèbre en l'honneur des citoyens soldats morts à Nancy en Septembre 1790"; II, pl. 134: "Entrée triomphale des monuments des sciences et arts en France. 9 Thermidor an VI." In the 2nd edition, by J. Duplessis and Bertaux (Paris, 1817), these plates are numbered I, 48; I, 52; II, 145.

586. Jean-Nicolas-Louis Durand, *Recueil et parallèle des édifices de tout genre, anciens et modernes* (Paris, *an* IX), pl. 42.

587. Prieur, *Tableaux historiques,* I, 154; pl. 39. Lenotre, *Quartiers,* part V, pl. 39, shows the celebration of the destruction of the emblems of feudalism. On this occasion an additional pyramid was erected between the altar and the Ecole Militaire. There is a description also in Jacques Antoine Dulaure, *Esquisses historiques des principaux événemens de la Révolution française* (Paris, 1823), I, 362; ill. opp. p. 488.

588. See note 585, above.

589. Harold A. Larrabee, *Joseph Jacques Ramée and America's First Unified College Plan* (New York, 1934), p. 5. C. Hislop and Harold A. Larrabee, "J. J. Ramée and the Building of North and South Colleges," *Union Alumni Monthly* XXVII, no. 4, p. 3. Christopher Tunnard, "Minerva's Union," *Architectural Review* CI (1947), p. 57–60.

590. *Athenaeum,* ed. Baltard (Paris, 1806), part 5, ill. foll. p. 10.

591. Vacquier, *Hôtels,* ser. 12, p. 8; pl. 20. Pugin, *Paris,* p. 11; ill. opp. p. 140.

592. Rue de Lille front: Legrand and Landon, *Description,* II, pl. 49. Saint-Victor, *Tableau historique,* III, ill. opp. p. 826. Pugin, *Paris,* ill. opp. p. 136. Vacquier, *Hôtels,* ser. 12, pl. 24.

593. Krafft and Ransonette, *Plans,* pl. 62, with date. Charles Lefeuve, *Anciennes Maisons de Paris* (Paris, 1870), part 15, p. 5. Hautecoeur, *Histoire de l'architecture,* IV, fig. 217, plan.

594. Krafft and Ransonette, *Plans,* pl. 11, plan no. 2.

595. See Part III, note 480, above.

596. Cf. Jean Mariette, *Architecture française* (Paris, 1727), II, pls. 236, 333, 347; III, pls. 365, 397. See Emil Kaufmann, "The Contribution of Jacques-François Blondel to Mariette's Architecture," *Art Bulletin* XXXI (1949), 58–59.

597. Krafft and Ransonette, *Plans,* pl. 11, plans 1 and 3.

598. Lefeuve, *Anciennes Maisons,* part 16, p. 46, dates it 1790.

599. Krafft and Ransonette, *Plans,* pl. 112, with date.

600. Legrand and Landon, *Description,* IV, 26; pl. 40. Dulaure, *Histoire de Paris* (7th ed.), IV, 37: 1781. F. Hoffbauer, *Paris à*

travers les ages (Paris, 1875), II, pt. 2, p. 11: 1788; ill. fig. 31. Lenotre, *Quartiers*, pt. 4, p. 35 bis: 1787. Albert Babeau, *Paris en 1789* (2nd ed., 1892), fig. 123. Hautecoeur, *Histoire de l'architecture*, IV, figs. 31, 32.

601. *Ibid.*, XVII, pl. 6.

602. *Ibid.*, XVII, pl. 5.

603. Landon, *Annales*, XIII, 39; pl. 16.

604. See Pt. I, p. 62, above.

605. Landon, *Annales*, III, 103; pls. 48, elevation, 49, section. Henry M. Fletcher, "The Harmony of the Spheres," *Journal of the Royal Institute of British Architects* XLII (1935), 774–777, presents the spherical houses of Sobre and Vaudoyer only, reproduced from *Annales*.

606. See Kaufmann, "Boullée," 212; figs. 1, 2. *Three Revolutionary Architects*, figs. 22, 23, 158, 271, 272.

607. See Part III, note 439, above.

608. [Jean Pierre Louis Laurent] Houel, *"peintre architecte,"* "Projet d'un monument public," *Journal de La République* (14 *brumaire an* VIII), recommends the sphere: "Un globe, en tous les tems, n'est égal qu'à lui-même; C'est de l'égalité le plus parfait emblême. Nul corps n'a, comme lui, ce titre capital, Qu'un seul de ses aspects à tout autre est égal." Ledoux, *Architecture*, p. 194.

609. Fletcher, "Harmony," ill. p. 775.

610. Landon, *Annales*, II, 124: "Ce n'est pas de la grande architecture, mais c'est ce qu'on appelerait en poésie un madrigal. . . ."

611. Kaufmann, *Three Revolutionary Architects*, fig. 64.

612. *Art Bulletin* XXI (1939), 212; fig. 2. Kaufmann, *Three Revolutionary Architects*, fig. 272.

613. *Collection des prix*, ed. van Cléemputte, XII, pl. 3, Délépine's project. *Projets d'architecture et autres productions de cet art qui ont mérités les grands prix*, ed. Allais, Detournelle and Vaudoyer, (Paris, 1806), pl. 98, Labadie's project.

614. Krafft and Ransonette, *Plans*, pl. 55, with date. The text states Rue Richer. Hautecoeur, *Histoire de l'architecture*, IV, fig. 216, plan.

615. Krafft, *Recueil*, p. 6: "un peu tour-

menté dans la forme de son plan"; pl. 13. See fig. 108.

616. Krafft and Ransonette, *Plans*, pl. 8, with date.

617. Lenotre, *Quartiers*, part I, pl. 11, dates it 1788, and comments: "une vaste construction plus bizarre que pratique." Michel, *Histoire de l'art*, VIII, fig. 1, elevation and plan. Louis de Loménie, *Beaumarchais et son temps* (Paris, 1856; New York, 1857), II, 426, respectively 409. Hautecoeur, *Histoire de l'architecture*, IV, fig. 214, plan.

618. Krafft and Ransonette, *Plans*, pl. 19, with date. Cf. note 649, below. Hautecoeur, *Histoire de l'architecture*, IV, fig. 213, plan.

619. Krafft and Ransonette, *Plans*, pl. 57, with date. Hautecoeur, *Histoire de l'architecture*, IV, fig. 247.

620. Krafft and Ransonette, *Plans*, pl. 26, with date.

621. *Collection des prix*, ed. van Cléemputte, I, pl. 5.

622. *Ibid.*, vol. II, pl. 1. See note 863, below.

623. *Ibid.*, vol. VII, pl. 1. Rietdorf, *Gilly*, fig. 131, shows a similar project, in a drawing by Friedrich Gilly, with the latter's remark: "nach Bondhorg architecte. Paris 88."

624. *Collection des prix*, ed. Van Cléemputte, I, pl. 5.

625. *Ibid.*, vol. I, pl. 1.

626. *Ibid.*, pl. 3.

627. Krafft and Ransonette, *Plans*, pl. 14, with date. See note 733, below.

628. *Ibid.*, pl. 60, below, with date. See note 654, below.

629. Krafft, *Recueil*, pls. 55, 56.

630. *Ibid.*, pls. 37, 39; p. 10, the disguise of the house as a temple is censured. Kaufmann, *Three Revolutionary Architects*, fig. 215.

631. Krafft and Ransonette, *Plans*, pl. 66, no. 1.

632. *Ibid.*, pl. 7, with dates.

633. *Ibid.*, pl. 33, with date. See note 473, above, for Dervieux house.

634. Krafft and Ransonette, *Plans*, pl. 50, with date.

635. Krafft, *Recueil*, pl. 19, elevation, with date; pl. 21, plans.

636. *Ibid.*, p. 7: "une disposition nouvelle, régulière et très pittoresque . . ."

637. *Ibid.*, pls. 25, 26, with date. Charles François Mandar, *Etudes d'architecture civile* (2nd ed.; Paris, 1826). pl. 1.

638. Krafft, *Recueil*, pl. 43.

639. Krafft and Ransonette, *Plans,* pl. 8. See note 616, above.

640. *Collection des prix,* ed. van Cléemputte, vol. III, pl. 2.

641. *Ibid.,* pl. 4.

642. *Ibid.,* vol. XVII, pl. 4.

643. *Ibid.,* vol. XV, pl. 2.

644. *Ibid.,* vol. XII, pl. 2.

645. Krafft and Thiollet, *Choix,* pl. 175. Pugin, *Paris,* ill. opp. p. 96, with the remark in the text: "plain, but impressive." I could not ascertain whether the builder of the Timbre was identical with Boullée's favorite pupil (*Art Bulletin* XXI, 215, note 19), or the prize winner of 1774 (Van Cléemputte, ed., *Collection des prix,* IX, pls. 1, 2.) W. I. Bicknell, *Public Buildings of Paris* (London, n.d.), I, ill. opp. p. 66.

646. Landon, *Annales,* IX, 93; pl. 43. Krafft and Thiollet, *Choix,* pl. 177. Paul Planat, *Style Louis XVI* (2nd ed.; Paris, n.d.), I; p. v, names only Antoine as the architect, but illustrates, pl. 113, the restoration by Clavareau.

647. Jean Charles Krafft, *Portes cochères* (Paris, 1810), p. 14; pl. 11.

648. Krafft, *Recueil,* pl. 52.

649. Krafft and Ransonette, *Plans,* pl. 19, with date. See notes 464, 639, above.

650. Krafft, *Recueil,* pl. 67.

651. See note 265, above.

652. See note 441, above.

653. Krafft and Ransonette, *Plans,* pl. 34, with date. Hautecoeur, *Histoire de l'architecture,* IV, fig. 249.

654. Krafft and Ransonette, *Plans,* pl. 58, with date. See Olivier's gatehouse, above, and Mangot's house, below.

655. Krafft and Ransonette, *Plans,* pl. 30. See note 471, above.

656. Krafft and Ransonette, *Plans,* pl. 53. Thieme-Becker, *Künstlertexikon,* ascribes the house to the younger Trepsat, Jean.

657. Krafft and Thiollet, *Choix,* pl. 60.

658. *Ibid.,* pls. 107, 108.

659. *Ibid.,* pl. 14.

660. *Ibid.,* pl. 12.

661. Joyant, "Les Gisors," p. 286, note, mentions the exhibition of the "Thermes" project in the *Salon de l'an XII.*

662. Krafft and Ransonette, *Plans,* pl. 60, with date.

663. Krafft, *Recueil,* p. 16: "d'une ordonnance et d'une composition bien entendues." Rietdorf, *Gilly,* fig. 76, illustrates a very similar façade "près la rue Montmartre," drawn by Gilly, 1797.

664. Landon, *Annales,* vol. XIII, pl. 52.

665. *Ibid.,* p. 111.

666. Charles Pierre Gourlier, Biet, Grillon, et feu Tardieu, *Choix d'édifices publics projetés et construits en France depuis le commencement du XIXe siècle* (Paris, 1825–1850), vol. I, pt. X, pl. 88.

667. Kaufmann, *Three Revolutionary Architects,* figs. 38, 39, 164, 188.

668. See Part III, note 234, above.

669. *Collection des prix,* ed. van Cléemputte, vol. V, pl. 2.

670. *Ibid.,* pls. 45.

671. *Ibid.,* vol. IX, pl. 5.

672. See Pt. III, note 472, above.

673. Krafft and Ransonette, *Plans,* pl. 3, with date.

674. Krafft, *Recueil,* p. 16; pls. 67, 68.

675. Hans Rose, *Spätbarock* (Munich, 1922), fig. 136.

676. Klopfer, *Von Palladio,* fig. 58. Brinckmann, *17. und 18. Jahrhundert,* p. 299: 1810. Thieme-Becker, *Künstlerlexikon:* 1817.

677. Charles Saunier, *Bordeaux* (Paris, 1925), ill. p. 101. Léon Deshairs, *Bordeaux* (Paris, n.d.), pl. 55.

678. Saunier, *Bordeaux,* ill. p. 99. According to p. 105 the house was built prior to 1790. Marionneau, *Victor Louis,* p. 471.

679. Auguste Bordes, *Histoire des monumens anciens et modernes de la ville de Bordeaux* (Paris, 1845), II, 124; ill. opp. p. 124. Saunier, *Bordeaux,* p. 105.

680. Kaufmann, *Three Revolutionary Architects,* figs. 77, 79.

681. Wollin, *Suède,* fig. 245.

682. Kaufmann, *Three Revolutionary Architects*, figs. 174, 120.

683. Andre-Jacques Roubo [the younger], *Traité de la construction des théâtres* (Paris, 1777), pl. III. Pierre Patte, *Essai sur l'architecture théâtrale* (Paris, 1782), p. 148. Hautecoeur, *Histoire de l'architecture*, IV, fig. 275.

684. Kaufmann, *Von Ledoux bis LeCorbusier*, ill. p. 25. *Three Revolutionary Architects*, fig. 259.

685. Boyer, "Projets," p. 174; ills. opp. pp. 172, 180.

686. S. Blondel, *L'Art pendant la Revolution*, p. 85.

687. P. F. L. Dubois, *Projet de réunion du Louvre au Palais des Thuileries* (Paris, n.d.), p. 1; first and fifth plates.

688. Krafft, *Recueil*, pls. 73–76.

689. Simond, *Paris de 1800 à 1900*, I, ill. p. 233.

690. Baltard, *Paris et ses monuments*, "Saint-Cloud," ill. p. 18.

691. *Collection des prix*, ed. van Cléemputte, VIII, pls. 1-3. Pierre Lelièvre, *L'Urbanisme et l'architecture à Nantes aux XVIIIe siècle* (Nantes, 1942), p. 70.

692. *Art Bulletin* XXI, 215. *Collection des prix*, ed. van Cléemputte, IX, pls. 1, 2, Bénard's "Bath," with the date 1774.

693. Lelièvre, *Nantes*, pl. VII, Corps de Garde; p. 156; fig. 25, layout of Place Royale, with date.

694. *Ibid.*, p. 277; fig. 74, plan; pl. XVIII, elevation.

695. *Ibid.*, p. 278; fig. 75, plan; pl. XXV, elevation.

696. *Ibid.*, p. 278.

697. *Ibid.*, p. 158, text and note; pl. XXV.

698. Kaufmann, *Three Revolutionary Architects*, fig. 166.

699. *Ibid.*, fig. 78.

700. *Ibid.*, fig. 198.

701. *Collection des prix*, ed. van Cléemputte, vol. XIII, pl. 2, Bernier; vol. XV, pl. 4, Lefèvre.

702. *Ibid.*, vol. XX, pls. 1, 2.

703. *Projets d'architecture*, ed. Allais and others, pls. 66, Elysée; 88, Prytanée.

704. Antoine-Laurent-Thomas Vaudoyer et

Louis-Pierre Baltard, *Grands prix d'architecture* (Paris, 1818), pl. 113, Brasserie. Louis-Marie Normand, *Paris moderne* (Paris, 1837), I, pl. 122, Thiais house.

705. Landon, *Annales*, I, 71; pl. 34.

706. *Collection des prix*, ed. van Cléemputte, vol. II, pl. 6.

707. *Ibid.*, vol. VI, pl. 2.

708. *Ibid.*, vol. X, pl. 4.

709. *Ibid.*, vol. VI, pl. 6.

710. J. and H. S. Storer, *Views in Edinburgh and its Vicinity* (London, 1820), vol. II, ill. of the church. (The book has no pagination.) Klopfer, *Von Palladio*, p. 39, fig. 15, ascribes the church erroneously to William Henry Playfair.

711. Klopfer, *Von Palladio*, fig. 16.

712. Storer, *Views*, vol. II.

713. *Collection des prix*, ed. van Cléemputte, vol. VII, pl. 2. Cf. Pt. III, p. 187, above.

714. *Ibid.*, vol. XVI, pl. 5.

715. Landon, *Annales*, V, 133 (signed "L. G."-Legrand); pl. 63, Phare, *Projets d'architecture*, ed. Allais and others, pl. 4, named Colonne rostrale.

716. Claude-Jacques Toussaint, *Traité de géométrie et d'architecture* (Paris, 1812), I, 32, pl. 13, fig. 6.

717. Kaufmann, *Three Revolutionary Architects*, fig. 235. The comparison of the Rendez-vous with Goodwin's Swiss cottage illustrated by Pilcher (see Pt. I, n. 599), fig. 88, is very elucidating.

718. Helen Rosenau, "Lequeu," *Architectural Review* CVI (Aug. 1949), 111–116, compares Lequeu's works with some of Soane. Comparisons with several less-known architects might be even more interesting, particularly with John Carter.

719. Gustav Pauli, *Kunst des Klassizimus und der Romantik* (Berlin, 1925), ill. p. 180. Klopfer, *Von Palladio*, fig. 123.

720. Klopfer, *Von Palladio*, fig. 138.

721. *Ibid.*, fig. 84.

722. Both Vienna buildings are in the *Enciclopedia Italiana*, vol. XXXV, pl. LXXVIII.

723. Kaufmann, *Three Revolutionary Architects*, fig. 190.

724. Normand, *Paris moderne,* vol. II, pls. 1–3.

725. Dubois, *Anciens Châteaux,* ser. 13, p. 10; pl. 31. Hautecoeur, *Histoire de l'architecture,* IV, fig. 263.

726. Dubois, *Anciens Châteaux,* p. 10.

727. *Ibid.*

728. Kaufmann, *Three Revolutionary Architects,* fig. 162.

729. See Pt. III, p. 159, above.

730. Cf. Pt. II, p. 195, about Valadier's pavilion, Giuseppe Valadier, *Raccolta di diverse invenzioni di no. 24 fabbriche* (Rome, n.d.), pl. 2.

731. Stern, *Belanger,* II, 191.

732. L. Dussieux, *Les Artistes français à l'étranger* (Paris, 1856), p. 191.

733. Cf. Pt. III, n. 627, above. Hautecoeur, *Histoire de l'architecture,* IV, fig. 46.

734. Krafft and Ransonette, *Plans,* pl. 14, with date.

735. *Ibid.,* pl. 12, with date.

736. *Ibid.,* p. 117, signed "L. G."

737. Cf. Pt. II, note 281, above.

738. Krafft, *Portes,* p. 30; pl. 37. Donnet, *Architectonographie,* p. 236.

739. Krafft, *Portes,* p. 30 (English text).

740. *Ibid.,* p. 29; pl. 34.

741. Kaufmann, *Three Revolutionary Architects,* fig. 165.

742. *Ibid.,* fig. 195.

743. *Ibid.,* fig. 110, Houses nos. 1, 2, 3.

744. Krafft, *Portes,* p. 31: "in the best and most agreeable manner." Dussieux, *Aristes français,* p. 191: "un chef-d'oeuvre du genre." Donnet, *Architectonographie,* p. 244: "Ce jolie édifice, dont l'aspect théâtral et pittoresque réunissait tout ce qui peut charmer la vue."

745. Dussieux, *Artistes français,* p. 191.

746. P. J. Goetghebuer, *Choix des monuments, édifices, et maisons les plus remarquables du Royaume des Pays-Bas* (Ghent, 1827), p. 13; pls. XX, XXI.

747. Kaufmann, *Three Revolutionary Architects,* fig. 88.

748. Goetghebuer, *Choix,* p. 14.

749. Cf. Pt. III, pp. 145, 146.

750. Jean Rondelet, *Traité théorique et pratique de l'art de bâtir* (Paris, 1802). The quotations are from the 8th edition, 1838.

751. *Ibid.,* vol. I, p. xxvi.

752. *Ibid.,* pp. iv–vii.

753. *Ibid.,* p. xiv.

754. Krafft, *Recueil,* pl. 13.

755. Krafft and Ransonette, *Plans,* pl. 56, with date.

756. *Ibid.,* pl. 58, with date.

757. Vacquier, *Châteaux,* ser. 7, pl. 13.

758. Dimier, *L'Architecture,* I, 2; pl. VII. Poète, *Vie de cité,* III, 135.

759. Lucien Lambeau, "Communication au sujet d'une petite maison . . . à Belleville, ayant appartenu à François Soufflot, dit le Romain," Ville de Paris, Commission municipale du Vieux Paris, *Procès-verbaux, 1902* (Paris, 1903), p. 65, with ill.

760. Krafft and Ransonette, *Plans,* pl. 67, with date.

761. Krafft, *Recueil,* pl. 16.

762. Landon, *Annales,* vol. V, pl. 63. *Projets d'architecture,* ed. Allais and others, pl. 4. Cf. Pt. III, note 715, above.

763. *Projets d'architecture,* ed. Allais and others, pls. 12 (plan), 14 (elevation).

764. *Ibid.,* pls. 19 (plan), 20 (elevation).

765. Landon, *Annales,* III, 13; with the date 1792; pl. 3.

766. *Ibid.,* III, 13.

767. *Ibid.,* 91; pl. 42.

768. *Ibid.,* pl. 10; p. 27: "On désirait une grande maison, distribuée à la française." *Ibid.,* pl. 26, house with Baroque gradation.

769. Charles [Pierre Joseph] Normand, *Recueil varié de plans et de façades* (Paris, 1815), pl. 32, fig. 3, "Château," resembling Villa Medici; pl. 50, fig. 2, "Salle de spectacle." See notes 303, 304, 551, above.

770. For Scheult, *Recueil,* see note 514, above. See also Constant Bourgeois, *Vues et fabriques d'Italie* (Paris, 1803). Pierre Clocher, *Palais, maisons et vues d'Italie* (Paris, 1809).

771. Detournelle, *Recueil,* pl. 11.

772. *Projets d'architecture,* ed. Allais and others, pl. 2, Orangerie; pls. 92 (plan), 93 (elevation) of the Arsenal.

773. Krafft, *Recueil,* pls. 40, 41. Further *Fabriques flamandes* pls. 5, 24. On p. 8 is the

description: "Les plans comme les élévations sont irréguliers; la construction en paraît rustique."

774. Vacquier, *Châteaux,* ser. 12, pl. 11. Cf. Pt. III, note 274, above.

775. Jean Charles Krafft, *Plans des plus beaux jardins pittoresques de France, d'Angleterre, et d'Allemagne* (Paris, 1809), p. 17, with date; pl. 27. Krafft, *Recueil,* pl. 246.

776. Krafft, *Plans,* pl. 30; *Recueil,* pl. 247.

777. Krafft, *Plans,* pl. 38; *Recueil,* pl. 201.

778. Emil Kaufmann, "Lequeu," *Art Bulletin* XXXI (1949), figs. 4–10.

779. See also Kaufmann, *Three Revolutionary Architects,* p. 552, fig. 239.

780. Cf. Part III, p. 169, above.

781. Joyant, "Les Gisors," p. 272; ill. opp. p. 280. *Collection des prix,* ed. van Cléemputte, vol. I, pls. 1, 2.

782. Joyant, "Les Gisors," p. 273, with ill. after an engraving by Berthault, with Gisors' name.

783. Stern, *Belanger,* I, 233.

784. Mariette, *Architecture françoise,* vol. III, pls. 434–436 (plans), 439 (section).

785. *Ibid.,* pl. 437.

786. Ferdinand Boyer, "Les Tuileries sous la Convention," *Bulletin de la Société de l'Histoire de l'Art Français* (1934), p. 216. According to Pierre Vignon's pamphlet, *Sur la nouvelle salle dans le palais des Tuileries* (Paris, an II), and Hoffbauer, *Paris,* II, 47, fig. 28, Boullée and Heurtier seem to have assisted Gisors. For assembly halls see *La Décade philosophique* VIII (an IV), 270, XIX (an VII), 295, with ills.

787. Boyer, "Projets," pp. 181, 183.

788. Boyer, "Tuileries," ill. opp. p. 220.

789. Kaufmann, *Three Revolutionary Architects,* fig. 158.

790. *Ibid.,* fig. 159.

791. *Ibid.,* fig. 85; p. 489. Patte, *Essai,* pp. 167, 175, holds views similar to those of Ledoux.

792. See Part III, pp. 167–168, above.

793. Frederick Nash, *Picturesque View of the City of Paris* (London, 1823), third plate from end. Ferdinand Boyer, "Le Conseil des Cinq-cents au Palais-Bourbon," *Bulletin de la Société de l'Histoire de l'Art Français* (1935), p. 71. See p. 160, above.

794. Boyer, "Conseil," ill. opp. p. 72.

795. *Ibid.,* ill. opp. p. 64. Legrand and Landon, *Description,* II, 71; pl. 43.

796. Landon, *Annales,* I, 137; pls. 67, 68.

797. Dupezard, *Le Palais-Royal,* p. 15, states that the hall was carried out by Beaumont after a plan by Blève. For the authorship, see *Journal des Bâtiments* XIV (an XII), 153, 189, 238.

798. Landon, *Annales,* X, 37, signed "L. G."; pls. 15, 16.

799. *Ibid.,* X, 37.

800. See Pt. III, notes 467, 469, above.

801. Joyant, "Les Gisors," p. 270.

802. See Pt. III, n. 469, above.

803. Alphonse de Gisors, *Le Palais du Luxembourg* (Paris, 1847), p. 98: "La nouvelle salle . . . est, contrairement à l'usage suivi jusqu'à présent, éclairée par des jours verticaux . . ."

804. Hustin, *Palais du Luxembourg,* ill. p. 25, Gisors' hall. Gisors illustrates the plan of the altered hall, *Palais du Luxembourg,* between pp. 94 and 95.

805. Landon, *Annales,* I, 47; pls. 18, 22.

806. *Ibid.,* XIV, 18.

807. Dubois, *Anciens Châteaux,* ser. 13, pl. 38. P. 12: "la pièce de plus haut intérêt: une salle à manger, carré . . . auquel deux hémicycles sont accolés . . . Ces hémicycles ont pour voûtes des coquilles. . . ."

808. Paul Jarry, *Vieux Hôtels . . . ,* ed. F. Contet (n.p., 1926/34), ser. 18, p. 14; pls. 35–40.

809. *Ibid.,* pl. 36.

810. *Ibid.,* pl. 37.

811. Vacquier, *Châteaux,* ser. 7, pl. 14.

812. Louis Ambroise Dubut, *Architecture civile* (Paris, 1803; 2nd ed., 1837). Dubut distinguishes his houses by numbers, which appear on each plate and in the comparative chart of the ground plans.

813. *Ibid.,* House No. 2, pl. III. (Kaufmann, *Three Revolutionary Architects,* fig. 203.)

814. Dubut, *Architecture civile,* introduction.

815. *Ibid.,* House No. 30, pl. L.

816. *Ibid.*, House No. 3, pl. V (Kaufmann, *Von Ledoux bis Le Corbusier*, ill. p. 55. *Three Revolutionary Architects*, fig. 202), House No. 13, pl. XXII.

817. Dubut, *Architecture civile*, House No. 14, pl. XXIV, elevation; pl. XXX, perspective (Kaufmann, *Von Ledoux bis Le Corbusier*), ill. p. 56.

818. Dubut, *Architecture civile*, House No. 25, pl. XLI, plan (Kaufmann, *Von Ledoux bis Le Corbusier*, ill. p. 56), elevation; pl. XLII, perspective.

819. Dubut, *Architecture civile*, House No. 24, pls. XL, XLVIII. In the perspective view it is erroneously labeled "23." (Kaufmann, *Three Revolutionary Architects*, fig. 204.)

820. Dubut, *Architecture civile*, House No. 9, pl. XVII (Kaufmann, *Von Ledoux bis Le Corbusier*, ill. p. 57.)

821. Dubut, *Architecture civile*, House No. 41, pl. LXXII, elevation, LXXIII, perspective. (Kaufmann, *Three Revolutionary Architects*, fig. 206.)

822. Dubut, *Architecture civile*, House No. 28, pl. XLVII (Kaufmann, *Von Ledoux bis Le Corbusier*, ill. p. 55. *Three Revolutionary Architects*, fig. 201.)

823. Dubut, *Architecture civile*, House No. 22, pl. XXXVI.

824. *Ibid.*, House No. 10, pl. XVI, plan; XVII, perspective, (Kaufmann, *Von Ledoux bis Le Corbusier*, ill. p. 57. *Three Revolutionary Architects*, fig. 205.)

825. Dubut, *Architecture civile*, House No. 21, pl. XXXIV, plan; (Kaufmann, *Von Ledoux bis Le Corbusier*, ill. p. 57); XLII, perspective.

826. Dubut, *Architecture civile*, House No. 1, pl. II. *Projets d'architecture*, ed. Allais and others, pls. 46, 47, show Dubut's prize-winning public granary.

827. Dubut, *Architecture civile*, House No. 6, pl. XI; House No. 12, pl. XX.

828. Landon, *Annales*, XV, 77: "Cet artiste, également recommandable par la solidité et la pureté de sa théorie, et par la manière dont il la met en pratique . . ."

829. Cf. *The First Proofs of the Universal Catalogue of Books on Art* (London, 1870),

I, 470, 471. For the influence of French revolutionary architecture on Germany see the excellent essay of Nikolaus Pevsner, "Schinkel," *Journal of the Royal Institute of British Architects* LIX (1952), 89–96.

830. Durand, *Précis*. My quotations are taken from the 1809 edition. Vol. I, p. vii.

831. *Ibid.*, I, 12.

832. *Ibid.*, I, 65: "les formes et les proportions . . . dont l'habitude nous a fait en quelque sorte un besoin, telles que les formes et les proportions des édifices antiques . . ."

833. *Ibid.*, I, 7 (against Vitruvius); I, 5 (against Laugier).

834. *Ibid.*, I, 10.

835. *Ibid.*, I, 12.

836. *Ibid.*, I, 11.

837. Jean-Nicolas-Louis Durand, *Partie graphique des cours d'architecture faits à L'Ecole Royale Polytechnique* (Paris, 1821), p. 25.

838. Durand, *Précis*, I, 91.

839. *Ibid.*, I, 4.

840. *Ibid.*, I, 21: "L'architecture est un art qui a un genre propre . . . Son but . . . est de satisfaire un grand nombre de nos besoins. . . ."

841. *Ibid.*, I, 71. Similarly, I, 15.

842. *Ibid.*, I, 83.

843. *Ibid.*, I, 22. "La décoration n'est point l'objet dont l'architecte doive s'occuper . . ." Similarly, I, 14, 23.

844. *Ibid.*, I, 64.

845. *Ibid.*

846. *Ibid.*, I, 17. Similarly, I, 14.

847. *Ibid.*, I, 3.

848. Durand, *Partie graphique*, p. 19: "Les élévations . . . ne sont et ne doivent être que des résultats naturels et nécessaires du plan et de la coupe."

849. Durand, *Précis*, I, 22.

850. *Ibid.*, I, 65.

851. Louis Hautecoeur, "Conférence," *Architecture Française* 37 (November 1943), 6: "Le Cours d'architecture de Durand . . . fut le manifeste des constructeurs."

852. Durand, *Précis*, I, 66.

853. *Ibid.*, I, 2.

854. *Ibid.*, I, 22.

855. *Ibid.*, I, 85.

856. *Ibid.*, I, 88.

857. *Ibid.*, II, 97.

858. Durand, *Partie graphique*, p. 6.

859. Cf. Part II, note 100, above.

860. Antoine Rondelet, "Notice historique sur la vie et les ouvrages de J. N. L. Durand" (Reprint from *Moniteur, Journal des Lettres* I, 1835; 101, according to *Dictionary of the Architectural Publication Society*), p. 5. Rondelet reports that Boullée endowed Durand with a lifelong income, after Durand had refused to accept an increase of his salary as Boullée's *dessinateur,* and names Panseron as Durand's teacher.

861. *Projets d'architecture,* ed. Allais and others, pls. 31, 32.

862. Landon, *Annales*, V, 47.

863. *Collection des prix,* ed. van Cléemputte, II, pls. 1, 2. See note 622, above.

864. *La Décade philosophique,* VI, 461, reports that Durand with his coworker Thibaud (Thibault) was awarded the First Prize for the Temple à l'Egalité, and adds: "La pensée de ce projet . . . a paru aux juges neuve, pleine de caractère." Rondelet, "Notice historique," p. 7, states that this design and several others were submitted by the two in a competition arranged by the Convention in 1793, and comments: "Leurs compositions fixèrent l'attention générale, tant par l'habileté avec laquelle elles étaient rendues, que par la marche neuve et hardie qu'ils y avaient observée."

865. Rondelet, "Notice historique," p. 7. Durand, *Précis*, vol. II, pl. 23. Legrand and Landon, *Description*, vol. IV, pl. 45. Krafft and Thiollet, *Choix,* pls. 83, 84. Hautecoeur, *Histoire de l'architecture*, IV, fig. 42.

866. Durand, *Précis*, I, 100. *Ibid.*, II, pls. 27, 28, 29, 30, 32.

867. *Ibid.*, I, pl. 19. The title of this plate reads: "Emploi des objets de la nature dans la composition des édifices."

868. *Ibid.*, II, 20.

869. *Ibid.*, I, plates in part II. Kaufmann, *Von Ledoux bis Le Corbusier,* ills. p. 55, with the following comments: "Der Vulgarisator der neuen Lehre war Durand . . . Das Grundmotiv seiner Pläne is die regelmässige Aufteilung des Rechteckes, die Kombinationen rechtwinkliger Koordinatensysteme . . . Die Durandschen Schemata bedeuten die Dogmatisierung der neuen Baugesinnung, die Erhebung der Idee in den Rang der gefestigten Lehrmeinung." Raval and Moreux, *C.-N. Ledoux,* pp. 45, 67, made these comments: "Durand en est le plus sûr continuateur. Ses plans obeissent bien à un trace craticulaire . . . nous les voyons érigés en méthode et en guide par Durand." Closely following my book, Raval and Moreux refer also at the end of their book to Boullée and Lequeu.

870. Walter Gropius, *The New Architecture and the Bauhaus* (London, 1935), p. 27.

871. Durand, *Précis*, II, pl. 31. Kaufmann, *Von Ledoux bis Le Corbusier,* ill. p. 53.

872. Durand, *Précis*, II, pl. 28. For Durand's *Recueil,* see note 586, above.

873. *Grands prix de Rome,* ed. Armand Guérinet (Paris, n.d.).

874. Leon Vaudoyer, "Histoire de l'architecture en France," in J. Aicard, *Patria. La France ancienne et moderne* (Paris, 1847), II, sect. xxvi, col. 2191.

875. *Croquis d'Architecture,* ed. Intime-Club (1884), ser. 2, vol. 8, no. 2, F. 6. For Antonelli, p. 118. *Croquis d'Architecture* present many other designs showing how close in spirit to the revolutionary period even the late nineteenth century could be.